D1249704

THE
DAVID WADE
COLLECTION

THE DAVID WADE COLLECTION

David Wade

EAKIN PRESS

Austin, Texas

FIRST EDITION

Copyright © 1986
By David Wade

Published in the United States of America
By Eakin Press, P.O. Box 23066, Austin, Texas 78735

ALL RIGHTS RESERVED. No part of this book may be reproduced in any form without written permission from the publisher, except for brief passages included in a review appearing in a newspaper or magazine.

ISBN 0-89015-554-2

This book is dedicated to a young gentleman who possesses all of the qualities and humanities that are dear to me. For the past six years I have shared a very close personal experience with him through the world of scouting. He is Silver Palm Eagle Scout Cameron Wade. The Lord has truly blessed my life with this beloved son.

David Wade

David Wade has been referred to many times as the Rembrandt of the kitchen, the Edison of the cookbook, and the gourmet that gourmets talk about. Through the mediums of radio, television, newspapers, and magazines, combined with public demonstrations around the world, David has demonstrated food during the past twenty-five years to more persons than anyone else. He recently received the food industry's top accolade as America's leading food demonstrator. This recognition was given him by the National Culinary Arts Society, the premier organization for recognizing artistic achievement in the realm of food. David conducts "The David Wade Show" television program (formerly titled "The Gourmet") in major cities across the country, and is the author of numerous cookbooks. He has been featured on the ABC radio network on a program called "Flair," originating in New York, and has given food reports on the radio program "Patterns," syndicated on 350 radio stations across the land. David conducted food demonstrations at two World's Fairs and is constantly staging many of the beautiful food photographs that are seen in national magazine advertising.

David launched a restaurant endorsement program comparable to the old Duncan Hines project, and his recognition of these restaurants can be seen across the country in the form of outdoor lighted signs. He has developed many marketing programs built around food, which are used by supermarket chains, and he travels extensively around the world collecting special recipes to be incorporated into his food reports. David is credited with teaching many famous motion picture stars, such as Gregory Peck and Charlton Heston, to cook. He is a personal friend of most of the top chefs in leading hotels and restaurants around the world.

Some years ago, David organized the nation's first Junior Gourmet Club, which has achieved much national recognition. "Dining with David Wade," a syndicated newspaper column, was a popular feature with American newspapers. Three of David's twelve published cookbooks have been best sellers across the country.

David Wade has an amazing array of talents that go far beyond his internationally recognized gourmet abilities. In fact, *Radio/Television Mirror* magazine titled an article showcasing his activities "He Led One Million Lives" and added this list: airplane pilot and experimental test inspector, radio hymn singer, championship tennis player, dog breeder and network radio and television host of "Canine Comments," author, lecturer, raconteur, talented painter, public relations counselor.

In addition, David works tirelessly as church layman and Sunday school teacher. He is a member of the executive board for the East Texas Area Council of the Boy Scouts of America; scout master of Troop 589 in Tyler, Texas; and honorary life member of the National Congress of Parents and Teachers. He is currently serving on the Texas State Advisory Board for the Prevention of Child Abuse and the board of directors of the Texas Girls' Choir. As a world traveler, he further demonstrates his concern for human beings everywhere by participating in United Nations efforts to bring about peace and order through improved communications.

David is a partner in David Wade, Ltd., a food company which features several products he developed. He was awarded the prestigious International Gold Medal Award from Monde Selection, presented in Luxembourg, Luxembourg and Geneva, Switzerland, and the Gold Medal in Paris, France for his personal contributions to world cuisine — the first individual ever to be so honored by Monde Selection.

Contents

Foreword

When I was asked to write the foreword for *The David Wade Collection* cookbook, I felt pleased and, indeed, honored. I remember our international friendship of many years and my visit with David and his lovely family in Dallas. During that visit, I celebrated with the finest food that I have ever tasted from the author's kitchen. When David, Becky and Cameron visited in my home in Bruxelles, Belgique, we were very apprehensive in presenting our special table fare, but David soon placed us at ease with his warm gentlemanly demeanor.

I first became acquainted with this fascinating man of the food world in 1976 in Luxembourg, Luxembourg during a world food conference. His charming personality took charge of us all during that meeting. Since that time, we have shared working experiences in Paris, London, Geneva, Vienna, Rome and other cities of Europe, and I have grown to appreciate the great knowledge and expertise of food that this man possesses. Few people are blessed by God with the taste and feeling for international food that David Wade has. His love for mankind is felt by all who learn from this exceptional teacher. Anyone who has spent an hour or two with David will understand what I am trying to say. His interests and talents go far beyond the world of food. He is active in many fields of endeavor.

David's contributions to the world of cuisine are a matter of record. He has done more, in my opinion, to elevate the taste of Americans for good food than any other. He cuts through the pretentiousness of fancy food preparation and serving procedure and presents elegant foods in a simple and understandable manner. Many of the recipes that are found in this book are today legend, not only in America, but in other countries of the world as well. This is because they have universal taste appeal and are easy to prepare. David also limits his recipes to those ingredients that can be found everywhere. This is just one more reason why they are so popular.

There are many outstanding cookbooks in print. I have found that most will have at least five or six recipes that I am interested in. This book *The David Wade Collection* has many more than one hundred that I find extremely special. This is one cookbook that I recommend to real food lovers everywhere. I hope to see it in print in many languages soon.

My expression of good will to David Wade, King of the American Food World, and all who read and enjoy this outstanding publication.

BARON GEORGE DEBRUYN
Director General
Monde Selection
Bruxelles, Belgique

America's Favorites

Veal

Escallops of Veal Bordelaise

1   stick of butter
4   escallops of veal
4   tablespoons of brandy

Melt butter in blazer pan then add veal. Sauté veal on both sides until done. Add brandy to blazer pan and heat. Then flambé and work brandy into butter. Spoon lightly over veal. Serve veal on heated plates topped with sauce.

Sauce Bordelaise

1   stick of butter
2   shallots chopped finely
1   cup of sliced mushrooms, drained
1   tablespoon Worcestershire powder
2   teaspoons garlic powder
1   tablespoon powdered dry mustard
2   cups demi-glaze or thick beef gravy
1   cup brandy
   Salt and cracked black pepper to taste

Melt butter in blazer pan and sauté shallots and mushrooms for 4 minutes. Add all other items and simmer until well blended and heated. Recipe serves 4.

Veal Rolls Parmigiano

8   pieces veal cutlet (about 1¹/₂ pounds)
2   tablespoons finely chopped parsley
1   teaspoon seasoned salt
¹/₄ teaspoon seasoned pepper
3   tablespoons grated Parmesan cheese
   Flour
2   tablespoons cooking oil
1   tablespoon butter or margarine
1   small clove garlic, minced
1   small onion, finely chopped
6   large mushrooms, sliced
2   teaspoons cornstarch
1   can (1 pound) stewed tomatoes
¹/₂ teaspoon crumbled oregano or rosemary
¹/₂ teaspoon seasoned salt
¹/₄ teaspoon seasoned pepper
¹/₄ pound mozzarella cheese, sliced

Have butcher cut 8 pieces veal cutlet ¹/₄-inch thick. Sprinkle on one side with parsley, seasoned salt and pepper, and grated Parmesan cheese. Roll up with cheese in center and fasten with wooden picks. Dust lightly with flour.

Heat cooking oil and butter or margarine in skillet over medium heat. Add veal rolls and fry until brown on all sides. Remove rolls from skillet and place on large rectangle of heavy duty foil, turned up around edges. Add minced garlic and finely chopped onion to drippings and cook over low heat until softened, stirring occasionally. Add mushrooms, cornstarch, stewed tomatoes, oregano or rosemary, seasoned salt and pepper; bring to simmer. Spoon sauce over rolls. Dot with sliced mozzarella cheese.

Close foil over meat, using double fold at edges and leaving room for steam which forms during cooking. Place in shallow baking pan. Bake in moderate oven (350 degrees) 35 minutes. Makes 4 servings.

Veal Scaloppine a la Marsala

1¹/₂ pounds veal round steak
³/₄ teaspoon MSG powder
¹/₂ teaspoon salt
¹/₈ teaspoon pepper
¹/₄ cup olive oil
1   clove garlic, minced
1   tablespoon chopped onion
1   tablespoon sliced mushrooms
¹/₂ cup Marsala wine
¹/₂ cup white wine
¹/₄ teaspoon chopped parsley
¹/₈ teaspoon salt
¹/₈ teaspoon pepper
1   large green olive, sliced

Pound round steak and cut into 6 pieces (cutlets). Combine MSG powder and salt and pepper and rub on cutlets. Heat olive oil in skillet over medium temperature and add minced garlic. Add cutlets and cook until brown on both sides. Combine onion, mushrooms, Marsala wine, white wine, parsley, salt, pepper, and green olive and add slowly to browned cutlets. Cover and simmer over low heat 20 minutes or until meat is tender. Makes 6 servings.

Vealuscious

3 tablespoons bacon drippings or fat
1 large onion, minced
3 pounds boneless veal shoulder, cubed
1 cup Rhine wine
1 4-ounce can sliced mushrooms and liquid
2 tablespoons chopped parsley
   Salt and pepper to taste
¹/₄ cup flour
¹/₂ cup water
1 4-ounce can pimiento, chopped
1 teaspoon Worcestershire powder
¹/₂ cup sour cream
   Buttered noodles

Heat the bacon drippings or fat in Dutch oven or heavy kettle over medium heat. Add minced onion and cubed veal and cook until meat is browned, stirring frequently. Add wine, mushrooms and liquid, parsley, salt and pepper to taste, flour, water, pimiento, and Worcestershire powder; cook, stirring constantly, until mixture boils. Cover and simmer over low heat 1 hour or until meat is tender. Just before serving, stir in sour cream. Serve with buttered noodles. Makes 8 servings.

Tangy Veal Cutlets

1 cup dry white wine
1 teaspoon grated orange peel
1 teaspoon grated lime peel
   Dash ground allspice
¹/₈ teaspoon dried rosemary leaves, crushed
1 pound veal cutlets (¹/₄-inch thick)
1 egg, beaten
1 tablespoon milk
¹/₂ cup fine dry bread crumbs (seasoned)
6 tablespoons butter or margarine

In small saucepan combine wine, orange peel, lime peel, allspice and rosemary. Heat until hot. (Do not boil.) Cool slightly. Place veal in medium mixing bowl or plastic food storage bag. Pour marinade over veal. Cover dish or close bag. Refrigerate at least 3 hours, turning veal occasionally.

In shallow dish blend egg and milk. Dip veal in egg mixture, turning to coat both sides. Dip in bread crumbs, turning to coat both sides. Set aside.

Preheat griddle on setting "8." Melt 3 tablespoons butter on griddle. Cook veal three minutes. Melt remaining 3 tablespoons butter on griddle. Turn veal. Cook 2 to 3 minutes longer, or until crisp. Four servings.

Wiener Schnitzel

2 pounds veal, prepared for schnitzel
   Lemon juice to cover meat
³/₄ pound butter
12 anchovy fillets, mashed
   Paprika
2 eggs
2 tablespoons water
1 cup fine dry bread crumbs mixed with
    ¹/₄ cup chestnut flour
   Lemon quarters

Marinate the pounded schnitzels in lemon juice to cover 1 hour. Just before sautéing them, prepare the sauce by melting ¹/₄ pound butter and adding mashed anchovies and paprika. Keep this sauce hot.

Beat eggs lightly in bowl, add water. Dip drained schnitzels into egg mixture, then dredge with mixed bread crumbs and flour and let stand 15 to 20 minutes.

In a good-sized skillet melt remaining ¹/₂ pound butter and let it foam well. Reduce heat, add schnitzels, and sauté 1 to 1¹/₂ minutes for each side. The slices are done as soon as the coating turns golden brown. Sprinkle lightly with lemon juice at once and pour the hot anchovy butter over them. Serve immediately with lemon quarters on the side, as garnish. Makes 8 servings.

Pork

Sicillian Pork Chops

6   pork chops
2   tablespoons oil
1   tablespoon chili powder
4   tablespoons flour
2   teaspoons salt
1   teaspoon Worcestershire powder
2   teaspoons A-1 sauce
$^1/_2$ bottle tomato catsup
1   catsup bottle of water
    Dash Tabasco
1   onion, sliced
2   green bell peppers, sliced

Combine the chili powder, flour and salt and coat the chops with the mixture, shaking off any excess flour. In a heavy skillet brown the chops on both sides in the oil. Transfer the chops to a baking dish, placing them side by side. Place an onion and green bell pepper slice on each chop. In a saucepan heat the remaining ingredients. Pour over the chops and bake at 350 degrees covered for 1 hour or until tender.

Dutch Chops

6   pork chops
$^1/_2$ cup flour
$^1/_2$ teaspoon salt
$^1/_2$ teaspoon MSG powder
$^1/_4$ teaspoon pepper
1   tablespoon shortening
$^1/_2$ cup water
2   tablespoons vinegar
$1^1/_2$ teaspoons sugar
1   small bay leaf
1   cup sour cream

Melt shortening in a skillet and brown chops on both sides after they have been coated in a mixture of flour, salt, MSG powder, and pepper. After they have browned remove from the skillet and arrange in a greased baking dish and pour over them the following mixture: water, vinegar, sugar, and bay leaf. Cover dish and bake for 1 hour in a 350-degree oven. Remove from oven and top with sour cream. Return dish to oven for about 15 minutes. Serve on curried rice. Serves 6.

Maui Pork

2   tablespoons shortening
2   pounds lean boneless pork shoulder, cut in $1^1/_2$-inch cubes
2   medium onions, thinly sliced
1   large green bell pepper, cut in strips
1   cup diced celery
1   clove garlic, chopped
$^1/_4$ cup orange juice
$^1/_4$ cup soy sauce
$^1/_4$ cup brown sugar, firmly packed
$^1/_2$ teaspoon salt
$^1/_4$ teaspoon ginger
2   teaspoons Worcestershire powder
$^1/_2$ cup white wine
3   medium carrots, cut in strips
$^1/_4$ pound mushrooms, halved (optional)
2   tablespoons plus $1^1/_2$ teaspoons cornstarch
2   tablespoons water

Heat shortening in Dutch oven over medium heat. Add pork cubes and cook until brown. Remove meat from pan. If necessary, remove excess fat from pan. Add onions, green bell pepper, celery, and garlic and cook until tender but not brown. Combine orange juice, soy sauce, brown sugar, salt, ginger and Worcestershire powder. Then add white wine and slowly pour over vegetables. Return meat to pan. Add carrot strips and bring to boil. Reduce heat to low, cover tightly and simmer until meat is tender, about 1 hour. Add mushrooms and cook 5 minutes.

Blend cornstarch and water and stir into meat mixture. Bring to boil and cook 5 minutes, stirring. Makes 5 or 6 servings.

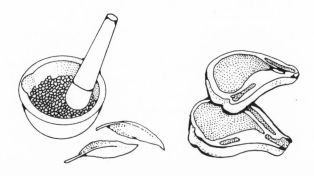

Ham and Macaroni Casserole

1   **pound cooked smoked ham, ground**
1   **small package macaroni, cooked**
    Salt and pepper to taste
2   **cups tomato sauce**
$^1/_2$ **cup bread crumbs**
$^1/_3$ **cup grated Romano cheese**

Alternate layers of ham and macaroni in casserole; season to taste. Cover with tomato sauce; sprinkle with crumbs. Top casserole with cheese. Bake at 350 degrees for 1 hour.

Pork Casserole with Cashews and Stir-Fried Vegetables

PORK:

1   **ounce dried Chinese mushrooms***
    (about 12)
3   **pounds lean pork, cut into $^1/_2$x$^1/_2$x1$^1/_2$-inch strips**
1   **two-inch length of fresh gingerroot, peeled and cut into $^1/_8$-inch julienne strips**

MARINADE:

1$^1/_2$ **cups (one 12-ounce can) apricot nectar**
$^1/_2$ **cup soy sauce**
2   **tablespoons dry sherry**
2   **teaspoons oyster sauce***
1$^1/_2$ **tablespoons honey**

VEGETABLE TOPPING:

3   **tablespoons peanut oil**
$^1/_2$ **cup coarsely chopped unsalted cashews**
$^3/_4$ **pound fresh snow peas, cut into $^1/_8$-inch julienne strips (about 3 cups)**
8   **scallions, cut into quarters lengthwise and then into 2-inch lengths**
1   **can (8-ounces) water chestnuts — drained, rinsed and cut into $^1/_8$-inch julienne strips**
$^1/_2$ **cup (one 4-ounce) bamboo shoots — drained, rinsed and cut into $^1/_8$-inch julienne strips**
$^1/_2$ **teaspoon Oriental sesame oil**

* Available at Oriental groceries

Prepare the pork: Place the mushrooms in a medium bowl and pour 1 cup hot water over them; let them rest for 15 minutes. Drain and discard the juice or reserve it for another use. In a shallow 4-quart casserole, combine the pork with the mushrooms and ginger.

Prepare the marinade: In a medium mixing bowl, combine all the marinade ingredients with $^1/_2$ cup of water. Pour the marinade over the meat and mushrooms, tossing them well. Marinate 1 hour. Preheat the oven to 350 degrees. Cover the casserole tightly and bake for 2 to 2$^1/_2$ hours, or until the meat is tender and easily pierced with a fork. Remove from the oven and set aside.

Stir-fry the vegetables: In a wok or large heavy skillet, warm the peanut oil over moderate heat. Add the cashews and stir-fry for about 30 seconds. Stir in the snow peas, scallions, water chestnuts and bamboo shoots; stir-fry until the vegetables are heated through but still crisp, 2 to 3 minutes. Stir in the sesame oil for flavoring. Transfer the pork and mushrooms to a platter and arrange the stir-fried vegetables in a crescent shape over half the dish.

Rum Roasted Pork

3   **to 5 pound boneless pork loin roast**
    Salt
    Coarsely ground black pepper
    Dried thyme, crumbled
    Garlic cloves, peeled and slivered
    Dark Jamaica rum
    Worcestershire powder

With a sharp knife, pierce surface of pork about 1$^1/_2$ inches deep in 6 to 10 places. With forefinger, press into each hole about $^1/_{16}$ teaspoon each salt, pepper, and thyme, and about $^1/_4$ clove garlic. Rub surface of roast with Worcestershire powder and enough rum to moisten. Place pork in a shallow pan. Pour over 6 to 10 tablespoons more rum. Cover and chill for 12 to 24 hours. Turn occasionally. Place on rack in roasting pan and bake in a slow oven (325 degrees), allowing about 40 minutes per pound or until meat thermometer registers about 185 degrees. Allow to stand for about 15 minutes. Meantime, remove from roasting pan all fat and any burned drippings; leave crusty brown drippings. Add $^2/_3$ cup water and 2 tablespoons rum, stir to loosen drippings, and cook and stir over high heat just to blend. Carve pork into thin slices. Pass rum sauce to ladle over. Makes 6 to 10 servings.

Braised Pork Chops with Fresh Tomato Sauce

6   pork chops, cut 1-inch thick (about 2¹/₂ to
    3 pounds)
    About ¹/₄ cup all-purpose flour, for
    dredging
¹/₄   cup olive oil
7   medium onions, chopped
5   garlic cloves, crushed and minced
4   pounds ripe tomatoes (about 10 medium)
    — peeled, seeded and coarsely chopped
1   tablespoon basil
2   teaspoons oregano
2   cups dry red wine or chicken broth
1   tablespoon sugar
1   tablespoon salt
¹/₂   teaspoon freshly ground pepper

Dredge the pork chops in the flour; shake off any excess. In a large, heavy noncorrodible skillet, heat the oil until almost smoking. Working in batches if necessary, add the pork chops and cook over moderately high heat, turning once, until crisp and golden brown, about 5 minutes on each side. Remove and set aside.

Add the onions to the pan drippings in the skillet, reduce the heat to moderate and sauté, stirring occasionally, until golden brown, about 20 minutes. Add the garlic and cook for 5 minutes longer. Add the tomatoes, basil, oregano, wine, sugar, salt and pepper. Bring to a boil, reduce the heat to low and simmer, stirring occasionally for 30 minutes.

Return the pork chops to the skillet. Cover them with the sauce, cover and simmer, basting occasionally, for 2 hours. Watch carefully during the last 30 minutes and stir to prevent the sauce from sticking or scorching.

Pecan-Stuffed Honey-Glazed Ham

6   to 8 pound boneless ham, fully cooked
2¹/₂   cups chopped onion
¹/₄   pound (1 stick) butter or margarine
1¹/₂   cups packaged corn bread stuffing mix
³/₄   cup chopped fresh parsley
2¹/₂   cups coarsely chopped pecans
3   teaspoons prepared mustard
3   eggs, lightly beaten
3   tablespoons frozen orange juice
    concentrate, thawed

Cut all skin and fat from ham. Make a cavity in the ham by cutting a 2-inch diameter cylinder through the length of the ham, beginning in the front and working toward the back. Remove ham from cylinder, leaving a 2-inch tunnel. (Save the center scraps of ham for another use.)

Make pecan stuffing: In large skillet, sauté onion in butter or margarine until soft. Remove to bowl and add corn bread stuffing mix, parsley, pecans, mustard, and egg; toss lightly. Stuff cavity of ham with two thirds of the stuffing, packing it in lightly. Score top of ham in diamond pattern, cutting about ¹/₄-inch deep. May be refrigerated for 2 days. Refrigerate remaining stuffing in covered bowl.

Bring to room temperature. Preheat oven to 325 degrees. Place ham on rack in roasting pan. Bake for 1¹/₂ hours.

While ham is baking, make glaze by mixing honey and orange juice concentrate in bowl. After 1¹/₂ hours, pour glaze over ham; bake 20 minutes. Remove ham from oven and spread the remaining stuffing evenly over the top. Baste with pan juices. Return to oven and bake 20 to 30 more minutes or until top is brown and crusty.

Pork Chops, Lisbon

6   loin pork chops, at least ¹/₂-inch thick
    Salt and pepper
2   tablespoons butter
1   bunch green onions, chopped
1   teaspoon brown sugar
¹/₄   cup chopped carrots
1   clove
4   peppercorns
1   sprig parsley
1   pinch thyme
1   tablespoon flour
¹/₂   cup white wine

Season the chops with salt and pepper and brown them on both sides in a skillet with 1 tablespoon of butter. Cover the pan and bake in a moderate oven until tender.

In a saucepan build a sauce by melting 1 tablespoon of butter to which you add the brown sugar and chopped onion, cooking together until the onion browns. Add ¹/₂ cup of hot water to the saucepan, and bring to a boil. Turn down to a simmer, add the carrots, clove, peppers, parsley and thyme.

Let the sauce simmer.

When the chops are done, remove from the pan, placing aside. Pour off the fat in the pan, except for about a tablespoonful. Into this, work 1 tablespoon of flour, blending flour and hot fat into a smooth paste.

Add 1 cup of hot water to the saucepan, containing the onions, etc., mix, and pour into the skillet with the thick paste, stirring all together until it thickens.

Now place the pork chops in the saucepan.

Place a sieve over the saucepan and pour the contents of the skillet through the sieve onto the chops. Add the white wine and bring up the heat, but not to the boiling point. Cook very slowly for 10 minutes, and serve.

Barbecued Pork Chops

4   pork chops
2   tablespoons pan drippings
1   can tomato sauce
$^1/_3$ cup diced celery
    Juice of $^1/_2$ lemon
$^1/_2$ teaspoon dry mustard
$^1/_2$ teaspoon salt
$^1/_2$ cup water
2   tablespoons brown sugar
$^1/_8$ teaspoon pepper

Brown chops in drippings; place in shallow greased baking dish. Combine remaining ingredients; pour over chops. Cover, bake at 350 degrees for 1 hour and 30 minutes, basting occasionally. Yield 4 servings.

Cornhuskers' Casserole

4   medium sized potatoes, peeled and sliced
        medium thick
2   Jonathan apples, cored and sliced thickly,
        but unpeeled
4   thick pork chops
1   large onion, sliced
    Salt and pepper to taste

Trim slices of fat from pork chops and place into skillet. Lightly heat until some fat is rendered from the pork slices. Brown pork chops slowly until light brown. Remove from skillet. Add $1^1/_2$ cups of water to the fat remaining in the skillet. Preheat oven to 375 degrees. Place sliced, peeled potatoes and sliced onion in 2-quart casserole. Salt and pepper to taste. Place apple rings and pork chops on top with small end of pork chop through the hole of apple ring. Pour contents of skillet over these ingredients and bake at 375 degrees for approximately 1 hour. Serves 4.

Stuffed Pork Chops

3   strips bacon
2   tablespoons chopped onion
1   cup soft bread crumbs
1   cup peeled, chopped raw apple
$^3/_4$ cup chopped cooked prunes
6   pork chops cut 1-inch thick
    Salt, pepper, and flour
$^1/_2$ cup pineapple juice
$^1/_2$ cup Sauterne

Mince bacon and cook until almost crisp. Add onion and cook 3 minutes (medium heat). Add crumbs, apple, and prunes. Cut a slit in each chop and fill with the stuffing. Fasten with a toothpick. Sprinkle with salt, pepper, and flour. Brown in a heavy skillet, pour off fat, and add the pineapple juice and wine. Cover and either bake at 325 degrees or cook on top of the stove at low heat until tender, about 1 hour. Add more juice if necessary, or water.

German Sausage Diabla

Cut into $^1/_4$-inch rounds, two 12-ounce packages of German sausage. Place these into a large skillet and add water to almost cover. Bring to a boil. Place tight-fitting lid on skillet and lower heat to medium. Continue cooking for about 10 minutes. Drain water completely. Add sauce and return to boiling point. Place lid on skillet again and reduce heat to simmer. Heat for about 40 minutes or until sausage is tender.

SAUCE

1   15-ounce bottle catsup
$^1/_2$ cup white Karo syrup
$^1/_4$ cup red wine vinegar
2   tablespoons liquid smoke
2   tablespoons A-1 Sauce
1   tablespoon Worcestershire powder
1   teaspoon salt
2   teaspoons black pepper
4   drops Tabasco sauce
1   tablespoon dry powdered mustard
2   teaspoons garlic powder

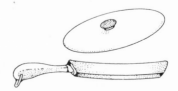

Dutch Ham Hofbrau Style

1	14-pound ham, with leg bone and skin removed
1	cup red wine
6	cups sifted flour
4	teaspoons double acting baking powder
$1/_4$	teaspoon powdered sage
2	teaspoons salt
1	teaspoon powdered mustard
1	cup shortening
$1^1/_2$	cups cold milk

Place the ham into a roasting pan and pour over it one cup of red wine. Cover the ham and place into a preheated oven at 325 degrees; roast about 20 minutes per pound. Baste ham from time to time while cooking.

While ham is roasting, prepare the following dough: Sift the 6 cups of flour twice. Resift the flour with baking powder, powdered sage, salt, and mustard. Into this mixture cut shortening with a pastry blender until the mixture resembles coarse meal. Gradually add cold milk to make a soft but not sticky dough. On a floured board, knead the dough for a minute and shape it into a ball. Roll the dough out about $1/_2$-inch thick.

When the ham has been roasted, remove it from the oven and, while it is still warm, enrobe it with the dough. Decorate the top with designs made from leftover dough. Then place the dough-covered ham onto a baking sheet and into a preheated oven at 450 degrees for 10 minutes. Then lower the heat to about 350 degrees and bake until the dough is delicately browned, brushing the crust twice with cold milk. This second baking time should require about 15 minutes. Before serving, the ham can be decorated with fresh flowers.

Chicken

New Haven Broccoli Chicken

12	halves deboned, skinned chicken breasts (cooked until tender)
3	packages frozen chopped broccoli (cooked and drained)
1	$10^3/_4$-ounce can condensed cream of chicken soup
$1^1/_2$	cups mayonnaise
1	tablespoon lemon juice
1	teaspoon curry powder
1	cup grated sharp Cheddar cheese
1	stick butter
	Dash of Tabasco
1	teaspoon Worcestershire powder
$1^1/_2$	cups cracker crumbs
	Salt and pepper to taste
1	teaspoon curry powder

Arrange broccoli in a casserole dish and place chicken breasts on top. Place soup, mayonnaise, lemon juice and cheese in a sauce pan. Over low heat melt cheese forming a sauce.

Blend in all seasoning, then top chicken and broccoli with the sauce. Sauté bread crumbs in the butter and sprinkle over casserole mixture — bake at 350 degrees for at least 30 minutes or until mixture bubbles around the outsides. Recipe serves 12.

Chicken Clemonceau

6	chicken breasts, skinned and boned
1	stick butter
1	yellow onion, sliced
1	green bell pepper, diced
1	6-ounce can sliced mushrooms
1	15-ounce can English peas
3	large raw potatoes, peeled and sliced
	Worcestershire powder
	Powdered dry mustard
	Garlic powder
	Tabasco
	Salt
	Pepper
2	cans beef consommé

Melt butter in a large skillet and brown chicken on both sides. Add onion, bell pepper and mushrooms, continue cooking slowly for 5 minutes. Add peas and potatoes then seasoning and consommé. Bring to a boil, place lid on skillet. Lower heat and simmer, stirring occasionally until chicken is tender. Recipe serves 6.

Chicken Livers Sautéed with Apples and Onion Rings

12 **chicken livers**
$^1/_2$ **teaspoon salt**
$^1/_4$ **teaspoon paprika**
2 **tablespoons butter**
3 **tablespoons flour**
$^1/_2$ **Spanish onion, peeled and sliced in rings**
4 **apple slices about $^1/_2$-inch thick**
2 **tablespoons sugar**

Rinse and drain livers; if very large, cut in half. Season lightly with salt and paprika, sprinkle lightly with flour. Cook gently in 2 tablespoons butter until browned. In another small pan cook onion in a little butter. Sprinkle over cooked livers.

In a third pan brown apple slices in remaining butter. Sprinkle with sugar to give glaze and flavor. Top liver and onions. Makes 2 servings.

Sautéed Chicken Livers with Thin Noodles

1 **pound fresh or frozen chicken livers**
4 **heaping tablespoons fresh sweet butter**
$^1/_4$ **cup olive oil**
$^1/_4$ **pound onions, peeled and sliced thin**
1 **garlic clove, mashed**
1 **teaspoon Worcestershire powder**
1 **bay leaf**
$^1/_3$ **teaspoon freshly ground black pepper**
$^1/_3$ **teaspoon salt**
$^2/_3$ **cup dry white wine**
  Juice of 1 lemon
6 **fresh parsley springs, leaves only, chopped fine**
1 **pound thin noodles**

Wash the chicken livers and dry gently. Combine butter and olive oil in a skillet; heat. Add the onions and garlic and sauté until light brown. Add chicken livers and cook slowly for 4 minutes. Add Worcestershire powder, bay leaf, pepper and salt, stir, and cook for 1 minute. Add the wine, stir, and cover. Cook slowly for 5 minutes. Add the lemon juice and parsley and simmer over medium heat for about 5 minutes. Taste for cooking and add more salt if necessary. Remove bay leaf.

Cook the noodles to your taste and drain. Add a little butter and cheese to noodles. Arrange livers over noodles on individual plates and spoon the sauce over top. Serve a salad of Bibb or Boston lettuce with Italian Salad Dressing. Serves 4.

Glazed Cornish Hens with Pears

2 **Cornish hens (16 to 24 ounces each), thawed if frozen**
2 **firm pears**
1 **cup whole cranberry sauce**

Remove giblets and necks from hens. Rinse and drain hens. With string, tie wings and legs close to bodies of hens.

Carefully skewer one pear on spit. Skewer hens on center of spit. Secure with meat holders. Skewer remaining pear on spit. Push pears close to hens. Cook on "Hi," 60 to 70 minutes, or until meat thermometer inserted in thigh registers 180 degrees to 185 degrees. Brush with cranberry sauce every 15 minutes. Remove spit and strings. Cut pears in half. Remove cores. Spoon any remaining warmed cranberry sauce in pear centers. Two servings.

Chicken au Gratin with Broccoli

1 **chicken ($3^1/_2$ to 4 pounds), poached**
$1^1/_4$ **pounds tender fresh broccoli**
$^1/_4$ **cup butter**
3 **tablespoons all-purpose flour**
$^1/_4$ **cup boiling chicken broth**
$^1/_2$ **cup heavy cream, warmed**
$^1/_2$ **cup dry white wine**
  Salt and pepper
$^3/_4$ **cup freshly grated Parmesan cheese**

Slice the breasts and thighs of the poached chicken and lightly pound the meat of the legs between 2 sheets of wax paper. Reserve any remaining chicken for other uses. Trim and wash the broccoli and steam it, heads up, in $1^1/_2$ inches of water for about 15 minutes. Drain.

Preheat oven to moderate (350 degrees). Place butter in a small saucepan and heat. Add flour and stir. Add chicken broth slowly. Stir until mixture thickens. Add the warmed cream and the wine and stir. Remove from the heat. Have 4 individual casseroles ready and warmed. Place a quarter of the drained broccoli in the center of each. Arrange chicken alongside broccoli. Grind a little pepper and a pinch of salt over the top. Now spoon sauce evenly over top. Sprinkle cheese on top and bake for about 20 minutes. Serves 4.

Country Style Hot Chicken Salad

4 cups cooked, cubed chicken
2 cups cooked rice
1 cup chopped celery
$^1/_2$ cup slivered almonds
$^3/_4$ cup mayonnaise
1 10$^3/_4$-ounce can condensed cream of chicken soup
1 2-ounce jar chopped pimiento, drained
3 hard cooked eggs, chopped
2 tablespoons chopped green bell pepper
2 tablespoons chopped onion
$^1/_4$ teaspoon salt
1 tablespoon lemon juice
$^1/_2$ cup crushed potato chips

Heat oven to 350 degrees. In large bowl stir together all ingredients except potato chips. Spread into greased 13x9 baking pan. Sprinkle with chips. Bake for 40 to 50 minutes or until heated through. Yield: 8 servings.

Chicken Salad Supreme

$2^1/_2$ cups diced cold chicken
1 cup celery, chopped fine
1 cup sliced white grapes
$^1/_2$ cup shredded browned almonds
2 tablespoons minced parsley
1 teaspoon salt
1 cup mayonnaise
$^1/_2$ cup whipping cream, whipped

Combine and serve in lettuce cups with thin slices of chicken on top, garnished with stuffed olives, sliced thin, or chopped ripe olives.

This same mixture can be made into a mold that is delicious. Use the same eight ingredients, plus:

$1^1/_2$ tablespoons gelatin
4 tablespoons water
$^1/_2$ cup chicken stock

Mix the chicken, celery, grapes, almonds, parsley, and salt. Soak gelatin in the cold water for 5 minutes and dissolve in hot chicken stock. When cold, add mayonnaise and whipped cream. Stir until thick and fold in the chicken mixture. Pack in individual molds or a large ring. Serve garnished. Allow at least 3 hours for gelatin to set — 6 hours is better.

Russian Chicken

$2^1/_2$ to 3 pounds chicken pieces
Garlic salt, to taste
1 teaspoon Worcestershire powder
1 8-ounce bottle of Russian dressing
2 ounces sherry wine (not cooking wine)
1 medium onion, sliced in rings

Preheat oven to 350 degrees. Season chicken with garlic salt. Arrange in 9x12-inch baking pan. Pour Russian dressing over chicken. Add sherry wine and top with sliced onions. Cover with foil and bake for 1 hour, 30 minutes. Can be frozen. Recipe serves 4.

Oven Fried Chicken

1 egg
2 tablespoons Miracle Whip, heaping
$^1/_2$ cup evaporated milk
1 teaspoon salt
$^1/_4$ teaspoon pepper
Ritz cracker crumbs

Dip each piece of chicken in the above mixture and roll in cracker crumbs. Makes enough batter for 2 chickens, cut up. Bake 1 hour at 400 degrees or a little longer.

Jean Baskin's Chicken Cutlets

3 cups flour
$1^1/_2$ teaspoons pepper
3 teaspoons salt
$1^1/_2$ teaspoons Worcestershire powder
3 cups milk
$1^1/_2$ cups cooking oil
3 pounds skinless chicken breasts

Mix together in a bowl the flour, pepper, salt and Worcestershire powder and set aside. Pour milk into a large bowl. Heat cooking oil in large skillet until frying hot.

Pound each chicken breast to about $^1/_8$-inch thickness. Roll breasts in seasoned flour, then dip in milk and roll again in the flour mixture. Carefully place chicken pieces into hot oil and cook until golden brown on both sides. (About 5 minutes on each side.)

Remaining flour mixture can be used with additional milk and residue from skillet to make sauce to be spooned over cooked chicken. Recipe serves 6.

Chicken Curry

2   chickens — cut up
5   large onions
1   minced garlic clove
3   tablespoons sugar
3   tablespoons chutney
12 whole black peppers, mashed
1/2 teaspoon powdered ginger
2 1/2 tablespoons Madras curry powder
1   cup coconut milk *
3   cups chicken stock or consommé
    Salt, oil, butter, flour

Dredge the chicken by shaking one piece at a time in a paper sack containing flour. Heat 4 or 5 tablespoons of oil in a frying pan and brown the dredged chicken. Remove the chicken to a pot, preferably a clay pot. Metal utensils affect the flavor of curry dishes. Stirring should be done with a wooden spoon. An enameled pot would do.

After removing the chicken from the frying pan, brown the onions and garlic in the same pan.

Work the curry into 4 tablespoons of melted butter, and have ready.

To the onions add chutney, salt, peppercorns, sugar, ginger, and the chicken stock or consommé. Simmer for a few minutes until the "brown" in the pan (created in the frying) has been absorbed by the liquids. Pour this over the chicken in the pot. Add the curry-butter mixture. Cover the pot and simmer 45 minutes, stirring occasionally.

Add the coconut milk. Cook until the chicken is tender and the liquids reduced. Remove the chicken pieces from the pot. Remove the meat from the bones and return the chicken to the pot. Keep piping hot until serving time.

The ideal method of serving is to present the clay pot over an alcohol flame on the buffet table. Serve with fluffy white rice.

* To produce 1 cup of coconut milk, combine 2 cups of grated coconut with 1 cup of boiling water in this way: Place a double layer of cheesecloth over a strainer. Put the grated coconut on, or in, the cloth. Pour the boiling water over the coconut, draining it into a bowl. That's coconut milk, as used in curry dishes.

Chicken Santa Fe

2   broiler-fryers (2 1/2 to 3 pounds each) cut in serving pieces
6   tablespoons butter or margarine
2   medium onions, sliced
1/2 pound mushrooms, sliced
1   cup dark or light raisins
1 1/4 cups water
4   teaspoons salt
1/4 cup lemon juice
2   teaspoons MSG powder
1/2 teaspoon ground cloves
1/2 teaspoon allspice
1/2 teaspoon ginger
1/4 cup brown sugar
1   cup walnut halves
4   teaspoons cornstarch
1/2 cup water
2   cups seedless grapes
2   cups orange sections
12 maraschino cherries, washed

Sauté chicken pieces in butter or margarine in heavy Dutch oven over medium heat until golden. Add onion, mushrooms, raisins, water, salt, lemon juice, MSG, ground cloves, allspice, ginger and brown sugar, cover and simmer over low heat 40 minutes or until tender, turning occasionally. Add walnut halves. Push chicken pieces to one side of pan.

Blend cornstarch and water and add to liquid in pan. Cook until liquid is thickened and smooth. Add grapes, orange sections and maraschino cherries and cook 2 minutes. Serve at once. Makes 8 servings.

Chicken Rotel

1   chicken, boiled, deboned, diced
1   can cream of mushroom soup
1   can cream of chicken soup
1   can Rotel tomatoes
1   pound Velveeta cheese, chipped
1   cup uncooked rice or cooked noodles

Combine all ingredients and place into casserole dish. Bake 1 hour at 350 degrees.

Creole Chicken

　　Fat from ¹/₂ pound of cooked bacon
2　medium onions, diced fine
1　green bell pepper, diced fine
1　large can of mushrooms
1　small can tomato paste
1　small can tomato sauce
1　No. 2 can of peeled tomatoes
1　tablespoon garlic salt
　　Dash of pepper
　　Dash of Tabasco
1　tablespoon Worcestershire powder
¹/₄　cup white wine
1　4-pound baking chicken
　　Salt and pepper
1　large supermarket paper bag
　　Cotton string

Place the bacon fat into a skillet. (Do not use the bacon.) In this bacon fat sauté onions, green bell pepper and mushrooms until soft. Then add tomato paste, tomato sauce, peeled tomatoes, garlic salt, pepper, Tabasco, Worcestershire powder and wine. Simmer for 12 minutes with the cover on the skillet.

Make sure baking size hen is a few degrees below room temperature. Lightly salt and pepper hen to taste. Place ¹/₂ of the sauce in the cavity and cover the chicken with the other half. Carefully place chicken inside paper bag and close the open end securely. Tie this end tightly with string then place paper bag containing the chicken and sauce into a lower section of a shallow roasting pan. Place roasting pan into a preheated 350-degree oven and cook for 1 hour and 30 minutes. Remove from oven and very carefully tear a hole in the top of the paper bag permitting live steam to escape then rip away paper. Serve the Creole Chicken on a platter of fluffy white rice. Recipe serves 6.

Chicken Delmonaco

¹/₂　stick of butter
6　boneless, skinned chicken breasts
2　large shallots, chopped fine
1　small green bell pepper, chopped fine
1　8-ounce can sliced mushrooms, drained
1　tablespoon Worcestershire powder
　　White pepper to taste
2　teaspoons garlic powder
2　teaspoons dry powdered mustard
2　tablespoons sugar
¹/₂　cup dry Vermouth
2　cups beef consommé
2　cups packaged seasoned croutons
1　tablespoon corn starch
¹/₂　cup beef consommé

Melt butter in a large skillet. Add chicken breasts and brown on one side. Turn chicken and blend in shallots, mushrooms, green bell pepper and continue browning chicken and vegetables for a few minutes. Add the 6 seasoning items. Blend in Vermouth and 2 cups of consommé. Cover with tight-fitting lid and simmer until chicken is fork tender.

Slur or blend cornstarch and ¹/₂ cup of consommé together. Mix into recipe. Place lid back on skillet and simmer until mixture thickens. Add croutons and continue to simmer covered for 4 more minutes.

Recipe can be served on a plate over toast or rice. Serves 6.

Chicken and Dumplings

3　pound chicken, cut into 8 pieces,
　　　giblets reserved
1　teaspoon salt
¹/₂　teaspoon freshly ground pepper
2　medium carrots, thinly sliced
2　medium onions, thinly sliced
2　celery ribs, thinly sliced
3　garlic cloves, crushed through a press
2　cups sifted all-purpose flour
1　tablespoon baking powder
1　teaspoon salt
2　eggs, lightly beaten
²/₃　cup milk
¹/₂　cup chopped parsley

Place the chicken pieces and giblets in a large flameproof casserole. Season with the salt and pepper. Add the carrots, onions, celery, 2 of the garlic cloves and water to

cover. Bring to a boil over high heat. Reduce the heat to moderately low and simmer for about 1 hour, or until the chicken is very tender. With a slotted spoon, remove the chicken pieces to a deep platter and cover with foil to keep warm.

In a medium mixing bowl, combine the flour, baking powder and salt. Add the eggs, milk, parsley and the remaining clove of garlic and stir well until blended.

Over moderately high heat, return the chicken stock to a boil. Drop the batter by rounded teaspoons into the broth. Cover the casserole and cook for 15 minutes.

To serve, place the dumplings on the platter around the chicken pieces and pour on the cooking liquid and vegetables.

Antoine's Chicken Creole

1	2^1/$_2$ to 3 pound chicken
	Milk
	Flour
1	cup olive oil
1	can (1 pound 4 ounces) tomatoes
1	tablespoon butter or margarine
1	teaspoon salt
^{1}/$_8$	teaspoon pepper
^{1}/$_8$	teaspoon cayenne
1	sprig thyme
1	tablespoon minced parsley
1	bay leaf
3	cloves garlic, minced
1	tablespoon butter or margarine
1	tablespoon flour
6	chopped shallots or ^{1}/$_2$ cup minced onion
5	tablespoons chopped green bell pepper
^{1}/$_2$	cup white wine

Cut chicken in serving pieces and wipe with damp cloth. Dip in milk then flour. Heat olive oil in skillet over medium heat, add chicken pieces and fry until brown. Remove from skillet and place in heat-proof baking dish.

Add tomatoes and butter or margarine to oil remaining in skillet and cook over low heat 10 minutes, stirring occasionally. Add salt, pepper and cayenne and continue cooking 10 minutes. Add thyme, parsley, bay leaf and minced garlic and continue cooking 15 minutes or until sauce is thickened. Pour over chicken in baking dish.

Melt butter or margarine in saucepan over very low heat. Stir in flour and cook until brown. Add white wine and continue cooking until slightly thickened, stirring constantly. Pour over chicken in baking dish. Bake in hot oven (400 degrees) 45 minutes or until chicken is tender. Serve on bed of cooked rice (approximately 2 cups). Makes 4 servings.

David Wade's Chicken Spaghetti

1	stick butter
6	large chicken breasts (skinned and deboned)
1	green bell pepper, chopped
1	large white onion, chopped
3	ribs celery, chopped
6	ounces chopped pimiento
12	ounces canned sliced mushrooms (drained)
6	drops garlic juice
5	drops Tabasco
1	tablespoon Worcestershire powder
1	tablespoon powdered mustard
2	teaspoons poultry seasoning
	White pepper to taste
4	cups instant vegetable bouillon
^{1}/$_2$	cup dry white wine
1	bay leaf
1	pound package thin spaghetti
2	tablespoons cooking oil
	Water
3	cups sour cream
1	cup heavy cream
1^1/$_2$	cups grated Velveeta cheese
	Seasoned salt to taste

Melt butter in a large skillet, add chicken and brown on one side. Turn chicken and add green bell pepper, onion, celery, pimiento, and mushrooms. When chicken is browned on all sides and vegetables are soft, add garlic juice, Tabasco, Worcestershire powder, powdered mustard, poultry seasoning, white pepper, vegetable bouillon and wine.

Bring to a boil, add bay leaf, cover skillet and lower heat to a simmer. Simmer until chicken is fork tender. Remove bay leaf and remove from heat. Place water and cooking oil in kettle and bring to a boil, add spaghetti and cook until tender. Drain away water and add stock from chicken to spaghetti. Cover and permit to stand for 30 minutes.

Cut chicken into ^{1}/$_2$-inch cubes and place with spaghetti along with stock, seasonings and vegetables. Mix completely.

Using a saucepan, heat sour cream and heavy cream. Blend in cheese. Pour mixture slowly over spaghetti and permit liquid to blend. The cheese will remain on top. Place kettle covered into a preheated oven at 375 degrees. Bake for 30 minutes or until bubbling around outside. Remove cover and continue baking for 10 to 15 minutes until cheese on top browns. Remove from oven and permit to stand uncovered for 20 minutes.

Serve on a large flat platter surrounded by ripe tomato slices. Recipe serves 8.

Breast of Chicken Viennese Style

8   chicken breasts (boned and skinned)
1   stick of butter
2   shallots, chopped fine
1   cup canned sliced mushrooms (drained)
²/₃ cup chopped green bell pepper
3   cups vegetable stock
¹/₂ cup dry vermouth
1   tablespoon Worcestershire powder
   White pepper to taste
   Seasoned salt to taste
2   teaspoons garlic powder
2   teaspoons powdered dry mustard
   Few drops Tabasco

Melt butter in a skillet and brown chicken on one side. Turn and add shallots, mushrooms, and green bell pepper. When chicken is brown on both sides and vegetables are soft, add vegetable stock and vermouth. Add all seasonings and bring to a boil. Place tight-fitting lid on the skillet and lower to a simmer. Simmer until chicken is fork tender. Tighten sauce with a small amount of flour slurred with a little stock, if desired.

Serve over cooked turmeric rice. Recipe serves 8.

Chicken Pie Creole

1   5-pound stewing chicken, cut up

Simmer chicken 2 hours or more or until tender. Remove meat from bones and arrange in baking dish.

SAUCE:

2   tablespoons butter or margarine, melted
¹/₄ cup flour
3   cups chicken stock
1   cup light cream
¹/₂ teaspoon salt
¹/₄ teaspoon pepper

Blend together melted butter and flour. Gradually add warm chicken stock, cream, salt and pepper. Cook, stirring constantly, until sauce comes to a boil. Pour 2 to 3 cups over chicken, reserving enough sauce for a gravy bowl.

CRUST:

2   cups sifted flour
4   teaspoons baking powder
1   teaspoon salt
2   tablespoons butter or margarine, melted
1   egg, well beaten
³/₄ to 1 cup milk

Sift together flour, baking powder and salt. Combine melted butter, egg and milk, and add, stirring quickly to make a soft dough. Drop by spoonfuls over chicken and sauce in baking dish. Bake at 425 degrees for 15 to 20 minutes. Serve with reserved sauce. Yield: 6 portions.

Chicken Croquettes

2¹/₂ cups ground, cooked chicken or turkey
1   cup Thick White Sauce
2   tablespoons chopped parsley
1   tablespoon minced onion
¹/₂ teaspoon lemon juice
¹/₈ teaspoon rubbed sage
   Salt
1   egg
1   tablespoon water
¹/₄ cup all-purpose flour
¹/₂ cup dried bread crumbs
   Salad oil
   Mushroom sauce or Cheese sauce

In medium bowl, blend well first 6 ingredients. Add salt to taste. Cover; chill several hours.

About 30 minutes before serving: Shape chilled mixture into 8 cones. In shallow dish with fork, beat egg with water. Place flour and bread crumbs on separate sheets of waxed paper. Coat each on separate sheets of waxed paper. Coat each croquette first in flour, then in egg, then in crumbs.

In 4-quart saucepan over medium heat, heat 1 inch oil to 370 degrees. Fry croquettes until golden brown, turning frequently. Drain on paper towels; serve with Mushroom or Cheese Sauce.

Chicken Shanghai

6   chicken breasts, boned and skinned; then cubed $^1/_2$ inch x $^1/_2$ inch
10 tablespoons peanut oil

Place 8 tablespoons peanut oil in wok or large skillet, add chicken and cook until all of the redness is gone and chicken is white. Drain all oil in a collander and wipe out skillet with paper towel. Return chicken to skillet and add the other 2 tablespoons of peanut oil.

1   large white onion sliced
1   large green bell pepper chopped
2   ribs celery sliced crosswise

Add these three items to skillet and sauté stirring with chicken. When items are slightly browned, add the following, stirring:

1   tablespoon Worcestershire powder
**   Salt and white pepper to taste**
2   teaspoons garlic powder
2   teaspoons MSG
2   teaspoons powdered ginger
2   teaspoons powdered dry mustard
2   teaspoons Mey Yen
2   teaspoons dry powdered horseradish
**   Few drops Tabasco sauce**
2   tablespoons soy sauce
2   tablespoons Plum Sauce
1   tablespoon Chinese Mustard (salad style or sauce)
2   tablespoons Red Wine Vinegar

Steam a few moments, stirring. Add a slur made with 1 tablespoon cornstarch blended with $^1/_4$ cup water. Stir and cook over low heat 2 minutes. Add:

1   15-ounce can bean sprouts, drained
1   7-ounce can sliced water chestnuts, drained
1   7-ounce can bamboo shoots, drained

Cook a few minutes and serve over cooked rice.

Chicken Elizabeth

**   Broiling chicken**
**   Salt and pepper**
**   Butter**
$^1/_2$ pint sour cream
4   ounces Roquefort cheese
1   clove garlic

Cut a tender young broiler in half, season it with salt and pepper, and brown it on all sides in butter. Arrange the chicken in a baking dish and pour over it a mixture of sour cream, crumbled Roquefort cheese, and garlic clove that has been forced through a press. Cover the dish and bake the chicken in a moderate oven (350 degrees) for about 45 minutes or until the bird is thoroughly cooked.

GARLIC

Pecan-Stuffed Chicken Breasts

3   cups toast crumbs
3   tablespoons butter or margarine, melted
$^1/_3$ cup chopped onion
$^1/_2$ cup chopped celery
2   teaspoons chopped parsley or parsley flakes
$^3/_4$ cup chopped pecans
$^3/_4$ teaspoon MSG powder
**   Water**
4   small chicken breasts
**   Lemon juice**
3   tablespoons butter or margarine, melted
**   Salt and pepper**

Combine toast crumbs, melted butter or margarine, onion, celery, parsley, pecans, MSG powder and enough water to moisten. Shape mixture in mounds on 4 squares of double thickness foil arranged on baking sheet. Brush chicken breasts with lemon juice and melted butter or margarine, and sprinkle with salt and pepper. Place a chicken breast over each mound of stuffing. Fold foil up around chicken to make individual packages. Bake in moderate oven (350 degrees) 40 minutes. Fold back foil and bake in hot oven (400 degrees) 20 minutes until brown. Makes 4 servings.

Chicken Raphael

3   tablespoons olive oil
3   tablespoons butter or margarine
1   broiler/fryer, cut in serving pieces
     Salt and pepper to taste
     Shallots, finely chopped
¼   cup white wine
¼   cup sherry
¼   cup chicken consommé
2   egg yolks
     Small amount heavy cream
     Minced chives
     Minced parsley
     Dash nutmeg

Heat olive oil and butter or margarine in skillet over medium heat. Add chicken pieces and fry until brown. Reduce to low heat and continue cooking until tender. Season with salt and pepper and shallots.

Drain excess fat from skillet. Pour white wine, sherry, and consommé over chicken and simmer for a few minutes.

Just before serving, beat egg yolks and heavy cream together and add to recipe, stirring constantly. Add minced chives, parsley and nutmeg. Makes 4 servings.

Chicken Moni

1   small onion, finely chopped
5   water chestnuts, chopped medium fine
1½   slices bread
¼   cup light cream
     Dash MSG powder
¼   pound ground beef
1   egg
2   teaspoons soy sauce
¼   teaspoon ginger
     Dash cayenne
¼   pound ground veal
¼   pound ground pork
2   tablespoons salad oil

4   chicken breasts, boned
6   teaspoons honey
     Sesame seeds
2   fresh coconuts
     Pineapple and fruit for garnish

Mix first group of ingredients together well, and use to stuff chicken breasts from which the bones have been removed. Secure with skewers and bake with top side up in

325-degree oven for 50 minutes or until done. Remove from oven, baste with honey and sprinkle with sesame seeds. Return to oven for 10 minutes at 400 degrees. Serve on halves of fresh coconut. Garnish with pineapple and fruit.

Mennonite Chicken Baked in Sour Cream

¼   cup butter or margarine
¼   cup flour
1   teaspoon salt
     Dash pepper
2   pound broiler/fryer, split in half
     Paprika
2   tablespoons dry white wine
1   tablespoon flour
¼   teaspoon salt
     Dash paprika
     Dash pepper
½   cup sour cream

Place butter or margarine in shallow oven-proof baking dish or oven-proof skillet and melt over very low heat. Combine flour, salt, and pepper. Roll the chicken in seasoned flour until coated. Dip coated chicken in melted butter and place in baking pan, skin side up. Sprinkle with paprika. Bake in moderate oven (325 degrees) 1½ hours or until chicken is tender and brown. Remove from pan and keep warm. Add wine to drippings in pan, mixing well. Blend in flour, salt, paprika, pepper, and sour cream. Over low heat, heat just to boiling, stirring constantly. Remove from heat and serve over chicken. Makes 2 servings.

Chicken Stroganoff in Peppers

6   large green bell peppers
1   cup raw rice
1   cup chicken consommé
1   cup water
¼   pound butter
1   medium onion, chopped
1   clove garlic, chopped
½   cup chopped mushrooms
2   cups cooked diced chicken
     Worcestershire powder
     Dash Tabasco
½   cup sour cream
½   cup heavy cream
1   tablespoon red vinegar
1   tablespoon flour
     Salt and pepper to taste

Rinse green bell peppers and cut away one third of top of pepper. Remove stems, fiber, and seeds. Drop bell peppers into boiling salted water and simmer about 4 minutes. Remove and drain. Boil rice in chicken consommé and water until soft and golden in color. Melt butter in a large skillet and sauté onion, garlic, and mushrooms until tender. Add chicken, Worcestershire powder, Tabasco, sour cream, heavy cream, vinegar, flour, and salt and pepper to taste. Add cooked rice and mix completely. Remove from heat and stuff mixture into the peppers. Place stuffed peppers into a greased baking dish and add a little water to dish. Preheat oven and bake at 350 degrees for about 25 minutes. Serves 6.

Beef

Tampico Steak

Marinate your choice of steak for 2 hours in the following mixture:

1   cup red wine
$^1/_2$ teaspoon black pepper
1   15-ounce can Rotel tomato puree
1   teaspoon coriander
1   teaspoon comino
1   teaspoon taragon leaves

After 2 hours, drain marinade and broil with melted margarine blended with juice of one lemon. Baste and turn steak.

Picadillo

1   pound ground beef
$^1/_2$ cup chopped onion
1   clove garlic, minced
1     $10^1/_2$ ounce can tomato puree
1   medium apple, peeled, cored, and chopped
$^1/_2$ cup raisins
$^1/_4$ cup snipped parsley
$^1/_4$ cup chopped toasted almonds
1   tablespoon vinegar
1   teaspoon sugar
1   teaspoon salt
$^1/_4$ teaspoon ground cinnamon
$^1/_4$ teaspoon ground cumin
$^1/_8$ teaspoon pepper

In 10-inch skillet cook ground beef, onion, and garlic until meat is brown and onion is tender. Drain off excess fat. Stir in remaining ingredients. Cover; simmer 20 to 25 minutes. Serve as a main dish or use as a filling for tacos or Empanaditas. Makes 4 cups.

Swiss Steak

$^1/_4$ cup flour
1   teaspoon salt
$^1/_4$ teaspoon pepper
1   teaspoon Worcestershire powder
2   pounds round steak, cut 1-inch thick
2   tablespoons shortening
1   4-ounce can mushroom pieces
$^1/_2$ cup finely chopped onion
$^1/_2$ cup finely chopped green bell pepper
1   cup tomatoes, canned or fresh or one 1-pound can whole tomatoes with juice

Combine flour with salt, pepper, and Worcestershire powder, and pound into meat.

In family skillet, melt shortening over medium heat, about 3 minutes. Do not allow shortening to smoke. Brown steak for 5 minutes per side.

Add mushrooms, onion, green bell pepper and tomatoes. Simmer over low heat, covered, for $1^1/_2$ hours, or until tender. Makes 4 to 6 servings.

Home Cured Corn Beef

6-9   pound brisket
4   quarts water
$1^1/_2$ cups pickling salt
1   tablespoon sugar
2   tablespoons pickling spices
$^1/_2$ ounce saltpeter
8   large bay leaves
8   cloves garlic
2   medium onions
2   ribs celery including leaves

Bring water to a boil, using a 6- to 8-quart pan. Add pickling salt, sugar, pickling spices, saltpeter and bay leaves and bring to a rolling boil for 5 minutes. Let cool to room temperature. While cooling, trim as much fat from brisket as possible.

Place meat in a 3-gallon earthenware crock (like you make home brew in). When saline solution has cooled, pour over the meat. Add the garlic which has been halved. Be sure meat is completely immersed in solution. If not, place a heavy bowl on it to weight it down. Put cheesecloth over the container and let stand at room temperature for 12 days. (Not above 75 degrees.)

After 12 days, there will be a grayish-green residue on meat. Scrape it off and discard. Wash meat under cold running water until all spices are off. Place in large kettle and cover with water. Bring to a boil. Taste meat. If meat tastes salty, pour out the water and rinse the meat with cold water. Again, place meat in pan and cover with water. Add onions that have been quartered and the celery. Bring to a boil. Let simmer until meat is tender, checking with sharp-tinned fork (about 3 hours).

Place meat on board or platter to cool. Refrigerate to firm up, usually overnight, then slice and serve.

Nevada Baked Steak

    2   pounds round steak, cut 1-inch thick
  $^1/_2$ teaspoon salt
        Dash pepper
    1   can (6-ounces) tomato paste
    1   teaspoon Worcestershire powder
 $1^1/_2$ cups water
    1   bay leaf
  $^1/_4$ teaspoon thyme
  $^1/_4$ cup vinegar
    1   clove garlic
        Salt and pepper
  $^1/_4$ cup flour
    3   tablespoons oil
    1   large onion, sliced and separated into
          rings
    1   green bell pepper, sliced in rings

Trim fat from round steak and cut into serving pieces. Place in shallow dish or pan. Combine salt, pepper, tomato paste, Worcestershire powder, water, bay leaf, thyme and vinegar and pour over meat. Refrigerate overnight. After removing from refrigerator drain sauce from meat and reserve. Rub meat with garlic clove then sprinkle meat with salt and pepper. With mallet or edge of heavy plate, pound flour into meat.

Heat oil in skillet over medium heat, add meat and cook until brown. Place meat in baking dish. Drain oil from skillet. Add reserved sauce and heat. Arrange sliced onion rings and green bell pepper rings on top of meat. Pour hot sauce over all. Cover tightly. Bake in moderate oven (350 degrees) $1^1/_2$ to 2 hours. Makes 6 servings.

Nutty Burgers

Patties:

    1   pound lean ground beef
  $^1/_2$ cup minced walnuts
  $^1/_4$ cup chopped green onions
    1   teaspoon sesame seed oil
    4   sesame seed hamburger buns, split and
          toasted

For patties: In medium mixing bowl combine all ingredients. Divide mixture into 4 equal portions. Shape each portion into $^3/_4$-inch thick patty.

Preheat griddle on setting "7." Lightly grease griddle. Cook patties 9 to 11 minutes, or until desired doneness. Turn about half the time. Serve in hamburger buns.

Tip: Grilled onions make a good addition to Nutty Burgers (or other burgers). Slice 1 large onion (about $^3/_4$ pound) crosswise into $^1/_4$-inch slices. Cook on griddle along with burgers until golden brown. Turn occasionally.

Gypsy Steak

  $^1/_4$ cup cooking oil
    4   small individual round steaks,
          approximately $^1/_4$-inch thick
        Flour, salt and pepper
  $^1/_4$ cup cooking oil
    1   large yellow onion, finely chopped
    1   medium green bell pepper, finely
          chopped
    1   can (4-ounces) sliced mushrooms
    1   can (4-ounces) tomato paste
    2   cans (8-ounces each) tomato sauce
    1   can (10-ounces) tomatoes, drained
    1   tablespoon Worcestershire powder
        Dash Tabasco
    1   teaspoon garlic salt
  $^1/_4$ teaspoon basil
  $^1/_2$ teaspoon oregano
        Salt to taste
        Pepper to taste
    2   cups cooked elbow macaroni
    1   cup grated Cheddar cheese

Heat oil in heavy skillet over medium heat. Score the edges of round steaks and dust each side with flour, salt and pepper. Add steaks to hot oil and cook until brown on each side. Remove from skillet. To oil remaining in skillet add $^1/_4$ cup cooking oil, chopped onion, green bell pepper and sliced mushrooms and cook until vegetables are tender. Add tomato paste, tomato sauce, tomatoes, Worcestershire powder, Tabasco, garlic salt, basil, oregano, salt and pepper. Reduce heat to low and continue cooking 5 minutes. Stir in cooked elbow macaroni. Spoon 2 tablespoons of mixture onto center of each steak and top with grated cheddar cheese.

Shape steaks into rolls by folding sides over mixture and securing with toothpicks. Arrange the four steak rolls in deep baking dish and pour over remaining sauce mixture. Cover and bake in moderate oven (350 degrees) 45 minutes or until meat is fork tender. Makes 4 servings.

Corned Beef 'n' Cabbage Casserole

1	can condensed celery soup
1/2	cup chopped onion
1	teaspoon dry mustard
1	cup diced cooked corned beef
4	cups coarsely shredded cabbage

Mix all ingredients in 1 1/2-quart casserole. Cover and bake in 375-degree oven for 45 minutes. Makes 3 or 4 servings.

German Braised Steak

3	pounds round steak, cut thick
	Flour
1/2	teaspoon salt
1/2	teaspoon pepper
1	tablespoon Worcestershire powder
3	tablespoons butter, margarine, beef or bacon fat
1 1/2	pounds red onions, peeled and sliced
1	pint beer

Cut round steak into 2-inch squares and sprinkle generously on one side with flour. Then sprinkle with salt, pepper and Worcestershire powder. With mallet or edge of heavy plate, pound seasoning into meat, flattening slightly. Turn and repeat flouring, seasoning and pounding on other side. Melt butter, margarine, beef or bacon fat in heavy skillet over medium heat. Add seasoned meat and onions and cook until brown on all sides. Add beer.

Cover tightly. Reduce heat to low and simmer 1 1/2 to 2 hours or until meat is tender and broth is thick. Serve with boiled potatoes with chopped parsley and butter, scalloped tomatoes and cucumber salad. Makes 4 to 6 servings.

Note: After adding beer, covered skillet may be placed in moderate oven (325 degrees) and baked 1 1/2 to 2 hours. Use oven-proof skillet.

Chinese Pepper Steak

1 1/2	pounds sirloin steak, 1-inch thick
1/4	cup fat or vegetable oil
1	clove garlic, crushed
1	teaspoon salt
1	teaspoon ground ginger
1/2	teaspoon pepper
3	large green bell peppers, seeded and sliced
2	large onions, thinly sliced
1/4	cup soy sauce
1/2	teaspoon sugar
1/2	cup beef bouillon
1	can (6-ounces) water chestnuts, drained and sliced
4	green onions, cut in 1-inch pieces
1	tablespoon cornstarch
1/4	cup water
	Cooked hot rice

Freeze sirloin steak for 1 hour, then remove from freezer and cut into 1/8-inch thick slices. Heat fat or vegetable oil in skillet over medium heat, add crushed garlic, salt, ground ginger and pepper and sauté until garlic is golden. Add steak slices and brown lightly for 2 minutes. Remove meat from pan. Add sliced green bell pepper and sliced onion and cook 3 minutes. Return meat to pan. Add soy sauce, sugar, bouillon, water chestnuts and green onion. Mix cornstarch and water together and stir into mixture. Simmer over low heat 2 minutes or until sauce is thickened. Serve over hot rice.

Salt Steak

5	cups coarse kosher salt
1 1/2	cups water
	Sirloin steak, 2 1/2 inches thick seasoned with Worcestershire powder

Mix salt and enough water to make a paste. Spread a layer half an inch thick on each side of steak. Place a wet paper towel on top of salt. Grill over hot coals about 25 minutes on each side for rare, longer for medium. Test by making a small cut in the center of the steak. Knock off salt crust and slice. Makes 5 or 6 servings. (Do not use a steak less than 2 inches thick or steak will be salty. Cook for about 20 minutes on each side for rare for a 2-inch steak.)

Rio Grande Meat Loaf

2   **pounds lean ground beef**
$1/2$ **pound lean ground pork**
$1/2$ **pound lean ground veal**
2   **eggs**
    Salt and pepper to taste
1   **pound Monterrey Jack cheese or mild Cheddar cheese**
$2^{1}/_{2}$ **cups Spanish sauce**

Mix meat thoroughly with eggs then add salt, pepper and $1/2$ of the cheese. Mix thoroughly. Stir in $1^1/_2$ cups Spanish Sauce. Place meat mixture into casserole dish and form into loaf. Top with remaining Spanish Sauce and place covered into a preheated 375-degree oven. Bake for approximately 45 minutes or until done. Remove lid and add remaining cheese. Return to oven and bake uncovered for 10 more minutes. Recipe serves 8 or recipe can be cut by $1/2$ to serve 4.

SPANISH SAUCE

    Fat from $1/2$ pound bacon
1   **cup onion, diced fine**
1   **green bell pepper, diced fine**
$1/2$ **cup celery, diced fine**
1   **clove garlic, diced fine**
$1/2$ **green chili pepper, diced fine**
    Dash of oregano
1   **tablespoon Worcestershire powder**
4   **drops Tabasco**
1   **bay leaf**
    Dash of thyme
1   **teaspoon garlic salt**
$1/8$ **teaspoon chili powder**
1   **cup brown sauce or canned beef gravy**
1   **cup tomato sauce**
1   **cup peeled tomatoes**
$1/2$ **cup tomato paste**
$1/4$ **cup sherry (Not cooking sherry)**
    Salt and pepper to taste

Place bacon fat into a skillet and sauté the onion, bell pepper, celery, garlic and chili pepper until soft. Stir in other ingredients and simmer slowly about 5 minutes. Remove bay leaf. Yield: 6 cups.

Ricotta Meat Loaf

2   **pounds lean ground beef**
2   **eggs**
    Salt and pepper to taste
1   **pound Ricotta cheese**

Mix meat thoroughly with eggs then add salt, pepper and Ricotta cheese. Stir in $1^1/_2$ cups tomato sauce. Place meat mixture into casserole dish and form into loaf. Top with remaining sauce and place uncovered, into a preheated 375-degree oven. Bake for about 45 minutes or until done. Serves 6.

TOMATO SAUCE:

2   **tablespoons cooking oil**
1   **large onion, finely diced**
1   **can (1 pound 1 ounce) tomatoes and liquid**
1   **(12 ounce) can tomato sauce**
1   **small can tomato paste**
    Few drops Tabasco sauce
2   **tablespoons Worcestershire powder**
$1/2$ **teaspoon salt**
$1/2$ **teaspoon pepper**
1   **teaspoon garlic powder**
$1/2$ **teaspoon oregano**
$1^{1}/_{2}$ **teaspoons sugar**

Heat cooking oil in saucepan then add onion. Sauté until onion is soft; add tomatoes with liquid, tomato sauce and tomato paste. Cook slowly until rawness is removed from tomatoes. Add Tabasco sauce, Worcestershire powder, salt, pepper, garlic powder, oregano and sugar. Simmer slowly for approximately 3 minutes.

Chicken Fried Steak and Country Gravy

Select 2 large round steaks $1/2$-inch thick. Trim outside fat and remove round bone. Cut each steak into 3 large cutlets. Pound lightly with meat pounder. Blend together 1 tablespoon salt, 2 teaspoons black pepper, 1 tablespoon Worcestershire powder, 2 teaspoons dry powdered mustard and 2 teaspoons garlic powder. Break 4 eggs into bowl and add enough milk to make "wash." Whip until well blended. In another bowl finely crumble $1/2$ to 1 pound Ritz crackers.

Using large skillet, heat $1/2$-inch cooking oil to 350 degrees. Dip seasoned cutlets into egg wash and then cover generously with crushed crackers. Place into skillet and fry until the coating is golden brown. Drain on paper towels. When steaks are fried, spoon enough flour into pan to absorb excess oil. Heat until flour is lightly brown. While stirring, add enough milk to create a medium thick gravy. Correct gravy seasoning with only salt and pepper.

Steak Diane

3 tablespoons butter
1 pound top sirloin steak, pounded to ¹/₄-inch thickness
1 teaspoon Worcestershire powder
2 tablespoons sour cream
1 tablespoon Diabla Sauce, Escoffier
1 tablespoon Robert Sauce, Escoffier
¹/₂ cup brandy

Melt butter in blazer pan. Place steak in butter and brown on one side. Turn and brown on other side. In separate blazer pan, melt ¹/₂ stick butter. Add sour cream, Worcestershire powder, Diabla and Robert sauces. Heat for a few minutes and then clean one side of pan. Add brandy. Heat a few moments and then flame. As the flame diminishes, work the brandy into the sauce. When steak is complete, serve on heated platter and top with the sauce. Makes 2 servings.

Embassy Grenadines

8 small grenadines of beef
   Flour
¹/₄ pound butter, melted
1 onion, diced
1 cup mushrooms
¹/₂ cup celery, diced
1 tablespoon parsley
1 carrot, diced fine
1 teaspoon Worcestershire powder
¹/₄ cup beef stock (or consommé)
   Salt and pepper to taste
1 tablespoon garlic salt
2 tablespoons wine vinegar
1¹/₂ cups sour cream

Melt butter in skillet over medium heat. Dredge grenadines in flour and brown on both sides in melted butter. Add onion, mushrooms, celery, parsley and carrot, and sauté until items begin to soften. Add Worcestershire powder, beef stock, salt and pepper, garlic salt, vinegar and sour cream and allow to simmer for 25 minutes, covered. Serve over a bed of cooked rice. Recipe serves 4.

Steak Madrid

4 small round steaks
1 cup flour
4 tablespoons shortening
2 cups Cheddar cheese, grated
1 small bottle pimiento, diced fine

Remove bone from steaks and score around edges. Lightly dredge steaks in flour and brown each one on both sides in shortening. Place ¹/₂ cup of grated Cheddar and 1 teaspoon diced pimiento on each steak and fold together the edges of each steak; secure with toothpicks. Place the steaks into a greased baking dish and cover with Spanish Sauce. Cover baking dish and place into a preheated oven (375 degrees) and bake for 1 hour or a little longer until tender. Makes 4 large servings.

SPANISH SAUCE

   Fat from ¹/₂ pound bacon
1 cup onion, diced fine
1 bell pepper, diced fine
¹/₂ cup celery, diced fine
1 clove garlic, diced fine
¹/₂ green chili pepper, diced fine
   Dash of oregano
1 tablespoon Worcestershire powder
¹/₂ cup tomato paste
4 drops Tabasco
1 bay leaf
   Dash of thyme
1 teaspoon garlic salt
¹/₈ teaspoon chili powder
1 cup brown sauce or brown gravy
1 cup tomato sauce
1 cup peeled tomatoes
¹/₄ cup sherry
   Salt and pepper to taste

Place bacon fat into a skillet and sauté the onion, bell pepper, celery, garlic, and chili pepper until soft. Stir in other ingredients and simmer slowly about 5 minutes.

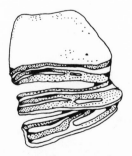 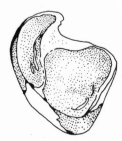

Filet Mignon with Dijon Brandy Sauce

4   filet mignon
    Salt and pepper
1   tablespoon butter or margarine
¹/₄ cup brandy
2   tablespoons finely chopped fresh onion
1   cup heavy cream
¹/₄ cup Grey Poupon Dijon Mustard
1   teaspoon Worcestershire powder

Sprinkle filets with salt and pepper to taste. In large skillet, melt butter. Cook filets as desired. Pour brandy over meat. Ignite carefully. When flame dies, remove meat to heated platter. Cook onion in drippings. Stir in heavy cream. Simmer until sauce slightly thickens. Mix in mustard and Worcestershire powder. Serve sauce immediately over filets. Makes 4 servings.

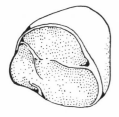 

Crock Pot Barbecued Brisket

Place a trimmed 4 to 8 pound brisket into a crock pot. Top brisket with the following items:

¹/₂ cup soy sauce
    Few drops Tabasco sauce
2   tablespoons liquid smoke
2   tablespoons A-1 sauce
    Black pepper to taste
1   teaspoon seasoned salt
2   tablespoons Worcestershire powder
2   tablespoons dry powdered mustard
1   tablespoon garlic powder

Cover crock pot with lid and cook on high temperature for 1¹/₂ hours. Lower heat to low and continue cooking for several hours or until meat is fork tender. Remove brisket to a platter and remove all but 1¹/₂ cups of stock. Stir before removing. Save the removed stock essence for later use. Return brisket to crock pot and the 1¹/₂ cups of stock. Add one 12-ounce bottle PLAIN barbecue sauce. Place lid on pot and cook at high temperature for 1¹/₂ hours. Serve brisket with sauce.

Blue Ribbon Teriyaki

2   pounds lean beef cut into 1-inch cubes
1   large can of button mushrooms
1   large can of chunk pineapple
1   bottle catsup
¹/₄ cup salad oil
¹/₂ cup wine vinegar
¹/₄ cup soy sauce
10 drops of Tabasco
2   tablespoons lemon juice
1   tablespoon garlic salt
1   tablespoon sauté onion powder
¹/₂ cup Grenadine syrup

Place the beef cubes, mushrooms and pineapple chunks alternately onto skewers. Marinate for 30 minutes in the following sauce and then broil, basting with the sauce.

Mix in a saucepan: catsup, salad oil, Grenadine syrup, wine vinegar, soy sauce, Tabasco, lemon juice, garlic salt, and sauté onion powder. Heat and mix thoroughly. Recipe serves 4.

Hungarian Goulash

2¹/₂ pounds beef, rump or round, or veal
¹/₃   cup suet, chopped
¹/₂   cup chopped onions
¹/₂   clove garlic, crushed
2   cups water
1   cup catsup
¹/₂   teaspoon dry mustard
1   tablespoon paprika
2   tablespoons brown sugar
1   tablespoon salt
1   teaspoon Worcestershire powder
1   teaspoon vinegar
2   tablespoons flour
1   package fine noodles

Cut meat into 1-inch cubes. Brown in suet with onion and garlic. Add water, catsup, and seasonings. Cover and cook at low heat until the meat is tender, about 2 hours. Mix flour with ¹/₃ cup of water and add to the hot mixture, stirring constantly, and cook until thick. In the meantime, cook noodles in boiling salted water. Drain, mix with part of the sauce from the meat, and serve with the meat over them.

Canadian Meat Balls in Cream Gravy

4	slices Canadian-style bacon, diced
$1/_2$	cup chopped onion
$1^1/_2$	pounds ground beef
1	egg
1	teaspoon salt
$1^1/_4$	teaspoon allspice
2	tablespoons butter or margarine
2	tablespoons flour
1	$10^1/_2$-ounce can condensed beef broth
1	6-ounce can evaporated milk

In large skillet, over medium heat, lightly sauté diced bacon. Add onion and cook until soft. Remove bacon and onion from skillet. Add ground beef, egg, salt, and all-spice, mixing together lightly. Shape meat mixture into 36 balls. Add butter or margarine to drippings in skillet. Add meat balls and fry until brown on all sides. Push meat balls to one side of skillet. Stir flour into drippings. Add beef broth gradually and cook, stirring constantly, until slightly thickened. Reduce heat to low and simmer 10 minutes. Add evaporated milk and heat just to boiling. Makes 6 servings.

Park Avenue Burgers

1	pound lean ground beef
1	onion, finely diced
$1/_2$	green bell pepper, diced
1	tablespoon garlic salt
1	tablespoon Worcestershire powder
1	teaspoon Tabasco
1	teaspoon MSG powder
	Salt and pepper to taste
$1^1/_2$	favorite pie dough recipe

Mix beef, onion, bell pepper, garlic salt, Worcestershire powder, Tabasco, MSG powder, and salt and pepper together. Form into 4 patties and broil under hot flame until done. Remove patties from broiler and drain on paper towel. Mix favorite pie dough recipe and roll out onto a board. Cut 4 circles from the pie dough that just fit bottom side of patties. Grease a cookie sheet and place meat patties onto circles of pie dough and then onto cookie sheet. With remaining dough form one-inch strips. Using several strips, criss-cross them over each patty, covering surface of meat. Dot a little melted butter on dough and place burgers into a preheated 350-degree oven and bake until crust turns brown. Remove burgers from oven and serve on a platter topped with Mushroom Sauce.

MUSHROOM SAUCE:

1	6-ounce can sliced mushrooms, drained
2	cups chicken broth
5	tablespoons butter
3	tablespoons flour
6	tablespoons heavy cream
	Salt and pepper to taste

Combine mushrooms and chicken broth in a saucepan. Simmer slowly for about 10 minutes. Using another saucepan, form a roux with butter and flour. Stir into roux the chicken broth and mushrooms. When sauce thickens add the heavy cream. Cook slowly for a few more minutes. If sauce is too thick, thin with a little cream. Season to taste.

New Fashion Beef Pot Pies

$1/_4$	pound butter
2	pounds top sirloin, cut into $1/_2$-inch cubes
	Flour
12	tiny onions
6	small carrots, sliced
1	4-ounce can sliced mushrooms
6	tiny potatoes, cooked
$1/_2$	cup diced celery
1	cup green beans, cooked
2	cups brown sauce (brown gravy)
$1/_2$	cup Burgundy
1	tablespoon English mustard
1	bay leaf
1	teaspoon garlic salt
	Dash Tabasco
1	tablespoon Worcestershire powder
	Salt and pepper to taste
1	recipe for pastry or puff paste
1	egg yolk and $1/_2$ cup milk, blended

Melt butter in a heavy skillet. Lightly dust meat in flour and place into hot fat. Brown on all sides; then add onions, carrots, mushrooms, potatoes, celery, and green beans. Allow these items to brown lightly; then add brown sauce. When brown sauce is well blended and heated through, add Burgundy, English mustard, bay leaf, garlic salt, Tabasco, Worcestershire powder, and salt and pepper to taste. Cover skillet and allow this recipe to simmer slowly until meat is tender. Remove bay leaf. Stir from time to time. Divide this cooked recipe into six small potpie dishes that have been lightly greased. Cover with a pastry top, fluting the edges securely. Cut several vent holes in the top of the pastry and brush on some of the egg yolk and milk mixture. Place these pies into a preheated 425-degree oven and bake for about 25 minutes or until crust is brown. Serves 6.

Meat-Za Pizza

1	pound ground round meat
$^2/_3$	cup condensed milk
$^1/_2$	cup bread crumbs
$^1/_2$	teaspoon garlic salt
1	small can tomato paste
1	small can sliced mushrooms
1	cup grated sharp cheese
3	tablespoons Parmesan cheese
1	tablespoon oregano

Mix thoroughly the ground round meat, condensed milk, bread crumbs, and garlic salt. With this mixture form a pie shell in a 9-inch pie pan. Cover the pie shell with tomato paste, mushrooms, grated sharp cheese, Parmesan cheese, and oregano. Place into a preheated oven at 350 degrees and bake for 30 minutes. Cut and serve like a pie.

Chinese Burgers

$1^1/_2$	pounds ground meat
3	tablespoons soy sauce
2	tablespoons garlic salt
2	tablespoons Worcestershire powder
2	tablespoons onion juice
1	tablespoon Kitchen Bouquet
1	4-ounce can mushrooms
1	3-ounce can bamboo shoots, drained and thinly sliced
	Salt and pepper to taste
6	slices bacon
12	toothpicks
6	slices pineapple

Place ground meat into a mixing bowl and work in soy sauce, garlic salt, Worcestershire powder, onion juice, Kitchen Bouquet, mushrooms, bamboo shoots, and salt and pepper. When thoroughly mixed, form into 6 meat patties and wrap each patty with one slice of bacon secured by 2 toothpicks. Top each patty with a slice of pineapple and broil in a preheated broiler until done. Serves 6.

Tenderloin of Beef Tips Diat

2	pounds lean cubed tenderloin of beef tips
$^1/_4$	pound butter
1	medium onion, finely diced
$^1/_4$	cup chopped celery
1	tablespoon chopped fresh parsley
1	16-ounce can tomatoes, drained
1	cup demi-glaze (brown gravy)
$^1/_4$	cup red wine
1	6-ounce can sliced mushrooms, drained
	Salt and pepper to taste
	Cooked rice for 4

Melt butter in a heavy skillet. Brown beef tips in butter on all sides. Remove beef tips from butter and set aside. In the remaining butter, sauté onion, celery, and parsley until onion is soft. Stir in tomatoes. Add demi-glaze, wine, mushrooms, and salt and pepper. Heat through. Return beef tips to mixture, cover. Simmer slowly until the beef tips are cooked through. Serve tips and sauce over a fluffy bed of white rice. Serves 4.

Spanish Pot Roast

2	tablespoons flour
$^1/_2$	teaspoon salt
3	or 4 pound roast (rump of veal, bottom round of beef, or chuck roast)
2	or 3 tablespoons Spanish olive oil
1	large onion, sliced
2	cloves garlic, crushed
1	teaspoon salt
2	whole cloves
1	teaspoon cinnamon
1	bay leaf or 1 tablespoon minced parsley
1	tablespoon vinegar
1	tablespoon catsup
2	cups water
$^1/_2$	square (1 ounce) unsweetened chocolate, grated

Combine flour and salt and dust over roast. In Dutch oven or flameproof casserole, over medium heat, brown meat in Spanish olive oil. Remove meat. Add sliced onion and crushed garlic to drippings and cook until yellow. Replace meat and add salt, cloves, cinnamon, parsley, vinegar, catsup, and water. Cover tightly and cook over low heat $2^1/_2$ to 3 hours or until meat is very tender. Remove meat and place on platter. If necessary, add liquid to make 2 cups sauce. Add grated chocolate and cook until thickened. Serve sauce in boat as accompaniment to roast. Makes 8 to 10 servings.

Cheeseburger Pie

1/2   cup strong coffee
1/2   cup evaporated milk
4 1/2   teaspoons instant minced onion
2 1/2   pounds lean ground beef
2   cups soft whole-wheat bread crumbs
2   eggs
2   teaspoons seasoned meat tenderizer
1   teaspoon Worcestershire powder
1   tablespoon prepared mustard
4   slices process American cheese

Combine the coffee, milk, and minced onion. Let stand for 10 minutes. Combine the ground beef, bread crumbs, and eggs. Now add the coffee mixture to the meat mixture. Add in meat tenderizer, Worcestershire powder and prepared mustard, mixing each ingredient well into the solid mixture.

Pack into a 10-inch pie pan and place in a 350-degree oven. After baking 1 hour cut cheese slices diagonally in half and place them around the edges of the pie. Broil 5 to 8 minutes until cheese melts and becomes lightly browned. Serves 8 to 10 people.

Sooner Scratch Hash

1   stick butter
2 1/2   pounds lean ground beef
2   white onions
1   tablespoon seasoned salt
1   tablespoon black pepper
1   tablespoon Worcestershire powder
4   drops Tabasco sauce
1   tablespoon sugar
5   peeled and sliced large potatoes
2   cups beef consommé or beef stock
   Salt to taste

Melt butter in large skillet. Add ground beef and brown. Blend in all other ingredients except salt. Cover and bring to a boil. Reduce heat to simmer and cook until potatoes are tender. Stir frequently. Add salt to taste if necessary. Recipe serves 8. (May need to remove excess liquid before serving.)

Seafood

Tuna Casserole

1   can tuna fish (8 ounces)
   Brown rice for 4 servings (follow package directions for cooking)
1   can cream of mushroom soup, undiluted
1   onion medium size
1   green bell pepper, medium size
3   shallots
1/4   teaspoon Worcestershire powder
1   medium size can sliced black olives
   Pepper to taste

Cook rice. Set aside. Drain tuna, open mushroom soup, peel onion, remove seeds from green bell pepper, slice black olives, peel shallots. Let these stand for 5 minutes.

Spoon out one layer of rice on the bottom of a 1 1/2-quart casserole dish, one layer of tuna, next a layer of thinly sliced onion, followed by thinly sliced green bell pepper, a layer of mushroom soup and the next layer is of black olives and shallots. Sprinkle on Worcestershire powder after olives and shallots. Repeat the layers until all the ingredients are in the casserole dish.

Preheat oven at 350 degrees. Cook casserole with cover on for about 1 hour. Garnish with parsley and serve directly from dish.

Spicy Catfish Fingers

5   pounds catfish fillets cut into 4-inch by 1-inch strips

Marinate in

1   quart Louisiana Hot Sauce
2   tablespoons cayenne pepper

for at least 3 hours

Coat with white self-rising cornmeal. Deep fry immediately until golden.

Serves 16 8-ounce servings.

Caviar

A good caviar-stretcher: Blend a small jar of caviar with cream cheese, tasting as you go to make sure you don't bury the caviar flavor. Add a few drops of onion juice. Heap on toasted fingers of bread; top with grated yolk of hard-cooked egg.

Shrimp Mousse

2   **pounds or more uncooked shrimp**
1   **can tomato soup**
3   **3-ounce packages cream cheese**
2   **tablespoons gelatin**
1   **cup water**
$^3/_4$ **cup finely chopped green bell pepper**
$^3/_4$ **cup finely chopped celery**
1   **cup mayonnaise**
   Salt
   Tabasco
   Worcestershire powder
   Grated onion

Boil and shell shrimp. Mash cheese in soup and heat in top of double boiler until cheese is melted and very hot. Soak gelatin in water for 5 minutes and add to soup mixture. When soup is cooled, add shrimp broken into small pieces, celery, green bell pepper, mayonnaise and grated onion to taste. Season highly with salt, Tabasco and Worcestershire powder. Pour into well-oiled mold and refrigerate until firm. Unmold on lettuce and serve with mayonnaise. Serves 20.

Skewered Shrimp and Prosciutto

9   **thin slices of prosciutto**
3   **dozen medium size raw shrimp, shelled and deveined**
2   **dozen pitted California black olives**
18 **thin lemon slices (2 or 3 lemons)**
$^1/_3$ **cup finely chopped Italian parsley**
2   **or 3 garlic cloves, peeled and finely chopped**
   Crushed dried red pepper, to taste
6   **tablespoons best quality olive oil, or more**

Preheat oven to 350 degrees.

Cut each slice of prosciutto lengthwise into halves and wrap 1 piece of prosciutto around each of 18 shrimp.

Slide 2 olives onto one of 6 skewers. Slide a wrapped shrimp onto skewer. Wrap a lemon slice around a plain shrimp and slide onto skewer. Repeat, using 2 more prosciutto-wrapped shrimp and 2 more lemon-wrapped shrimp. End with 2 more olives. Repeat skewering procedure with remaining shrimp, lemons and olives.

Lay each skewer on a piece of foil. Sprinkle with parsley, chopped garlic and red pepper to taste. Drizzle each skewer with a tablespoon or so of olive oil and seal the packets. Set on a baking sheet.

Bake for 10 minutes, or until shrimp are done. Do not overcook. Transfer packets to plates and allow guests to open them at table. Six portions.

Twice-Baked Potatoes with Lobster

4   **large baking potatoes**
   Salt and freshly ground black pepper, to taste
4   **tablespoons sweet butter**
$^1/_2$ **cup chopped yellow onion**
$^1/_2$ **cup finely chopped fresh mushrooms**
2   **cups cooked lobster meat (crab or tuna may be used)**
1   **cup dry white vermouth**
$^1/_2$ **cup grated Jarlsberg cheese, plus additional cheese for topping potatoes**
1   **to 2 tablespoons heavy cream (optional)**

Scrub and dry the potatoes. Cut a small, deep slit in the top of each potato. Set potatoes on the middle rack of a preheated 375-degree oven and bake for about 1 hour, or until potatoes are tender when pierced with a fork.

Let potatoes cool slightly, cut off and discard the tops, and scrape the potato pulp into a bowl. Do not scrape so deeply that you tear the potato skin. Salt and pepper the potato shells; reserve. Mash the potato pulp; reserve.

Melt the butter in a small skillet and sauté the chopped onion, covered, until tender and lightly colored, about 25 minutes. Add the mushrooms and sauté for another 5 minutes. Stir in the lobster or crab. Season with salt and pepper, add the vermouth, then raise heat to a boil. Stir frequently over high heat until all liquid has boiled away. Remove from heat.

Combine lobster mixture with the reserved mashed potato pulp and $^1/_2$ cup Jarlsberg. Taste, correct seasoning; add heavy cream if the mixture seems too dry.

Stuff the mixture into the reserved potato skins; mound the filling slightly. Sprinkle additional grated cheese on top and place on baking sheet.

Bake again, at 400 degrees, until potatoes are hot and cheese is bubbling. Serve immediately. Four portions.

Company Creamed Tuna

2 tablespoons finely chopped onion
2 tablespoons margarine
3 tablespoons flour
1/4 teaspoon salt
Dash pepper
1 1/4 cups milk
1/2 cup sour cream
1 can (7 ounces) tuna, drained
3 tablespoons dry white wine
2 tablespoons snipped parsley
Toasted slivered almonds, optional
Toast points

Sauté onion in margarine until tender, but not browned. Blend in flour, salt, and pepper. Add milk and cook, stirring constantly until the mixture thickens and bubbles. Stir in sour cream; add tuna, wine and parsley. Heat through. Sprinkle with almonds if desired. Spoon over buttered toast points. Serves 4.

Fisherman's Pie

1 quart water
1 small carrot, pared
4 peppercorns
1 strip lemon rind
3 sprigs parsley
1 bay leaf
1 pound flounder or haddock, cut in 1-inch cubes
1 1/2 pounds shrimp, shelled and deveined
1/2 cup chopped onion (1 medium)
3/4 cup sliced celery
3 tablespoons butter or margarine
1/3 cup flour
1 cup light cream
1/2 teaspoon dill weed
1 can (3 to 4 ounces) chopped mushrooms, drained
3 cups hot mashed potatoes
2 egg yolks
2 tablespoons butter or margarine
2 to 4 tablespoons milk
Melted butter or margarine

Simmer water, carrot, peppercorns, lemon rind, parsley, and bay leaf 10 minutes. Strain; return to saucepan; add fish and shrimp; simmer 5 minutes. Drain; reserve 1 3/4 cups broth. Sauté onion and celery in 3 tablespoons butter or margarine; blend in flour; add broth slowly; add cream and dill. Cook over medium heat, stirring constantly, until thickened; stir in fish, shrimp, and 1/2 can mushrooms. Turn into 1 1/2-quart greased casserole. Heat oven to 375 degrees. Mix potatoes, egg yolks, 2 tablespoons butter or margarine, enough milk to make smooth, and remaining mushrooms. Spoon potato mixture onto fish mixture; brush with melted butter or margarine. Bake 25 minutes or until lightly browned. Makes 6 servings.

Panfried Catfish with Walnuts and Bacon

8 thick slices hickory-smoked bacon
1/2 cup coarsely chopped walnuts
1 egg
1/2 cup milk
1 cup all-purpose flour
1 cup yellow cornmeal
4 catfish (about 1 pound each) — skinned, cleaned and head removed
1/2 teaspoon salt
1/2 teaspoon freshly ground pepper
4 tablespoons fresh lemon juice
1/2 cup (1 stick) unsalted butter
1/4 cup vegetable oil
Lemon halves, for garnish

Preheat the oven to 350 degrees. Cook the bacon slices on a baking sheet with sides until crisp, about 20 minutes. (Drain off grease midway in cooking.) Drain on paper towels, then cut into 1/2-inch pieces.

Meanwhile, roast the walnuts on a cookie sheet in the oven until lightly browned, about 15 minutes. Set aside. Leave the oven on.

In a medium bowl, beat the egg and milk until blended. In a shallow pan or dish long enough to hold one fish, mix together the flour and cornmeal.

Rinse the catfish under cold running water; pat dry. Sprinkle the fish inside and out with the salt, pepper and 2 tablespoons of the lemon juice.

In a large skillet, melt 4 tablespoons of the butter in the oil over moderately high heat. Dip the fish into the egg-milk mixture and then into the cornmeal-flour mixture to coat lightly. When the butter and oil are sizzling, add the fish and cook, turning once, until golden brown on each side, about 5 minutes total.

Transfer the fish to a baking pan large enough to hold them in a single layer. Bake for 8 to 10 minutes, until the fish has lost its pink color next to the bone. Place on a warmed platter or plates. Sprinkle the bacon pieces and walnuts over the fish.

Place the remaining 4 tablespoons butter in a small saucepan and cook over high heat until it foams and turns nut brown. Add the remaining 2 tablespoons lemon juice, then pour over the fish. Garnish with lemon halves.

Escargots — Snails in Garlic Butter

1   package (4²/₅ ounce) extra large snails
      with shells
¹/₄   cup soft butter or margarine
1   tablespoons finely minced shallots or
      onion
1   clove of garlic, minced
1   tablespoon chopped parsley
¹/₄   teaspoon salt
      Dash of pepper
      Dash Worcestershire powder
1   tablespoon Vermouth

Wash and drain snails. Combine remaining ingredients; put about ¹/₄ teaspoon butter mixture into each shell. Place each snail in a shell; pack remaining mixture into shell to seal in snail. Place in shallow baking dish or snail pan. Bake at 450 degrees for 10 minutes. Serve with crusty bread. Makes 3 servings.

Shrimp Salad

6   slices of Italian salami ¹/₄-inch thick
1   large green, red or yellow pepper
20   jumbo shrimps, boiled
2   celery ribs with leaves, diced
6   whole fresh green scallions, diced
3   hard-cooked eggs, quartered
3   medium-sized hard tomatoes, quartered
      Pinch of salt
      Pinch of freshly ground black pepper
6   heaping tablespoons Shrimp Sauce

Cut the salami into strips 1¹/₄ inches long, and slice the peppers into long thin strips. Place in a large bowl with shrimps, diced celery and scallions; refrigerate. Refrigerate eggs and tomatoes separately. When ready to serve, add salt and pepper and toss. Arrange eggs and tomatoes over top. Spoon shrimp sauce over all. Serve on the antipasto or as a main course. Serves 4 or 5.

SHRIMP SAUCE

2   whole green scallions or 1 tablespoon
      grated sweet onion
6   tablespoons finely chopped fresh green or
      red pepper
2   tablespoons Spanish capers, chopped fine
2   tablespoons prepared horseradish
1   cup mayonnaise, preferably homemade
      with virgin olive oil
¹/₂   cup chili sauce
¹/₂   teaspoon crushed red pepper
¹/₂   teaspoon freshly ground black pepper
¹/₂   teaspoon salt
1   garlic clove, mashed

Slice scallions lengthwise and chop fine, or grate the sweet onion. Place scallions or onion, green or red pepper, capers and horseradish in a strainer and drain for 15 minutes. Combine mayonnaise and chili sauce in a bowl. Add red and black pepper, salt and garlic. Whip well together with a whisk. Add drained ingredients and beat or mix well. Taste for salt. Refrigerate. Use over shrimps, crabmeat, or cold chicken lobster. Makes about 2 cups.

Chilled Fresh Salmon with Herb Mayonnaise

2   pounds fresh salmon
      Pinch of black pepper
      Pinch of salt
1   cup wine vinegar
1   medium onion, sliced
2   celery stalks with leaves, cut into halves
      Herb Mayonnaise

Have fishman prepare fish for cooking. Place salmon in a shallow pan and cover with warm water. Add all other ingredients except mayonnaise. Bring to a boil. Lower heat and simmer for 30 to 40 minutes. Check to see if fish is cooked. Remove from water, drain, and allow to cool. Split down the center and remove all bones. Arrange salmon on platter. Cover with Herb Mayonnaise. Serves 6 to 8.

HERB MAYONNAISE

2   garlic cloves, mashed
2   cups mayonnaise
10   fresh parsley sprigs, leaves only
2   whole fresh green scallions
1   can (5 ounces) pimientos
8   ounces fresh peas, cooked, or 8 ounces
      canned peas, drained
1   teaspoon dried oregano

Mixed mashed garlic into mayonnaise, then discard the bits of garlic. Chop parsley leaves fine and dice entire scallions. Drain pimientos and cut into cubes. Mix all ingredients together and blend well. Spoon over the top of salmon.

Broiled Fresh Oysters

10 fresh parsley sprigs, leaves only
6 leaves of fresh or dried basil
1 garlic clove, mashed
2 shallots, chopped very fine
$^{1}/_{4}$ cup olive oil
$^{1}/_{2}$ cup fresh creamery butter, melted
$^{1}/_{2}$ cup sifted bread crumbs
$^{1}/_{4}$ cup grated Parmesan cheese
Pinch of black pepper
Pinch of crushed red pepper
Pinch of salt
36 large juicy oysters on half shell, freshly opened

Chop together the parsley, basil and garlic. Mix with shallots, oil and butter. Then add all the other ingredients except oysters and mix well. Place oysters in their half shells on an open pan and cover each oyster with some of the dressing. Cover tightly with aluminum foil. Place pan in preheated slow oven (300 degrees) and bake for 15 minutes. Uncover and place pan under preheated medium broiler for 5 minutes. Serves 6.

Fresh Crabmeat Sautéed in Cream Sherry

6 tablespoons sweet butter
1 pound fresh Maryland lump crabmeat
6 tablespoons good cream sherry
10 fresh parsley sprigs, leaves only chopped fine
Pinch of crushed red pepper
Pinch of freshly ground black pepper
Salt

Place butter in a skillet and heat. Add crabmeat and sherry and sauté slowly for about 5 minutes. Add parsley, red and black pepper and a sprinkle of salt. Cover and simmer for 10 minutes. Serve over toast. This also makes a delicious main course. Serves 4 or 5.

Chilled Maryland Crabmeat

1 garlic clove, mashed
6 tablespoons olive oil
3 tablespoons wine vinegar
Juice of $^{1}/_{2}$ lemon
1 teaspoon Worcestershire powder
Pinch of salt
Pinch of crushed red pepper
Pinch of freshly ground black pepper
$^{1}/_{2}$ teaspoon powdered mustard
6 fresh parsley sprigs, leaves only, minced
1 pound fresh lump crabmeat
Boston lettuce leaves

Mix garlic into the oil with a fork. Add vinegar to garlic and oil; then add lemon juice, Worcestershire powder, salt, red and black pepper, mustard and parsley. Mix well together. Discard bits of garlic. Arrange crabmeat on chilled lettuce leaves. Spoon the dressing over. Serves 4 to 6.

Light and Crispy Fish Fillets

Oil for deep fat frying
1 cup pancake mix
$^{1}/_{3}$ cup club soda
1 pound package frozen fish fillets (not breaded), thawed, drained
$^{1}/_{2}$ cup buttermilk

Heat oil in deep fat fryer or 3-quart saucepan to 375 degrees. In medium bowl stir together $^{1}/_{2}$ cup pancake mix and club soda. Dip fillets in buttermilk, then coat with remaining $^{1}/_{2}$ cup pancake mix. Dip coated fish into pancake and club soda mixture. Fry, turning once, until deep golden brown (3 to 4 minutes). Yield 4 servings.

Oyster Stuffing

1 onion
$^{1}/_{2}$ cup chopped celery
$^{1}/_{4}$ cup butter, melted
1 bud garlic
1 pint small oysters, drained
2 tablespoons chopped parsley
4 cups soft bread crumbs
1 teaspoon salt
$^{1}/_{4}$ teaspoon white pepper
$^{1}/_{2}$ cup light cream
1 teaspoon Worcestershire powder

Sauté the onions and celery in the butter with the garlic until soft. Remove the garlic, add the oysters and parsley, and cook until the oysters begin to curl. Add the bread crumbs and seasonings. Stir in the cream; stuff turkey cavity, well rubbed with butter.

Deviled Crab

3   cups crabmeat
2   hard-boiled eggs, chopped
$^1/_2$ cup cream
$^1/_2$ teaspoon dry mustard
1   teaspoon salt
$^1/_2$ teaspoon pepper
1   teaspoon Worcestershire powder
1   tablespoon lemon juice
      Bread crumbs
      Butter

Blend the crabmeat and chopped eggs together in a bowl, and moisten with the cream. Add the seasonings and toss lightly as if it were a salad.

Wash the crab shells, and pack them with the mixture. Spread bread crumbs over each. Dot with butter. Bake for 10 minutes at 450 degrees. Individual casseroles are alternates to the crab shells.

Brazos River Catfish and Tartar Sauce

3   catfish fillets
1   cup salad-style mustard
1   cup cornmeal
1   cup pancake mix
2   teaspoons instant minced onion
$2^1/_2$ teaspoons salt
$^1/_2$ teaspoon white pepper
2   teaspoons parsley flakes
1   tablespoon Worcestershire powder
3   slightly beaten eggs
      Shortening or cooking oil

Slightly coat fillets of catfish with mustard. Combine cornmeal, pancake mix, instant minced onion, salt, white pepper, parsley flakes and Worcestershire powder in mixing bowl. Blend thoroughly. Dip mustard-coated fish fillets in slightly beaten egg wash. Then coat thoroughly with dry mixture.

Fry in heavy skillet in $^1/_2$-inch hot oil or shortening (approximately 350 degrees) until brown on all sides. Serve with tartar sauce. Recipe yields 6 portions.

TARTAR SAUCE:

2   cups mayonnaise
$^1/_2$ cup salad-style mustard
2   tablespoons sweet pickle relish

Combine all the above ingredients and chill thoroughly.

Seafood Gumbo

$^1/_4$ cup butter
$^1/_2$ cup diced green bell pepper
1   cup diced celery
$^1/_2$ cup chopped onions
9   tablespoons flour
4   cups chicken stock, made with bouillon cubes
2   cups canned tomatoes
1   bay leaf
1   teaspoon thyme
$^1/_2$ teaspoon Tabasco sauce
1   tablespoon salt
$^1/_2$ teaspoon pepper
3   tablespoons dried parsley
1   tablespoon Worcestershire powder
1   can crabmeat or 6 ounce frozen, with juice
$1^1/_2$ pounds frozen shrimp, cleaned
1   20-ounce package frozen sliced okra
1   jar oysters (optional)
      Gumbo file powder
$1^1/_2$ cups cooked rice

Sauté green bell pepper, celery and onions in $^1/_4$ cup butter. Meanwhile, slowly brown flour in the remaining $^1/_2$ cup butter, to make a roux. Add chicken stock to roux, then tomatoes and other vegetables. Add seasonings, crabmeat and juice, and cook slowly for about 45 minutes. Add frozen shrimp, okra and oysters, if desired, and cook about 15 minutes, or until the shrimp curls slightly. Turn off heat and let set. Remove bay leaf. Reheat just before serving, sprinkle file powder over the top (at least 1 tablespoon) and ladle over a generous spoonful of rice in each bowl. Serves 6 to 8.

Crab Crescents with Veloute Sauce

1　stick butter
1　pound lump crabmeat
1　yellow onion, finely minced
1　cup mushrooms, sliced
　　Salt and pepper to taste
1　tablespoon Worcestershire powder
2　teaspoons garlic powder
　　Dash Tabasco
$\frac{1}{2}$　teaspoon Thyme
2　cups fish stock or veal stock
$\frac{1}{2}$　cup dry vermouth
　　Crepes

Melt butter in skillet. Add crabmeat, onion and mushrooms. Sauté quickly then add all other ingredients except crepes. Heat through until alcohol is removed from vermouth.

Using a strainer spoon, lift tablespoon of the crab mixture and permit to drain. Fold mixture into a crepe. When completed, place the crepes onto a cookie sheet and heat in preheated 400-degree oven for just a few moments. Remove and serve on a canape dish topped with the veloute sauce remaining in the skillet.

Dishwasher Fish

If you enjoy poached fish the way that I do, you will thoroughly enjoy this recipe and have much fun in the process.

Select as many fish fillets (any type) as may be desired for serving. Make certain the fish is just slightly below room temperature. Sprinkle approximately 1 tablespoon of lemon juice over each fillet. Brush approximately 1 tablespoon of melted butter over each fish selection. Sprinkle $\frac{1}{2}$ teaspoon of Worcestershire powder over each fillet. Securely seal each fillet, with seasoning, in freezer bags (the type used in freezing foods). Carefully place the individual pouches in the top racks of your automatic dishwasher. Close the dishwasher and set control to full cycle. (DO NOT use detergent.) Activate dishwasher and remove fish 15 minutes following the termination of the dishwasher operation. You will find these poached fish to be delightful.

Various seasoned vegetables can be sealed in freezer bags and placed in the lower racks to cook during the process. These vegetables will be served crisp tender.

Red Snapper Pontchartrain

2　eggs
4　10-ounce portions fillet of red snapper
4　tablespoons white flour
　　Salt and pepper to taste
8　uncooked jumbo shrimp
1　stick sweet butter
1　clove garlic, crushed
3　green onions, finely chopped
$\frac{1}{2}$　cup chopped green parsley
$1\frac{1}{2}$　cups fresh or canned mushrooms
　　Juice of $1\frac{1}{2}$ lemons
1　cup dry vermouth

Beat whole eggs and set aside. Dip red snapper fillets into beaten eggs. Place flour, salt and pepper into a small paper sack and insert fish fillets and jumbo shrimp. Shake sack until fish is well coated.

Melt butter in a heavy skillet and add crushed garlic. Place red snapper fillets and shrimp into the butter and cook slowly for 3 to 5 minutes. Turn fish to other side and cook until red snapper starts to flake slightly. Add finely chopped green onion and chopped parsley, then add mushrooms and lemon juice. Cook slowly until mushrooms and green onions are lightly browned, then add dry vermouth. Permit this sauce to reduce by cooking for approximately 1 additional minute. Serve on a heated plate garnished with parsley and a slice of lemon.

Crab Louis in Avocado Halves

1　egg yolk
2　teaspoons prepared imported mustard
$\frac{1}{2}$　teaspoon Worcestershire powder
2　teaspoons red wine vinegar
$\frac{1}{2}$　cup peanut, vegetable or corn oil
1　tablespoon chili sauce
$\frac{1}{4}$　cup finely chopped scallions, including
　　　green part
4　large stuffed green olives, chopped (about
　　　$\frac{1}{4}$ cup)
　　Salt and pepper
1　pound lump crab, all trace of shell and
　　　cartilage removed
4　ripe avocados
　　Lettuce leaves
2　hard-cooked eggs, sliced (optional)

Put the yolk in a mixing bowl and add the mustard, Worcestershire powder and vinegar. Beat with a wire whisk. Add the oil gradually, beating rapidly.

When thickened and smooth, add the chili sauce, scallions and olives. Mix well and season to taste with salt and pepper.

Put the crab in a mixing bowl and add half the sauce. Mix gently so as not to break up the crab lumps more than necessary.

Split the avocados in half and discard the pits. Pile equal portions of the crab into the avocado halves. Spoon the remaining sauce over. Serve on a bed of lettuce leaves. Garnish the crab filling with egg slices, if desired, or trimmed scallions. Makes 4 servings.

Crabmeat Soufflé

1¹/₃   cups grated Cheddar cheese
1¹/₂   cups thick cream sauce
  1   pound crabmeat (approximately 3 cups; pick shell pieces out carefully)
  4   eggs, whites and yolks beaten separately

Melt cheese in cream sauce. Add crabmeat and egg yolks. Fold in the stiffly beaten egg whites, pour into buttered baking dish or individual casseroles, set in a pan of hot water, and bake at 325 degrees for about 1 hour. Serve on slices of broiled canned pineapple, or with a thin cream sauce (make with cream) and bits of finely chopped watercress.

Salmon Croquettes

  2   15-ounce cans salmon (use a good grade as there is a big difference)
  2   eggs
  2   cups Ritz crackers
     Few drops Tabasco
  1   teaspoon seasoned salt
     Black pepper to taste
  2   teaspoons Worcestershire powder

SAUCE:

²/₃   stick butter
¹/₂   cup flour
  3   cups milk
     Salt and pepper to taste
  1   8-ounce can green peas

Pick out all bones in salmon, even though they are soft. Now make a cream sauce medium thick by melting butter in saucepan, add flour, mixing well with butter. Pour milk in slowly and stir until sauce cooks to medium thickness. Salt and pepper to taste.

Add ²/₃ cup of cream sauce to salmon. Mix in eggs, crushed Ritz crackers, Tabasco, seasoned salt, black pepper, and Worcestershire powder. Blend well and form 8 croquettes. Cover with waxed paper and chill for 30 minutes in refrigerator. Place enough oil to cover skillet with a fraction of an inch depth. Using medium heat, fry until croquettes are golden brown.

Add peas to remaining cream sauce, heat for just a few moments, then top croquettes with sauce.

Dover Sole Braganza

1   stick of butter
4   fillets of sole (large)
4   tablespoons brandy

Melt butter in blazer pan then sauté sole fillets until golden brown on both sides and seafood flakes. Add brandy, heat then flambe. Spoon sauce over sole. Remove fillets of sole to a platter of Rice Tumeric and top with Braganza Sauce.

BRAGANZA SAUCE

     Fat from ¹/₂ pound bacon
¹/₂   cup sliced mushrooms
  1   cup onion, diced fine
¹/₂   cup celery, diced fine
  1   green bell pepper, diced fine
  1   clove garlic, diced fine
¹/₂   green chili pepper, diced fine
     Dash of oregano
  1   tablespoon Worcestershire powder
  4   drops Tabasco
  1   bay leaf
     Dash of thyme
  1   teaspoon garlic salt
¹/₈   teaspoon chili powder
  1   cup brown sauce or canned beef gravy
  1   cup tomato sauce
  1   cup peeled tomatoes
¹/₂   cup tomato paste
¹/₄   cup sherry
     Salt and pepper to taste

Place bacon fat into a skillet and sauté the mushrooms, onion, bell pepper, celery, garlic and chili pepper until soft. Stir in other ingredients and simmer slowly about 5 minutes. Remove bay leaf. Yield 6 cups. Recipe serves 4.

Barbecued Shrimp

Juice of 1 lemon
1 tablespoon onion juice
1 cup catsup
2 tablespoons Worcestershire powder
1 teaspoon chili powder
1 teaspoon salt
2 dashes liquid red pepper seasoning
¹/₄ cup white wine
2 pounds cleaned, deveined jumbo shrimp

Combine lemon juice, onion juice, catsup, Worcestershire powder, chili powder, salt, red pepper seasoning, and white wine in saucepan and heat over very low heat until mixture begins to bubble. Remove from heat and let stand 10 minutes. Place the jumbo shrimp in single layer in shallow pan or on foil-covered broiler pan and top with sauce. Broil 3 inches from medium heat until shrimp is golden brown. Makes 4 servings.

Shrimp and Green Bean Casserole

3 5-ounce cans shrimp
1 9-ounce package frozen French-style green beans
1 10¹/₂-ounce can condensed cream of celery soup
2 tablespoons chopped parsley
1 teaspoon grated onion
1 teaspoon lemon juice
¹/₂ cup grated cheese
Paprika

Drain and rinse shrimp in cold water. Cook the green beans according to package directions, omitting salt. Remove from heat and drain well. Place beans in greased shallow 1¹/₂-quart casserole. Cover with drained shrimp. Combine cream of celery soup, parsley, onion, and lemon juice and pour over shrimp. Top with grated cheese and sprinkle with paprika. Bake in moderate oven (350 degrees) 20 to 25 minutes. Makes 6 servings.

Buffet Tuna Hot Dish

1 10¹/₂-ounce can condensed cream of mushroom soup
1 10¹/₂-ounce can condensed cream of chicken soup
¹/₂ cup mayonnaise
2 7-ounce cans tuna
1 8-ounce can cut green asparagus
¹/₂ cup slivered almonds
1 4-ounce can sliced mushrooms
1 cup American cheese, grated
1 green bell pepper, chopped
1 8-ounce package fine noodles, cooked
Paprika

Heat cream of mushroom soup and cream of chicken soup in saucepan over low heat and add mayonnaise. In 3-quart casserole, arrange tuna, asparagus, almonds, mushrooms, grated cheese, green bell pepper, and cooked noodles in alternate layers, ending with grated cheese and using soup mixture every other layer. Sprinkle with paprika. Bake in moderate oven (350 degrees) 45 minutes. Serve with green salad and garlic bread. Makes 6 servings.

Pepper Pan Oyster Roast

¹/₂ cup butter or margarine
1 pint Olympia oysters or 2 dozen New York oysters, shucked
4 tablespoons minced onion
4 slices bacon, crisply cooked and chopped
4 tablespoons chopped green bell pepper
¹/₂ cup white wine
Juice of 1 lemon
Salt to taste

Heat butter or margarine in heavy pan over medium heat. Add oysters, onion, bacon, and green bell pepper and fry until edges of oysters curl. Add wine, lemon juice, and salt. Pour into heated casserole or individual casseroles. Bake in moderate oven (350 degrees) until oysters are plump. Garnish with chopped parsley to serve. Makes 4 servings.

Lobster Tails Reginald Denny

6　4-ounce frozen South African rock lobster
　　tails
　　Lemon juice
　　Butter

Place frozen lobster tails into lemon juice and marinate until they are at room temperature. Coat in melted butter and broil under hot flame until golden in color. Top with sauce.

SAUCE:

3　tablespoons butter
3　tablespoons flour
$^1/_2$　cup dry white wine
$1^1/_2$　cups heavy cream
1　teaspoon chopped parsley
1　teaspoon dry minced onion
　　Salt and pepper
3　egg yolks, lightly beaten

Melt 3 tablespoons butter in saucepan. Remove from flame and stir in 3 tablespoons flour. Return to low flame and mix in wine, heavy cream, parsley, minced onion, salt and pepper. Blend in egg yolks and heat through, but be sure to remove from flame before egg yolks start to cook.

Pompano en Papillote

3　pompano or other fish
2　cups fish stock
7　tablespoons butter or margarine
2　shallots, chopped
$2^1/_4$　cups dry white wine
1　cup cooked crabmeat
1　cup diced cooked shrimp
$^1/_2$　teaspoon garlic purée
1　bay leaf
　　Pinch thyme
2　tablespoons flour
2　well-beaten egg yolks

Clean pompano, removing head and backbone, and cut into 6 fillets. Cover fish heads and bones with salted water and cook over very low flame until tender. Strain. Measure and add water if necessary to make 2 cups fish stock. Heat 3 tablespoons butter or margarine in skillet. Add shallots and fillets; sauté. Add 2 cups dry wine; cover and cook over very low heat 5 to 8 minutes or until fillets are tender. Remove from heat. In another skillet heat 2 tablespoons butter and sauté cooked crabmeat,

shrimp, and garlic purée. Add $1^3/_4$ cups fish stock, bay leaf, and thyme; simmer slowly for 10 minutes. Remove bay leaf. Blend together 2 tablespoons butter, $^1/_4$ cup fish stock and flour. Combine with crabmeat shrimp mixture and wine stock from fish fillets. Cook, stirring constantly until thickened. Slowly stir half the mixture into well-beaten egg yolks combined with $^1/_4$ cup dry white wine. Beat egg mixture into remaining hot mixture. Chill in refrigerator until firm. Cut 6 parchment paper hearts 8 inches wide and 12 inches long. Oil well. Put a spoonful of sauce near edge of heart, place a fillet on top, fold over and hand seal. Place filled hearts on greased baking sheet. Bake in hot oven of 450 degrees for 15 minutes or until brown. Serve in paper hearts.

Tuna a la Geisha

$^1/_4$　cup butter or margarine
2　tablespoons minced onion
1　teaspoon salt
$^1/_8$　teaspoon pepper
$^1/_4$　cup flour
$1^1/_2$　cups milk
1　7-ounce can tuna, drained and broken in
　　chunks
$^3/_4$　cup mandarin orange sections, drained
4　cups cooked rice
2　tablespoons chopped peanuts or almonds

Combine butter or margarine, minced onion, salt, and pepper in saucepan and heat over very low temperature until fat is melted. Stir in flour. Add milk quickly and cook until smooth and thickened, stirring constantly. Add tuna and orange sections and continue cooking until thoroughly hot. Place in serving dish the cooked rice and pour tuna mixture over rice. Sprinkle with chopped peanuts or almonds. Makes 4 servings.

Cheese Tuna Puff

PIE SHELL:

1　cup sifted flour
$^1/_2$　teaspoon salt
$^1/_3$　cup shortening
3　to 4 tablespoons cold water

Sift flour and salt into bowl. With a fork or pastry blender, cut in shortening until mixture is the size of small peas. Sprinkle cold water over mixture. Blend with fork until mixture will hold together. Roll out on floured surface to 11-inch circle. Fit into 9-inch pie pan. Fold edge to form standing rim; flute.

TUNA FILLING:

1 tablespoon butter or margarine
3 tablespoons flour
1 14$^1/_2$-ounce can evaporated milk
1$^3/_4$ cups Cheddar cheese, grated
2 6$^1/_2$-ounce cans tuna
$^1/_2$ cup chopped celery
2 tablespoons chopped green bell pepper
$^1/_2$ teaspoon Worcestershire powder
Salt and pepper to taste

Melt margarine over low heat; blend in flour. Gradually add evaporated milk, stirring constantly. Cook until thickened. Add Cheddar cheese and stir until melted. Combine tuna, chopped celery, chopped green bell pepper, Worcestershire powder, and salt and pepper to taste. Reserve 1 cup cheese sauce for topping. Combine remaining sauce with tuna mixture and blend well. Spoon into pastry shell. Bake in hot oven (425 degrees) for 15 minutes. Remove from oven and cover pie with cheese puff topping. Decrease heat to 375 degrees. Bake 20 to 25 minutes. Sprinkle with $^1/_4$ cup grated cheddar cheese. Serve at once.

CHEESE PUFF TOPPING:

2 egg whites
2 egg yolks
1 cup cheese sauce

Beat egg whites until stiff but not dry. Combine egg yolks, slightly beaten, with cheese sauce and fold into egg whites. Serves 6.

New Bedford Scallops Jambalaya

2 pounds fresh or thawed frozen sea scallops
4 slices bacon, diced
1 small onion, minced
1 clove garlic, halved
$^1/_2$ cup thinly sliced celery
$^1/_2$ teaspoon thyme
1 teaspoon salt
Few drops liquid red pepper seasoning
2 16-ounce cans whole tomatoes, drained
2 cups cooked or canned peas
2 cups cooked rice

Cut scallops in half. Combine bacon, onion, garlic and celery in large skillet and cook over low heat until soft but not brown. Discard garlic. Stir in thyme, salt, red pepper seasoning, scallops, tomatoes, peas, and cooked rice. Simmer 15 minutes. Makes 6 servings.

Catfish Courtbouillon

6 pounds of catfish fillets
2 tablespoons salt
1 tablespoon red pepper
$^1/_3$ cup cooking oil
1 cup chopped onion
1 cup chopped celery
$^1/_2$ cup chopped bell pepper
$^1/_2$ cup chopped green onion tops
$^1/_3$ cup chopped parsley
1 clove garlic
1 can tomato sauce
$^3/_4$ cup tomato catsup
$^1/_2$ cup water

Season fillets of catfish with salt and red pepper. Add the cooking oil to the bottom of a heavy metal cooker. Mix together onion, celery, bell pepper, green onion tops, parsley, and garlic. Place a layer of these mixed vegetables on the bottom of the kettle, then a layer of catfish. Repeat the procedure until all of the fish and vegetables are in the kettle. If possible, have a layer of the mixed vegetables on top. Mix the tomato sauce, catsup, and water together and pour evenly over the ingredients in the kettle. Cover the kettle and cook in a 450-degree oven for 1$^1/_2$ hours. Recipe serves 6.

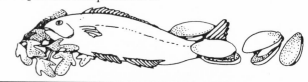

Salmon Soufflé

3 tablespoons butter
3 tablespoons flour
$^1/_2$ teaspoon curry powder
Pinch of thyme (optional)
Salt and pepper
1 cup milk
1$^1/_2$ cups fresh or canned salmon flakes
4 eggs, separated

Melt the butter; add the flour and seasonings and cook until bubbly. Add the milk; bring to a boil and boil for 1 minute, but start counting when it boils, stirring constantly. Remove from stove. Add egg yolks beaten until light and the salmon flaked and free from bones and skin. Cool. Fold in the egg whites stiffly beaten. Pour into a buttered casserole and bake at 375 degrees for 45 minutes in a hot-water bath. (Use the same recipe for leftover chicken or ham or any cooked fish.) Serve with:

BENGAL SAUCE

1 tablespoon butter
1 tablespoon flour
1 cup half-and-half (or whole milk)
  Salt
1/2 teaspoon curry powder
2 teaspoons grated coconut
1/4 cup slivered blanched almonds

Melt butter, add flour, and cook a few seconds. Add milk and cream mixture and cook until smooth and thickened. Add seasonings, coconut, and nuts. A good sauce for any soufflé or for croquettes.

Mexican

Sour Cream Enchiladas

2 tablespoons cooking oil
2 pounds lean ground beef
1 onion diced finely
1 green bell pepper, diced finely
  Salt and pepper to taste
4 tablespoons canned chili without beans
    (slightly thinned with water)
2 tablespoons Picante sauce
1 tablespoon chili powder
1/2 teaspoon cumin powder
1/2 teaspoon coriander
1 tablespoon garlic powder
1 tablespoon Worcestershire powder
4 drops Tabasco sauce
1/2 cup ripe, sliced, pitted olives
12 corn tortillas
1/4 cup Picante sauce
2 cups water
1/4 pound butter
4 tablespoons flour
1 1/2 cups milk
1 pint sour cream
1 pound grated mild Cheddar cheese
1/2 cup whole, pitted ripe olives

In a large, heavy skillet or Dutch oven, heat oil, then brown ground beef, stirring constantly. Add onion and green bell pepper and continue cooking until soft. Add salt, pepper, chili, Picante sauce, chili powder, cumin powder, coriander, garlic powder, Worcestershire powder, Tabasco sauce and sliced ripe olives. Continue stirring while recipe simmers for approximately 5 minutes.

Using mixing bowl, place 1/4 cup Picante sauce in 2 cups water and blend with fork. Place tortillas in Picante water and permit to soak for a few minutes.

In separate saucepan, melt butter and stir in flour. Add milk and continue to stir until sauce is slightly thickened. Blend in sour cream and continue to heat slowly for 1 minute.

Select a large casserole dish and grease lightly. Drain each tortilla slightly and fill with 2 tablespoons of meat mixture. Sprinkle some grated Cheddar cheese (reserving 1/2 pound) over meat mixture and fold over in enchilada style. Arrange the stuffed tortillas in the dish and top thoroughly with sour cream sauce. Sprinkle remaining 1/2 pound of grated Cheddar over top of enchiladas. Locate whole ripe olives on surface and place enchiladas into a preheated 375-degree oven. Bake for 25 minutes or until sauce is bubbling. Remove from oven and serve immediately on heated plates. Makes 12 enchiladas.

Huevos Rancheros

3 tablespoons olive oil
1 large onion, sliced
1 large green bell pepper, sliced
1 clove garlic, crushed
1 tablespoon flour
3 1/2 cups peeled, cooked tomatoes
  Salt and pepper
  Chili powder
  Cumin
  Oregano
2 tablespoons dry white wine
6 eggs
  Sharp Cheddar cheese, cubed
  Pitted black olives

Heat olive oil in saucepan over low heat. Add onion, green bell pepper, and garlic and cook 3 minutes. Blend in flour. Add tomatoes and cook, stirring, for a few minutes. Add salt and pepper, chili powder, cumin and oregano to taste. Add wine and cook 5 minutes.

Pour sauce into shallow baking dish. Break eggs into shallow dish, one at a time, and slip into depression in sauce. Between eggs, place cubed Cheddar cheese and black olives. Bake in moderate oven (350 degrees) 12 minutes or until eggs are set. Makes 6 servings.

David Wade's Tacos

12   **taco shells**
1   **pound ground beef**
1   **large onion, chopped**
2   **large tomatoes, diced**
1   **small head lettuce, chopped**
1   **pound mild Cheddar cheese, grated**
1   **pint David Wade Gourmet Chili**

Heat chili to serving temperature. Place ground beef in a skillet and brown. Place meat into a colander and drain the fat. Wipe out skillet with paper towel then return the drained meat. Add chili and blend.

Place meat mixture into taco shells and then into an open baking dish. Bake in a preheated 375-degree oven for five minutes. Remove and top each taco with onion, lettuce, tomato and grated cheese.

Yield 12 tacos.

David Wade's Chalupas

8   **chalupa shells**
$^1/_2$ **cup minced onion**
1   **pint David Wade Gourmet Chili**
$^1/_2$ **pound Monterey Jack Cheese, grated**

Heat chili to serving temperature. Spread chili on each chalupa shell. Sprinkle with minced onion. Top with cheese. Place chalupas on a broiling pan then under broiler for just a few minutes until cheese melts.

Recipe serves 4.

South of the Border Stuffed Peppers

6   **green bell peppers**
1   **15-ounce can hominy (drained)**
$^1/_2$ **pound mild Cheddar cheese, grated**
1   **pint David Wade Gourmet Chili**

Cut $^1/_4$ of each green pepper from the top. Remove seeds and fibers from each pepper cavity. Drop peppers into boiling water and blanch for just 2 minutes. Remove peppers and dry with paper towels.

Heat chili to serving temperature and blend in hominy. Stuff each pepper with mixture and top with grated cheese. Bake in preheated 375-degree oven for 25 minutes.

Recipe serves 6.

NOTE: Top of each pepper can be festooned with sliced jalepeño peppers, sliced olives or chopped onion.

Mary Judges's Mexican Peas

1   **16-ounce can English peas**
$^1/_2$ **10-ounce can Rotel tomatoes and green chilies**
1   **large onion, sliced**
     Diced, cooked ham
     Cheese
1   **large tomato**

Drain liquid from peas into saucepan; add tomato. Cook onion in this mixture; then add desired amount of ham and cheese, and heat until cheese melts. Add peas and heat through. Serves 6.

For the Sweet Tooth

Becky's Cheesecake

PASTRY:

1	cup sifted all-purpose flour
$^1/_4$	cup sugar
1	teaspoon grated lemon rind
1	egg yolk
$^1/_4$	cup butter or margarine
1	teaspoon vanilla extract

CHEESE FILLING:

$2^1/_2$	pound cream cheese
$1^3/_4$	cups sugar
3	tablespoons flour
$1^1/_2$	teaspoons grated orange rind
$1^1/_2$	teaspoons grated lemon rind
$^1/_4$	teaspoon vanilla extract
5	eggs
2	egg yolks
$^1/_4$	cup heavy cream

Mix flour, sugar, lemon rind and vanilla extract in a bowl. Make a well in the center, add unbeaten egg yolk, butter or margarine and work mixture together with your hands until it forms a ball. Wrap in waxed paper and chill in refrigerator for at least 1 hour.

When thoroughly chilled, get out a 9-inch spring-form pan and oil bottom. Start your oven at 400 degrees or moderately hot. Cut off about one-quarter of the dough, roll dough directly on bottom of pan $^1/_8$-inch thick. Trim the edges even. Bake this bottom crust 10 minutes or until golden. Cool.

Now divide remaining dough in 3 sections and roll each part $^1/_8$-inch thick in a narrow strip on a lightly floured board. Fit these thin strips around the oiled sides of spring-form pan and press the joining edges together to line sides completely. Trim top edge of dough neatly so that dough reaches $^3/_4$ of the height of the pan. NOTE: This amount of dough is exactly right providing it is rolled thin enough. Chill dough in refrigerator until filling is made.

Turn your oven up to 550 degrees or very hot. Mix cream cheese, sugar, flour, grated orange and lemon rind, vanilla extract in a large bowl. Beat until mixture is smooth and well blended — use your electric mixer if you have one. Now drop in the eggs and extra egg yolks one at a time and stir lightly after each addition. Mix in the cream last of all.

Assemble spring-form pan with baked crust on the bottom (still in the pan, of course) and the unbaked pastry around the sides. Pour in cheese filling and bake 10 minutes at this high temperature. Then reduce heat to 200 degrees or very, very low and continue baking 1 hour longer. Cool on cake rack until completely cold. Release sides of pan, remove and serve cold without removing bottom of pan.

For topping, use your favorite fruit pie filling such as cherry, blueberry, strawberry, etc.

Crazy Pudding

1	cup dates, cut fine
1	cup nuts, scant
1	cup sugar
1	cup flour
1	teaspoon baking powder
1	teaspoon vanilla
$^1/_2$	cup milk
1	cup brown sugar
2	cups water
1	tablespoon butter

Mix together dates, nuts, sugar, flour, baking powder, vanilla, and milk. In a 2-quart baking dish, mix and heat together brown sugar, water, and butter. Add this mixture by the teaspoonful to date mixture. Bake at 350 degrees in preheated oven for about 45 minutes. Serves 12.

Impossible Pie

2	cups milk
1	cup coconut
$^1/_2$	cup flour
$^3/_4$	cup sugar
4	eggs
$^3/_4$	stick margarine
$^1/_4$	teaspoon salt
1	teaspoon vanilla

Place all ingredients in a blender and mix. Pour mixture into greased and floured pie plate. Bake at 350 degrees for 45 minutes. This pie forms its own crust as it bakes.

Walnut Divine Cake

$^3/_4$ cup sifted flour
2   teaspoons cinnamon
1   teaspoon salt
9   eggs, separated
$1^1/_2$ cups sugar
2   teaspoons vanilla
2   cups walnuts, finely chopped

Sift flour with cinnamon and salt. Beat egg whites in large bowl until soft peaks form. Gradually add $^3/_4$ cup of the sugar and beat until stiff straight peaks form. Do not underbeat. Combine egg yolks, remaining $^3/_4$ cup sugar and vanilla in small bowl. Beat until thick and lemon-colored. Stir in dry ingredients. Fold batter gently and thoroughly into egg whites using spatula or wire whip. Blend in walnuts. Pour into ungreased tube pan and bake at 350 degrees for 55 to 60 minutes. Invert immediately. Cool completely before removing from pan. Ice with vanilla glaze.

VANILLA GLAZE

3   cups sifted powdered sugar
3   tablespoons milk
2   tablespoons butter
$^1/_2$ teaspoon vanilla

Heat butter and milk over low heat, stirring constantly until butter melts. Remove from heat. Add to sugar, blending until smooth. Stir in vanilla.

Maxine's Chocolate Cake

1   pound bitter sweet cooking chocolate
1   tablespoon flour
1   tablespoon granulated sugar
$^1/_2$ cup ($^1/_4$ pound) butter
4   eggs, separated

Do not bake any longer than time given. Cake will harden as it cools. Cut chocolate into small pieces and melt slowly with a very small amount of water. When it is the consistency of thick cream, remove from heat and add to the sugar, flour and softened butter, stirring constantly.

When the mixture is very smooth, add the egg yolks and mix thoroughly. Beat egg whites until stiff and fold lightly into chocolate mixture.

Line pudding mold with buttered paper. Pour in batter and bake for 15 minutes in a hot (425-degree) oven. Cool on rack.

Calories, Inc. (Dessert Squares)

1   yellow cake mix
1   cup pecans, finely chopped
2   eggs
1   stick butter, melted
1   16-ounce box powdered sugar
2   eggs
8   ounces cream cheese, softened

Mix together dry cake mix, pecans, 2 eggs and butter. Spread into 9x12 greased baking dish or pan. Then thoroughly mix cream cheese, 2 eggs and powdered sugar. Pour on top of cake mixture. Bake for 1 hour at 275 degrees.

Judy's Lemon Pie

$^1/_4$ cup cornstarch
3   tablespoons flour
$1^3/_4$ cup sugar
$^1/_4$ teaspoon salt
$^1/_2$ package unflavored gelatin
4   egg yolks, slightly beaten
$^1/_2$ cup lemon juice
1   tablespoon grated lemon peel
1   tablespoon butter

In medium-sized saucepan, combine cornstarch, flour, sugar, salt and gelatin. Mix well. Gradually add 2 cups water and stir until mixture is smooth. Bring to a boil over medium heat. Boil 1 minute then remove from heat and quickly stir some hot mixture into slightly beaten egg yolks. Return to hot mixture. Cook over low heat 5 minutes, stirring constantly. Remove again from heat and stir in lemon juice, lemon peel and butter. Pour mixture into baked pie shell. Top with meringue and brown meringue. Cool completely before serving.

MERINGUE

4   egg whites, room temperature
$^1/_4$ teaspoon cream of tartar
$^1/_2$ cup sugar

Add cream of tartar to egg whites and beat mixture until stiff but not dry. Add sugar slowly.

Oatmeal Cake

1　cup oatmeal
1½　cups hot water
½　cup butter

Mix above ingredients and set aside for 20 minutes.

1　cup brown sugar
1⅓　cups flour
1　teaspoon soda
1　scant teaspoon salt
1　cup white sugar
1　teaspoon baking powder
2　eggs, well beaten
1　teaspoon vanilla

Mix well and add to oatmeal mixture. Bake at 350 degrees for 35 minutes in 9x13 inch pan.

TOPPING

1　cup brown sugar
1　tablespoon milk
6　tablespoons butter

Bring to boil and cook 1 minute.

Add 1 cup chopped pecans and 1 can flaked coconut. Spread on top of cake. Broil until slightly brown.

Miracle Cake

1¾　cups flour
1　cup sugar
3　tablespoons cocoa
2　teaspoons baking soda
1　cup cold water
1　cup Miracle Whip Salad Dressing
1　teaspoon vanilla
½　teaspoon salt

Sift together the flour, sugar, cocoa, and soda and mix well. Then, add water, Miracle Whip, vanilla, and salt. Bake 30 minutes at 350 degrees in a 13x9 inch pan which has been greased and floured, or may make 18 cupcakes.

Easy Caramels

½　pound butter or margarine
2　cups light corn syrup
2　cups sugar
2　15-ounce cans Borden's Eagle Brand Sweetened Condensed Milk
½　cup sifted flour
1　teaspoon vanilla

In heavy saucepan, melt butter; add corn syrup and sugar. Boil for 5 minutes over medium heat, stirring constantly. Add 1½ cans of milk, mix flour thoroughly with remaining milk, then add to corn syrup mixture. Boil until mixture darkens and forms hard ball (240 degrees). Stir constantly or mixture will stick. Add vanilla and pour into buttered 9x13x2 inch pan. Allow to cool. Cut into 1-inch pieces with a sharp buttered knife. Wrap in small squares of waxed paper. Makes about 5 dozen pieces.

Sour Cream Raisin Pie

2　eggs, slightly beaten
¾　cup sugar
¼　teaspoon salt
1　teaspoon cinnamon
½　teaspoon nutmeg
¼　teaspoon cloves
1　cup sour cream
1　cup seeded raisins
　　Pie shell

Combine all ingredients and pour mixture into a pie shell. Bake at 450 degrees for 10 minutes, reduce heat to 350 degrees for 30 minutes or until knife comes out clean.

Vinegar Butter Pie

4　egg yolks
1　cup sugar
1　cup water
4　tablespoons flour or cornstarch
10　tablespoons strong vinegar
1　teaspoon lemon juice
　　Butter, size of large egg
4　egg whites
2　tablespoons sugar
1　pie shell, baked

Combine first 7 ingredients and cook until thick. Pour into baked pie shell. Use remaining egg whites beaten until stiff, and 2 tablespoons sugar stirred in to make meringue topping for pie. Brown top of meringue in oven.

Sour Cream Apple Pie

CRUST:

$2^1/_2$	cups unbleached all-purpose flour
5	tablespoons granulated sugar
$^3/_4$	teaspoon salt
$^3/_4$	teaspoon ground cinnamon
6	tablespoons sweet butter, chilled
6	tablespoons shortening, chilled
4	to 6 tablespoons apple cider or juice, chilled

Sift flour, sugar, salt and cinnamon into a bowl. Cut in butter and shortening with a fork or pastry cutter until mixture resembles rolled oats.

Moisten with just enough cider, tossing ingredients lightly with a fork, to permit the dough to be formed into a ball. Wrap and refrigerate for 2 hours.

Cut off one third of the dough and return it to the refrigerator. Roll out the other two thirds between 2 sheets of wax paper. Line a greased 9-inch pie pan with the dough. Trim overhang and crimp decoratively. Preheat oven to 350 degrees.

FILLING:

5	to 7 tart apples
$^2/_3$	cup dairy sour cream
$^1/_3$	cup granulated sugar
1	egg, lightly beaten
$^1/_4$	teaspoon salt
1	teaspoon vanilla extract
3	tablespoons unbleached all-purpose flour

Peel, core and thinly slice apples; drop slices into a mixing bowl. Whisk together sour cream, sugar, egg, salt, vanilla and flour in a small bowl. Pour mixture over apples and toss well to coat. Spoon apples into pastry-lined pie pan.

TOPPING:

3	tablespoons brown sugar
3	tablespoons granulated sugar
1	teaspoon ground cinnamon
1	cup shelled walnuts, chopped

Mix sugars, cinnamon and walnuts together and sprinkle evenly over apple filling. Roll out remaining pastry between sheets of wax paper to form a 10-inch circle. Cut into $^1/_2$-inch strips, and arrange these lattice-fashion over apples; trim ends of strips and crimp edge of crust decoratively.

Set pie on the middle rack of the oven and bake for 55 to 65 minutes. If crust browns too quickly, cover loosely with foil. Pie is done when juices are bubbling and apples are tender. Serve warm or cool, topped, if you like, with whipped cream or vanilla ice cream. Six portions.

Coconut Macaroons

$^1/_3$	cup unbleached all-purpose flour
$2^1/_2$	cups shredded coconut
$^1/_8$	teaspoon salt
$^2/_3$	cup sweetened condensed milk
1	teaspoon vanilla extract

Preheat oven to 350 degrees. Grease a cookie sheet well.

Mix flour, coconut and salt together in a bowl. Pour in condensed milk and vanilla and stir well to make a thick batter.

Drop batter by quarter-cupfuls onto the well-greased cookie sheet, allowing an inch of space between cookies. Bake for 20 minutes, or until golden brown. Remove from pan at once, and cool on racks. About $1^1/_2$ dozen macaroons.

Apricot-Raisin Bread

1	cup boiling water, approximately
$^3/_4$	cup coarsely chopped dried apricots
$^1/_2$	cup raisins
3	tablespoons plus $^1/_2$ cup granulated sugar
$^1/_3$	cup oil
2	eggs, beaten
$2^1/_4$	cups unbleached, all-purpose flour
1	tablespoon baking powder
$^1/_2$	teaspoon salt
$^2/_3$	cup milk
$^3/_4$	cup unprocessed bran

Preheat oven to 350 degrees. Grease a 9x5x3 inch bread pan.

Pour boiling water over apricots and raisins just to cover. Let sit for 10 minutes. Drain well and add 3 tablespoons sugar. Mix well.

While fruit is soaking, add the remaining $^1/_2$ cup sugar to the oil and beat well. Add eggs, one at a time, beating until well mixed.

Sift flour, baking powder and salt together and add alternately with milk and bran to oil mixture. Fold in fruits.

Pour mixture into prepared pan. Bake for 1 hour, or until a cake tester inserted in the center comes out clean.

Remove from oven and cool for 10 minutes. Remove from pan and cool on a cake rack. Makes 1 loaf.

Ice Box Graham Cracker Roll

8 ounces graham crackers, crushed
8 ounces marshmallows, cut fine
8 ounces chopped dates
$^1/_2$ cup half and half cream
20 cherries, chopped

Mix together and roll on wax paper; add a few additional cracker crumbs. Let stand in refrigerator until nearly ready to serve. Garnish with colored candies or cherries and serve with or without whipped cream. Rich, but delicious.

Potato Chocolate Cake

1 cup hot unseasoned mashed potatoes
2 cups sugar
$^2/_3$ cup shortening
4 eggs
1 teaspoon vanilla extract
2 cups all-purpose flour, sifted
1 cup cocoa powder
3 teaspoons baking powder
1 teaspoon each powdered cinnamon and
      nutmeg
$^1/_2$ teaspoon salt
$^1/_4$ cup milk
1 cup chopped walnuts

Prepare mashed potatoes. An easy way is to follow directions for 2 servings on package mashed potatoes. Measure, set aside. Start oven at moderate (350 degrees). Line bottoms of two 9-inch layer pans, or oblong pan 13x9x2 inches, with waxed paper cut to fit; grease paper lightly. Gradually beat sugar into shortening until fluffy. Add eggs, one at a time, beating well. Add vanilla and potatoes. Sift all dry ingredients together 3 times; add about $^1/_4$ of dry ingredients to egg mixture, beat, add $^1/_4$ of milk, beat well; continue adding dry ingredients and milk alternately until all are used. Stir walnuts in. Pour into pans. Bake layers in moderate oven 40 to 45 minutes, or loaf cake 50 minutes, or until done when tested. Let stand 5 minutes in pans. Turn out on racks, peel off paper. Let cool. Frost with Butter Cream or other favorite frosting and sprinkle thickly with chopped walnuts. Makes 8 or more servings.

Pumpkin Pound Cake

1 cup margarine or vegetable shortening
3 cups sugar
3 eggs
2 cups pumpkin (16-ounce can)
3 cups sifted flour
1 teaspoon baking powder
1 teaspoon soda
1 teaspoon cinnamon
1 teaspoon nutmeg
1 teaspoon ground clove
1 teaspoon allspice

Cream together shortening and sugar. Add eggs and pumpkin and mix well. Sift dry ingredients together and add slowly to the creamed mixture. This is a heavy pound cake type batter; thorough mixing is necessary. Add no additional liquid. Pour into a greased and floured angel food tube pan. Bake at 325 degrees for $1^1/_4$ hours. If not done, bake an additional 15 minutes. Cool in pan. Dust with powdered sugar or drizzle with thin glaze. Serve with whipped cream or ice cream.

Black Walnut Cake

2 sticks butter or margarine
2 cups sugar
4 eggs
2 teaspoons baking powder
1 cup milk
1 can finely cut coconut
16 ounces graham cracker crumbs
1 cup chopped black walnuts

FILLING:

1 pound of powdered sugar
1 stick melted butter
1 small can crushed pineapple

Cream butter and sugar thoroughly. Beat in eggs one at a time. Stir in coconut. Mix the baking powder with cracker crumbs. Add alternately with milk. Stir in the nuts last. Divide batter between 3 large round cake pans, that have been lined with wax paper. Bake for 25 to 30 minutes in a 350-degree oven. When cool, frost between layers and on top. Combine filling ingredients. This cake is much better if made a day ahead of serving.

Zabaglione

For four, beat 6 egg yolks, then add 1 teaspoon vanilla extract or 1 vanilla stick, 6 tablespoons of brandy or white wine, 6 tablespoons granulated sugar. Place in top of double boiler over but not in hot water. Stir constantly from here out. Cook slowly at first, bringing the water in the bottom pan to a boil, then gradually increase the heat, always stirring, until the sauce thickens. It will fluff up. Pour into sherbet or parfait glasses and serve warm. Zabaglione may also be served cold: line a bowl with ladyfingers, sprinkle them with wine, and pour in the cooled zabaglione. Decorate with pistachio nuts and chill.

Buttercream Icing for Cake Decorating

$^2/_3$ **cup sweet butter**
2   **cups powdered sugar**
1   **egg yolk**
     Vanilla or other flavoring to taste
     Coloring to suit

Cream the butter until it is as light and fluffy as you can get it. Add the egg yolk and mix. Beat in the sugar a little at a time. Vanilla is the standard flavoring, but this is a matter of choice, as is the coloring.

To apply, squeeze through a pastry bag, or parchment paper cones.

For a pure white icing, use uncolored margarine instead of butter.

Chocolate Pie Spectacular

PECAN CRUMB CRUST:

1   **cup fine graham cracker crumbs**
$^1/_2$ **cup finely chopped pecans**
$^1/_2$ **cup brown sugar, firmly packed**
$^1/_3$ **cup melted shortening**

FILLING:

1   **envelope unflavored gelatin**
$^1/_4$ **cup cold milk**
$^2/_3$ **cup sugar**
2   **eggs, separated**
$^1/_4$ **teaspoon salt**
$1^1/_4$ **cup scalded milk**
1   **teaspoon vanilla**
1   **cup heavy cream, whipped**
1   **square semi-sweet chocolate, shaved**
     Chocolate Topping

Crust: Combine ingredients and press firmly into 9-inch pie pan. Make even layer on bottom and sides of pan. Bake in slow oven (300 degrees) 10 minutes. Cool.

Filling: Soften gelatin in cold milk. Combine $^1/_2$ the sugar, slightly beaten egg yolks, salt and scalded milk. Cook, stirring over very low heat until mixture coats a metal spoon. Remove from heat. Blend in softened gelatin and vanilla. Chill mixture until it begins to thicken. Beat until light. Beat egg whites until frothy; gradually add remaining $^1/_3$ cup sugar, beating until glossy, firm peaks form. Fold into gelatin mixture. Fold in whipped cream and shaved chocolate. Heap filling into cool Pecan Crumb Crust. Chill until firm. Drizzle on Chocolate Topping and refrigerate or freeze until serving time. Makes 6 to 8 servings.

Chocolate Topping: Heat $^1/_2$ (6 ounce) package semi-sweet chocolate pieces ($^1/_2$ cup) and 2 teaspoons butter or margarine over hot, not boiling, water, until chocolate is just melted. Remove from heat; add 1 tablespoon hot water and stir until smooth. Immediately drizzle over top of pie.

Bananas Foster

3   **tablespoons butter**
1   **tablespoon brown sugar**
1   **teaspoon cinnamon**
2   **tablespoons banana liqueur**
1   **tablespoon rum**
2   **tablespoons brandy**
1   **banana, quartered**
1   **tablespoon brandy**
2   **dishes vanilla ice cream**

Blend butter, brown sugar, cinnamon, banana liqueur, rum, brandy and quartered banana in skillet and bring to simmer over low heat. Simmer about 1 minute. Add brandy. Ignite sauce with match. Spoon over ice cream and serve immediately. Makes 2 servings.

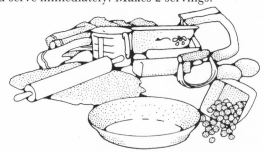

Orange Slice Cookies

Combine and mix the following ingredients:

1   **cup brown sugar**
1   **cup flour**
1   **teaspoon baking powder**
$^1/_2$ **teaspoon cinnamon**
1   **cup orange slices (diced)**
1   **cup chopped pecans**
2   **eggs (well-beaten — beat the mischief out of them)**

Place mixture into a sheet cake pan and bake for 20–25 minutes at 350 degrees. Cool and cut into wedges.

Vinegar Pie Crust

Blend

3   **cups flour**
8   **teaspoons milk powder**

Add just until lumpy

$1^3/_4$ **cup butter**

Dissolve and add to above mixture

3   **teaspoons salt**
$^3/_4$ **teaspoon soda**
3   **teaspoons vinegar (may substitute syrup)**
$^1/_2$ **cup water (or just enough to barely mix)**

Peanut Brittle

$^1/_2$ **cup water**
2   **cups sugar**
2   **cups Planters Cocktail Peanuts**
$^1/_2$ **cup butter**
2   **teaspoons soda**
1   **teaspoon vanilla**
1   **cup corn syrup**

Bring water to a boil, add sugar and syrup. Cook to 260 degrees stirring constantly. Add butter and peanuts. Keep stirring and cook to 305 degrees. Remove from heat. Add soda and vanilla. Stir in thoroughly. Pour onto buttered cookie sheets. As it cools, stretch until very thin. Let cool until hard, then break into pieces.

Buttermilk Pie

$3^3/_4$ **cups sugar**
$^1/_4$ **cup flour**
2   **sticks of butter**
5   **or 6 eggs**
2   **cups of buttermilk**
2   **teaspoons vanilla extract**
    Pinch of salt

Blend all items until creamy. Pour into 2 unbaked pie shells in 9-inch pie pans.

Preheat oven to 350 degrees and bake until pies are brown.

Easy Puff Pastry

$^1/_4$ **cup butter or margarine**
$^1/_2$ **cup hot water**
$^1/_2$ **cup flour**
$^1/_4$ **teaspoon salt**
$^1/_4$ **teaspoon sugar (increase to 1 teaspoon for dessert puffs)**
2   **eggs**

Combine butter, water, salt and sugar in a saucepan and bring to a boil. Reduce heat and dump in flour. Immediately stir vigorously and continue stirring for 2 minutes. Let pan stand off the heat for 5 minutes.

Place the flour mixture in a food processor and process for 10 seconds. Add the eggs and process for 30 seconds. (Dough can be baked right then, or kept in the fridge for one or two days until needed.) For small appetizer puffs, drop the mixture by teaspoonfuls onto a buttered or non-stick baking sheet. For the larger puffs, use heaping tablespoonfuls. Leave space between them as they will swell as they bake.

Bake the puffs in a preheated 425-degree oven for about 20 minutes until they are puffed and a light, golden brown. Cool completely before cutting them open to fill. Recipe yields 16 small or 8 large puffs.

Peanut Butter Pie

Cream together:

1   **cup peanut butter**
1   **8-ounce package cream cheese**
1   **cup sugar**
2   **tablespoons melted butter**

Then add:

1   **cup whipping cream (whipped) DO NOT USE COOL WHIP!**
1   **tablespoon vanilla**

Mix together. Pour into a graham cracker crust and chill overnight. May be topped with hot fudge but chill again for 30 more minutes.

Top of the Sixes Cherries Jubilee

1   **lemon**
$^1/_2$ **cup confectioners' sugar**
1   **can (1 pound) tart red cherries and liquid**
2   **tablespoons Triple-Sec**
$^1/_4$ **cup Triple-Sec**
    Vanilla ice cream

Heat chafing dish blazer pan or skillet over very low heat. Cut lemon in half and squeeze into warmed pan, reserving shells. Lift pan and revolve so lemon juice covers surface. Add confectioners' sugar, stirring constantly until dissolved. Add cherries and liquid and continue cooking and stirring until liquid is reduced by half. Rub bottom of pan with cut sides of lemon shells, tilting as necessary to avoid liquid. Add 2 tablespoons Triple-Sec and cook until alcohol is evaporated, stirring constantly. Turn heat to high and add $^1/_4$ cup Triple-Sec. When slightly warmed, ignite with match. Flame until alcohol is greatly evaporated. Place vanilla ice cream in 4 dessert dishes and make a well in top of each scoop ice cream. Pour cherries over ice cream. Serve immediately. Makes 4 servings.

Cherry Cobbler

1   **package white cake mix with pudding**
2   **21-ounce cans cherry pie filling**
    Juice of 1 lemon
1   **stick butter**
    Cinnamon (optional)
$^1/_2$ **cup chopped pecans**

Butter baking dish. Spoon cherry pie filling into baking dish and sprinkle over top with lemon juice. Melt butter in saucepan. Add cake mix and stir until crumbly. Add nuts. Spread cake mixture over cherry filling. Bake at 350 degrees for 50–60 minutes. Top with Cool Whip or whipped cream.

Other fruits (canned) may be substituted in the same amount.

Baked Pineapple Alaska

Fresh pineapple
Brick ice cream
Meringue

Select one fresh pineapple for every 2 persons. Divide pineapple with a sharp knife into 2 halves. With a spoon, core out some of the heart of each section. Place brick ice cream into the cored-out sections and top with meringue, being careful to seal completely to edges of pineapple. Brown meringue with cooking torch or put pineapple halves into preheated 500-degree oven for about 5 minutes, or until meringue is lightly browned.

For meringue: Combine 5 egg whites with 1 teaspoon sugar and 1 teaspoon vanilla extract and whip until very stiff.

Becky Wade's Snicker Doodle Cookies

1   **cup shortening**
$1^1/_2$ **cups sugar**
2   **eggs**
$2^3/_4$ **cups sifted flour**
2   **teaspoons cream of tartar**
1   **teaspoon soda**
1   **teaspoon salt**

Mix thoroughly the shortening, sugar and eggs. Sift together the remaining ingredients and stir in. Chill dough, then roll into walnut size balls. Roll each ball into a mixture of:

2   **tablespoons sugar**
2   **tablespoons cinnamon**

Place 2 inches apart on ungreased baking sheet. Bake until lightly brown at 400 degrees for 8–10 minutes. Makes 5 dozen.

Blue Ribbon Oatmeal Cookies

1½   cups sifted all-purpose flour
½   teaspoon baking soda
½   teaspoon salt
     Dash of ground mace
1   cup vegetable shortening
1¼   cups firmly packed brown sugar
1   egg
¼   cup milk
1¾   cups quick-cooking rolled oats
1   cup chopped pecans

Measure flour, soda, salt and mace into a sifter. Cream shortening with brown sugar until fluffy in a large bowl; beat in egg and milk. Sift in flour mixture, blending well to make a thick batter. Fold in rolled oats and pecans. Drop by teaspoonfuls, 3 inches apart, on greased cookie sheet. Remove from cookie sheets and cool completely on wire racks. Yields about 3½ dozen.

Japanese Fruit Cake

2   cups sugar
1   cup butter
1   cup milk
4   cups flour
3   teaspoons baking powder
1   teaspoon salt
1   teaspoon cinnamon
1   teaspoon cloves
1   teaspoon allspice
8   eggs
1   box raisins
1   box currants
1   large box dates
1   small box citron
1   cup walnuts
1   cup pecans
1   box candied pineapple
1   box candied cherries

Cream butter and sugar. Sift spices, baking powder and flour together. Add milk and dry ingredients alternately. Add fruit and nuts and well-beaten eggs last. Bake in four 9-inch layers at 250 degrees about 2½ hours.

FILLING:

3   cups sugar
1½   cups boiling water
4½   tablespoons cornstarch
3   large oranges
3   lemons
1   can coconut

Grate rind of one orange and one lemon. Peel fruit and dice. Mix all ingredients together. Cook until thick. Spread on cake and add nuts for decoration.

Vanilla Ice Cream

5 cups heavy cream, whipped until stiff. 1 long vanilla bean stick. Remove bark and scrape with a sharp knife or grate 2 teaspoons full. Sift grated fresh vanilla with 4 cups of sugar. Blend 3 cups of milk with 2 beaten eggs then blend into the sugar mixture. Fold mixture into whipped cream and turn into ice trays. When almost half frozen, stir completely and return to freezer and freeze until stiff. Yields approximately 1 gallon.

Divinity

First Part

1   cup sugar
¼   cup water

Cook to 242 degrees on candy thermometer. Fold in

3   beaten egg whites

Second Part

3   cups white sugar
1   cup white syrup
½   cup hot water
     Pinch of salt
     Pinch of Cream of Tartar

Cook to 252 degrees on candy thermometer.

Pour slowly over first part. Beat, beat, beat. Add 2 cups nuts and 1 teaspoon vanilla. Drop on wax paper.

Peanut Butter Cookies

1 cup chunky peanut butter
1 cup sugar
1 egg
¹/₂ teaspoon vanilla

Mix well all of the above ingredients. Drop by spoonful on ungreased cookie sheet. (Or place foil on the cookie sheet and bake cookies on foil.) Bake at 325 degrees until brown. Slide off cookie sheet very gently as cookies are tender.

Chewy Pralines

³/₄ cup canned evaporated milk
¹/₄ cup water
3 cups sugar
2 cups pecans, large pieces

Carmelize 1 cup of sugar in heavy skillet. At the same time heat the liquid in a large heavy kettle. When the sugar is carmelized thoroughly, pour into hot (not boiling) milk and stir. Sugar will form a large hard lump which will dissolve. Add the other 2 cups of sugar, stir at frequent intervals and let cook over medium flame. Test in cold water after mixture has reached foamy consistency. When it forms decidedly hard, but not brittle ball, take from flames and place in a pan or sink of cool water. Add pecans and stir thoroughly. It is not necessary to beat. When the mixture begins to thicken and crackle when stirred, it is ready to dip. Dip by teaspoonful onto waxed paper and allow to cool.

Macedonne au Creme

2 tablespoons butter
1 cup brown sugar
1 · cup red bing pitted cherries (reserve ¹/₂ cup syrup)
1 cup melon balls
2 bananas, sliced in rounds
1 cup fresh strawberries, hulled and sliced
1 cup fresh peaches, sliced
1 teaspoon cinnamon
1 teaspoon nutmeg
1 cup moist, flaked coconut
1 cup sour cream
¹/₄ cup banana liqueur
¹/₂ cup macadamia nuts or almonds
2 tablespoons brandy

Melt butter in skillet and add brown sugar, stirring until dissolved. Add cherries and syrup. Cook 1 minute. Add fruits, cinnamon, nutmeg and coconut. Blend in sour cream and banana liqueur. Heat and add nuts and brandy. Flame and serve over vanilla ice cream.

Strawberries Romanoff

2 pints red, ripe strawberries
¹/₃ cup plus 2 tablespoons sugar
¹/₃ cup Grand Marnier or Cointreau
1 orange
³/₄ cup heavy cream

Remove the stems from the strawberries. Rinse well and drain. Pat dry with paper towels.

Place the strawberries in a bowl and add ¹/₃ cup of the sugar and the Grand Marnier.

Using a swivel-bladed potato peeler, cut around the orange to produce a very thin spiral of peel. Do not cut into the white pulp. Cut the peel into wafer thin shreds. Add to the strawberries and fold together gently. (Use the orange in another dish.)

Cover the bowl and refrigerate until ready to serve.

Whip the cream and flavor it with the remaining 2 tablespoons of sugar. Serve the cream with the strawberries.

Makes 8 servings.

South Louisiana Pecan Torte

6 tablespoons butter or margarine
1¹/₂ cups brown sugar
4 eggs, separated
3¹/₂ cups ground pecans
1 teaspoon vanilla extract
2 cups whipped cream
¹/₂ cup ground pecans

Cream butter and sugar. Mix in well-beaten yolks of eggs. Stir in the 3¹/₂ cups ground pecans and vanilla. Fold in stiffly beaten whites. Turn into two 9-inch layer pans lightly oiled. Bake at 350 degrees for about 25 minutes. Cool. Just before serving, layer with whipped cream, cover top with whipped cream and sprinkle with remaining pecans. Yield 8 portions.

Cherries Manhattan

3   tablespoons butter
1   cup brown sugar
1/2   cup heavy cream
1   15-ounce can dark sweet pitted cherries
4   tablespoons Kirch (white cherry brandy)

Blend in order and flame in blazer pan. Serve over vanilla ice cream.

Serves 6.

Cheese Blintzes

FILLING:

1   pound dry cottage cheese
2   eggs, beaten
1   tablespoon sugar
   Pinch cinnamon

Combine all ingredients and mix until of smooth consistency.

Ginger Ale Chiffon Pie

1   envelope unflavored gelatin
2½   cups ginger ale
1   cup instant dry milk
²⁄₃   cup sugar
4   egg yolks
1   tablespoon butter or margarine
¼   teaspoon salt
1   teaspoon vanilla
¼   teaspoon almond extract
4   egg whites
4   tablespoons sugar
   Shaved unsweetened chocolate
1   baked 9-inch pastry shell

Soften gelatin in ½ cup ginger ale. Combine 2 cups ginger ale with instant dry milk, stirring until milk is dissolved. Stir in ²⁄₃ cup sugar. Beat egg yolks in saucepan. Blend in ginger ale-milk mixture. Cook over very low heat until thickened, stirring occasionally (about 12 minutes). Add softened gelatin and continue cooking 2 to 3 minutes, stirring constantly. Add butter or margarine. Remove from heat. Add salt, vanilla and almond extract. Cool. Chill in refrigerator until thickened. Beat vigorously with rotary beater. Stiffly beat 2 egg whites and fold into the chilled mixture. Place into refrigerator once more and chill until thickened. Pour into cold, baked 9-

inch pastry shell. Cover top of pie with shaved unsweetened chocolate. Chill once more until firm. Beat 2 egg whites until foamy. Gradually add 4 tablespoons sugar, beating until egg whites are stiff. Spread on pie, being careful to seal meringue onto edge of pastry to prevent shrinkage. Bake in hot oven, 450 degrees, for 4 minutes or until meringue is brown. Remove from oven and decorate top with shaved chocolate. Cool. Chill in refrigerator until served.

CREPES OR PANCAKES:

1   quart milk
3   eggs, beaten
1   cup sifted flour
   Sour cream or applesauce

Mix milk, beaten eggs and flour together to form smooth batter. Heat 6-inch skillet over medium temperature until very hot. Wipe inside of skillet with oil, leaving very thin coating. Pour batter into skillet immediately pouring off excess. Fry until light brown. Pull lightly at edges until pancake rolls. Loosen from skillet and place, browned side up, on hot platter or cloth. Repeat until batter is used.

Place a tablespoonful of filling on browned side of each pancake. Fold in edges, envelope fashion, sealing in filling. Pour oil in skillet to half the depth of each blintz. Fry blintzes over medium heat until brown on all sides. Remove from skillet and dry in cloth. Serve with sour cream or applesauce. Fruit fillings may also be used. Makes 15 to 20.

Fresh Strawberry Chiffon Pie

1   tablespoon (1 envelope) unflavored gelatin in
¼   cup cold water
3   egg yolks
½   cup sugar
¼   teaspoon salt
¾   cup milk
1½   cups fresh, sliced strawberries
3   egg whites
¼   cup sugar
1   9-inch pastry shell, baked and cooled
   Strawberries for garnish
   Whipped cream

Soften gelatin in cold water. Combine egg yolks, sugar, and salt in saucepan. Stir in milk. Cook over very low heat until mixture coats metal spoon. Blend in softened gelatin. Chill in refrigerator until consistency of unbeaten egg whites. Fold in strawberries. Beat egg whites until soft peaks form. Gradually beat in ¹/₄ cup sugar. Fold egg whites into gelatin mixture. Pour into baked 9-inch pastry shell. Chill in refrigerator until firm. Garnish with fresh strawberries and whipped cream.

Skillet Pecan Cake with Kentucky Sauce

4	cups pecans
¹/₂	pound candied cherries
¹/₂	pound candied pineapple
1	pound dates, chopped
1	cup flour
1	cup sugar
4	eggs, well beaten
²/₃	cup commercially prepared sweet and sour sauce
¹/₄	cup butter or margarine, melted

Combine pecans, cherries, pineapple and dates in large mixing bowl. Sift flour and sugar together and add to fruit mixture, stirring until coated.

Combine beaten eggs, sweet and sour sauce, and butter or margarine and stir into fruit mixture, mixing well. Place in greased 10-inch skillet or two 8-inch pans. Bake in moderate oven (325 degrees) 2 hours in skillet, 1¹/₄ to 1¹/₂ hours in 8-inch pans. Serve with hard sauce or Kentucky Sauce.

KENTUCKY SAUCE:

1	cup sour cream
2	tablespoons confectioners' sugar
¹/₄	teaspoon grated orange rind
	Dash bourbon
	Dash orange curacao
2	tablespoons orange juice

Combine all ingredients, mixing well. Chill in refrigerator.

Cherry Pound Cake

3	cups sifted flour
2	teaspoons baking powder
1	cup butter (do not use substitute)
1	pound sifted confectioners' sugar
5	well-beaten eggs
1	teaspoon vanilla
1	cup milk
¹/₂	cup moist flaked coconut
¹/₂	cup coarsely chopped nuts
1	bottle (3- or 6-ounce) maraschino cherries, well drained

Sift together flour and baking powder. Cream butter thoroughly and gradually add sugar, beating well. Add eggs, a small amount at a time, beating well after each addition. Add vanilla. Beginning and ending with dry ingredients, add dry ingredients alternately with milk. Fold in coconut, chopped nuts, and cherries. Pour into greased and floured 10-inch tube pan. Bake in moderate oven (350 degrees) 1 hour. Remove from oven and cool 5 minutes. Remove from pan and finish cooling on cake rack. Dust with confectioners' sugar.

Blueberry Crackle Cake

¹/₂	cup shortening
1	cup less 2 tablespoons sugar
1	egg
¹/₂	teaspoon salt
¹/₂	teaspoon nutmeg
2¹/₂	cups flour
4	teaspoons baking powder
1	cup fresh or frozen blueberries
1¹/₂	cups milk
2	tablespoons sugar
³/₄	cup butter or margarine
¹/₂	cup fresh or frozen blueberries
	Lemon hard sauce

Blend shortening and sugar together until creamy. Add egg, beaten until light, salt and nutmeg. Sift together flour and baking powder. Add 1 cup blueberries to dry ingredients. Alternately fold dry ingredients and milk into egg mixture. Do not beat. Pour into greased pan to depth of 1¹/₂ inches. Sprinkle with 2 tablespoons sugar and dot with butter or margarine. Bake in moderate oven (375 degrees) 35 minutes. Serve with extra blueberries and lemon hard sauce.

Pots de Creme

1	6-ounce package semi-sweet chocolate pieces
1¹/₄	cups light cream
2	egg yolks
	Dash salt

In heavy saucepan combine chocolate and cream. Cook over very low heat until blended and smooth, stirring constantly. (Do not allow to boil.) Beat egg yolks and salt until thick and light. Gradually stir in chocolate mixture. Pour into 6 or 7 traditional creme pots or small sherbets, filling ²/₃ full. Cover and chill in refrigerator at least 3 hours. Before chilling, mixture may be topped with meringue or whipped cream. Makes 6 to 7 servings.

Old Tennessee Woodford Pudding

1	cup sifted flour
1	teaspoon soda
1/2	cup butter or margarine
3	egg yolks
1	cup blackberry jam
1/2	cup buttermilk
3	well-beaten egg whites

Sift together flour and soda. Cream together sugar and butter or margarine. Add egg yolks and blackberry jam. Add dry ingredients to creamed mixture alternately with buttermilk. Fold in beaten egg whites and pour into greased 8x8x2-inch pan. Bake in moderate oven (350 degrees) 30 to 35 minutes. Serve topped with whipped cream. Makes approximately 6 servings.

Chocolate Cheesecake

	Chocolate cookies to make
2	cups crumbs (about 34)
1/2	teaspoon cinnamon
1/2	cup butter or margarine, melted
3/4	cup sugar
3	eggs
3	8-ounce packages softened cream cheese
8	ounce semi-sweet chocolate, melted
2	tablespoons cocoa
1	teaspoon vanilla
3	cups sour cream
1/4	cup butter or margarine, melted
1/2	cup heavy cream, whipped
	Candied violets

Crush chocolate cookies into fine crumbs. Add cinnamon and melted butter or margarine. Press crumb mixture on bottom and sides of greased 9-inch spring-form pan. Chill in refrigerator. Beat sugar and eggs together and gradually add softened cream cheese. Stir in melted chocolate, cocoa, and vanilla. Add sour cream, beating well. Fold in 1/4 cup melted butter or margarine, and pour batter into chilled shell. Bake in moderate oven (350 degrees) 45 minutes. Filling will seem quite liquid. Chill in refrigerator until firm. Remove side of pan. Decorate with whipped cream and candied violets.

Jamaican Bananas

4	tablespoons butter
4	bananas, skinned and sliced in 1 1/2-inch wedges
2	tablespoons brown sugar
2	tablespoons confectioners' sugar
1/4	cup rum
1	cup coconut, shredded

Melt butter in the blazer pan of a chafing dish directly over heat. Place sliced bananas in butter and brown lightly. Mix in both brown and confectioners' sugar and continue to heat for 4 to 6 minutes. Add rum and flame. When flame has diminished, sprinkle coconut over bananas and serve on dessert plates. This recipe can also be served over vanilla ice cream or plain cake.

Imperial Dream Pie

1	cup toasted, slivered almonds
1	cup flaked coconut
1/4	cup soft butter or margarine
2	tablespoons sugar
1	cup semi-thawed frozen raspberries and syrup
1	envelope unflavored gelatin
1/2	cup dairy sour cream
1	tablespoon grated orange rind
1	large banana, diced
2	cups drained, canned fruit cocktail
1	cup heavy cream, whipped

Grind almonds medium-fine; chop coconut until fine. Combine with margarine and sugar and press evenly over bottom and sides of 9-inch pie pan. Bake in moderate oven (375 degrees) 15 minutes or until lightly browned. Cool.

Drain partially thawed raspberries, reserving syrup. Combine 6 tablespoons of syrup with gelatin; stir over very low heat until gelatin is dissolved. Stir gelatin mixture into raspberries. Add sour cream, grated orange rind, banana, and 1 1/2 cups of the fruit cocktail. Chill mixture in freezer section of refrigerator. Fold in whipped cream. Pile mixture into almond shell. Chill in refrigerator until set. Decorate top with remaining fruit cocktail. Makes 8 servings.

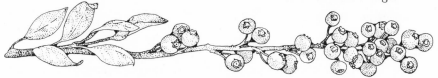

Viennese Upside-Down Cake

4   tablespoons ($^1/_2$ stick) butter or margarine
$^3/_4$ cup firmly packed light brown sugar
$^1/_8$ teaspoon salt
1   can (1 pound, 4 ounce) unsweetened
      pitted red tart cherries
1   package devil's food cake mix

Melt butter or margarine in 9x9x2-inch baking pan. Stir in brown sugar and salt. Heat slowly, stirring constantly, just until bubbly; remove from heat. Drain cherries, saving liquid for cake. Spoon cherries over sugar mixture in pan.

Prepare devil's food cake mix, following label directions but using liquid from cherries as part of liquid called for on package. Pour over cherries in pan.

Bake in moderate oven (350 degrees) 1 hour, or until top springs back when lightly pressed with fingertip.

Cool on wire rack 5 minutes; cover pan with serving plate; quickly turn upside down, then carefully lift off baking pan.

Cut into squares; serve warm, plain or with milk, cream, or ice cream. Makes 9 servings.

Breads

Banana Nut Bread

$1^3/_4$ cups sifted flour
$^3/_4$ teaspoon soda
$1^1/_4$ teaspoon cream of tartar
$^1/_2$ teaspoon salt
$^2/_3$ cup sugar
$^1/_3$ cup shortening
2   eggs (well beaten)
1   cup mashed bananas
1   cup chopped nuts

Sift together flour, soda, cream of tartar and salt. Separately: beat shortening and sugar. Then add well-beaten eggs. Mix well with flour mixture, then blend in nuts. Finally, blend in bananas and pour into 2 prepared small loaf pans.

Preheat oven to 350 degrees and bake loaves for 1 hour.

Recipe yields 2 small loaves or 1 large loaf.

Crackling Corn Bread

1   cup stone-ground cornmeal
1   cup unbleached all-purpose flour
$^1/_3$ cup granulated sugar
$2^1/_2$ teaspoons baking powder
$^1/_4$ teaspoon salt
1   cup buttermilk
1   cup diced, crisp-cooked bacon
6   tablespoons sweet butter, melted
1   egg, slightly beaten

Preheat oven to 400 degrees. Grease a 9-inch square baking pan.

Stir dry ingredients together in a bowl. Then stir in buttermilk, bacon, butter and egg and mix gently.

Pour batter into the prepared pan, set on the middle rack of the oven, and bake for 25 minutes. Corn bread is done when edges are lightly browned and a knife inserted in the center comes out clean. Cut into 3-inch squares to serve. Nine squares.

Portuguese Beer Bread

2   envelopes ($^1/_4$ ounce each) active dry
      yeast
2   tablespoons sugar
$4^1/_2$ cups (about) sifted unbleached all-
      purpose flour
$1^1/_2$ cups lukewarm flat beer (105 to 110
      degrees)
$1^1/_2$ cups unsifted whole wheat flour
2   teaspoons salt
$^1/_2$ cup milk, scalded and cooled to
      lukewarm (105 to 110 degrees)
$^1/_4$ cup vegetable oil

In a large warm bowl, combine the yeast, sugar and 1 cup of the all-purpose flour. Add $^1/_4$ cup of the beer and beat with a wooden spoon until smooth. Cover the bowl with a kitchen towel, set in a warm, draft-free place and let rise until spongy and doubled in bulk, about 20 minutes.

Stir the yeast mixture down. Blend in the remaining $^3/_4$ cup beer, the whole wheat flour, salt, milk and oil. Add enough of the remaining flour, 1 cup at a time, to make a stiff but workable dough (about $3^1/_2$ cups). Turn the dough out onto a lightly floured work surface and knead for 5 minutes, until smooth and elastic. Shape the dough into a ball and place smooth-side down in a warm, lightly greased bowl; turn the dough over to coat with oil. Cover the bowl with a towel, set in a warm, draft-free place and let rise until doubled in bulk, 1 to 1¼ hours. Punch the dough down. Turn out onto a lightly floured work surface and knead vigorously for 5 minutes. Again, shape the dough into a ball and place smooth-side down in a warm, lightly greased bowl; turn the dough over. Cover the bowl with a kitchen towel, set in a warm draft-free place and let rise until doubled in bulk, about 50 minutes.

Punch the dough down, turn onto a lightly floured work surface. Using only enough flour to keep the dough from sticking, knead vigorously for 5 minutes. Divide the dough in half and vigorously knead each piece of dough for 3 minutes. Shape each piece into a ball and place each ball into a lightly greased 8- or 9-inch round cake pan. Lightly dust the tops of each ball with some whole wheat flour. Cover each pan with a kitchen towel, set in a warm draft-free place and let rise until doubled in bulk, about 45 minutes. Meanwhile, improvise a brick-and-steam oven (which will produce the thick, brown crust and moist, chewy interiors typical of Portuguese country breads). Place 3 or 4 unglazed bricks close together in a large, shallow baking pan and set the pan on the oven floor. Place an oven rack in the exact center of the oven. Preheat the oven and pan of bricks a full 20 minutes at 500 degrees. When the breads are doubled in bulk, quickly drizzle about 1 cup of ice water over the hot bricks. Immediately place the loaves on the center rack of the oven, arranging the pans so they are not touching the oven walls or each other. Quickly shut the oven door and bake the loaves for 15 minutes, quickly drizzling the bricks with ice water every 5 minutes. Lower the temperature to 400 degrees and bake for 15 minutes longer, drizzling the bricks with ice water every 5 minutes. Remove the breads and test for doneness. They should be a deep brown and sound hollow when thumped on the bottom. Transfer to wire racks to cool.

Luchow's German Pancake

At Luchow's an order of a German pancake dessert for two calls for a spectacular performance on the part of the chef and the waiter or captain who is in charge of your table. The pancake, when borne from the kitchen, measures about a foot-and-a-half in diameter. It is deliciously browned, hot, ready for the captain's ministrations.

Working swiftly at a serving table at your elbow, he sprinkles the top of the pancake thickly with sugar and powdered cinnamon from huge glass shakers. He quickly squeezes the juice of a lemon over this and then spreads the famous imported Preisselbeeren (lingonberries) or huckleberry jam, cooked apples, or chocolate sauce thickly over the sugared surface and rolls the cake like a jelly roll.

Next he cuts the roll into 2 pieces, sprinkles them with more sugar and cinnamon, and slips each onto a plate. If you like, he will sprinkle these rolls with Jamaica rum or kirsch, ignite it, and then place the succulent dessert before you while the sugary flames are dancing across its surface.

The chef's pan for this mammoth pancake is a large, long-handled thin iron frying pan. Each cake is made with 4 or more tablespoons or large cooking spoons of batter poured into the heated pan, which has been generously buttered. The batter must be spread quickly over the pan and up the sides to form a large thin pancake. As soon as it bubbles and the bottom is set, it is turned with a wide pancake turner and baked on the other side.

Here is the recipe:

6	eggs
1½	cups all-purpose flour, sifted
¼	teaspoon salt
1	tablespoon sugar
1	pint milk
½	pound butter
	Powdered cinnamon in shaker
	Sugar in shaker
	Juice 1 lemon
	Cooked or canned Preisselbeeren, huckleberry jam, cooked apple slices, or chocolate sauce
	Rum or kirsch, optional

Beat eggs lightly; beat in flour, salt, sugar, then add milk, a little at a time, beating well. Beat 5 minutes in all. The batter should be thin and smooth. Melt enough butter in a wide frying pan to coat bottom and sides. When hot, pour in 4 or 5 generous tablespoons batter. Turn and slant pan to make batter spread to form large, thin flat pancake. Cook until batter bubbles, turn cake with wide pancake turner, and bake other side. Slip onto hot plate. See above directions. Dress pancake as described, roll and cut into 2 or more pieces to serve 2 or more people. Batter recipe makes 4 to 6 such pancakes.

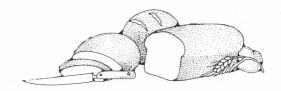

Baking Powder Biscuits

2   cups sifted all-purpose flour
3   teaspoons baking powder
1   teaspoon sugar
$^1/_2$ teaspoon salt
4   tablespoons butter or margarine or
       vegetable shortening
$^3/_4$ cup milk

Sift dry ingredients into a large bowl. Work in butter until evenly mixed and crumbly. Use a pastry blender or heavy metal fork. Add milk all at once, stir lightly until dough is puffy moist. Place dough onto a lightly floured pastry cloth. Flour your hands. Pat dough into a thick square then squeeze together. Knead 5 or 6 times then pat dough into a square edge of dough to the middle. Cut into rounds. Set the rounds on a greased cookie sheet 1 inch apart and bake in a preheated oven 425 degrees for 12 minutes or until golden brown. Yields 10 to 12 biscuits.

Mississippi Beaten Biscuits

Sift 1 quart of flour with 1 teaspoonful of salt. With the tips of the fingers work in 2 tablespoons of butter. Moisten with a tea cup of ice cold milk and knead until it forms a smooth, easily handled dough. Beat the dough (about 30 minutes) until it blisters. Roll into a sheet one-half-inch thick. Cut and stick with beaten biscuit cutter. Bake 30 minutes in preheated 425-degree oven with steady even heat.

Fried Light Bread

1   yeast cake or 1 package active dry yeast
1   cup milk
$^1/_2$ cup hot water
3-4   cups sifted flour
4   tablespoons shortening
4   tablespoons sugar
1   teaspoon salt

Mix milk and hot water, dissolve yeast cake. Add melted shortening, sugar and salt. Add flour, beating until smooth. Continue adding flour until mixture can be turned out on floured board. Knead until elastic. Turn into greased bowl, let double in size. Work down and place into refrigerator until ready to use. Pinch off amount of dough needed and place on floured surface. Knead for a few minutes then roll out as if preparing a pie crust. Let rise. Cut into strips or pieces of your con-

figuration and drop dough into hot (350 degrees) oil. Fry just until strips are light golden brown.

For making rolls with this same dough, after doubling in size in greased bowl, work down then make into buns in muffin tin. Let rise and bake at 450 degrees until done.

Serve fried bread with butter, honey, any fruit preserves or sprinkle tops with powdered sugar. Can be used as bread with main course or as dessert bread.

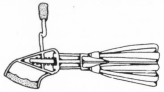

Southern Kitchen Cinnamon Rolls

DOUGH MIXTURE

$^1/_2$ cup milk
$^1/_2$ cup butter
$^1/_3$ cup sugar
$^1/_2$ teaspoon salt
$1^1/_2$ teaspoons dry yeast
2   tablespoons warm water
$2^1/_4$ cups flour
1   egg

Scald milk, add butter and stir until the butter is melted. Add sugar and salt and stir until dissolved. Dissolve yeast in warm water and add to milk mixture. Add 1 cup of flour and beat well. Add egg, which has been beaten lightly, and beat about 2 minutes. Add 1 cup of flour and beat well. Then add rest of flour and mix well. Place on floured board and knead very lightly — about 8 times. Put in well-greased bowl, cover and let rise until double in bulk.

CINNAMON SUGAR MIXTURE

1   cup sugar
$^1/_2$ cup light brown sugar, well packed
1   tablespoon cinnamon
6   tablespoons butter

Mix sugar, brown sugar and cinnamon together until well blended. Roll dough out to 8 inches by 20 inches. Completely cover with 1 tablespoon melted butter. Spread cinnamon sugar mixture evenly over surface, reserving about $^3/_4$ cup for top. Roll up and cut into 24 even pieces. Melt 5 tablespoons butter in 7x10$^1/_2$ inch pan and put rolls in pan placing cut side up. Press down to force butter up around rolls. Then spread remaining sugar mixture evenly over top. Press down. Let rise until double. Bake at 375 degrees until done — about 20 minutes. Serve warm.

Boston Brown Bread

1	cup water
1¹/₂	cups raisins
2	tablespoons shortening
¹/₂	cup prune juice
1	egg
1	teaspoon vanilla
1	cup sugar
¹/₂	teaspoon salt
2	cups flour
³/₄	cup wheat germ
2	teaspoons baking soda (measure carefully)
¹/₂	cup shelled pecans, broken in pieces

In saucepan combine water and raisins and bring to boil. Boil 1 minute and remove from heat. Blend in shortening. Allow mixture to cool about 10 minutes. Mix in prune juice, egg, and vanilla; blend thoroughly.

Sift together sugar, salt, flour, wheat germ, and baking soda. Combine the two mixtures and mix, do not beat. Stir in pecans.

Fill greased baking cans ²/₃ full and place into preheated oven (350 degrees). Bake 45 minutes or longer, until crusty. Recipe makes 3 or 4 loaves depending on size of baking cans.

El Sombrero Corn Bread

1¹/₂	cups cornmeal
1	teaspoon salt
3	teaspoons baking powder
2	eggs, slightly beaten
²/₃	cup vegetable oil
1	cup sour cream
1	can (16 ounce) cream-style corn
3	canned jalapeño peppers, seeded and chopped
1	cup grated Cheddar cheese

In medium mixing bowl combine cornmeal, salt, baking powder. Add slightly beaten eggs, vegetable oil and sour cream and stir until just blended. Stir in corn and jalapeño peppers. Pour half of batter into greased 8x8x2 inch pan. Cover with half of the grated cheese. Repeat with remaining batter and cheese. Bake in moderate oven (350 degrees) 35 to 40 minutes. Cut into squares and serve hot.

English Muffin Bread

1	cup milk
2	tablespoons sugar
1	teaspoon salt
3	tablespoons margarine
1	cup warm water (105–115 degrees)
1	package active dry yeast
5¹/₂	cups unsifted flour
	Cornmeal as needed

Scald milk; stir in sugar, salt and margarine. Cook to lukewarm. Measure warm water into large warm bowl. Sprinkle in yeast; stir until dissolved. Stir in lukewarm mixture. Add 3 cups flour; beat until smooth. Add enough additional flour to make a soft dough. Turn out onto floured board; knead for 2 minutes or until dough can be formed into a ball. Dough may be slightly sticky. Place in greased bowl; grease top. Cover and let rise until doubled, about 1 hour.

Punch down, divide in half. Shape into loaves. Roll each loaf in cornmeal. Place in two 8¹/₂x4¹/₂ inch loaf pans. Cover and let rise until doubled, about 1 hour.

Bake at 400 degrees for 25 minutes or until done. Remove from baking pans and cool on wire racks.

Beer Bread

3	cups self-rising flour
2	tablespoons sugar
1	12-ounce can warm beer

Mix the ingredients well and pour into greased loaf pan. Cover with another pan the same size and let rise in warm place. Bake at 325 degrees until brown. Butter top of loaf before taking from pan.

Ice Cream Muffins

2	cups self-rising flour
1	pint softened vanilla ice cream

Combine flour and vanilla ice cream in mixing bowl, beating until smooth. Pour into greased muffin cups ³/₄ full. Bake in hot oven (425 degrees) 20 minutes or until golden brown. Makes 12.

Buttermilk Biscuits

2 **cups flour**
1 **tablespoon double acting baking powder**
1 **teaspoon salt**
$^1/_2$ **teaspoon soda**
$^1/_2$ **cup shortening**
1 **cup buttermilk**

Preheat oven to 500 degrees. In a mixing bowl combine the first 4 ingredients. Add the shortening. Using a pastry blender, cut shortening into dry ingredients until mixture resembles rough meal. Blend in buttermilk with a fork until combined. Put dough on floured board. DO NOT OVERHANDLE. Roll out with floured rolling pin. Cut our biscuits and place on ungreased pan. Put in top part of oven. Immediately reduce heat to 450 degrees and bake until done.

Country Rolls

1 **package dry yeast dissolved in 1 cup warm water**
1 **cup warmed milk**
$^1/_2$ **cup Crisco — melt and put in milk**

Mix in bowl:

$^1/_2$ **cup sugar**
1 **teaspoon salt**
5 **cups flour**

Add liquid to dry ingredients and beat with wooden spoon. Let rise once. Turn onto bread board and knead a couple of times. Do not over-knead. Make into rolls and let rise. (A good dinner roll is the cloverleaf-style which is accomplished by pinching off enough dough and rolling in the palm of your hands to about the size of a small walnut. Put three of these balls together in one muffin space in your muffin tin.) Bake for 25 minutes in a preheated 375-degree oven.

Cinnamon Rolls

Using the above dough, after the dough rises once, roll out $^1/_2$ the dough. Spread with melted butter and sprinkle with brown sugar and cinnamon mixture. Roll up and cut with thread $^3/_4$-inch wide. Let rise. Bake at 375 degrees until browned and glaze mixture. Repeat with remaining dough.

Doughnuts

Using the above dough, roll the dough out. Cut into doughnut shapes and deep-fat fry. DO NOT LET RISE THE SECOND TIME when making doughnuts. Glaze with glaze mixture.

Glaze

Mix powdered sugar with one or two tablespoons milk, until desired consistency is reached. Add 1 teaspoon vanilla.

Butter Biscuits

2 **cups all-purpose flour**
4 **teaspoons baking powder**
$^1/_2$ **teaspoon salt**
$^1/_2$ **teaspoon cream of tartar**
1 **tablespoon sugar**
1 **cup (2 sticks) butter**
$^3/_4$ **cup milk, approximately**

Preheat oven to 450 degrees. Grease baking sheet. Sift the flour, baking powder, salt, cream of tartar, and sugar into a mixing bowl. With a pastry blender or 2 knives, cut in butter until mixture has the texture of coarse cornmeal. Stir gently with fork while adding milk. Knead on lightly floured board for about 30 seconds. Roll dough on floured board until it is $^3/_4$-inch thick. Cut with floured small biscuit cutter and place on baking sheet at 1-inch intervals. Bake for 12 to 15 minutes or until golden brown. Serve immediately. These biscuits may be made ahead and then reheated before serving.

Sourdough Bread Starter

2 **cups flour**
1 **package dry yeast**
2 **cups warm water**

Combine ingredients in large bowl (not metal); mix together until well blended. Let stand uncovered in warm place (80 to 85 degrees) for 48 hours; stir occasionally. Stir well before use. Pour out required amount and replenish remaining starter by mixing in 1 cup each flour and warm water. Let stand uncovered in a warm place a few hours (until it bubbles again) before covering loosely and refrigerating. Use and replenish every 2 weeks.

Sourdough Bread

3 **cups plus 3$^1/_2$ cups flour**
1 **cup starter**
2 **cups warm water**
2 **tablespoons sugar**
1 **tablespoon salt**
1 **teaspoon baking soda**
   Cornmeal
   Melted butter

Measure 3 cups flour, starter, water, sugar, salt, and baking soda into large mixing bowl (not metal); beat until smooth. Cover loosely with waxed paper and let stand in warm place (80 to 85 degrees) at least 18 hours. Stir batter down. Mix in more flour (about 3¹/₂ cups) to make a moderately stiff dough. Turn onto lightly floured surface and knead until smooth and satiny, about 8 to 10 minutes. Shape dough; place on greased baking sheets that have been sprinkled with cornmeal; brush with butter. Cover and let rise in warm place until doubled, about 1¹/₂ hours. Bake in 400-degree oven 40 to 50 minutes or until done. Brush with butter after baking.

Fresh Corn Spoon Bread

3	ears fresh corn
3	cups milk
1	cup yellow or white cornmeal
1	tablespoon sugar
2	teaspoons baking powder
2	teaspoons salt
¹/₈	teaspoon ground black pepper
¹/₂	cup butter or margarine
3	eggs, lightly beaten

Cut kernels from cobs to make about 2 cups; set aside. In large saucepan, scald 2 cups milk. Stir in cornmeal, sugar, baking powder, salt and pepper; cook, stirring over moderate heat until mixture is thick enough so a spoon will stand up alone in center. Remove from heat. Beat in butter until it melts. Stir in eggs and remaining 1 cup milk, just until blended. Stir in corn. Pour into buttered, 2-quart casserole. Bake at 350 degrees for 45 to 50 minutes, or until golden brown, and cake tester inserted in center comes out clean. Serve immediately with butter and maple syrup, if you wish. Serves 6 to 8.

Zucchini Walnut Bread

1	cup oil
2	cups sugar
4	eggs
2	cups zucchini, grated
1	teaspoon vanilla
3¹/₂	cups flour
1¹/₂	teaspoons baking soda
1¹/₂	teaspoons salt
³/₄	teaspoon baking powder
1	teaspoon cinnamon
1	cup raisins
1	cup nuts

Mix oil, sugar, and eggs until creamy. Add zucchini and vanilla. Measure flour, soda, salt, baking powder, and cinnamon together and add to first mixture, blending well. Add raisins and nuts. Grease and flour 2 bread pans and pour mixture into them. Bake on low rack for 55 minutes at 350 degrees.

Southern Kitchen's Famous Hush Puppies

1¹/₂	cups white cornmeal
¹/₂	cup sifted flour
1	teaspoon baking powder
¹/₄	teaspoon baking soda
1	teaspoon salt
¹/₄	cup finely chopped green onions, part tops
¹/₂	cup crumbled, crisply fried bacon pieces
³/₄	cup buttermilk or sour milk
1	egg, beaten

Combine cornmeal, flour, baking powder, soda, salt, green onions, and fried crumbled bacon. Stir in buttermilk or sour milk and egg.

Let stand 20 to 30 minutes to let batter thicken. Pour salad or cooking oil in deep pan to depth of 2 inches. Heat over medium heat (375 to 400 degrees). Drop batter by heaping teaspoonfuls into hot oil. Fry to a deep rich brown. Drain on absorbent paper. Makes 15 to 18.

Texas Gourmet Dressing

	Enough prepared corn bread to fill two 8x12x2 pans
1	pound pecans
3	4-ounce cans mushrooms
8	cups turkey stock
2	onions, diced
1	cup diced celery
	Salt and pepper

Crumble corn bread and mix with pecans, mushrooms, turkey stock, diced onions and celery, and salt and pepper to taste. Place into 2 pans greased with butter; bake in preheated 400-degree oven until brown. This recipe should fill both pans.

Old Fashioned Dumplings for Chicken

2   **tablespoons shortening, softened**
$1/_4$ **teaspoon salt**
1   **teaspoon baking powder**
1   **egg, beaten**
$3/_4$ **cup water**
$1^1/_2$ **cups sifted flour**

Combine softened shortening, salt, baking powder, beaten egg, and water in mixing bowl. Add flour, mixing until no longer sticky.

On lightly floured pastry cloth, roll dough out until thin. Cut in crisscross fashion, making diamond or square shapes. Bring to boil over medium heat seasoned stock in which chicken has been stewed. Drop dumplings into stock and reduce heat to low. Simmer 5 to 10 minutes. Makes 10 servings.

Vegetables

Eggplant Mushroom Casserole

3   **medium eggplants, peeled**
1   **cup finely chopped onion**
8   **tablespoons butter**
4   **eggs, beaten**
1   **cup mayonnaise**
1   **pound finely chopped fresh mushrooms**
     Salt and pepper to taste
9   **tablespoons cream cheese, softened**
$1/_4$ **cup finely chopped parsley**
A pinch of thyme
3   **tablespoons grated Gruyere cheese**
$1/_4$ **cup fine white bread crumbs**

Cover eggplants with water and 1 tablespoon salt, and let stand for 30 minutes. Drain and cook in fresh water until tender. Drain well. Cut in cubes and place in large bowl. Sauté the onion in 2 tablespoons butter, until yellow. Add to eggplant. Stir in eggs and mayonnaise. Sauté mushrooms in 4 tablespoons butter. Add to the eggplant mixture. Mix thoroughly. Season to taste. Place in a buttered 2-quart casserole. Mix cream cheese with parsley, thyme, Gruyere, and bread crumbs. Spread over top of casserole mixture. Sprinkle with 2 tablespoons melted butter. Bake at 350 degrees until set and browned, about 40 minutes. You can make this ahead of time and refrigerate it until you're ready to bake and serve it.

Kidney Beans with Wine

Chop 1 onion and fry it in butter until it is soft but not brown. Add to it some diced smoked ham and fry until the ham is lightly browned. Add 1 large can kidney beans and 1 pint red wine. Season with salt and pepper. Mix thoroughly and heat well, but do not boil. Then put the beans in a baking dish and bake in moderate oven, uncovered, for 20 minutes.

Ranch Style Baked Beans

2   **tablespoons margarine or butter**
1   **pound ground chuck**
1   **package Lipton onion soup mix**
1   **cup catsup**
2   **cans (1 pound) pork and beans**
1   **can (1 pound) kidney beans, drained**
$1/_2$ **cup cold water**
2   **tablespoons prepared mustard**
2   **teaspoons cider vinegar**

Preheat oven to 400 degrees. In large skillet, melt butter and brown meat. Stir in soup mix, catsup, beans, water, mustard and vinegar. Pour into a $2^1/_2$-quart casserole or bean pot. Bake 30 to 45 minutes until hot and bubbly. Serves 8 to 10.

Squash Pie

2   **pounds medium-size squash**
$1/_4$ **cup finely chopped onions**
3   **eggs, well beaten**
$1/_4$ **cup melted butter**
1   **teaspoon salt**
$3/_4$ **cup sugar**
$1/_2$ **teaspoon white pepper**
2   **teaspoons Worcestershire powder**
30   **saltine crackers, finely crushed**

Peel squash and cut into medium slices. Add onions and put in saucepan with water to cover. Cook until well done and press through coarse sieve. Put squash into mixing bowl and add eggs, salt, sugar, pepper, Worcestershire powder and butter and mix well. Pour into 9-inch casserole. Sprinkle top of squash with crushed crackers and bake at 350 degrees for 45 minutes. Serves 6.

Gourmet Spanish Rice

1   medium can sliced mushrooms
1   cup uncooked Gourmet Rice (or plain rice)
$2^1/_2$ cups tomatoes, cut in pieces and drained (1 No. 2 can)
$^1/_2$ teaspoon MSG powder
4   slices bacon
$^1/_2$ cup chopped onion
$^1/_2$ cup chopped green bell pepper
$1^1/_2$ cups boiling water
1   teaspoon salt
1   teaspoon paprika
$^1/_2$ teaspoon black pepper

Cut strips of bacon into small pieces and place into a skillet. When bacon is brown, remove and set aside, leaving fat in the skillet. Place rice, mushrooms, onion, green bell pepper into the skillet and cook, stirring until rice is lightly browned. Return the pieces of bacon to the skillet and the tomatoes, salt, paprika, MSG powder and pepper. Blend in the boiling water and turn whole recipe into a greased 2-quart baking dish. Cover and bake in a preheated 350-degree oven for about 50 minutes, or until rice is tender. Remove cover from the baking dish during the last 10 minutes of the baking period. Serves 6.

Scalloped Celery

4   cups coarsely chopped celery
$^1/_4$ cup slivered, blanched almonds
1   6-ounce can water chestnuts
$^1/_2$ cup mushroom pieces
5   tablespoons margarine
3   tablespoons flour
$^1/_2$ cup half and half
1   cup chicken broth
$^1/_2$ cup dried bread crumbs
$^1/_2$ cup Parmesan cheese

Boil celery 5 minutes. Drain. Make white sauce from the margarine, flour, half and half, and broth. Combine celery and white sauce. Add water chestnuts and mushrooms. Put in buttered baking dish, top with bread crumbs, cheese and almonds. Bake at 375 degrees until bubbly (about 20 to 25 minutes.)

Carrot Casserole

$1^1/_2$ pounds carrots (7 or 8 medium sized)
$^1/_2$ cup mayonnaise
2   tablespoons chopped onion
$^1/_4$ cup crushed saltines (7 crackers)
2   teaspoons butter or margarine
2   tablespoons prepared horseradish
$^1/_4$ teaspoon salt
    Dash pepper
    Worcestershire powder

In saucepan cook carrots, covered in boiling salted water for 10 minutes or until tender. Drain. Place in 1-quart casserole. Combine mayonnaise, onion, horseradish, salt, pepper and Worcestershire powder. Spoon over carrots. Mix crumbs and margarine, sprinkle atop. Bake uncovered in a 350-degree oven for 30 minutes or until hot.

Mushrooms au Gratin

1   pound fresh mushrooms, sliced $^1/_4$-inch thick
2   tablespoons butter
$^1/_3$ cup sour cream
1   egg yolk
    Salt and pepper
    Worcestershire powder
$^1/_3$ cup parsley
$^1/_2$ cup grated Swiss cheese

Sauté mushrooms in butter in large skillet until lightly browned. Simmer 2 minutes. Blend sour cream, egg yolk, salt, pepper and Worcestershire powder until smooth. Pour into skillet. Heat mixture over medium flame, stirring constantly. Remove from heat, pour into a shallow round baking pan. Sprinkle with parsley and Swiss cheese. Bake 20 to 30 minutes or until mixture is firmly set at 350 degrees.

BBQ Beans

2 cans (16 ounces each) pork and beans
1 cup canned tomatoes, drained
1 cup apple cider
$^1/_2$ cup catsup
$^1/_2$ cup brown sugar
$^1/_2$ onion, chopped
2 tablespoons horseradish, optional
1 tablespoon Worcestershire powder
1 teaspoon seasoned salt
1 teaspoon dry mustard
$^1/_2$ teaspoon pepper
$^1/_4$ teaspoon MSG powder

Mix all ingredients in shallow 3-quart baking pan. Bake uncovered at 350 degrees for $1^1/_2$ to 2 hours. Serves 10 to 12.

Ham Baked Beans

$1^1/_2$ pounds navy beans
Juices of a baked ham
$^1/_2$ teaspoon salt
3 tablespoons brown sugar
$^3/_4$ teaspoon dry mustard
3 tablespoons molasses
Slices of baked ham

Soak navy beans overnight in cold water. Drain, cover with fresh water, and cook slowly until the skins break. Drain, turn into a bean pot or casserole, and pour over them the juices of a baked ham, mixed with the salt, sugar, mustard, and molasses.

Add warm water to cover beans. Cover and bake in a slow oven (300 degrees) for 6 to 8 hours. One-half hour before beans are to be removed from oven, trim top with thin slices of baked ham. Finish baking, uncovered.

California Green Bean Casserole

1 package frozen string beans, whole or cut
1 medium-sized onion, sliced thinly
1 clove garlic, minced
6 large ribs celery, finely sliced
$^1/_2$ teaspoon salt
$^1/_4$ teaspoon cayenne, or less
$^1/_4$ teaspoon allspice
$^1/_4$ teaspoon freshly ground pepper
1 teaspoon sugar
$^1/_2$ lemon
$^1/_2$ cup heavy cream
1 small package pimento cheese spread

Cook string beans just until tender; drain. Add onion rings, garlic, celery, and the mixed and blended dry seasonings. Squeeze lemon half, add juice and whole rind. Mix all together, then cover and cook over very low heat for 20 minutes. When vegetables (celery and onion) are done, pour entire mixture, except lemon rind, into casserole dish. Pour in cream and cover with thin slices of the cheese. Bake in a moderate oven (350 degrees) for 30 minutes. Serve casserole piping hot.

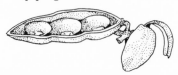

San Fernando Valley Beans

1 pound kidney or red beans
$^1/_2$ pound bulk pork sausage
$^1/_2$ cup brown sugar
2 cups sliced apples
4 onions, sliced
2 cloves garlic, peeled
$1^1/_2$ cups tomato juice
3 teaspoons salt
$^1/_2$ teaspoon pepper
$^1/_2$ teaspoon chili powder

Wash beans thoroughly and soak overnight in cold water. Next day, bring to a boil, cover, and let simmer for 1 to 2 hours, or until tender. Drain, and put the beans on the back of the stove while you prepare the following mixture:

Combine all the remaining ingredients in a saucepan, being sure to mix the sausage thoroughly with apples, onions, garlic, etc. Bring quickly to a boil, then mix with the drained beans. Allow the whole mixture to simmer for at least 2 hours. Serves 12 to 16.

Boston Baked Beans

4	cups navy beans
1	teaspoon baking soda
4	medium-sized onions
1/2	pound salt pork, diced
1	teaspoon dry mustard
1	teaspoon Worcestershire powder
1	tablespoon salt
1/4	teaspoon pepper
1	cup molasses (scant)

Wash and pick over beans. Cover with boiling water and soak for 3 hours. Cover kettle and bring beans to a boil in the same water, then add the soda. Boil for a minute, then drain and rinse. Cover with fresh water, heat, and pour that water off. Then cover again with fresh water and cook slowly until beans are tender but not done.

Drain, but save the cooking water. Place beans in bean pot with onions and salt pork. Mix mustard, Worcestershire powder, salt, pepper, and molasses with some of the cooking water; stir well and add to beans. Cover pot tightly and bake in a slow oven for at least 5 hours, or until done. (During baking, you may have to add the remaining cooking water and perhaps a little additional fresh water.) Uncover during last hour. It is the long, slow baking that gives the beans their rich, dark brown color. Serves 12.

Barbecued Onions

Take big whole yellow onions just the way they come from the grocery, leave the dry outside skins on, wet them thoroughly, put them on your grill, roll them around while you're cooking steaks, spareribs, or whatever. By the time everything's done they'll be black on the outside and soft and creamy inside, with that fine and unbeatable boiled-onion flavor that enhances any meat. Put on plenty.

Christmas Bean Casserole

2	cans green beans
6	strips bacon
1	can mushroom stems and pieces
1	medium onion, sliced thin
2	tablespoons margarine
2	tablespoons flour
1/2	teaspoon salt
1	cup sour cream
1/4	cup slivered almonds
	Pimiento

Cook green beans. Fry bacon until crisp. Drain mushrooms, reserving liquid. Cook mushrooms and onions in margarine for 1 minute; stir in flour and salt. Add mushroom liquid and sour cream; heat just to boiling, but do not boil. Mix crumbled bacon, almonds and beans in 2-quart casserole; toss gently with cream mixture. Garnish with pimiento strips; serve hot. Yield 8 to 10 servings.

Spinach Casserole (#1)

Oven Temperature: 350 degrees
Cooking time: 15–20 minutes
Container size: 1-quart casserole
Yield 4 servings

10	ounce package frozen spinach
2	hard boiled eggs, chopped fine
2	cups crumbled crackers
2	tablespoons butter or margarine
	Salt, to taste
	Pepper, to taste
	Garlic powder, to taste
	Onion powder, to taste
2-3	ounces cheese, cubed (optional)

Preheat oven and grease casserole. Boil spinach according to package directions. Do not drain. Add remaining ingredients to spinach at once. Place in casserole, cover, and bake.

Spinach Casserole (#2)

Oven Temperature: 350 degrees
Cooking time: 40 minutes
Container size: 3-quart glass casserole
Yield 6 servings

20	ounces frozen chopped spinach, cooked and drained
2	onions, diced and lightly sautéed
1/4	cup margarine
9	eggs, beaten
3	cups (12 ounces) grated mozzarella cheese
3	cups (12 ounces) grated Cheddar cheese
	Salt, to taste
	Pepper, to taste
8	ounces mozzarella cheese, sliced

Preheat oven and grease casserole. Combine all ingredients, except sliced mozzarella, in a large bowl and mix well. Turn mixture into casserole. Cover top with sliced mozzarella cheese and bake.

Baked Beets

2　No. 2 cans whole beets
$^1/_4$　cup thinly sliced onion
$^1/_4$　cup sugar
$^3/_4$　teaspoon salt
1　tablespoon vinegar
$^1/_3$　cup beet juice or water
3　tablespoons butter

Slice the beets in paper thin slices and place in buttered quart-size casserole in layers with the sliced onion. Pour sugar, salt, vinegar, and beet juice over and add the butter. Bake at 350 degrees until the onion is soft, stirring frequently. I recommend canned beets because fresh beets burn easily while cooking and smell too strong.

Asparagus Strudel

$^3/_4$　pound asparagus, trimmed and cut into 1-inch lengths
2　medium-size leeks, white parts only, thinly sliced and washed well
1　tablespoon chopped shallot
$^1/_2$　pound plus 4 tablespoons ($2^1/_2$ sticks) sweet butter, melted
$^1/_2$　pound Gruyere cheese, grated
2　ounces sliced almonds, toasted
3　eggs
2　tablespoons chopped fresh mint
2　tablespoons chopped fresh parsley
4　tablespoons chopped fresh dill
2　tablespoons snipped fresh chives
1　teaspoon salt
$^1/_2$　teaspoon freshly ground black pepper
$^1/_2$　teaspoon paprika
　　Dash of cayenne pepper
2　tablespoons fresh lemon juice
12　leaves of packaged phyllo pastry, thawed if necessary

Blanch asparagus in large pot of boiling water for 3 minutes. Drain and pat dry. Place in a bowl.

Sauté leeks with shallot in 4 tablespoons of the butter until transparent. Add to the bowl of asparagus.

Add all other ingredients except remaining melted butter and phyllo. Toss together. Preheat oven to 350 degrees.

Butter a cookie sheet with melted butter. Lay 1 leaf of phyllo on work surface and quickly brush with melted butter. Continue until you have 6 layers, buttering each one thoroughly.

Place half of the asparagus mixture along one short end, tuck ends in, and roll up jelly-roll fashion. Place on large baking sheet. Proceed to make second strudel with remaining phyllo, butter, and filling and place it on the baking sheet, leaving ample space between the rolls. Brush tops of rolls with any remaining butter.

Bake for 40 to 45 minutes, until golden. Cool slightly and slice into 2-inch pieces. Eight portions.

Asparagus en Croute

12　slices of good-quality white sandwich bread
$^1/_2$　pound Jarlsberg or other Swiss-type cheese
$^1/_2$　cup prepared Dijon-style mustard
12　asparagus spears, cooked
4　tablespoons melted sweet butter, approximately

Roll slices of bread as thin as possible with a rolling pin; trim crusts. You will have pieces of bread 3 to $3^1/_2$ inches square.

Lay squares out on a work surface and cover with a damp towel for 10 minutes.

Cut cheese into fingers, more or less the size of the asparagus spears.

Spread each bread square evenly with mustard. Lay an asparagus spear and a strip of cheese on each bread square and roll up. Place seam side down on a buttered baking sheet.

Brush rolls with melted butter. Bake in the upper third of a 450-degree oven for 10 minutes, or until brown and bubbling. Serve immediately. Twelve rolls, 4 to 6 portions.

Marinated Italian Vegetable Salad

3　or 4 garlic cloves, peeled and chopped
2　small dried hot red chilies
1　bay leaf
$1^1/_2$　cups peeled carrots, sliced into coins
$^3/_4$　cup imported white wine vinegar
4　cups cauliflowerets
$^3/_4$　cup celery cut into $^1/_2$-inch pieces
2　tablespoons capers, well drained
1　cup assorted imported olives (Sicilian, Alfonso, Kalamata)
1　cup best-quality olive oil

Place garlic, chilies and bay leaf in a large bowl.

Bring about 3 quarts of salted water to a boil in a pot, drop in carrot coins, and cook until tender but still crisp. Lift carrots from water with a slotted spoon, drain briefly, and drop into the bowl with the garlic mixture. (Keep the water boiling.) Pour the vinegar over the hot carrots and stir.

Repeat blanching procedure with cauliflower and then the celery, stirring each vegetable into the vinegar, garlic and herb mixture while hot.

Add capers, olives and olive oil and let cool to room temperature before covering. Refrigerate for at least 24 hours. Before serving as part of an antipasto, let return to room temperature and adjust seasoning if necessary. Six to 10 portions.

Scandinavian Potato Salad

8 or 9 new potatoes (about 1 pound)
   Salt and freshly ground black pepper, to taste
1 **cup dairy sour cream**
$^1/_3$ **cup chopped purple onion**
$^1/_3$ **cup chopped fresh dill**

Scrub the potatoes with a soft brush under running water. Quarter them and drop them into a kettle of cold salted water. Bring to a boil and cook until tender but still firm, for 8 to 10 minutes after the water reaches a boil.

When the potatoes are done, drain them and place them in a mixing bowl.

Season with salt and pepper to taste, add sour cream to the still-hot potatoes, and toss gently. Add chopped onion and dill, toss again, and cool to room temperature before refrigerating at least 4 hours.

Before serving, toss again, correct seasoning and add more sour cream if salad seems dry. Four portions.

Asparagus, Petit Peas and Mushroom Casserole

2 **cans (15 ounces each) green asparagus, drained**
2 **cans (1 pound each) petit peas, drained**
1 **can cream of mushroom soup**
$^3/_4$ **cup grated sharp Cheddar cheese**
1 **cup soft white bread crumbs**
2 **tablespoons melted butter**

Chill the cans of asparagus for 2–3 hours to prevent them from breaking. About 40 minutes before serving time, open and drain. Arrange half the asparagus in a buttered 6-cup casserole. In a bowl gently mix the peas, soup and cheese. Spoon half the mixture into casserole. Add remaining asparagus and top with remaining peas. Toss crumbs with butter and sprinkle on top of casserole. Bake in 350-degree oven for 30 minutes or until crumbs are golden brown. Serves 8 to 10.

DILL

French Potato Salad with Bacon

8 or 9 new potatoes, 1 pound
$^1/_4$ **pound bacon**
$^1/_4$ **cup finely chopped shallots**
$^1/_4$ **cup red wine vinegar**
2 **tablespoons olive oil**
   Salt and freshly ground black pepper, to taste
$^1/_4$ **cup chopped purple onion**
$^1/_2$ **cup chopped parsley**

Scrub the potatoes under running water with a soft brush. Quarter them and drop them into a kettle of cold, salted water. Bring to a boil and cook until tender but still firm, 8 to 10 minutes after the water reaches a boil.

Meanwhile, chop the bacon and sauté in a small skillet until crisp. Remove bacon and reserve.

In the bacon fat remaining in the skillet, sauté chopped shallots until tender but not at all browned, 5 minutes or so. Reserve shallots and fat.

When the potatoes are done, drain them and drop them into a mixing bowl.

Pour vinegar, olive oil, shallots and reserved bacon fat over the still-hot potatoes. Season with salt and pepper to taste, and gently toss. Add purple onion and parsley and toss again. Cool to room temperature, cover, and refrigerate.

Before serving bring back to room temperature, toss, correct seasoning and add additional oil and vinegar if the salad seems dry. Sprinkle reserved crisp bacon on top. Four portions.

Molded Gazpacho Salad

2   envelopes unflavored gelatin
3   cups tomato juice
1/4   cup wine vinegar
1   clove of garlic, crushed
2   teaspoons salt
1/4   teaspoon pepper
    Dash of cayenne
2   large tomatoes, peeled, seeded, chopped, and drained
1/2   cup finely chopped onion (1 medium)
3/4   cup finely chopped green bell pepper
3/4   cup finely chopped cucumber, well drained
1/4   cup finely diced pimiento
1   small avocado
1   tablespoon lemon juice
1/2   cup dairy sour cream
1/2   teaspoon salt
    Dash of cayenne
    Crisp greens

Soften gelatin in 1 cup tomato juice 5 minutes. Heat until mixture simmers and gelatin is dissolved. Remove from heat; add remaining tomato juice, vinegar, garlic, 2 teaspoons salt, pepper, and dash of cayenne. Chill until mixture begins to set; fold in tomatoes, onion, green bell pepper, cucumber, and pimiento. Pour into 6-cup mold. Chill about 3 hours or until firm. Unmold onto serving plate. Mash avocado with lemon juice in small bowl. Stir in sour cream, 1/2 teaspoon salt, and dash of cayenne. Spread on top of unmolded salad. Garnish with crisp greens. Makes 6 to 8 servings.

Potato Patties with Cheese

4   tablespoons butter
2   tablespoons minced raw onion or
2   teaspoons instant minced onions
2   cups cold, left-over mashed potatoes
3/4   cup grated Cheddar or American cheese
1   teaspoon dried dillweeds
1   teaspoon salt

Preheat skillet for 2 minutes over medium-low heat. Melt 2 tablespoons butter.

Sauté onion until golden, about 2 minutes. Remove from skillet and combine with potatoes in mixing bowl.

Blend cheese, dillweed, and salt into potatoes. Divide mixture into 4 portions and shape into patties.

In skillet, melt 2 tablespoons butter over medium-low heat. Fry patties over medium-low heat until golden on each side, 2 to 3 minutes per side. Makes 4 patties.

Cabbage Slaw

3   cups finely chopped, grated or shredded cabbage
1/2   cup grated carrot
1/2   cup diced celery
1   teaspoon salt
    Cooked Salad Dressing

Place cabbage, carrot and celery in vegetable crisper or covered dish and refrigerate for 1 to 2 hours. Then sprinkle with salt.

Moisten with cooled Cooked Salad Dressing. Toss lightly with fork. Serve immediately. Makes 6 servings.

Cooked Salad Dressing

3   tablespoons flour
1 1/2   teaspoons salt
1   teaspoon dry mustard
1   tablespoon sugar
1   tablespoon paprika
1 1/2   cups milk
2   egg yolks, beaten
1/3   cup vinegar
2   tablespoons butter

In 1-quart saucepan, combine flour, salt, mustard, sugar and paprika. Gradually blend in milk, stirring until smooth.

Cook over low heat, stirring constantly, until mixture thickens and boils. Boil 1 minute. In small bowl, add a little of the hot mixture to the beaten egg yolks. Stir into hot mixture in saucepan. Bring to a boil, stirring constantly. Cool. Dressing will keep in covered jar in refrigerator. Makes 2 cups.

Carrots with Bacon

4   strips bacon, cut into 1/2-inch slices
2   tablespoons butter
8   carrots, cut in half lengthwise
4   green onions, finely chopped
1/2   teaspoon salt
1/4   teaspoon pepper

In skillet, fry bacon slices until crisp over medium-low

heat. Drain bacon on paper toweling and remove drippings.

Melt butter in skillet over medium-low heat. Add carrots, onions, salt and pepper. Increase heat to medium and cover. When cover is hot to touch, reduce heat to low. Cook for 20 to 25 minutes.

Add bacon just before serving. Makes 4 servings.

Scalloped Tomatoes

3   slices crisp toast, cut in $^1/_4$- to $^1/_2$-inch cubes
1   No. 2$^1/_2$ can tomatoes, drained and cut in pieces with a spoon
1   teaspoon seasoned salt
2   tablespoons butter
1   cup chopped onion
$^1/_2$ cup cheese cracker crumbs
1   tablespoon parsley flakes
1$^1/_2$ teaspoons sugar
1   cup thick sour cream
    Parsley flakes

Grease a shallow 1$^1/_4$-quart baking dish. Mix the onion, tomatoes, cracker crumbs, and a mixture of parsley flakes, sugar, and seasoned salt in the baking dish. Spoon sour cream evenly over mixture. Heat butter in a skillet. Add toast cubes and toss until sides are coated. Top sour cream with toast cubes. Sprinkle with parsley flakes. Heat thoroughly in a 325-degree oven about 20 minutes. Serve in sauce dishes. Makes 6 servings.

Cauliflower with Almonds

1   large cauliflower
$^1/_2$ cup slivered almonds
1   cup soft bread crumbs
1   garlic clove, minced
4   tablespoons butter

Steam cauliflower for 20 minutes or until tender. Sauté remaining ingredients in butter until the almonds are golden and crumbs crisp. Serve over cauliflower. Serves 6.

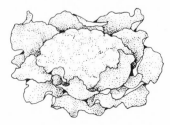

Potatoes Boulangere

1   pound potatoes, pared and sliced
$^1/_4$ pound Gruyere cheese, sliced thin
1   pound onions, peeled and sliced thin
    Salt and pepper
$^1/_2$ cup stock or bouillon
$^1/_2$ cup bread crumbs
$^1/_4$ cup grated cheese
4   tablespoons butter, melted
    French mustard

Start oven at moderate (350 degrees). Grease 2-quart casserole. Arrange a layer of sliced potatoes in casserole, add thin slices cheese, and layer of onion slices. Sprinkle with salt and pepper; repeat layers until dish is full. Press down well, pour stock or bouillon over all.

Sprinkle with bread crumbs and a little grated cheese. Pour melted butter over. Cover with piece of buttered waxed paper. Bake in moderate oven 20 minutes, remove paper, continue baking 10 to 15 minutes longer, or until potatoes are done and browned. Serve at once. Makes 6 servings.

Potato Skins with Cheese and Bacon

2   baking potatoes, preferably Idaho (about 8 ounces each)
1$^1/_2$ tablespoons unsalted butter, melted
$^1/_2$ cup finely shredded Cheddar or Parmesan cheese
4   strips of cooked bacon, crumbled

Preheat the oven to 400 degrees. Scrub and dry the potatoes. Pierce each one with a fork. Bake for 1 hour and 10 minutes, or until very tender when pierced with a knife. Remove the potatoes from the oven; reduce the oven temperature to 375 degrees.

As soon as the potatoes can be handled, using a mitt if necessary, cut in half lengthwise. Scoop out the potatoes, leaving a $^1/_4$-inch shell. (Reserve the scooped-out potato for another use.)

Brush the insides of the skins generously with the melted butter. Sprinkle on the cheese and top with the crumbled bacon.

Return the potatoes to the oven and bake for 30 minutes, or until the tops are golden and the skins are very crisp. Serve as a side dish, or cut into strips and serve as an hors d'oeuvre. Makes 4 pieces.

Fried Rice

$^1/_2$ cup chopped onion
1   cup rice
2   tablespoons butter
$2^1/_2$ cups canned consommé
$^1/_2$ teaspoon salt

Chop the onions, add rice, and sauté in the butter until the rice is brown. Add consommé and salt; cover, and cook over low heat until dry, about 25 minutes. Try this with chicken prepared any way.

Vichyssoise

Chop fine the white parts of 4 leeks, place in a pot with a lump of sweet butter and brown very lightly. Add 1 finely chopped small onion, 4 finely sliced potatoes, and 1 quart chicken broth or consommé. Salt to taste. Simmer for at least a half hour. When the potatoes and leeks are soft, take the pot off the fire, crush the vegetables, and pass the soup through a fine sieve. Return to the fire and add 2 cups milk, 2 cups cream, and a tiny lump of butter. Correct seasoning, bring to a quick boil, cool, and again rub through a fine strainer. Add a cup of heavy cream and chill. Just before serving, top with finely chopped chives. Serves 6 generously.

Squash Soufflé

$^3/_4$ cup finely diced onion
4   tablespoons butter
4   pounds yellow or white squash
2   cups fine bread crumbs
1   6-ounce jar chopped pimiento
1   tablespoon salt
1   teaspoon black pepper
$^1/_2$ teaspoon garlic powder
2   eggs beaten

Sauté onion in butter. Cut up squash and boil in hot water until soft. Drain squash and place all items into a food processor. Blend thoroughly and turn into a buttered casserole dish. Bake 30 minutes in a 350-degree oven preheated. Recipe serves 6 to 8.

Potatoes au Gratin

6   to 8 baking potatoes, baked in oven with the skins on
1   pound Velveeta cheese, cut in chunks
1   cup mayonnaise
1   onion, chopped
1   teaspoon Worcestershire powder
   Salt and pepper to taste
6   strips bacon, chopped and sautéed until half cooked
$^1/_4$ cup pimiento-stuffed olives, sliced

Remove skin from cooked potatoes and cut into large dice pieces. Toss with the next 5 ingredients. Pour into greased casserole. Sprinkle with bacon and olives. Bake at 325 degrees for 1 hour.

Cabbage Rolls

8   large cabbage leaves
$^1/_2$ pound ground beef
$^1/_2$ cup cooked rice
1   egg
$^1/_3$ cup milk
1   teaspoon salt
2   teaspoons Worcestershire powder
   Dash of pepper
2   tablespoons chopped onion
2   tablespoons cooking oil
$^1/_2$ cup cooked tomatoes
$^1/_4$ cup chopped onion
4   whole cloves
1   bay leaf

Cook cabbage in boiling salted water for 5 minutes; drain. Combine beef, rice, egg, milk, seasonings and onion. Place spoonful of mixture on each leaf and fold over. Place in saucepan. Add tomatoes, oil, onion, bay leaf and cloves. Cover and simmer 45 minutes. Remove bay leaf. Serves 4.

Eggplant Maison

1   eggplant
4   cups dry bread crumbs
1   egg
1/2   cup water
1   diced onion
1   green bell pepper, diced
2 1/2   cups fresh or canned tomatoes
1   teaspoon salt
1/2   teaspoon pepper
1   teaspoon sugar
1   teaspoon Worcestershire powder
1   cup Romano cheese

Peel eggplant and slice in 1/4-inch slices. Add 1/4 cup water to egg and beat in a bowl. Dip each slice of eggplant into bread crumbs then egg mixture and again into bread crumbs. Fry coated eggplant in cooking oil until brown. Remove eggplant, then sauté onion and green bell pepper until soft. Add tomatoes, salt, pepper, sugar and Worcestershire powder and simmer until well blended. Place eggplant into a casserole dish in alternate layers with cheese and sauce with a sauce and cheese layer on top. Cover dish and bake in a preheated 350-degree oven for 15 minutes. Remove cover and continue baking until recipe is brown and crusty. Serves 6.

Creamed Celery Amandine

2   cups celery, sliced crosswise
    Salt and freshly ground pepper to taste
2   tablespoons butter or margarine
1   tablespoon chopped onion or 1/2 teaspoon
        chopped chives
2   teaspoons flour
1/2   cup cream
1/4   cup chicken broth
1/4   cup toasted almonds

Place sliced celery, salt and freshly ground pepper and butter or margarine in saucepan with tight-fitting cover. Cover and cook over low heat until celery is almost tender, about 15 minutes, shaking pan frequently. Add chopped onion or chives and continue cooking until tender. If lid is not tight-fitting, add small amount water, if necessary. Celery should be almost dry at end of cooking time.

Blend in flour, then gradually add cream and chicken broth. Bring to boil and cook until thickened, stirring. Add toasted almonds. Makes 4 servings.

Belgian Smothered Potatoes

6   large potatoes
1/2   cup butter
3   tablespoons dry white wine
1   teaspoon onion powder
3/4   teaspoon salt
1/4   teaspoon coarse ground black pepper
1   tablespoon freeze-dried chives

Peel and quarter potatoes. In a heavy skillet melt butter. Add potatoes and remaining ingredients except chives. Cover tightly. Cook over low heat for 45 minutes; remove cover; add chives. If any cooking liquid remains, turn heat high so that moisture evaporates.

Cabbage a la Bretonne

2   cups beef stock
1   medium head cabbage, cut into 8 wedges
2   eggs, well beaten
3/4   cup light cream
1/2   teaspoon salt
    Freshly ground pepper
    Nutmeg
3   tablespoons olive oil
3   tablespoons tarragon vinegar
2   teaspoons sugar
    Paprika

Place beef stock and cabbage wedges in saucepan and cook over low heat until cabbage is tender. Drain and keep warm. Mix beaten eggs, light cream, salt, freshly ground pepper and nutmeg to taste together in mixing bowl.

Bring olive oil, tarragon vinegar and sugar to boil in saucepan over low heat. Add this mixture to egg mixture, stirring. Return to saucepan and cook over very low heat until thickened, stirring constantly. Remove core from cabbage and place in warm bowl. Pour sauce over cabbage. Sprinkle with paprika. Let stand for a few minutes before serving.

Potato and Sour Cream Casserole

8   to 10 potatoes, peeled
8   ounces cream cheese, softened
1   cup sour cream
6   green onions, chopped
1/2   stick butter, melted
    Salt and pepper

Cook potatoes in boiling, salted water until tender. Drain. Beat cream cheese, sour cream and onions with mixer until well blended. Stir in the hot potatoes and butter and beat until fluffy. Salt and pepper to taste. Transfer to a 2-quart buttered baking dish and bake at 350 degrees for 30 minutes.

Peas European

2   tablespoons butter or margarine
1   cup sliced fresh or canned mushrooms
$^1/_4$ cup minced onion
$^1/_4$ teaspoon salt
    Dash pepper
$^1/_4$ teaspoon nutmeg
$^1/_8$ teaspoon dried marjoram
2   tablespoons sherry (optional)
2   cups drained, hot, cooked or canned peas

Melt butter or margarine in skillet over medium heat. Add mushrooms and minced onion and sauté 5 minutes or until tender. Add salt, pepper, nutmeg, marjoram and sherry. Add peas and mix well. Makes 4 servings.

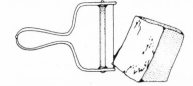

Cauliflower with Cheese Sauce

1   large head cauliflower, separated into
       flowerets
3   tablespoons butter or margarine
1   medium onion, chopped
1   small green bell pepper, seeded and
       chopped
1   can (2 ounces) mushroom stems and pieces
1   cup shredded sharp Cheddar cheese
2   cans (10$^1/_2$ ounces each) white sauce
2   tablespoons toasted sesame seeds

Cook cauliflower in covered saucepan in small amount boiling salted water 10 minutes or until barely tender. Melt butter or margarine in skillet over medium heat and sauté onion, green bell pepper and mushroom pieces until onion is clear.

Place in alternate layers in greased 2-quart casserole, drained, cooked cauliflower, sautéed vegetables, shredded Cheddar cheese and white sauce. Sprinkle with toasted sesame seeds and bake in moderate oven (350 degrees) 30 minutes or until bubbly. Makes 8 servings.

Good Luck Black-Eyed Peas

2   cups black-eyed peas
8   cups water
$^1/_2$ pound salt pork
2   onions, diced finely
1   medium size can tomatoes
1   bell pepper, diced fine
1   clove garlic, diced fine
1   tablespoon powdered mustard
2   teaspoons chili powder
1   tablespoon Worcestershire powder
2   teaspoons powdered ginger
    Salt and pepper to taste

Clean peas and place into a kettle with the 8 cups of water. Boil slowly for 2 hours until peas are tender. Remove the floaters (the peas that come to the top of the water). Add the salt pork, onions, bell pepper, tomatoes, garlic, mustard, chili powder, Worcestershire powder, ginger and salt and pepper to taste. Boil slowly for about 2 or more hours.

Cauliflower a la Polonaise

1   medium-sized head cauliflower
    Boiling salted water
$^1/_2$ cup ($^1/_4$ pound) butter or margarine
$^1/_3$ cup fine dry bread crumbs
1   hard-cooked egg, chopped
    Parsley sprigs

Cut out thick core from cauliflower; break into flowerets and wash. Cook, drain and arrange in a serving dish.

Heat butter in a saucepan until bubbly; pour over cauliflower, leaving about 3 tablespoons remaining in saucepan. Stir crumbs into remaining butter until combined; add to cauliflower with the chopped egg. Using 2 forks, mix lightly until well combined. Garnish with parsley; serve at once. Makes 4 servings.

Athenian Moussaka

2   small (1 pound each) eggplants
$^1/_2$ cup olive oil or salad oil
    Meat Sauce
    Custard Topping
$^1/_2$ cup shredded Parmesan cheese

Trim stem ends from eggplant and cut lengthwise in $^1/_4$-inch thick slices. Pour oil into two large baking pans and turn eggplant slices in it, coating both sides. Arrange in a single layer. Bake in a 425-degree oven for 30 minutes, or until tender, turning occasionally.

To assemble, arrange half eggplant in a 9x12-inch baking pan. Spoon on the meat sauce and top with remaining eggplant. Pour on custard topping and sprinkle with Parmesan. Bake, uncovered, in a 350-degree oven for 1 hour. Makes 12 servings.

MEAT SAUCE. Chop 2 medium-sized onions and sauté in 2 tablespoons salad oil. Add $2^1/_2$ pounds ground beef and cook, stirring, until crumbly. Add 2 teaspoons salt, 2 cans (6 ounces each) tomato paste, $1^1/_4$ cups dry red wine, $^1/_4$ cup finely chopped parsley, 1 stick cinnamon, and 2 cloves garlic, minced. Cover and simmer 30 minutes. Uncover and remove cinnamon stick; cook down until liquid is evaporated. Stir in 3 tablespoons fine dry bread crumbs and 1 cup shredded Parmesan cheese.

CUSTARD TOPPING. Melt $^1/_3$ cup butter and blend in $^1/_2$ cup all-purpose flour; cook, stirring, 2 minutes. Gradually stir in 1 quart milk and cook, stirring, until it boils and thickens. Add 1 teaspoon salt, $^1/_4$ teaspoon ground nutmeg, and $^1/_2$ cup shredded Parmesan cheese. Stir hot sauce into 6 slightly beaten eggs.

Laredo Ranch Beans

2	cups pinto beans
8	cups water
$^1/_2$	pound salt pork
2	onions, diced finely
1	medium size can tomatoes
1	bell pepper, diced fine
1	clove garlic, diced fine
1	tablespoon powdered mustard
2	teaspoons chili powder
1	tablespoon Worcestershire powder
2	teaspoons powdered ginger
	Salt and pepper to taste

Clean beans and place into a kettle with the 8 cups of water. Boil slowly for 2 hours until beans are tender. Remove the floaters (the beans that come to the top of the water). Add the salt pork, onions, bell pepper, tomatoes, garlic, mustard, chili powder, Worcestershire powder, ginger and salt and pepper to taste. Boil slowly for about 2 more hours.

Broccoli Lorraine

$1^1/_2$	pounds broccoli
3	slices bacon, cooked crisp, and crumbled
$^3/_4$	teaspoon salt
$^1/_8$	teaspoon each pepper and ground nutmeg
$^1/_2$	teaspoon dry mustard
4	eggs
$1^1/_2$	cups half-and-half (light cream)
3	tablespoons freshly shredded Parmesan cheese

Trim and cut broccoli; drain well and turn into a 2-quart shallow baking dish; sprinkle with bacon.

In a bowl, combine the salt, pepper, nutmeg, and mustard. Add eggs and beat lightly with a fork, then stir in half-and-half and Parmesan and pour over the broccoli.

Set baking dish inside a pan of hot tap water so that water comes to within $^1/_2$ inch of dish rim. Bake in a 350-degree oven for 25 to 30 minutes or until you can shake the pan back and forth and only a 3-inch circle in the center moves. Serve at once. Makes about 6 servings.

Lima Bonne Femme

3	cups lima beans, cooked and drained
2	tablespoons melted butter
$^1/_2$	large onion, diced fine
$^1/_2$	pimiento, diced fine
1	cup sour cream
	Salt and pepper

Melt butter in skillet. Add onion and pimiento and sauté until soft. Add lima beans and allow to heat through by simmering for about 4 minutes. Add sour cream and salt and pepper to taste. Recipe can be simmered for two more minutes after the sour cream has been added.

Heavenly Hominy

1	large onion, minced
	Butter
5	cups canned hominy
$^1/_2$	can cream of mushroom soup
1	can cream of celery soup
1	large can Parmesan cheese
1	tablespoon Worcestershire powder
	Juice of one lemon
1	small jar pimiento, minced
	Salt, pepper, and paprika to taste
	Bread crumbs

Melt butter over low heat; sauté onion. Add hominy and heat through. Add soups; blend in Parmesan cheese, Worcestershire powder, lemon juice, and minced pimiento. Season to taste with salt, pepper, and paprika. Place mixture in oblong casserole, 12x8x2, and cover with bread crumbs. Bake 45 minutes in 350-degree oven. Recipe serves 4.

Eggplant Soufflé

1	large or 2 small eggplants
1/4	cup butter or margarine
1/4	cup flour
2	cups milk, scalded
1 1/2	cups shredded Cheddar cheese
4	eggs, well beaten
1/2	teaspoon salt
1/2	teaspoon white pepper
1	cup cracker crumbs
1/2	cup grated Cheddar cheese

Peel and dice eggplant. Cook in salted water until tender. Drain and mash. Melt butter or margarine in saucepan over very low temperature; stir in flour. Scald milk and stir in flour. Continue to cook until thickened, stirring occasionally. Remove from heat. Add shredded Cheddar cheese. Cool. Add well-beaten eggs, salt and white pepper. Combine mashed eggplant and cheese sauce. Add cracker crumbs and pour into greased 2-quart casserole. Sprinkle with grated Cheddar cheese.

Bake in moderate oven (350 degrees) 30 minutes or until firm. Makes 8 servings.

Artichokes with Ninon Sauce

Wash and remove tough or discolored leaves from artichokes. Cut off 1/2 inch of top leaves with knife or scissors. Using sharp knife, trim base and stem so it is flat. Place slice of lemon on base of artichokes to keep them white. Tie with fine cord to secure leaves and lemon slice while cooking. Cook, uncovered, in large quantity of well-salted water over medium heat 10 minutes. Cover and continue cooking 40 minutes or until leaf pulls out easily. Remove cord and turn upside down to drain. Serve on individual dishes with Ninon Sauce in sauceboat as accompaniment.

NINON SAUCE:

5	tablespoons peanut oil
2	tablespoons vinegar
1	shallot, finely chopped
1	hard-cooked egg, sieved
1	tablespoon prepared mustard
1 1/2	teaspoons minced parsley
1 1/2	teaspoons minced chives
	Salt and pepper to taste

Combine all ingredients and mix well.

Barbecued Sweet and Sour String Beans

1	pound green beans, snapped, or 1 16-ounce can French-style wax beans
1	teaspoon salt
	Pepper and cayenne to taste
4	slices white fatback
1	apple, peeled and sliced
2	onions, sliced
1	tablespoon flour
2	tablespoons brown sugar
1/4	teaspoon dry mustard
	Salt and pepper to taste
1	cup bean liquid
2	tablespoons garlic or apple vinegar

Cook beans, salt, pepper and cayenne to taste in just enough water to cover until tender. Drain beans reserving 1 cup liquid. Cook in heavy skillet over medium heat, slices of fatback until fat is rendered from meat. Remove meat. Add apple slices and onion slices; fry until tender but not brown. Remove apple and onion slices and keep warm. Combine flour, brown sugar, dry mustard, salt and pepper; stir quickly into hot fat. Add reserved bean liquid and vinegar and continue cooking until slightly thickened, stirring constantly. Add drained beans and cook until thoroughly heated, stirring constantly. Serve on platter with onion and apple rings. Makes 4 to 5 servings.

Swiss Beans

2 tablespoons butter or margarine
2 tablespoons flour
1 teaspoon salt
$1/4$ teaspoon pepper
1 teaspoon sugar
$1/2$ teaspoon grated onion
1 cup sour cream
4 cups green beans, sliced lengthwise
2 cups Kellogg's Special K
$1/2$ pound process Swiss cheese, grated

Melt margarine or butter. Blend in flour, salt, pepper, sugar, and grated onion. Add sour cream gradually and cook until thickened, stirring occasionally. Fold in green beans which have been sliced lengthwise. Pour into greased $1\frac{1}{2}$-quart casserole. Combine Kellogg's Special K and grated cheese; sprinkle over beans. Bake in hot oven, 400 degrees, for 20 minutes. Serves 6.

Yam Peanut Puffs

4 cups mashed yams
3 tablespoons butter or margarine
2 tablespoons brown sugar
$1/2$ teaspoon ground nutmeg
$1/2$ teaspoon ground cinnamon
$1/2$ teaspoon salt
$1/16$ teaspoon ground black pepper
1 egg, lightly beaten
2 apples, peeled, cored and cut into 12 wedges
1 cup peanuts, coarsely chopped
2 tablespoons butter or margarine, melted

Combine yams, butter, sugar, nutmeg, cinnamon, salt, black pepper, and egg. Mix well. Surround each apple wedge with a portion of the mixture and shape into balls. Roll each yam ball in peanuts. Place on greased baking dish. Pour melted butter over each ball. Bake in pre-heated moderate oven (350 degrees) 25 to 30 minutes.

Recipe makes approximately twelve $1\frac{1}{2}$-inch balls.

Spanish Artichokes Antiqua

4 artichokes
  Water to cover artichokes
1 tablespoon salt
  Juice and rind of 2 lemons
2 teaspoons butter or margarine
1 green onion, finely chopped
1 pound crabmeat, flaked
  Salt and pepper to taste
3 or 4 drops liquid red pepper seasoning
4 crackers, crumbled
1 tablespoon cream sauce

Cut off stem and, with scissors, cut off top of each leaf from the artichokes. Tie with soft cord to keep the leaves from spreading out. In a large saucepan, over medium heat, bring to boil enough water to cover artichokes. To this water add one tablespoon of salt and the juice and rind of 2 lemons. Add artichokes and cook until bottoms are tender. Remove from heat. Drain and core, leaving leaves and bottom intact.

Melt in saucepan over low heat the butter or margarine. Add the green onions and cook until tender. Add crabmeat, salt, pepper, liquid red pepper seasoning, crackers, and cream sauce, cooking until thoroughly hot.

Now fill the cored artichokes with the blended crab mixture. This recipe serves 4.

Patio Potatoes

$2\frac{1}{2}$ pounds potatoes, cooked
3 cups medium white sauce
2 cups shredded milk Cheddar cheese
1 4-ounce can peeled green chilies, rinsed and cut in pieces
2 teaspoons salt
2 cloves garlic, puréed
  Buttered bread crumbs

Peel, slice, or cube cooked potatoes; place in $1\frac{1}{2}$-quart baking dish. Combine white sauce, shredded Cheddar cheese, green chili pieces, salt, and puréed garlic in saucepan. Cook over very low heat until cheese is melted. Pour cheese mixture over potatoes. Sprinkle buttered bread crumbs over top. Bake in moderate oven (350 degrees) until thoroughly hot and crumbs are brown. Makes 6 to 8 servings.

Pennsylvania Tomatoes

6   large tomatoes (about 3 pounds)
$^{1}/_{2}$ cup unsifted flour
$^{1}/_{2}$ cup butter or margarine
$^{1}/_{2}$ teaspoon light brown sugar
1   teaspoon salt
$^{1}/_{4}$ teaspoon pepper
     Brown sugar
$1^{1}/_{2}$ cups heavy cream

Cut thin slices from top and bottom of tomatoes, and cut each tomato in 3 crosswise slices. Dip cut sides of slices in flour.

In large skillet over medium heat melt butter or margarine and sauté tomato slices until browned on one side. Sprinkle each uncooked side with $^{1}/_{2}$ teaspoon brown sugar. Turn and sprinkle with salt, pepper and small amount of brown sugar. Sauté until browned. Turn again. Add heavy cream and cook, uncovered, 5 minutes or until tomatoes are tender. Makes 6 servings.

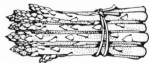

Asparagus Supper Casserole

1   pound fresh asparagus or 1 10-ounce package frozen asparagus
4   or 5 hard-cooked eggs, sliced
$^{1}/_{4}$ cup butter or margarine
$^{1}/_{4}$ cup flour
$1^{1}/_{2}$ cups milk
$^{1}/_{2}$ cup sauterne
$^{3}/_{4}$ teaspoon seasoned salt
3   tablespoons frozen chopped chives
$^{1}/_{2}$ cup grated Cheddar cheese
1   large tomato, thinly sliced
$^{1}/_{4}$ cup fine, dry bread crumbs
1   tablespoon melted butter or margarine

Cook asparagus until tender, drain and cut into bite-size pieces. Place asparagus in $1^{1}/_{2}$-quart casserole. Place sliced hard-cooked eggs over asparagus. Melt butter or margarine in saucepan over very low heat. Blend in flour. Gradually stir in milk and cook until thickened, stirring occasionally. Blend in sauterne, seasoned salt, chopped chives, and grated Cheddar cheese. Pour sauce over eggs in casserole. Arrange thinly sliced tomato over sauce. Combine bread crumbs and melted butter or margarine and sprinkle over top. Bake in moderate oven (375 degrees) 25 minutes. Makes 4 servings.

Baked Fresh Corn Casserole

2   cups fresh corn, cut off the cob
1   tablespoon flour
1   tablespoon sugar
1   tablespoon butter or margarine
3   eggs, beaten
$1^{1}/_{2}$ teaspoons salt
$^{1}/_{8}$ teaspoon ground black pepper
1   cup milk
$^{1}/_{2}$ cup heavy cream

Combine all ingredients. Turn into buttered 6-cup casserole. Place in pan of hot water. Bake in preheated oven (325 degrees) $1^{1}/_{2}$ hours or until knife inserted in center comes out clean. Recipe serves 6.

Spinach in Madeira

2   pounds fresh spinach
2   tablespoons butter or margarine
$^{1}/_{4}$ cup heavy cream
     Salt and pepper to taste
     Dash nutmeg
$^{1}/_{4}$ pound fresh mushrooms, thinly sliced
2   tablespoons Madeira
     Croutons

In covered pan, cook spinach over low heat until barely tender, in water clinging to leaves. Drain; put through food chopper, using finest blade. Add butter or margarine and heavy cream, beating well. Add salt, pepper, and nutmeg and set aside, keeping warm.

Sauté mushrooms in butter or margarine over medium heat until tender. Combine spinach and mushrooms, and add Madeira. Heat over low heat until very hot but not boiling. Garnish with croutons fried in butter or margarine. Makes 6 servings.

Fresh Tomato-Cheese Strata

12 slices white bread
2 cups creamed cottage cheese
1 teaspoon salt
1 teaspoon Worcestershire powder
1/4 teaspoon oregano, crushed
1/8 teaspoon pepper
6 eggs
4 medium tomatoes, sliced
1 tablespoon minced onion
1/4 teaspoon salt
1/8 teaspoon pepper
1 1/2 cups milk
1/2 cup grated sharp Cheddar cheese

Place 6 bread slices on bottom of 12x8x2-inch baking dish. Beat together cottage cheese, salt, Worcestershire powder, oregano, pepper, and 2 of the eggs; spread over bread. Cover cottage cheese mixture with half the sliced tomatoes and sprinkle with minced onion, salt, and pepper. Cover tomatoes with the remaining 6 bread slices. Beat 4 remaining eggs and milk together and carefully pour over bread. Cut the remaining tomato slices in half and arrange around edge of dish in scalloped effect; sprinkle with grated sharp Cheddar cheese. Chill in refrigerator 1 hour. Bake in moderate oven (350 degrees) 50 minutes or until puffed and brown. Makes 6 to 8 servings.

Fireside Stuffed Potatoes

Large, white California potatoes
Bacon, cooked and broken in small pieces
Cheddar cheese, diced
Chopped onion

Select large white California potatoes and scrub until thoroughly clean. With an apple corer drill a hole, starting from the long end, through the center of the potato to about 1/4 inch from the opposite end. With the corer, remove enough pulp from the center of the potato to form a rather large cavity. Stuff bacon pieces, diced Cheddar and chopped onion into the cavity. Alternate ingredients until potato is full. Then, with a plug of the removed potato pulp, seal the entrance hole. Grease the potato surface lightly and wrap in aluminum foil. Bake in preheated oven (375 degrees) for approximately 45 minutes or until potato is done.

Gingered Belgian Carrots

4 tablespoons sugar
1 can (1 pound, 13 ounces) Belgian-style
   carrots
1/2 teaspoon ground ginger
   Carrot juice

In heavy skillet, over medium heat, caramelize sugar (cook until melted and of rich brown color) stirring frequently. Drain carrots, reserving liquid. Add carrots to caramelized sugar and shake over heat until carrots are coated with sugar. Dissolve ground ginger in small amounts of carrot juice. Add to carrots and shake pan again. Recipe serves 4.

Stuffed Carrots

6 or 8 large carrots
2 hard-boiled eggs, chopped
1 tablespoon mayonnaise
1 tablespoon celery, finely chopped
1 tablespoon minced onion
1 tablespoon minced pickle
   Paprika
   Grated Parmesan cheese

Boil carrots whole (unscraped) until tender. Peel, then split down the center. Scoop out core of each carrot half; mash cores with fork in separate bowl. Add chopped eggs, mayonnaise, celery, onion, and pickle; mix well with carrot center. Stuff carrot boats and sprinkle with paprika and grated Parmesan cheese.

Steamed Fresh Broccoli with Mousseline Sauce

2 pounds fresh broccoli
1 teaspoon salt
2 packages Hollandaise sauce mix
2 teaspoons fresh lemon juice
1/2 cup heavy cream, whipped

Wash and trim broccoli. Cut large stalks in halves or quarters. Make lengthwise gashes in stalks to cook uniformly. Place on collapsible steamer rack and lower into large saucepan containing hot water to level of upper part of feet of the rack. Cover securely and cook over low heat 15 to 20 minutes until stalks are crisp-tender.

To make Mousseline Sauce: Prepare Hollandaise sauce mix according to package directions. Then stir in lemon juice and cook until thickened. Fold in whipped cream. Serve broccoli hot with Mousseline Sauce. Recipe yields 6 servings broccoli, 2 cups sauce.

Cheese Puffed Potato Casserole

4   **egg yolks**
4   **cups well-seasoned mashed potatoes**
1   **cup shredded sharp cheddar cheese**
4   **teaspoons finely chopped onion**
4   **teaspoons finely chopped green bell pepper**
1   **teaspoon celery salt**
1   **teaspoon Worcestershire powder**
    Salt and pepper to taste
4   **egg whites**
    Paprika

The day before serving beat together egg yolks and mashed potatoes until well mixed. Stir in shredded Cheddar cheese, onion, green bell pepper, celery salt, Worcestershire powder and salt and pepper to taste. Refrigerate until ready to bake.

Just before serving, beat egg whites until soft peaks form and fold into potato mixture. Spoon lightly into greased 7x13-inch baking dish. Sprinkle with paprika. Bake in moderate oven (375 degrees) for 25 minutes. Makes 6 servings.

Company Potato Casserole

6   **medium potatoes, peeled**
1   **cup sour cream**
1   **can (10½ ounces) condensed cream of chicken soup, undiluted**
1   **teaspoon salt**
¼   **teaspoon pepper**
¼   **teaspoon curry powder**
4   **hard-cooked eggs, sliced**
½   **cup soft bread crumbs**
½   **cup shredded sharp Cheddar cheese**

Cook potatoes in covered saucepan in small amount of boiling, salted water over low heat until tender. Drain and cut in ¼-inch thick slices. Combine sour cream, cream of chicken soup, salt, pepper and curry powder. Place in 2-quart casserole in alternate layers, in order given using ⅓ of quantity for each layer the sliced potatoes, sliced hard-cooked eggs and cream mixture. Combine bread crumbs and shredded Cheddar cheese and sprinkle over top.

Bake in moderate oven (350 degrees) 30 minutes or until thoroughly hot and brown on top. Makes 6 servings.

Broccoli and Rice Casserole

1   **cup rice, cooked**
1   **box (10 ounce) frozen, chopped broccoli, cooked and drained**

SAUTÉ:

1   **stick butter**
½   **cup chopped onion**
1   **cup chopped celery**

ADD:

1   **can mushroom soup**
½   **pound Velveeta cheese (or American)**

Stir until cheese is melted. Add rice and broccoli to soup and cheese mixture. Put into casserole dish and bake at 350 degrees for 30 minutes.

Miscellaneous

Eggs Parisienne

2   large eggs
1   tablespoon chopped chives
1   tablespoon sour cream
2   teaspoons grated Parmesan cheese
$1/4$ teaspoon salt
    Butter or margarine

Beat eggs, chopped chives, sour cream, Parmesan cheese, and salt together until well mixed. Heat butter or margarine in skillet over low temperature. Add egg mixture and cook, stirring constantly, until eggs are set. Makes 1 serving.

Crazy Crust Pizza

1   cup flour
1   teaspoon salt
1   teaspoon leaf oregano
$1/8$ teaspoon pepper
2   eggs
$2/3$ cup milk
$1^1/2$ pounds ground beef or 1 cup sliced
         pepperoni
$1/4$ cup chopped onion
1   cup drained mushroom pieces
1   cup pizza sauce, or 1 can tomato sauce
         plus 2 teaspoons oregano and $1/4$
         teaspoon pepper
1   cup shredded mozarella cheese

Brown ground beef. Drain. Grease a 12-inch pizza pan. Combine first 6 ingredients and mix until smooth. Pour batter into the pan to cover the bottom. Arrange topping of meat, mushrooms, and onions and drizzle with pizza sauce. Sprinkle with cheese. Bake at 425 degrees 25 to 30 minutes until crust is brown.

Almond Rice Casserole

$1/4$ cup blanched almonds, slivered
2   tablespoons butter
$1/2$ cup chopped onion
$1/2$ cup chopped celery
2   cups chopped cooked spinach, drained
2   cups cooked rice
1   chicken bouillon cube
$1/3$ cup boiling water
1   can mushroom soup

Toast almonds in butter and remove from pan. Sauté celery and onion in remaining butter. Dissolve bouillon cube in boiling water and combine with soup, using rotary beater; add celery and onion. Combine half the sauce with spinach and half the sauce with rice. Place spinach in bottom of buttered $1^1/2$-quart casserole. Top with rice, sprinkle with almonds. Bake at 350 degrees for 40 minutes. Serves 5 to 6.

Baked Egg Casserole

$1/4$ pound margarine
1   onion, diced
1   8-ounce can mushrooms, stems and
         pieces, drained
1   tablespoon vegetable oil or margarine
12   eggs
1   pound dry cottage cheese (if unable to
         obtain dry cottage cheese, eliminate the
         milk)
$1/2$ cup milk
1   teaspoon Worcestershire powder
       Salt, to taste
       Pepper, to taste
8   slices American cheese

Preheat oven. Put $1/4$ pound margarine in baking dish and place in oven to melt. Sauté onion and mushrooms in frying pan in oil or margarine until soft. Set aside. Beat eggs well. Stir in cottage cheese, milk and seasonings. Beat well until all ingredients are blended. Fold in sautéed onions and mushrooms. Pour egg mixture into heated baking dish and bake until eggs begin to set. This will take about 20–25 minutes but bears watching since oven temperatures vary. Place cheese slices over eggs and bake until cheese melts. Check frequently so that cheese does not burn. This can be sliced and served directly from baking dish. Can also be refrigerated and reheated.

Huckleberry Waffles

Sift together: 2 cups sifted cake flour, 2 teaspoons baking powder, $^1/_2$ teaspoon salt. Melt 6 tablespoons butter; add to the butter $1^1/_4$ cups milk and 2 well-beaten egg yolks. Add to flour, stirring to keep batter creamy. Beat 2 egg whites until stiff, then blend into batter. Wash, dry, and add to batter 1 cup fresh huckleberries. Bake on waffle iron according to manufacturer's directions. Serve with clover honey.

Wild Rice Stuffing

1   cup wild rice
    Giblets (liver, gizzard, and heart)
2   cups hot broth or water
$^1/_2$ cup finely chopped onion
$^1/_2$ cup butter or margarine
2   quarts oven toasted dry bread crumbs
1   teaspoon salt
$^1/_4$ teaspoon ground sage
$^1/_4$ teaspoon pepper
2   eggs, beaten

Cook the rice according to directions on the package. Chop the giblets fine and cook in water until done. Sauté onion in the butter until yellow in color, add the bread crumbs with the giblets and broth. Add the seasonings and mix lightly. Cover and let stand until the bread is moist. Add the wild rice and eggs, and mix lightly. Pour into a buttered baking dish and bake for 25 minutes at 325 degrees, or stuff whatever fowl you are roasting and cook during the last 20 minutes of its cooking.

Chestnut Dressing

$1^1/_2$ cups raisins (white ones are best)
1   cup melted butter
2   tablespoons salt
2   cups cream
$2^1/_2$ quarts crumbled white bread
$1^1/_2$ cups finely diced celery
4   cups chestnuts, toasted and broken up
1   teaspoon Worcestershire powder

Mix together and stuff into the turkey cavity, or bake in buttered casserole at 325 degrees for 1 hour.

Sour Cream Substitute

$^1/_4$ cup milk
1   8-ounce carton cream cottage cheese
1   tablespoon lemon juice
$^1/_4$ teaspoon salt

Put all ingredients in blender and mix. This can be used just as regular sour cream is used. Add a sprig of parsley when blending if it is to be used with baked potatoes.

Savory Dressing

1   quart white bread, crumbled in small pieces
$^1/_4$ cup butter, melted
1   teaspoon salt
$^1/_2$ tablespoon poultry seasoning (use more if you like)
$^3/_4$ cup chopped onion
$^1/_4$ pound bacon
$^1/_4$ teaspoon pepper
1   egg
2   tablespoons chopped parsley
1   teaspoon Worcestershire powder

Dice the bacon and fry with the onions until crisp. Add parsley, crumbled bread, butter, and seasonings. If you like a moist dressing add enough cold water to moisten. Beat and fold in the egg; stuff the fowl with it, or bake in a buttered casserole until brown. I prefer a dry, crunchy dressing, so I do not add any liquid or egg.

Corn Bread Dressing

$^1/_2$ cup onion, chopped fine
$^1/_2$ cup green bell peppers, chopped fine
$^1/_2$ cup celery, diced fine
$^2/_3$ cup butter
2   quarts corn bread crumbs (and be sure the corn bread is well browned)
6   hard cooked eggs, chopped
$^1/_2$ cup chopped pimiento
    Salt and pepper
    Chicken or turkey stock (or canned consommé)
$^1/_2$ cup broken pecans
1   teaspoon Worcestershire powder

Sauté the onions, green bell peppers, and celery in the butter; add corn bread, hard-cooked eggs, and pimiento. Season with salt and pepper, and moisten with chicken or turkey stock, or canned consommé. Turn into a shallow well-buttered casserole and bake at 350 degrees until brown on top.

Chestnuts en Casserole

3 cups shelled chestnuts*
3 cups chicken stock
2 tablespoons butter
1¹/₂ tablespoons flour
Salt and pepper

Melt the butter in the bottom of the casserole and work in the flour, adding as much of the chicken stock as may be required to make a thin paste. Add the chestnuts, pour in the rest of the stock, season well, and bake slowly for 3 hours. Serve as a side dish with baked ham.

* To shell chestnuts, cut a slit ¹/₂ inch deep in each chestnut. For each cup of chestnuts take a teaspoon of butter. Cook the chestnuts in a frying pan for 5 minutes, tossing them, and then place the pan in the oven for 5 minutes. The shells and skins are now easily peeled off with a paring knife.

Impossible Quiche

¹/₂ cup cooked ham or bacon cut into small pieces or 1 cup seafood (shrimp or crab)
3 eggs
¹/₂ cup biscuit mix
¹/₄ pound melted butter or margarine, cooled
1¹/₂ cups whole milk
¹/₄ teaspoon salt
Dash of pepper
1 cup shredded Swiss cheese

Place all ingredients, except the cheese and meat or seafood, in a blender. Mix for a few seconds to blend. Sprinkle cheese and meat or seafood in well-greased 9-inch pie pan. Pour egg mixture over cheese and meat. Pan will be very full. Bake at 350 degrees for about 45 minutes or until set. Allow quiche to "sit" about 10 minutes before cutting.

Grilled Vegetarian Sandwich

¹/₂ cup mayonnaise
2 teaspoons Dijon-style mustard
¹/₈ teaspoon garlic powder
8 slices bread
1 cup alfalfa sprouts
1 medium-size ripe avocado (thinly sliced)
4 thin slices Cheddar or mozzarella cheese
4 thin slices tomato
1 cup sliced mushrooms
8 thin slices green bell pepper
4 thin slices onion
softened butter or margarine

In small bowl blend mayonnaise, mustard and garlic powder. Spread generously on bread slices. Top each of 4 bread slices with one-fourth of the sprouts, avocado, cheese, tomato, mushrooms, green bell pepper and onion. Top with remaining bread slices. Spread both sides of sandwich with butter. Preheat griddle on setting "8." Cook sandwiches 8 to 10 minutes, or until cheese melts and bread is golden brown. Turn after half the time.

Mexican Cheese Appetizers

4 flour tortillas (8-inch diameter)
1 cup shredded Cheddar cheese
1 cup shredded Monterey Jack cheese
¹/₄ cup chopped green onion
¹/₄ cup chopped pitted ripe olives
Sour cream or taco sauce

Preheat griddle on setting "8." Lightly grease griddle with vegetable oil. Place 2 tortillas on griddle. Top each with one fourth of cheeses, onion and olives. Cook tortillas 1¹/₂ to 3 minutes, or until cheese melts. With pancake turner, roll each tortilla jelly roll fashion. Remove from griddle. Cut cross-wise into 4 pieces. Repeat with remaining tortillas. Serve with sour cream or taco sauce.

Grilled Deli Sandwich

1 thin slice Swiss cheese
2 bread slices
1 slice ham
1 slice bologna
2 thin slices tomato
1 slice cotto salami
Italian dressing
1 thin slice Cheddar cheese

Place Swiss cheese on one bread slice. Top with ham, bologna, tomato and salami, brushing with dressing between each layer. Top with Cheddar cheese and remaining bread slice. Preheat griddle on setting "8." Brush top of sandwich with dressing. Place dressing-side down on griddle. With pancake turner, lightly press down sandwich. Brush other side of sandwich with dressing. Cook sandwich 4 to 8 minutes, or until cheese melts and bread is golden brown. Turn after half the time.

Quesadillas

6   ounces Monterey Jack cheese
1   4-ounce can green chili peppers, rinsed and seeded
$^3/_4$ cup Frijoles Refritos or canned refried beans
12   6-inch tortillas
2   tablespoons cooking oil

Cut cheese into twelve 3x1x$^1/_4$-inch strips. Quarter chili peppers lengthwise. Spread 1 tablespoon of the beans on each tortilla. Top each with a piece of cheese and a piece of chili pepper. Fold tortillas in half; secure each with a wooden pick. In skillet heat oil; cook quesadillas, a few at a time, in the hot oil about 2 minutes per side or until lightly browned and cheese is melted. Makes 12.

Spicy Tomato Marmalade

12   medium-size firm, ripe, red or yellow tomatoes
2   large lemons
7   cups sugar
$^1/_4$ cup chopped candied ginger

Prepare 7 half-pint jars and covers. Scald, peel and core tomatoes; cut into eighths. Cut lemons in half lengthwise; slice paper thin. Combine tomatoes, lemons, and sugar in glass or pottery bowl; cover; refrigerate overnight. Next day drain off liquid, cook liquid and any undissolved sugar rapidly until syrup spins a thread from tip of spoon. Add tomatoes, lemons and ginger; cook over medium heat about 30 minutes or until tomatoes are transparent and stir constantly during last few minutes of cooking. Remove from heat. Makes 7 half pints.

Cucumber Sandwiches or Dip

4   cucumbers
2   packages (8-ounce) Philadelphia cream cheese
1   garlic clove, grated
   Dash paprika
1   tablespoon onion juice
$^1/_2$ cup chopped nuts
1   teaspoon sugar
1   teaspoon salt
   Pinch celery salt
1   teaspoon Worcestershire powder
$^1/_2$ cup mayonnaise

Grind cucumber in food grinder or blender. Mix in the other ingredients. Let sit at least 24 hours before serving. It is best not to combine the cucumber and the other ingredients in the blender. Filling will become too thin. This makes 24 sandwiches or a large amount of dip. Sandwiches will freeze.

Green Tomato Relish

12   quarts green tomatoes, cut up
$^1/_2$ gallon onions, cut in squares
1   quart green long hot peppers, cut with scissors
6   cups sugar
$^1/_2$ gallon vinegar
1   teaspoon salt

Combine all ingredients and bring to a boil. Remove from heat and seal in hot jars. Makes 20 pints.

Southern Frankfurter Dinner

1   large onion, cut into rings
1   cup diced green bell peppers
   Shortening
$^1/_2$ pound frankfurters, thinly sliced
2   cups tomatoes and juice
   Salt and pepper
$^1/_2$ cup cornmeal
1   teaspoon soda
$^1/_2$ teaspoon baking powder
1   egg
$^2/_3$ cup buttermilk

Fry onion and green bell peppers in shortening; add frankfurters, tomatoes, salt and pepper. Bring to a boil; pour into 8x8-inch baking dish. Sift cornmeal with soda, baking powder and 1 teaspoonful salt; cut in 2 table-spoonsful shortening. Beat egg with buttermilk; stir into dry mixture. Mix well; spoon over meat mixture. Bake at 425 degrees for 25 to 30 minutes or until top is golden brown. Serve from baking dish. Yield 6 servings.

Tamale Balls

1	**pound ground beef**
1	**pound ground pork**
1½	**cups cornmeal**
¾	**cup tomato juice**
¼	**cup flour**
3	**cloves garlic, crushed**
1	**tablespoon chili powder**
2	**teaspoons salt**

Grind beef and pork together twice. Add all other ingredients and form into small balls, about 150. Drop in sauce and simmer 2 hours.

SAUCE:

3	**cans (#2) tomatoes**
2	**teaspoons salt**
1	**tablespoon chili powder**

Heat ingredients together in large roaster. (May use electric). Let sauce come to a boil and drop in balls. Simmer.

To serve keep hot in chafing dish and pick up with toothpicks.

Boned Broiled Quail

12	**quail, backbone removed and birds deboned, leaving the wings intact (ask your butcher to do this if you wish)**
⅓	**cup Dijon-style mustard**
3	**tablespoons gin**
1	**tablespoon olive oil**

Skewer a plain toothpick through the top of each bird to pin the wings to the breast meat; with another toothpick, skewer the two legs together.

Preheat the broiler. In a small bowl, stir the mustard, gin and olive oil until blended. Brush the quail all over with about one-third of the mixture. Place the birds, breast-side up, on a rack over a broiler pan.

Broil the quail 4 inches from the heat for 4 minutes, basting once with half of the remaining mustard mixture. Using tongs, turn the birds over, brush with the remaining mustard mixture and broil for an additional 2 min-

utes, or until the breast meat is a light pink color. Remove the toothpicks before serving.

Spanish Venison

Chop 2 large onions and brown them in bacon fat. Remove onions. In the same fat, sear a venison flank steak on both sides. Put the steak in a buttered casserole and sprinkle it with salt and pepper. Spread the onions over the meat and top with a chopped green bell pepper, a thinly sliced carrot, and a stalk of sliced celery. Cover the whole with tomato juice and bake in a 350-degree oven, covered, for 1 hour. If you like, thicken the liquid with browned flour and pep it up with a little Worcestershire powder. Good with potato pancakes, a very sour apple-sauce with a jigger of brandy stirred in, a green salad, oven-toasted rolls, bottles of cold ale.

Venison de Chasseur

Make marinade of claret flavored with bay leaves, onion slices, carrot strips, whole black pepper, garlic clove, marjoram, and thyme. Add ¼ teaspoon ground cardamon and several juniper berries. Heat to simmering. Place venison in marinade for 48 hours, then dice the meat and sauté in olive oil until brown. Add chopped Canadian bacon, 3 minced onions. Sprinkle with flour. Add 2½ cups of marinade and a bundle of fresh herbs. Simmer gently until tender. Serve at once.

Chinese Spareribs

3½	**pounds spareribs**
	Accent
	Ginger and garlic powder
	Salt and pepper
	Catsup
	Molasses
	Soy sauce

Cut spareribs into strips. Place in pan, edge up, side by side. Cover with a coating of catsup. Sprinkle with salt and pepper to suit taste. Sprinkle with Accent. Sprinkle with small amounts of ginger powder and garlic powder. Shake soy sauce generously over ingredients. Thread dark molasses back and forth over pan (do not use too much, to avoid being oversweet). Bake in a 350-degree oven for 1 to 1¼ hours, watching carefully after 1 hour to avoid burning. Serves 4.

Venison Casserole

Roll bite-sized pieces of venison tenderloin in a flour seasoned with powdered sage, rosemary, and marjoram. Slowly sauté the pieces in butter until brown. Meantime, slice thin slivers of fat, country-cured ham and use them to line a big casserole. When the venison pieces are brown, arrange them in a layer in the bottom of the casserole. Top with a layer of small potato balls, a layer of onion rings, then more venison. Place the casserole in a moderate oven for 30 minutes, then add sweet cream to cover the meat. Meantime, simmer diced mushrooms in some claret. When the cream is fully absorbed and the venison tenderized, half-cover with the claret and the mushrooms. When the wine is absorbed (in about half an hour), the dish is ready to serve. With it, cauliflower Hollandaise, salad, hot scones, Burgundy.

Chili con Queso

¹/₂	cup finely chopped onion
1	tablespoon butter or margarine
2	medium tomatoes, peeled, seeded, and chopped
1	4-ounce can green chili peppers, rinsed, seeded, and chopped
¹/₄	teaspoon salt
1¹/₂	cups shredded Cheddar cheese
	Milk
	Tortilla chips

In medium skillet cook onion in butter or margarine until tender but not brown. Stir in tomatoes, chili peppers, and salt. Simmer, uncovered, for 10 minutes. Add cheese, a little at a time, stirring until cheese is melted. Stir in a little milk, if mixture becomes too thick. Serve immediately with tortilla chips or corn chips. Keep warm in fondue pot over low heat. Makes 1³/₄ cups.

Egg Croquettes

³/₄	cup chopped fresh or canned mushrooms
3	tablespoons butter or margarine
4	tablespoons flour
1	cup milk
¹/₂	teaspoon Worcestershire powder
	Salt, pepper, and cayenne to taste
1	teaspoon minced chives or onion
4	hard-cooked eggs, minced
	Fine bread crumbs
1	egg yolk, beaten

Cook mushrooms in butter over medium heat until tender but not browned. Remove mushrooms and save. Stir flour into butter or margarine that remains. Gradually add milk, Worcestershire powder, salt, pepper, and cayenne and cook over very low heat until thick, stirring constantly. Remove from flame. Add cooked mushrooms, minced chives or onion, and minced hard-cooked eggs. Chill in refrigerator.

Form into croquettes. Roll in fine bread crumbs, then roll in beaten egg yolk. Roll again in bread crumbs. Fry in deep hot fat (375–400 degrees) until golden brown. Drain on absorbent paper. Serve plain or with hot sauce. Makes 4 servings.

Home Cured Jerky

1¹/₂	to 2 pounds lean, boneless meat
¹/₄	cup soy sauce
1	tablespoon Worcestershire powder
¹/₄	teaspoon pepper
¹/₄	teaspoon garlic powder
¹/₂	teaspoon onion powder
1	teaspoon hickory smoke flavored salt
	Hot sauce or Tabasco, optional

Trim and discard all fat from meat. Cut meat into ¹/₈- to ¹/₄-inch thick slices. In a bowl, combine soy sauce, Worcestershire powder, pepper, garlic powder, onion powder and smoke flavored salt. Stir until seasonings are dissolved. Add all the meat strips and work them thoroughly into the mix until all surfaces are well coated. The meat will absorb most, if not all, of the liquid. Cover lightly and let stand overnight in the refrigerator. Shake off any excess liquid, sprinkle coarse ground black pepper on both sides. Arrange strips of meat close together, but not overlapping, directly on oven racks or cake racks set in shallow, rimmed pans. Dry meat in oven at the lowest possible oven setting, 150 to 200 degrees, until it turns brown, feels hard and is dry to the touch. This will take 5 hours for chicken and turkey, 4 to 7 hours for beef and venison. Pat off any beads of oil. Cool and store in airtight plastic bags or in jars with tight-fitting lids. Keeps in refrigerator or at room temperature indefinitely. Men love to make this! This particular jerky can be made from beef flank, brisket or top round steak, venison or the white meat from chicken or turkey. Partially freezing meat makes it easier to slice evenly. Cut with the grain for chewy jerky, across the grain for more tender, brittle jerky.

Roast Calf Liver

1	**3-pound calf liver**
12	**slices bacon**
1	**tablespoon grated onion**
$^1/_2$	**teaspoon salt**
	Freshly ground black pepper
	Bearnaise sauce

Put 6 slices of bacon on bottom of baking dish and place liver on top of it. Spread liver with grated onion, sprinkle with salt and pepper. Put 6 remaining bacon slices on top of liver. Bake in a moderate oven (325 degrees) for 1 hour. Serve with bearnaise sauce. Serves 6.

Bearnaise Sauce

1	**cup dry white wine**
3	**egg yolks, beaten**
2	**tablespoons tarragon vinegar**
1	**tablespoon chopped parsley**
1	**tablespoon minced shallots**
1	**teaspoon tarragon**
1	**teaspoon chervil**
1	**cup butter, melted**
$^1/_2$	**teaspoon salt**
	Freshly ground black pepper

Beat 2 tablespoons of the wine into egg yolks. Set aside. Combine the remaining wine with vinegar, parsley, shallots, $^1/_2$ teaspoon tarragon, $^1/_2$ teaspoon chervil, salt and pepper and cook for 15 minutes, stirring occasionally. Remove from heat and add egg yolk mixture slowly, stirring briskly. Add butter 2 tablespoons at a time, beating thoroughly after each addition. Strain through a fine sieve. Add the remaining tarragon and chervil and stir well. Makes about 2 cups.

Sautéed Calf's Liver with Avocado

$1^1/_2$	**pounds calf's liver**
2	**tablespoons butter or margarine**
2	**medium avocados**
2	**tablespoons butter or margarine**
$^1/_4$	**cup butter or margarine**
$^1/_2$	**cup chicken broth**
$^1/_3$	**cup white wine**
$^1/_4$	**cup lemon juice**
1	**tablespoon snipped chives**
1	**teaspoon snipped parsley**
2	**teaspoons Worcestershire powder**

Slice calf's liver in 12 thin slices. Heat 2 tablespoons butter or margarine in skillet over medium heat and add liver, cooking until brown on both sides. Remove liver to platter and keep warm. Peel and slice avocados into 9 whole slices each. Add 2 tablespoons butter or margarine to skillet in which liver was cooked and add avocado slices; cook approximately 1 minute on each side. Remove to platter with liver and keep warm. Add $^1/_4$ cup butter or margarine to drippings in skillet and cook until brown. Add chicken broth, white wine, lemon juice, chives, parsley and Worcestershire powder and bring to boil. Pour mixture over liver and avocado slices and serve. Makes 6 servings.

Dove Brazos Valley

6	**doves**
$1^1/_2$	**sticks melted butter**
1	**teaspoon Worcestershire powder**
1	**teaspoon garlic salt**
$^1/_3$	**cup cooking sherry**
1	**cup chopped mushrooms**
$^1/_2$	**teaspoon nutmeg**
	Salt and pepper to taste
$^1/_3$	**cup flour**
	Fresh grapes

Brown doves on all sides in melted butter in a large skillet. After doves become brown add Worcestershire powder, garlic salt, cooking sherry, chopped mushrooms, nutmeg, and salt and pepper. Cover skillet and allow to simmer for about 15 to 20 minutes. Remove the doves from the skillet; add to the sauce $^1/_3$ cup of flour, forming a roux. Place the doves on toast and top with the sauce. Garnish with fresh grapes. Serves 3.

Gouda Luncheon Supreme

4	**small Gouda cheeses**
1	**cup baked or boiled ham, diced**
1	**cup chicken or turkey, cooked and diced**
$^1/_4$	**cup onion, minced very fine**
$^1/_4$	**cup celery, minced very fine**
$^1/_2$	**cup French dressing**
	Salt and pepper to taste
1	**head lettuce**
2	**tomatoes cut into wedges**

Core out each of the Gouda cheeses, leaving a thickness of about $^1/_4$ inch. Remove the protective red wax coating also. Mix in a bowl the diced ham, diced chicken or turkey, onion, celery, French dressing, and salt and pepper. Stuff each of the cored-out cheeses with the ham-chicken mixture. Place the filled cheese onto a lightly greased cookie sheet and into a preheated oven at 375 degrees. Bake until the cheeses are melted through, but not out of shape. Remove and serve on a large leaf of lettuce. Place tomato wedges into the cheese for garnish. Each cheese serves 1 person.

Dirty Rice

$1/2$	pound ground beef
1	pound chicken livers, chopped
1	pound small frozen shrimp
1	small green pepper, chopped
2	small onions, chopped
2	ribs celery, chopped
2	cloves of garlic, minced
$1^1/_2$	teaspoons salt
1	teaspoon pepper
$1/2$	cup salad oil
2	cups rice, cooked
1	can beef bouillon

Cook all ingredients except rice and bouillon in salad oil until tender, but not brown. Stir in rice and bouillon. Simmer for 10 minutes. Bake at 350 degrees for 15 to 20 minutes. Yield 6 servings.

Macaroni and Cheese Supreme

1	24-ounce package large elbow macaroni
3	tablespoons cooking oil
1	tablespoon salt
2	pounds mild Cheddar cheese, grated
1	stick of butter
$1/2$	pint sour cream
1	pint heavy cream
$1/4$	cup grated Parmesan cheese
2	teaspoons seasoned salt
4	teaspoons Tabasco sauce
2	teaspoons white pepper
$1/3$	cup chopped pimiento

Cover macaroni with water, add cooking oil and salt. Bring to a boil and cook until tender. Drain in a colander and rinse in cold water to remove starch. Place macaroni in a 3-quart baking dish. Blend in all but 1 cup of the grated Cheddar cheese and pimiento.

Melt butter in a saucepan and add heavy cream, Parmesan cheese, seasoned salt, white pepper and Tabasco sauce. Heat slowly, stirring until well blended. Blend this mixture in with the macaroni and cheese and top with 1 cup of reserved grated Cheddar cheese. Place the baking

dish covered into a preheated 375-degree oven and bake for approximately 40 minutes until mixture is bubbling. Remove cover and continue baking for 10 more minutes. Serves 8.

Tuna Casserole Supreme

1	can tuna fish (8 ounces)
	Brown rice for 4 servings (follow package directions for cooking)
1	can cream of mushroom soup, undiluted
1	onion medium size
1	green bell pepper, medium size
3	shallots
$1/4$	teaspoon Worcestershire powder
1	medium-sized can sliced black olives
	Pepper to taste

Cook rice. Set aside. Drain tuna, mushroom soup, peel onion, remove seeds from green bell pepper, slice black olives, peel shallots. Let these stand for 5 minutes.

Spoon out one layer of rice on the bottom of a $1^1/_2$-quart casserole dish, one layer of tuna, next a layer of thinly sliced onion, followed by thinly sliced green bell pepper, a layer of mushroom soup and then a layer of black olives and shallots. Sprinkle on Worcestershire powder after olives and shallots. REPEAT THE LAYERS UNTIL ALL THE INGREDIENTS ARE IN THE CASSEROLE DISH.

Preheat oven at 350 degrees. Cook casserole with cover on for about 1 hour. Garnish with parsley and serve directly from dish.

DC's Shepherd's Pie

2	pounds potatoes
2	tablespoons butter
1	medium onion, chopped
$1^1/_2$	pound ground chuck
	Salt and pepper to taste
$1/2$	teaspoon chili powder
$1/2$	teaspoon garlic powder
1	teaspoon Worcestershire powder
$1/2$	teaspoon cumin
$1/2$	teaspoon coriander
1	small can tomato paste
1	small can tomato sauce
1	large can whole tomatoes, drained
1	15-ounce can French-style green beans
1	15-ounce can whole kernel corn
8-10	ounce Cheddar cheese

Peel, cube and cook potatoes in salted water until tender. Drain and whip with a little milk and butter. Sauté the onions in butter until they are tender. Crumble in ground meat and cook thoroughly. Add seasonings one at a time and stir after each addition. Pour in tomato paste and sauce. Add whole tomatoes that have been cut into pieces. Simmer this mixture until rawness is cooked out of tomato products. Add drained cans of green beans and corn. Turn mixture into greased casserole dish and top with whipped potatoes. Sprinkle top with grated Cheddar cheese.

Bake in moderate oven (350 degrees) for about $1/2$ hour or until mixture is bubbly. Allow to sit for about 10 minutes before serving. Serves 6.

American Family Baked Spaghetti

6	slices bacon
$1^1/_2$	pounds ground lean beef
	Salt
	Pepper
1	large onion, diced
1	medium-sized green bell pepper, diced
1	large can sliced mushrooms, drained
1	tooth garlic, crushed
1	tablespoon Worcestershire powder
5	drops Tabasco sauce
$1/2$	teaspoon basil
$1/2$	teaspoon oregano
$1/2$	teaspoon dehydrated parsley flakes
1	can (1 pound 1 ounce) peeled tomatoes
1	can (8 ounces) tomato sauce
1	can (6 ounces) tomato paste
1	pound package spaghetti
	Grated Parmesan cheese

Fry bacon in large metal skillet or Dutch oven until brown and remove bacon from container. Place ground beef into the bacon fat and lightly brown, stirring constantly. Salt and pepper meat to taste. Add onion, green bell pepper, drained mushrooms and crushed garlic. Continue to cook slowly, stirring until onion and green bell pepper become soft. Add Worcestershire powder, Tabasco sauce, basil, oregano and parsley flakes. Add tomatoes, tomato sauce and tomato paste. Lower heat to simmer and continue stirring and cooking slowly for 15 minutes. Cook spaghetti according to directions on package, place in colander and thoroughly wash away starch. Combine spaghetti with meat sauce in a large ovenware baking dish. Place lid on dish and into preheated 350-degree oven and bake for 45 minutes. Remove from oven and let stand for 15 minutes before serving. Top with Parmesan cheese if desired. Recipe serves 8.

Turkey Noodle Casserole

3	pounds cooked and cubed turkey
1	$10^3/_4$-ounce can cream of mushroom soup
1	$10^3/_4$-ounce can cream of chicken soup
1	$10^3/_4$-ounce can cream of celery soup
1	6-ounce jar of chopped pimientos
1	6-ounce can sliced water chestnuts (drained)
1	8-ounce package noodles (cooked)
1	package American cheese slices
1	yellow onion diced fine
1	large green bell pepper diced fine
1	teaspoon garlic powder
	Dash of Tabasco
1	teaspoon dry powdered mustard
	Salt and pepper to taste
1	stick of butter

Sauté onion and green bell pepper in butter, then blend and turn into casserole dish with all other items except cheese slices. Place cheese slices over top and bake 45 minutes in a 375-degree oven. Recipe serves 12.

David Wade's Jalapeño Cheese Ball

1	8-ounce package cream cheese
1	pound Velveeta cheese
1	pound sharp Cheddar cheese
3	jalapeño peppers, chopped
$1/4$	cup white wine

Place all items into a food processor and blend until smooth. Remove and form a cheese ball. Roll ball in finely crushed snack crackers such as Wheat Thins or finely crushed nuts. Cover with foil and refrigerate overnight.

Party Stuffed Mushrooms

12	large fresh mushrooms with stems removed
2	tablespoons butter
$1/4$	cup Cheddar cheese, grated
2	tablespoons Parmesan cheese, grated
2	tablespoons Romano cheese, grated
1	tablespoon butter, softened
2	pitted green olives, chopped
1	anchovy filet, mashed
$1/2$	teaspoon anchovy paste
1	tablespoon lime juice
1	tablespoon soy sauce

Sauté the mushrooms in butter until they are golden. Mix together the cheeses with the softened butter. Blend in the olives, anchovy, anchovy paste, lime juice and soy sauce. Stuff the mushrooms and bake at 350 degrees for 15 minutes or until bubbly.

Buffet Stuffed Mushrooms

20   large fresh mushrooms, remove stems, chop and set aside
$^1/_2$ cup bread cubes
2   tablespoons parsley, chopped
2   garlic cloves, chopped
$^1/_2$ onion, chopped
2   eggs, lightly beaten
$^1/_2$ cup cottage cheese
$^1/_4$ teaspoon cumin
$^1/_4$ cup olive oil
$^1/_4$ cup Parmesan cheese, grated
1   teaspoon Worcestershire powder

Soak bread crumbs in water, squeeze dry and shred in a mixing bowl. Add the mushroom stems. Add the remaining ingredients in except the oil and the Parmesan cheese. Stuff the mushroom caps and place on a lightly greased cookie sheet. Sprinkle the olive oil and the cheese over the mushrooms and bake at 400 degrees for 20 minutes or until puffed.

Egg Rolls

FILLING:

1   pound celery, shredded or finely cut
1   pound bean sprouts
      Boiling water
$^1/_3$ cup cooking oil
$^1/_2$ cup chopped green onions
2   cloves garlic, crushed
$^1/_4$ pound water chestnuts, finely cut
$^1/_4$ pound bamboo shoots, finely cut
6   ounces cooked shrimp, pork or chicken, finely cut
      Salt and pepper to taste
1   tablespoon MSG powder
3   tablespoons soy sauce

Fill saucepan to level of $^1/_2$ inch with boiling water. Add celery and bean sprouts and cook 5 minutes over low heat. Drain well. Heat cooking oil in large skillet over medium heat; add green onions and fry 30 seconds with crushed garlic cloves. Add drained celery and bean sprouts, water chestnuts, bamboo shoots, cooked shrimp,

pork, or chicken, salt and pepper, MSG powder and soy sauce, mixing well. Remove from flame. Drain and cool.

EGG WRAPPERS:

2   cups flour
$^3/_4$ cup cornstarch
$^1/_2$ teaspoon salt
3   eggs
3   tablespoons cooking oil
2   cups water (approximately)

Sift together flour, cornstarch, and salt. Beat eggs and cooking oil together until smooth. Add dry ingredients to egg mixture alternately with water. Beat well. (Batter should be thin enough to fall from spoon in drops. Add more water, if necessary.)

Heat oiled, 6-inch skillet over very low heat. Pour in batter to cover bottom. When bottom of egg wrapper is firm, pour off excess batter. Continue cooking until thoroughly dried. Fry on one side only. Quickly turn skillet over to remove wrapper. Continue in same manner until all batter is used. In center of each wrapper, place spoonful of filling. Roll up, tucking in ends. Brush edge of wrapper with beaten egg to seal roll. Chill in refrigerator. Just before serving, heat oil, 2 inches deep, in large skillet over medium heat. Fry egg rolls on one side 15 minutes or until golden brown on other side. Drain on absorbent paper.

Jalapeño Black-Eyed Pea Dip

6   cups cooked drained black-eyed peas
1   4-ounce jar yellow or green chilis, drained
1   3-ounce jar sliced jalapeño peppers, drained but reserve 1 tablespoon jalapeño juice
1   medium onion
2   cloves, peeled garlic
$^1/_2$ pound butter (2 sticks)
2   small jars Old English Cheese spread

Place chilis, jalapeños, 1 tablespoon jalapeño liquid, onion (cut into pieces), peeled garlic cloves into a blender. Purée. Place this mixture into a large saucepan. In a separate saucepan melt butter, then add in the Old English Cheese spread over low heat, blend thoroughly. Then add to the saucepan with the jalapeño blend. Sprinkle 1 teaspoon of salt and $^1/_2$ teaspoon of black pepper into the same mixture. Purée the black-eyed peas in the blender and add to the mixture. Heat while stirring constantly (over low heat) until the mixture is thoroughly blended. Remove from heat. Cover and chill overnight and reheat for serving with chips.

To add a touch of color to the recipe 1 teaspoon of Spanish paprika can be added in the original pepper mixture.

Peanut or Pecan Brittle

2¹/₂   cups sugar
    2   tablespoons butter
    1   teaspoon baking soda
    3   cups unsalted peanuts or broken pecans
¹/₂   teaspoon vanilla extract

Melt sugar in a heavy skillet over low heat, stirring constantly. When butter is melted, stir in all other ingredients. Pour hot mixture onto a greased flat platter and allow to cool Break into pieces. Recipe yields approximately 1 pound.

David Wade's Pimento Cheese Spread

Place in double boiler:

    1   tablespoon butter
    1   tablespoon sugar
    1   tablespoon sifted flour
    2   tablespoons red wine vinegar
¹/₂   cup heavy cream or canned evaporated
        milk (cream preferred)

Cook, stirring constantly, until well blended and mixture starts to thicken.

Add and blend:

    2   tablespoons finely grated onion
¹/₂   pound sharp Cheddar cheese (grated)
    8   ounce jar chopped pimientos with liquid
        Dash cayenne pepper
        Dash salt

Blend thoroughly.

Store in refrigerator until chilled.

Brennan's Eggs Benedict

Canadian-style bacon
Crisp rusk or English muffin
Soft poached egg
Hollandaise Sauce
Paprika
Truffle slices
Parsley

Place slice of grilled Canadian-style bacon on crisp rusk or English muffin. Place soft poached egg on bacon slice. Top with generous amount of Hollandaise Sauce. Sprinkle with paprika. Garnish with truffle slices and sprigs of parsley. Serve immediately.

SOFT POACHED EGGS

Fill saucepan with water to depth of 3 to 4 inches. Bring just to boiling over low heat. Add small amount of vinegar and salt. Break each egg into small sauce dish. Stir simmering water to make a swirl, following direction of swirling water. Reduce heat to very low and cook 3 to 5 minutes or until desired doneness. Do not let water boil. Remove egg from water with slotted spoon or pancake turner. To keep hot until serving time, place egg in lukewarm water, 3 inches deep.

HOLLANDAISE SAUCE

4   egg yolks
1   to 2 tablespoons lemon juice
1   cup butter, melted
    Salt and pepper to taste

In saucepan or top of double boiler, beat egg yolks slightly and stir in lemon juice. Place over very low heat or over hot water in lower part of double boiler (do not let water touch bottom of upper pan). Add butter, a small amount at a time, stirring constantly with wooden spoon. Add salt and pepper to taste. Continue cooking until mixture thickens, stirring constantly. Makes 1 cup.

Lamb Chops a L'Orange

    1   10-ounce jar orange marmalade
    2   tablespoons butter or margarine
    1   tablespoon dry sherry
    1   garlic clove, minced
1¹/₂   teaspoons salt
    8   lamb shoulder arm chops, each cut about
        1-inch thick

Preheat broiler if manufacturer directs. In 1-quart saucepan over low heat, heat all ingredients except chops until marmalade melts, stirring.

Place chops on rack in broiling pan; broil 10 to 15 minutes until of desired doneness, turning once and brushing occasionally with marmalade mixture.

Ratatouille

Cut medium eggplant in ¹/₂-inch slices, sprinkle with salt and let stand 15 minutes. Simmer in ¹/₂ cup tomato juice with 2 each of celery ribs, onions, green peppers, tomatoes and small zucchini, all cut in cubes. Add 1¹/₂ tablespoons each of basil and marjoram, 1 teaspoon sugar, 1 large clove garlic (crushed) and simmer 35 minutes or until thick. Serve cold as appetizer or hot as a vegetable.

Honeydew Game Hens

6   Rock Cornish Game Hens
6   honeydew or Crenshaw melons
**   Salt and pepper**
2   1-pound cans fruit salad
6   tablespoons Worcestershire powder

Permit game hens to reach a few degrees below room temperature. Season the cavities and outside with salt and pepper to taste. Fill each cavity with approximately 4 tablespoons of fruit salad. Rub 1 tablespoon of Worcestershire powder all over the surface of each hen.

With a sharp knife, cut each melon in half. Using a large spoon, remove all but $1/4$ inch of ripe fruit from each melon half. Place game hen in half of a melon. Put the top half of the melon back in place covering the game hen. You can tie a cotton string around the melon in both directions to tightly secure the top half. Place the 6 melons and game hens enclosed into a shallow baking pan approximately 3 inches tall. Do not use a lid for the pan. Preheat your oven to 400 degrees. Place the pan into the center of the oven and cook for 1 hour. Lower the temperature to 300 degrees and continue cooking for 3 hours.

When you remove the melon game hens from the oven, the melons will appear perfectly horrible but once you remove the top half, you will be surprised at the astonishing results found within. Recipe serves 6.

Melon au Jambon de Bayonne

Take really ripe melon — a Crenshaw, honeydew, Argentine, Spanish, Persian, casaba, or prime cantaloupe — and cut into balls, saving the juice. Put in small dishes set in cracked ice, lace generously with Cointreau, chill a full hour. Ring each serving plate, around melon dish, with 6 paper-thin curls of Bayonne ham (or its nearest equivalent, prosciutto). Eat two spoons of melon, then the ham. The flavor blend is delightful.

Noodles Romanoff

$1/4$ pound noodles
1   cup cottage cheese
$1/2$ cup thick sour cream
$1/4$ cup finely chopped onion
1   clove garlic, finely cut
2   teaspoons Worcestershire powder
**   Dash of Tabasco sauce**
1   teaspoon salt
$1/2$ cup shredded American Cheddar cheese
$1/2$ cup soft bread crumbs

Cook the noodles in salted boiling water until tender. Drain. Add the cottage cheese, sour cream, onion, garlic, Worcestershire powder, Tabasco sauce, and salt. Place in a 1-quart casserole. Cover with a mixture of the shredded cheese and bread crumbs. Bake in a moderate oven, 350 degrees, 30 minutes.

Cornish Hens with Walnut Sauce

2   Cornish hens ($1^1/_4$ pound each)
1   large clove garlic, split
**   Juice of 1 lemon**
1   tablespoon flour
1   teaspoon Worcestershire powder
$1/4$ cup Gray Poupon Dijon Mustard
1   cup chicken broth
2   tablespoons dry white wine
1   tablespoon honey
$1/3$ cup chopped walnuts
**   Cooked wild rice**

Rub hens inside and out with garlic. Sprinkle inside and out with lemon juice. Bake in 400-degree oven 1 hour or until tender. Remove hens to warm platter. Stir flour and Worcestershire powder into drippings in pan. Cook 2–3 minutes. Combine mustard, broth, wine and honey. Gradually add to flour mixture, stirring constantly. Bring to boil. Mix in nuts. Split hens. Place on bed of wild rice. Spoon sauce over all. Garnish with fresh strawberry and kiwi, if desired. Serves 4.

David Wade's Korean Egg Roll

4   pounds ground chuck meat — chili grind
1   pound ground pork — chili grind
4   fresh eggs
4   medium onions (white)
2   bunches fresh green onions (ends too)
3   pounds fresh bean sprouts (or 4 cans of bean sprouts)
1   tablespoon Worcestershire powder
2   teaspoons garlic powder
$1/4$ teaspoon MSG powder
$1/4$ cup soy sauce
**   Salt and pepper**

1. Chop onions (green and white)
2. Place fresh bean sprouts in boiling water and take out immediately and squeeze water out of bean sprouts. Chop into small pieces.
3. Mix all ingredients together. Place 1 tablespoon mixture on unfloured side of pastry (egg roll skin)

Old English Prime Rib, page 149

Liver Naish, page 145

Turkey in a Sack

Chicken Santa Fe, page 10

Steak Diane, page 20

Bar Harbor Fish Platter

French Onion Soup Escoffier, page 135

Tamale Bake

Sour Cream Enchilada, page 35

Chicken Salad Oriental, page 92

Salad Leone, page 91

Chili con Carne, page 111

Hong Kong Sauté Peas, page 137

Lima Bonne Femme, page 67

David Wade's Prune Cake, page 158

Bananas Foster, page 42

4. Place a little water around edges of pastry and roll up. Pinch end to seal.

5. Fry in deep fat until golden brown.

Fried egg rolls can be wrapped in foil and frozen for future use. To reheat, unwrap foil and heat in oven about 30 minutes at 400 degrees.

This recipe yields 40 egg rolls. Serve with Chinese Mustard and plum sauce.

Tempura

2	**cups flour**
1	**egg**
2/3	**cup water**
1/2	**teaspoon salt**
	Shrimp for 4 servings
	Fillet of whitefish for 4 servings
	Parsley sprigs
	Fresh spinach leaves
1	**bunch green onions**
1	**large white onion**
1	**bunch carrots**
2	**medium-sized baking potatoes**
1	**pound fresh string beans**
	Several hot red peppers
	Soy sauce

Combine flour and egg in mixing bowl. Blend in water and salt and mix until batter resembles white paste. In the order listed, dip each of the following into batter and fry in deep fat over medium heat until fish is lightly browned and vegetables are crisp: cleaned and deveined shrimp; fillet of whitefish; parsley sprigs; fresh spinach leaves; green onions, most of tops removed; white onion, cut in medium-sized slices; carrots, scraped and cut into julienne strips; baking potatoes, peeled and sliced; fresh string beans, ends removed; hot red peppers. Serve with soy sauce as hors d'oeuvres or as main dish. Recipe serves 6.

David Wade's
Blue Ribbon Cheese Soufflé

6	**eggs**
	Butter
	Grated Parmesan cheese
6	**tablespoons unsifted all-purpose flour**
1 1/2	**teaspoons salt**
	Dash cayenne
1 1/4	**cups milk**
1/2	**cup coarsely grated natural Swiss cheese**
1/4	**teaspoon cream of tartar**

Separate eggs, placing whites into one large bowl and yolks into another. Let whites warm to room temperature for about 1 hour. Butter a 1 1/2-quart straight-sided soufflé dish (7 1/2 inches in diameter). Dust lightly with grated Parmesan cheese (approximately 1 1/2 tablespoons).

Fold a sheet of waxed paper 26 inches long, lengthwise into thirds. Lightly butter one side. Wrap waxed paper around the soufflé dish making sure the buttered side is against the dish and a 2-inch rim extending above the top edge to form a collar. Secure the waxed paper to the soufflé dish by tying with tight string.

Preheat oven to 350 degrees.

Melt 5 tablespoons butter in a medium saucepan then remove from heat. Using a wire whisk, stir in the flour, 1 teaspoon salt and the cayenne. Beat until smooth. Gradually stir in milk. Bring this mixture to boiling temperature, stirring constantly.

Reduce the heat to simmer and continue stirring until the mixture is thick and leaves bottom and sides of pan.

Beat egg yolks with a wire whisk or wooden spoon. Gradually beat cooked mixture into yolks. Beat in 1/2 cup Parmesan cheese and the grated Swiss cheese.

At high speed, beat egg whites with 1/2 teaspoon salt and the cream of tartar until stiff peaks form when beater on mixer is slowly raised. With wire whisk, using under and over motions, gently fold 1/3 of the whites into warm cheese mixture and combine well.

Carefully fold in remaining egg whites just until combined. Turn into prepared soufflé dish.

Bake 40 minutes or until soufflé is puffed and golden brown. Carefully remove collar just before serving. Serve soufflé at once. Recipe makes 4 servings.

Soufflés should be served at once when removed from oven. Soufflé can be prepared in advance and placed into a refrigerator for chilling. The mixture will stay in good condition for approximately 3 hours.

Once your dinner party has started, while cocktails are still being served, remove the soufflé to the oven and bake as directed; however, the baking time should be increased from 10 to 15 minutes as the soufflé will be cold.

A light, airy cheese soufflé is the hallmark symbol of a good "kitchen technician." This gourmet delicate dish is ideal for luncheons or supper and provides an excellent dinner party main course when served with Crab Newburg or Turkey a la King.

This cheese soufflé is extremely low cost and provides a good source of protein.

Soufflés can be very tricky but by following the above directions carefully, you should enjoy success.

Monto Cristo Sandwich

18	slices bread
6	thin slices cooked ham
3	eggs
	Dash of salt
6	thin slices turkey or chicken
6	thin slices Swiss cheese
6	teaspoons milk
	Pineapple slices
	Currant or raspberry jelly or jam

For each sandwich, butter 1 slice of bread and cover with 1 slice of turkey, top with 1 slice of ham, and cover with second slice of buttered bread. Butter top of second slice of bread and cover with Swiss cheese. Close sandwich in half and fasten with wooden pick. Beat eggs with milk and salt and dip sandwich into mixture. Grill or sauté in butter until brown on both sides, or deep fry, with fryer heated to 375 degrees. Remove pick and serve with pineapple slices and jelly or jam. Serves 6.

Meat-Stuffed Green Peppers

6	large green bell peppers
$1/4$	cup olive oil
$1/2$	cup chopped onion
1	clove garlic, chopped
$3/4$	pound ground veal, beef or pork, or combination of all three
2	cups cooked rice
$3/4$	cup grated Parmesan cheese
3	tablespoons chopped parsley
3	tablespoons Burgundy or claret
	Salt and pepper to taste
$3/4$	cup tomato juice

Remove tops and seeds from green bell peppers. In large skillet heat olive oil over medium heat. Add onion and garlic and sauté until onion is transparent. Add meat and cook until no longer red. Stir in cooked rice, cheese, parsley, Burgundy or claret, and salt and pepper to taste. Remove from heat and cool slightly. Stuff peppers with mixture. Place in greased baking dish. Pour tomato juice around peppers.

Bake in moderate oven (350 degrees) 30 to 40 minutes, or until peppers are tender. Baste occasionally with juice in pan, adding more liquid, if necessary. Makes 6 servings.

Sauces

David Wade's Barbecue Sauce

1	6-ounce can tomato paste
2	8-ounce catsup
2	8-ounce tomato purée
2	tablespoons Worcestershire powder
	Juice of one lemon
$1/4$	cup molasses
1	teaspoon black pepper
$1/4$	cup garlic vinegar
2	teaspoons salt
$1/2$	teaspoon rosemary
$1/2$	teaspoon sweet basil
$1/2$	teaspoon dry mustard
	Few drops of Tabasco
1	teaspoon chili powder
3	tablespoons liquid smoke essence drained into a clean container from inside the pit

Combine all ingredients in saucepan and heat to a boil. Continue to simmer for a few minutes. Add water if too thick.

Tartar Sauce

1	cup mayonnaise
2	tablespoons minced sweet gherkins
1	tablespoon grated or minced onion or 1 teaspoon instant minced onion
1	tablespoon minced parsley
3	pimiento-stuffed green olives, chopped
1	teaspoon vinegar, or $1/2$ teaspoon lemon juice

To mayonnaise, add remaining ingredients in order given. Serve as a sauce for fish, or, mixed with tuna, as a sandwich filling. Makes about $1^{1}/_{4}$ cups.

Marinara Sauce

For 6, chop fine 3 cloves garlic and 1 sprig parsley. Fry together for a few minutes in $^1/_2$ cup hot olive oil, stirring the mixture; don't let it get brown, just soft. Add 1 large can tomatoes, salt, pepper, and a hefty pinch of oregano. Cook over low flame for 45 minutes, uncovered, stirring now and then; the sauce should get thick and smooth. Serve over spaghetti, with a meat course such as veal scallopine or meat balls. Use grated cheese on top.

Le Grande French Dressing

1	egg yolk
2	teaspoons salt
1	teaspoon cracked black pepper
1	teaspoon paprika
$^1/_2$	teaspoon powdered sugar
$^1/_2$	teaspoon dry powdered mustard
$^1/_8$	teaspoon cayenne
$^1/_4$	cup vinegar
$^1/_2$	teaspoon garlic juice
$^1/_2$	cup olive oil
$^1/_2$	cup salad oil

Combine all dry ingredients with vinegar. Beat egg yolk and add to mixture. Next add garlic juice, olive oil and salad oil. Pour mixture into blender or mixer and blend slowly until creamy. Chill covered in refrigerator for at least 1 hour before serving. Yields $1^1/_2$ cups.

Roquefort Cream Dressing

$^1/_2$	cup crumbled Roquefort or blue cheese
1	3-ounce package cream cheese
$^1/_2$	cup cream
$^1/_2$	cup mayonnaise
1	tablespoon lemon juice
1	tablespoon wine vinegar

Blend the Roquefort or blue cheese with the cream cheese. Gradually blend in the cream; then add the mayonnaise, lemon juice, and vinegar. Recipe yields $1^1/_4$ cups.

Soups

Brown Derby Split Pea Soup

$^1/_4$	cup butter or margarine
1	medium onion, sliced
2	small ribs celery, sliced
1	pound green split peas, quick-cooking variety
1	ham hock or whole ham bone
3	pints chicken or beef stock
$^1/_2$	bay leaf
$1^1/_2$	teaspoons black peppercorns
	Salt to taste
1	cup heavy cream, heated
$^1/_2$	cup croutons

Melt butter or margarine in heavy saucepan or kettle over low heat, add onion and celery and simmer 4 minutes. Add peas, ham hock or bone, chicken or beef stock, bay leaf, peppercorns and salt and cook $1^1/_2$ hours. Strain through fine sieve. Add heated cream and pour into heated tureen. Sprinkle with croutons. Makes 8 servings.

Note: If using regular split peas, soak overnight in water.

Minestrone

2	cups dried navy beans
1	cup chopped celery with leaves
1	cup finely chopped onion
1	garlic clove, minced
$^1/_2$	cup olive oil
$2^1/_2$	cups canned tomatoes
$^1/_4$	cup chopped parsley
2	cups shredded cabbage
1	zucchini, thinly sliced
2	cups cut macaroni
1	tablespoon salt
4	peppercorns
2	teaspoons Worcestershire powder

Soak beans in 10 cups of water overnight. Bring to a boil in the same water, reduce heat, add salt, peppercorns, and Worcestershire powder. Cover and simmer for 1 hour. Sauté celery, onion and garlic in olive oil for 10 minutes or until onion is lightly browned. Add to beans with tomatoes and parsley. Bring to a boil, reduce heat, cover and simmer for 1 hour. Add cabbage, zucchini and macaroni and simmer uncovered for 15 minutes, stirring occasionally. Serve with grated Parmesan cheese. Serves 6.

Oxtail Soup

Cut 1 large oxtail in small pieces; sauté it in butter with 1 diced onion. After 10 minutes add 2 chopped carrots, 4 ribs finely diced celery, 1 tablespoon minced parsley, and $1/2$ pound chopped lean beef. When all have browned, sprinkle with 1 tablespoon flour and slowly add 3 quarts of consommé and 3 whole cloves. Cover and simmer 4 hours. Strain through coarse strainer, add 1 large glass red wine and reheat. Serve as soon as it reaches the boil. Serves 8.

Dutch Country Soup

$1/2$ **pound frankfurters, cut into $1/2$-inch slices**
$1/4$ **teaspoon basil leaves, crushed**
2   **tablespoons butter or margarine**
1   **can ($11^1/2$ ounces) condensed Split Pea with Ham soup**
1   **can ($10^3/4$ ounces) condensed Cream of Potato soup**
1   **soup can water**
1   **can (about 8 ounces) canned tomatoes, cut up**

In large saucepan, brown frankfurters with basil in butter. Add soups; gradually stir in water. Add remaining ingredients. Heat; stir occasionally. Makes about 5 cups.

Golden Cauliflower Soup

2   **(10-ounce) packages frozen cauliflower or 1 small head fresh cauliflower, separated into small flowerets**
2   **cups water**
$1/2$ **cup chopped onion**
$1/3$ **cup margarine or butter**
$1/2$ **cup unsifted flour**
2   **cups milk**
2   **tablespoons Chicken Flavor Instant Bouillon or 2 Chicken Flavor Bouillon Cubes**
2   **cups (8 ounces) shredded mild Cheddar cheese**
$1/8$ **to $1/4$ teaspoon ground nutmeg Chopped green onion or parsley**

In medium saucepan, cook cauliflower in 1 cup water until tender. Reserve 1 cup cooked flowerets. In blender or food processor, blend remaining cauliflower and liquid; set aside. In large heavy saucepan, cook onion in margarine until tender; stir in flour. Gradually add remaining 1 cup water, milk and bouillon, stirring until well blended and thickened. Add cheese, puréed cauliflower, reserved flowerets and nutmeg; cook and stir until cheese melts and mixture is hot (do not boil). Serve garnished with green onion. Refrigerate leftovers. Makes about $1^1/2$ to 2 quarts.

Holiday Sweet Soup

1   **quart apple cider**
1   **cup dried apricots**
    Juice of one lemon
$1/4$ **teaspoon nutmeg**
    Pinch salt
6   **whole cloves for garnish**
1   **cup prunes**
2   **tablespoons sugar**
$1/4$ **teaspoon cinnamon**
    Dash ground cloves
6   **lemon slices for garnish**

Wash apricots and prunes and dry. Combine fruit with cider in a kettle and heat to boiling. Lower heat and simmer for 30 minutes or until fruit is tender. Add sugar, lemon juice, spices and salt. Serve soup chilled or hot and garnish with a lemon slice and a whole clove. Recipe serves 6.

Lentil Soup

1	pound dried lentils
4	quarts water
3	garlic cloves, mashed
1	celery rib, diced
1/4	cup olive oil
4	ounces salt pork, diced
1 1/2	pounds onions, peeled and diced
1/2	teaspoon black pepper
1	teaspoon salt
2	good-sized ripe tomatoes or 1 cup canned peeled plum tomatoes, chopped
1	pound potatoes, peeled and diced
1/4	pound carrots, scraped and diced
2	large leeks, diced
1	can (9 ounces) pitted black olives
1/4	cup butter
8	slices of boiled Italian salami or mortadella, diced

Wash the lentils and soak in 2 quarts water overnight. Drain and discard the water. Bring the 4 quarts water to a boil and add all the ingredients except the olives, butter and salami. Cook slowly for 1 1/2 hours. Add olives, salami or mortadella, and butter. Cook for 30 minutes longer. Taste for seasoning and add more if necessary. Serves 6.

Cream of Spinach Soup

5	cups washed, chopped fresh spinach
3	tablespoons butter
1/3	cup chopped scallions, white part only
1/2	teaspoon salt
1/8	teaspoon black pepper
2	tablespoons flour
4	cups chicken stock
3	egg yolks, lightly beaten
1	cup heavy cream

GARNISH:

2	tablespoons chopped egg white
2	tablespoons chopped scallions, green part only

Melt the butter in a heavy stainless steel or enameled saucepan and sauté the scallions over moderate heat for 5 minutes. Add the spinach and cook gently for 3 minutes, stirring occasionally. Stir in the salt, nutmeg, freshly ground pepper, and flour. Cook 2 minutes. Add the chicken stock, stir, bring slowly to a boil, and simmer 5 minutes.

Mix the egg yolks with the cream. Add a few tablespoons of the hot stock to the egg mixture, then return to the saucepan and heat, stirring, until the soup thickens. Do not boil, or the soup will curdle. Garnish with chopped egg white and the green scallions.

David Wade's Potato Soup

1	stick butter
1	large white onion, chopped
2	tablespoons flour
6	large potatoes, peeled and halved
	Salt to taste
1	quart milk
1	tablespoon seasoning salt
1	tablespoon Worcestershire powder
2	teaspoons Tabasco sauce
1	tablespoon garlic powder
	Pepper to taste

Melt butter in large skillet. Sauté finely chopped onion. Add flour, blend and cook rawness out of flour. Set mixture aside.

In separate pan, cover potatoes with water and a little salt. Boil until potatoes are tender. Drain off 3/4 of the potato water, reserving 1/4 for the soup mixture.

In a large dutch oven or container, combine both mixtures. Slowly add milk. Heat while stirring until soup begins to thicken then season with remaining seasonings. Blend thoroughly and continue cooking until soup is nice and thick. Correct seasoning for salt and pepper. Serve hot. Recipe serves 8.

Baked Bean Soup

2	cans (16-ounce) pork and beans in tomato sauce
4	cups water
1	can (16-ounce) whole tomatoes
1/2	cup chopped onion
1/2	cup chopped celery
1/2	teaspoon chili powder
1/4	teaspoon salt
1	cup sliced smoked sausage

In a large saucepan, combine pork and beans, water, tomatoes, onion, celery, chili powder and salt. Bring to a boil, reduce heat and simmer partially covered for 30 minutes. Transfer soup to blender or food processor and blend until smooth. Return to saucepan, add sausage and continue simmering 15 minutes or until sausage is heated through.

Tortilla Soup

10	tortillas, cut in julienne strips
1/4	cup oil
4	green bell peppers, quartered
2	tomatoes, peeled, seeded and chopped
1	onion, minced
1	teaspoon garlic powder
1	tablespoon Worcestershire powder
1/4	cup oil
8	cups chicken broth
3	cups sharp Cheddar cheese, grated
	Salt and pepper to taste

In a skillet, fry tortillas in oil, adding more if needed. When brown, drain on paper towels. Sauté the green bell peppers in the remaining oil until they are browned. Drain on paper towels. Sauté tomatoes, onion, garlic powder and Worcestershire powder in 1/4 cup oil until soft. Add chicken broth and bring to a boil. Salt to taste. Divide the tortilla strips, peppers and cheese among 6 soup bowls and pour the boiling soup over them.

Beer-Cheese Soup

8	cups beef broth
1/2	cup chopped carrots
1/2	cup green bell pepper, chopped
	Salt and pepper to taste
1	tablespoon Worcestershire powder
2	cups beer (not lite beer)
1	pound grated Swiss cheese
1/4	cup sifted flour

Heat beef broth, carrots and bell pepper to boiling. Add pepper, seasoned salt and Worcestershire powder. Blend 1/2 cup beer with flour to form a slur. Add to stock, stirring constantly. Lower heat to just under boiling point then slowly sprinkle in grated Swiss cheese, stirring constantly. When dissolved, add remaining beer. Serve with croutons.

Canadian Cheese Soup

1/4	cup butter or margarine
1/2	cup finely diced onion
1/2	cup finely diced carrots
1/2	cup finely diced celery
1/4	cup flour
4 1/2	teaspoons cornstarch
1	quart chicken stock
1	quart milk
1/8	teaspoon soda
1	cup process American cheese, grated
	Salt and pepper
2	tablespoons finely chopped parsley

Melt butter or margarine over medium heat. Add diced onion, carrots and celery and cook until soft. Blend in flour and cornstarch and cook until bubbly. Blend in chicken stock and milk to make smooth sauce. Add soda and grated cheese; season with salt and pepper. Just before serving, add chopped parsley. Makes 8 servings.

Cream of Asparagus Soup

2	tablespoons butter or margarine
1/2	cup chopped onion
1/2	cup chopped celery
2	16-ounce cans green asparagus spears
6	chicken bouillon cubes
4	tablespoons butter or margarine
1/4	cup flour
1	cup light cream
	Salt and pepper to taste

Melt butter or margarine in saucepan over low heat. Add onion and celery and cook until tender. Drain the 2 cans of asparagus spears, reserving liquid. Cut tips and set aside. Dice stalks and add to cooked vegetables along with asparagus liquid and water to make 5 cups. Add bouillon cubes. Bring to boil and cook 5 minutes. Remove from heat and put through sieve or food mill. Melt 4 tablespoons butter or margarine in saucepan over very low heat and stir in flour. Stir in light cream, continuing to cook until thickened, stirring constantly. Add sieved asparagus mixture, asparagus tips, salt and pepper, and heat to serving temperature. Makes approximately 1 1/2 quarts.

Salads

That's It Salad

1   package lime Jell-O
1   8-ounce can crushed pineapple
$^1/_2$ pint (carton) cottage cheese
1   small carton non-dairy whipped topping
1   cup pecans

Do NOT use water to make Jell-O. Dissolve Jell-O in the pineapple and blend well. Add cottage cheese and blend once more. Mix in topping and pecans then refrigerate until firm. "THAT'S IT!"

Belgian-Endive and Radish Salad

1   good-sized head of Belgian endive per
        person
3   good-sized red radishes per person
6   tablespoons olive oil
2   tablespoons white-wine vinegar
     Juice of 1 fresh lemon
1   garlic clove, mashed
$^1/_3$ teaspoon freshly ground black pepper
$^1/_3$ teaspoon salt
2   tablespoons heavy cream
3   hard-cooked egg yolks, mashed with a
        fork

Trim the endives, wash, and dry well. Scrape the radishes lightly at the tops and trim the roots. Wash and dry radishes and cut into $^1/_4$-inch slices. Combine dressing ingredients in a bowl. Mix well. Discard bits of garlic. Add sliced radishes and refrigerate. When ready to serve endive, separate leaves and arrange on a serving plate. Spoon dressing over top. Serves 4 to 6.

Salad Leone

Pour this dressing over a green salad made up of half chicory and half escarole: Into 1 cup olive oil, put bit (tip of teaspoon) freshly ground pepper and the same amount of French mustard. Add 2 scallions well cut up (green part, too) or 1 slice of onion chopped fine. Mash and add 1 hard-boiled egg, 2 cloves of garlic. Beat in $^1/_2$ cup wine vinegar and pinch of salt, then remove what is left of the mashed garlic. Dice 6 slices of Italian-style salami and mix thoroughly into dressing.

Tapioca Salad

1   cup pearl tapioca
$^1/_2$ cup pineapple, cubed
$^1/_2$ pound grapes
$^1/_2$ pound marshmallows
$^1/_2$ pint whipping cream
$^1/_2$ cup sugar
1   package strawberry Jell-O
     Nuts
     Maraschino cherries

Soak tapioca in 2 cups water for 1 day, then leave water on it. Place in double boiler and simmer until almost done. Add juice from pineapple and sugar and finish cooking. Set aside. Prepare Jell-O as usual and set aside to jell. When thick, add tapioca, grapes, marshmallows, pineapple, and whipped cream. Serve by scoops on a lettuce leaf. Top with whipped cream, maraschino cherries.

Pink Champagne Salad or Dessert

1   8-ounce package cream cheese (softened)
$^3/_4$ cup sugar
1   large can crushed pineapple (drained)
1   10-ounce package frozen sliced
        strawberries (thawed)
2   bananas, quartered and sliced
1   9- or 10-ounce package Cool Whip
     Nuts, if desired

Mix together cream cheese and sugar. Add other ingredients and freeze. Cut into 2- or 3-inch squares and serve. If used as a salad, serve on lettuce leaves. Serves 12 to 14.

Hot Pineapple Cheese Salad

2   No. 2 cans pineapple chunks
$^2/_3$ cup sugar
$^2/_3$ cup flour
$^3/_4$ pound Cheddar cheese, grated
$^1/_3$ cup pineapple juice
     Dash of lemon juice

Layer mixture of pineapple chunks, sugar, flour and then cheese, making 3 layers (always put sugar mixture on top of pineapple, then end with cheese). Pour pineapple juice and lemon over mix. Bake uncovered at 325 degrees for 1 hour.

Cherry Salad Supreme

1	package raspberry Jell-O
1	21-ounce can cherry pie filling
1	package lemon Jell-O
1	3-ounce package cream cheese
1/3	cup salad dressing
1	cup crushed pineapple
1/2	cup heavy cream
1	cup miniature marshmallows
2	tablespoons chopped nuts

Dissolve raspberry Jell-O in 1 cup boiling water, stir in pie filling. Turn into 9-inch square pan, chill until partly set. Dissolve lemon Jell-O in 1 cup boiling water. Beat cream cheese and salad dressing. Gradually add lemon Jell-O. Stir in undrained pineapple. Whip cream. Fold into lemon mixture with marshmallows. Spread on top of cherry layer, top with nuts. Chill until set.

Hot Chinese Salad

Coat a wok or large skillet, with a lid, with 1/4 cup walnut oil. When the oil has heated, add one 6-ounce can of water chestnuts, sliced and drained, two ribs of celery, sliced, 2 tablespoons of peeled and chopped diakon, 2 tablespoons peeled and chopped jicama.

Blend these items into the oil thoroughly then add 2 small shallots, peeled and minced, 1 tablespoon powdered ginger, 2 teaspoons Worcestershire powder, 1 teaspoon garlic powder, 1 teaspoon cracked black pepper, 1 teaspoon seasoned salt and mix thoroughly.

Tear 1 medium head of chinese cabbage into small sections and add to the salad. Slice 1 green bell pepper, removing seeds and fiber, and toss lightly with the salad. Pour 1/2 cup of Oriental Sauce or Oriental Oyster Sauce over the recipe. Blend thoroughly and place tight fitting lid on wok or skillet. Steam over low heat approximately 5 minutes.

Recipe serves 6.

Mickey Mantle Salad

1	7-ounce can tuna, drained and flaked
1	teaspoon salt
1/2	teaspoon onion juice
1/2	cup shell macaroni, uncooked (about 1 cup when cooked)
1/2	cup finely diced green bell pepper
1/2	cup chopped salted pecans
2	hard-cooked eggs, sliced
6	tablespoons lemon juice
1/2	teaspoon black pepper
1	teaspoon celery seed
3	tablespoons salad oil
1/2	cup sliced ripe olives
1 1/2	tablespoons chopped pimiento
1/2	cup diced celery
1	cup mayonnaise

Mix salad oil, lemon juice, salt, pepper, onion juice, and celery seed together in a bowl until well blended. Add tuna and toss lightly. Cover and chill in refrigerator about 2 hours. To complete salad, combine remaining ingredients in a bowl. Add tuna mixture and lightly toss all ingredients together. Chill thoroughly.

Chicken Salad Oriental

4	cups cooked chicken breasts, cubed
1	cup celery, sliced fine on bias
1/2	cup water chestnuts, diced medium fine
1	cup green onion tops
1	cup (small jar) pimiento drained and chopped
1/2	cup macadamia nuts, diced and toasted (or almonds)
1/2	cup bamboo shoots, shredded
	Dash pepper and seasoning salt

Top with Poppy Seed Dressing, toss and chill.

POPPY SEED DRESSING:

2	cups Poppy Seed Dressing
1/2	cup sour cream
1	teaspoon powdered ginger
2	teaspoons rice wine vinegar
	Few drops soy sauce
2	or 3 drops Tabasco

TO SERVE SALAD: Mound on lettuce bed and sprinkle lightly with paprika. Garnish platter with slices of avocado brushed with lime juice, rounds of hard-cooked eggs and cherry tomato halves.

Gazpacho Salad

2 cucumbers, peeled and finely diced
4 tomatoes, seeded and finely diced
2 green bell peppers, seeded and finely
    slivered
1 onion, finely chopped
    Salt and pepper to taste
5 or 6 rolled anchovies
5 or 6 black olives
2 garlic cloves
    Pinch of ground cumin seed
$^1/_4$ cup vinegar
$^1/_2$ cup olive oil
1 tablespoon finely chopped parsley
2 teaspoons finely chopped shallots
    Juice of one lemon

In a deep bowl or glass jar, arrange alternate layers of cucumber, tomatoes, green bell peppers and onion. Sprinkle the layers lightly with salt and pepper and intersperse the vegetables with the anchovies and olives. In a wooden mixing bowl, mash to a paste the garlic cloves with a little salt and cumin seed, beat in vinegar and olive oil and stir in parsley and shallots. Pour the dressing over the salad and chill it for 2 or 3 hours. Sprinkle the vegetables with the lemon juice and serve in chilled bowls as an hors d'oeuvre.

Festive Potato Salad

3 cups boiled potatoes, diced
2 tablespoons oil
1 tablespoon vinegar
1 teaspoon salt
$^1/_2$ cup ripe olives
$1^1/_2$ cups finely shredded cabbage
$^1/_4$ cup chopped dill pickle
$^1/_2$ cup coarsely grated carrot
2 tablespoons diced pimiento
2 tablespoons diced green bell pepper
$^2/_3$ cup mayonnaise
2 teaspoons grated onion
1 teaspoon prepared mustard
    Black pepper to taste

Dice hot, freshly boiled potatoes to make 3 cups. Blend oil and vinegar with salt and sprinkle over potatoes. Mix lightly and let stand until cold. Cut olives into large pieces. Combine olives, potatoes, cabbage, pickle, carrot, pimiento and green bell pepper. Blend mayonnaise, onion, mustard and pepper; pour over salad mixture and blend lightly. Serve well chiled. Yields 6 servings.

Chunky Egg Salad

6 hard-cooked eggs, cut in large pieces
1 cup sliced celery
2 tablespoons minced green bell pepper
1 teaspoon minced onion
$^1/_4$ cup mayonnaise
$^1/_2$ teaspoon Worcestershire powder
    Dash Tabasco
1 tablespoon vinegar
1 teaspoon salt
$^1/_8$ teaspoon pepper

Combine all ingredients. Chill in refrigerator. Serve on salad greens. Recipe makes 6 servings.

Italian Green Bean Salad

$^3/_4$ cup oil
$^1/_2$ cup vinegar
$^1/_2$ cup spaghetti sauce
2 16-ounce cans cut green beans, drained
3 cups shredded lettuce
6 slices bacon, diced and fried crisp

Combine the oil, vinegar, and spaghetti sauce. Add the green beans and chill. Just before serving, top with the lettuce and the crisp bacon.

Fiesta Melon Salad

    Cored-out melon halves
1 fresh pineapple, cut into small chunks
1 pint of fresh strawberries, hulled
1 bunch of romaine lettuce, cut into small
    pieces
3 oranges, peeled and sectioned
1 cup mayonnaise
1 cup honey

Divide one large Crenshaw melon in half (a honeydew or other melon may be used). Scoop out the centers and fill the cavities of the melons with the salad mixture tossed together.

Cranberry Dream Salad

1   cup heavy cream, whipped
1   cup crushed pineapple, drained
1   16-ounce can whole cranberry sauce,
      broken
2   tablespoons mayonnaise
2   tablespoons sugar
2   3-ounce packages cream cheese, quartered
3/4   cup walnuts

Combine whipped cream and pineapple in large mixing bowl. Blend cranberry sauce in blender until smooth. Add mayonnaise, sugar and cream cheese, blending well. Add walnuts and continue blending until chopped. Fold cranberry mixture into whipped cream mixture. Pour into shallow pan or tray and freeze. To serve, let stand at room temperature 15 minutes. Turn out on lettuce and slice. Makes 8 to 10 servings.

Avocado Potato Salad

6   slices bacon, diced and fried crisp
2 1/2   cups potatoes, cooked, peeled and diced
2   hard-cooked eggs, chopped
1/2   onion, finely chopped
2   green onions, tops and bottoms chopped
1   tablespoon pimientos, drained and sliced
1   teaspoon Worcestershire powder
      Salt and pepper to taste
1/2   cup mayonnaise
2   tablespoons lime juice
2   avocados, peeled, seeded and cubed

In a bowl, combine the crisp bacon, potatoes, eggs, onions, pimientos, Worcestershire powder and salt and pepper to taste. Toss the mixture and chill, covered, for 1 hour. Combine the mayonnaise and lime juice. Fold the dressing into the potato mixture and gently mix until well blended. Add the avocados.

Crunchy Tuna Salad

1/4   cup mayonnaise
2   tablespoons diced sweet pickle
1   tablespoon pickle juice
1   cup canned tuna or salmon, cooked or
      canned chicken or turkey
1/2   cup sliced celery
1/2   cup chilled cooked or canned peas
1   cup coarsely crushed corn or potato chips

Toss together mayonnaise, sweet pickle, pickle juice, celery, and peas, and your choice of tuna, salmon, chicken, or turkey. Add corn or potato chips. Serve at once on salad greens. Serves 4.

David Wade's Hot German Potato Salad

6   large baking-size potatoes cooked and
      peeled
1/2   pound bacon
2   white onions, finely chopped
1   cup beef consommé
1/4   cup sugar
1   tablespoon salt
2   teaspoons garlic powder
1   teaspoon nutmeg
1   tablespoon white pepper
1/2   cup salad oil
2/3   cup white vinegar

Scallop potatoes while hot and place in a large skillet. Fry bacon until crisp and add to potatoes, including bacon fat from the pan. Thoroughly blend in all other ingredients. Place skillet uncovered, over low heat. Cook slowly, stirring occasionally, until extraneous liquid has evaporated and mixture is heated through. Serves 6.

Restaurant Cole Slaw

4   cups cabbage, shredded
1/2   cup green bell pepper, chopped
1/4   cup green onions, finely chopped
1   cup carrots, shredded
2   teaspoons celery seed

DRESSING:

2/3   cup sour cream
2/3   cup mayonnaise
2   teaspoons lemon juice
2   teaspoons vinegar
      Dash of Tabasco
2   teaspoons prepared horseradish
      Salt to taste
1/4   teaspoon white pepper

Combine cabbage, green bell pepper, green onions, carrots and celery seed.

To make dressing, the cream may or may not be whipped, although whipping gives a fluffier texture. Combine mayonnaise and other ingredients and stir in cream. Just before serving, combine both mixtures, mixing lightly but well. Serve immediately. Six servings.

Most Requested Recipes

From The Print Media

This section is devoted to the reproduction of a selection of David Wade's weekly syndicated newspaper column, "Dining With David Wade." Many readers across America have requested that these columns be placed in book form. Mr. Wade, through the years, has championed the idea that food preparation is one of the most romantic endeavors known to man. The color and historical background that embraces each famous recipe is in itself worthy of editorial space.

ANGEL CORN

Have you ever stopped to think that you might not be here today if it were not for the American Indians' knowledge of growing corn? Have you stopped to think that America might not be a great country today, or a country at all, except for the Indians' willingness to share, in friendliness, knowledge of growing this wondrous new food — corn?

We have always heard that wheat is the staff of life, but to those early Americans, corn was the staff of life. At Jamestown, Virginia, Captain John Smith traded for corn with the Indians to keep the settlement from starving to death. At Plymouth, the pilgrims had exhausted every food staple they had, when desperately hunting in the wilderness they came upon corn cached in bushels and pots in the woods. (The Indians were shrewd enough to know that there would be periods of feast and famine, and like Joseph of the Old Testament, prepared for the worst by finding ways to store the plenty of other years in safe places while they migrated to other areas in search of game.)

Later, as the westward march began, it was corn which sustained the pioneers, and the Indians who showed them how to grow it. There was no beef from Texas then, no dairy herds in Wisconsin, no bacon from Iowa to sustain them. All of the plenty came later. Today as we seem to sustain a major part of the world with our over-production of food, we pause to remember that it was not always so. In the beginning, we were on the receiving end of other men's generosities.

So Thanksgiving is really a time to serve corn, not turkey. It is doubtful that there were many turkeys around even that first year of good harvest, following the winter of near starvation. There may have been pumpkins, and squashes; maybe there was fish and apples and chestnuts. But there must have been corn. People do not so easily forget a food that has given them life.

Corn is still a very popular food with Americans, but mostly they like it either on or off the cob. If off the cob is his desire then corn usually appears at the table in only three other forms: plain, creamed, or corn bread.

Let's do a little different something with corn this Thanksgiving as we observe the ritual of our ancestors' survival in this great new land, and appropriately, let's call it Angel Corn.

Here are the ingredients you will need:

Angel Corn

2	cups cooked corn, cut from the cob
1	cup heavy cream
3	tablespoons melted butter
3	beaten eggs
3	egg whites beaten stiff
	Dash of nutmeg
	Salt and pepper to taste
4	tablespoons grated Swiss cheese

Blend corn, heavy cream, nutmeg, salt and pepper to your own particular taste, and beaten eggs. Fold in egg whites and turn into buttered baking dish. Top with grated Swiss cheese. Place into preheated oven at 300 degrees and bake for 30 minutes. Increase oven to 375 degrees and brown the top of the Angel Corn for about 10 minutes. Recipe will serve 4.

AVOCADO AND CHEESE STUFFED CELERY

Celery was known for centuries only as a medicine. Its taste was bitter. In the seventeenth century, some unknown gardener in Italy or southern France, who set a great store by celery as a cure-all, transplanted wild celery (or "smallage") to a choice garden spot where the soil was deep, rich and moist. To his amazement the ribs and leaves from these plants had a pleasing taste. The flavor was so pleasing, in fact, that this gardener's family began munching ribs of the fragrant plants.

Celery is one of the most recently developed of all the world's popular vegetables. In the early seventeenth century still a medicine; in the twentieth, one of America's most popular vegetables, so highly esteemed that it takes an annual total of 1.5 billion pounds to satisfy our appetite.

Celery growing is tricky. The soil must be of medium texture, constantly moist, neither acid nor alkaline. Temperature during its growing season must average somewhere in the sixties. It takes its good old time about growing, even at that, requiring some 125 days from seed to harvest.

A celery grower needs a great deal of equipment, most of all he needs a "mule train," a huge tractor-drawn packing shed which moves along the length of the rows at harvest time. The crew of about seventy-five people who work this "mule train" cut, trim, wash and grade stalks twenty-four rows at a time. Conveyor belts, like outspread arms, carry the cut stalks from each row to the machine, then to a truck being pulled by the machine.

As each truck is filled with boxed, graded celery, it is

sped to the nearby hydrocooler. Here it is traveled slowly through an ice-cold shower to remove field heat. Before it is packed for transportation to our food markets a blizzard of snow-ice is blown over the layers of celery crates. This is how our celery reaches us so fresh, crisp and sweet.

Celery growers point out that there is still a certain amount of confusion in some cookbooks which call for "stalk" of celery when they mean "ribs." A "stalk" or "bunch" is the whole plant. The "rib" is only a part of the stalk — the part we eat with such gusto and a sprinkling of salt.

There are hundreds of good dishes which require celery — appetizers, salads, soups, stews, sandwich fillings, stuffings, and many cooked vegetable dishes. Get into the habit of using the leaves, too, for they are good, healthful food.

Avocado and Cheese Stuffed Celery

$^1/_3$ **cup cream cheese**
$^1/_3$ **cup mashed avocado**
$^1/_4$ **teaspoon salt**
$^1/_2$ **teaspoon lime juice**
$^1/_{16}$ **teaspoon ground white pepper**
16   **three-inch celery lengths**
     Thin radish slices for garnish

Combine cream cheese, mashed avocado, salt, fresh lime juice and ground white pepper. Mix until smooth. Stuff 3-inch celery lengths with mixture and garnish with radish slices. Yields 16 pieces of celery.

BACON FLAVORED CORN CASSEROLE

It was peppery eighteenth-century Jonathan Swift who said "Whoever could make two ears of corn . . . grow upon a spot of ground where only one grew before, would deserve better of mankind, and do more essential service to his country, than the whole race of politicians put together."

He might have been talking about present-day Florida where some 10,769 refrigerator cars of sweet corn were shipped north last year compared with 744 cars twenty years ago. Florida grows more sweet corn than any other state. From the rich black soil of the Sunshine State comes corn-on-the-cob almost the entire year.

Actually, it has taken many men to double and redouble this supply of sweet corn. First credit goes to the plant breeders who succeeded in developing strains of corn which would thrive in southern fields; strains which can develop and mature despite the shorter days of winter,

which even come to sub-tropical areas.

It takes all the resources of big business, too, to rush sweet corn to market in best condition. Huge motorized packing sheds or "mule trains" as they are called, move down the long fields with crews of about seventy-five workers picking the tender corn, crating it then and there and speeding it to hydrocoolers where the temperature is immediately dropped from field heat to 40° F. This prompt cooling slows down enzyme action which would otherwise change sugar to starch.

Time and temperature are of the essence, too, on road and rail. The crates of corn, showered with snow ice, can be sped from a Florida field to a table full of hungry corn-eaters a thousand miles away in forty-eight hours. Florida sells its corn mostly to the eastern half of the country, while Texas and California corn is enjoyed in the west.

Corn has been a cultivated crop in the Western Hemisphere for at least 4,000 years. The first mention of corn in what is now the United States described it as growing in Florida. This was 1528. Ten years later, De Soto landed in Florida and found "maes" not only in that peninsula, but all along the route to the Mississippi River.

We will never know how much, if any, of this corn was what we would now call sweet corn, for the earliest written record of this delicacy was dated 1801. (It began to be listed in seed catalogues in 1828, but was still unnamed.) It is possible, however, that sweet corn originated among the high civilizations of the Andes and that they ate it as a green vegetable and used its sweet juices in a beverage called "chicha." Today Andean gardeners are likely to hide their planting of sweet corn right in the center of fields of non-sweet maize. This is to keep unwelcome visitors from helping themselves to the delicious corn.

As is obvious from all the new sweet corn varieties developed for Florida, corn is very easily hybridized. Corn historians single out Golden Bantam as the one most important ancestor of most of today's corn varieties. A sweet corn resembling Golden Bantam was grown a century ago, but wasn't called that until 1902.

I suggest this great corn recipe:

Bacon Flavored Corn Casserole

6	ears fresh Florida corn
$1/4$	cup chopped onion
$1/3$	cup diced green bell pepper
2	tablespoons bacon fat
6	strips crisp bacon
1	cup soft bread crumbs
1	cup milk
1	egg, beaten lightly
1	teaspoon salt
$1/8$	teaspoon ground black pepper
2	tablespoons butter or margarine

Remove corn kernels from cob (makes about 2 cups); set aside. Sauté onions and green bell pepper in bacon fat. Add corn and cook 3 to 4 minutes. Break bacon into small pieces and add along with $1/2$ cup of the bread crumbs, beaten egg, milk, salt and black pepper; mix well. Turn into a buttered 1-quart casserole. Sprinkle with remaining bread crumbs. Dot with butter. Bake in a preheated moderate oven (375 degrees) 20 minutes or until crumbs are deep brown. Yield 6 portions.

BAKED LAKE BASS

Cooks gifted with a flair for seasoning have always agreed that basil is one of the most delightful of culinary herbs.

Not so, however, the doctors and herbalists of ancient times. As medicine and magic, basil was a bone of contention. That may be mixing metaphors a bit, but these old-time medicine men disagreed violently on the curative values of basil. Nicholas Culpepper, in his seventeenth-century herbal, says, "This is the herb which all authors are together by the ears about, and rail at one another like lawyers." He agreed that it might be good for the "bite of venomous beasts," but beyond that, he didn't think much of it as a medicine.

On the other hand, John Gerard, who'd lived at the time of Shakespeare, loved the fragrant herb and wrote in his herbal, "A smell of Basil is good for the heart and head — cureth the infirmities of the heart, taketh away sorrowfulness which cometh of melancholic, and maketh a man merrie and glad."

When it came to basil as a symbol, people really dug in their heels. In Italy, it was — and still is — a symbol of love. (They call it Kiss-Me-Nicholas in some parts of Italy.) Any girl carrying a basil sprig is encouraging her beau to propose. In Romania, the same thing is true! If a young man reaches out his hand and takes the sprig of basil offered by a girl, he may as well consider himself engaged to her.

In Greece, on the other hand, basil has always been the symbol of hate. The word "basil" has two possible origins. One from the Greek for "royal" or "kinglike." The other from a tongue-twister, also Greek, meaning "lizard." In Greek mythology, this was a very special lizard. The basilisk (bass-uh-lisk) had but to look at or breathe on his victims to kill them! These two different word origins started all the argument among the men of the medical profession.

Basil is an herb of the mint family. There are some sixty varieties, but here in the United States, we like the sweet basil best. The shiny leaves are a sort of golden green and the entire surface of the leaf is spotted with tiny wells filled with this exquisitely fragrant oil. The fields in which basil grows have a heavenly scent, especially if someone brushes up against a basil bush. Or, for that matter, if the wind stirs the leaves. Once you've become familiar with the smell — and flavor — of basil, you'll find more and more exciting ways of using it.

Basil rivals oregano as a pizza herb. Use it in all other dishes which include tomatoes or cheese. Broiled tomato halves, for instance, are excellent and easy to prepare. Dab tomato halves with butter. Sprinkle with salt, pepper and grated Italian cheese. Then, as a finishing touch, scatter a little pinch of basil over each half and broil.

Next time you're preparing sautéed zucchini, add a little basil, about one teaspoonful for six servings, just minutes before the zucchini is done. Cucumbers are very good prepared the same way. Slice them about 1/4-inch thick and sauté three or four minutes. They're done so quickly you'd better put the basil on as they begin to cook.

I suggest that fishermen try this recipe:

Baked Lake Bass

1	pound bass
2	teaspoons salt
$1/2$	teaspoon ground black pepper
1	teaspoon basil leaves
1	teaspoon instant minced onion
$1/4$	cup olive or salad oil
$1/2$	cup fine dry bread crumbs

Place the cleaned bass in dish. Combine salt, black pepper, basil, instant minced onion and oil. Mix well and pour over bass. Marinate 2 hours. Place in a 8x8x2-inch baking dish. Pour the marinade over the fish. Sprinkle with the bread crumbs and bake in a preheated oven (400 degrees) for about 20 minutes. Serve at once. Yield 6 servings.

BARBECUE

President Lyndon Johnson was, no doubt, our most popular salesman of the meat and sauce wedding of flavors we call barbecue. Popular it has always been, but just perchance there breathed a man in the world who had not heard of this Western taste experience, he has now been informed via the communications media from the LBJ Ranch fiestas where the great, the near-great, and the soon-to-be-great have been most graciously entertained in true Western style.

Really, barbecue is not a food. It is a method of cooking meaning literally, "to roast from snout to tail." We don't often, if ever, have the opportunity to barbecue such a huge piece of meat today so we concentrate on the smaller cuts with great emphasis on the sauce. The grandfather of all barbecue sauces is chili. So it was in the beginning, at least, but we have sought out a great many inventions. Today, there are hundreds of variations of barbecue sauce; everyone has a favorite. This interest in sauce, possibly, is what caused the visitor from the East to remark that "out West they barbecue everything except ice cream."

Barbecuing was introduced to us by the early French explorers. Those Frenchmen lived off the game of the land, cooked and ate outdoors; there being nothing else for them to do in this unexplored, unsettled country of ours. This is probably why barbecue still brings to mind a picture of outdoor dining, and indeed it is very much suited for the great outdoors still.

The Frenchmen were looking for gold which they didn't find, and it is more likely that the really great discovery was the barbecue which Americans discovered from the French.

This recipe for country pork ribs can be cooked in your oven and served inside by the fire, or outside on the patio.

Begin by selecting the desired amount of country pork ribs and marinating them for thirty minutes in lemon juice.

Make the sauce as follows:

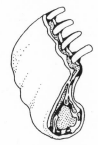 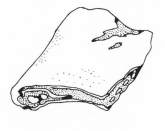

Country Pork Ribs

1	**15-ounce bottle catsup**
½	**cup white Karo syrup**
¼	**cup red wine vinegar**
2	**tablespoons liquid smoke**
2	**tablespoons A-1 sauce**
1	**tablespoon Worcestershire powder**
1	**teaspoon salt**
2	**teaspoons black pepper**
4	**drops Tabasco sauce**
1	**tablespoon dry powdered mustard**
2	**teaspoons garlic powder**

Blend all of these ingredients in saucepan and heat until mixture is hot. Pour over country pork ribs (about 20) which have been placed in a roaster. Bake ribs covered at 400 degrees for about 1 hour and 20 minutes, or until ribs are nice and tender. Remove lid and continue baking at 400 degrees for about 10 minutes, or until nicely browned. Turn ribs to other side and continue baking at 400 degrees until browned again.

BEEF STROGANOFF

Preparation of food enjoys first place as America's number one avocation. Movie stars, politicians, teenagers, and business executives have nudged the chef over and joined the ranks with some culinary claim to fame of their own.

When appreciation of fine food reaches such a peak of general interest we are no longer just eating. We are dining. Today, America is dining in a large and fancy way. Last year sales of gourmet foods totaled more than $3.1 billion. Supermarkets now have fancy food sections, department stores have joined the parade and are featuring such items as rattlesnake meat from Florida, grasshoppers (fried, of course) from Japan, truffles and snails from France, caviar from the Balkans, and almost everything which is considered an eatable delicacy in other parts of the world.

We are dining in more exclusive, more specialized restaurants, and dining out in ever increasing numbers, too. Tastes are favoring the international cuisines, emphasizing traditional Old World foods. The art of turning ordinary groceries into haute cuisine is the goal of every true gourmet. Mark Twain once said of writing, "All the words are in the dictionary." We might paraphrase his statement and, applying it to cooking, say that, "All the ingredients are in the supermarket." Ah, but there's the catch. How shall we put them together? We must have a plan, a blueprint, a recipe.

Here's my interpretation, my blueprint, for a traditional Old World favorite: beef stroganoff. A recipe which will haunt your hungry moments for weeks to come.

Beef Stroganoff

2	**pounds lean beef cubes, diced into 1-inch squares**
1/2	**pound butter**
1	**onion, diced**
1	**cup mushrooms**
	Dash Tabasco
1	**tablespoon Worcestershire powder**
1/2	**bell pepper, diced**
1	**clove garlic, diced**
1	**tablespoon garlic salt**
1	**cup sour cream**
1	**cup heavy cream**
2	**tablespoons wine vinegar**
2	**tablespoons flour**
	Rice
	Beef consommé
	Water

Sauté beef cubes in butter until brown. After meat begins to brown, add onions, mushrooms, Tabasco, Worcestershire powder, bell pepper, garlic and garlic salt. When these ingredients begin to soften, add sour cream, heavy cream and wine vinegar. Now add the flour. Let this mixture continue to simmer for 1 hour or until meat cubes are completely tender. Serve beef stroganoff over rice which has been boiled in one part beef consommé and one part water until golden brown. Garnish. Recipe serves 4.

BOMBAY TURKEY IN CLAY

It's just as the nursery rhyme has it,

> "Peas-porridge hot, peas-porridge cold;
> Peas-porridge in the pot, nine days old.
> Some like it hot; some like it cold;
> Some like it in the pot nine days old."

In countries near the equator they tend to serve foods very pungently spiced. People who have grown up in India, Brazil or Indonesia offer several explanations for this preference: "The spices which go into the making of a good curry grow best in tropical heat. People usually eat what grows near at hand — we've loved good, nippy spicing since childhood."

A native of India tells me, "Our foods just wouldn't taste right without plenty of spice. Eating hot dishes promotes perspiration which helps keep the body cool."

Here in the United States we eat curries and such bravely spiced foods because they are delicious. The curry powder ground and blended in this country is richly aromatic, but mild compared with curry powders packed for India and the Far East.

It's amazing to know that curry powder is no Johnny-come-lately to the American spice shelf. Actually, curry powder has been sold for generations. In a rare old cookbook printed in Philadelphia in 1792, I found a recipe for "Curry of Chicken" which directs, "Get a bottle of curry powder. Strew it over the chicken when frying. If it is not seasoned highly enough, put in a little cayenne." Other cookbooks more than a century old add more proof that this intriguing bouquet has been known for a very long time.

They were eating curries in India almost 1,500 years ago. Curries are mentioned in an Indian tale wherein one of the characters ate "rice dressed in butter, with its full accompaniment of curries." Naturally these early curries wouldn't have been seasoned with curry powder such as we know. In India, even today, the housewife generally grinds or bruises whole spices as they are needed for the day's meals.

Even more important: Those ancient curries would have been made without red peppers. "Chilies," the Indians call these pungent peppers and add them in generous numbers. These originated in the Western Hemisphere and would not have reached India until America was discovered a thousand years later. Today, of course, any curry dish without the snap of red peppers would be unthinkable!

All curry powders are a rich blend of spices, although almost all formulas differ somewhat (some are even well-kept family secrets in India). Cumin, coriander, fenugreek, turmeric, and red pepper are used in varying amounts. In addition, manufacturers may use one or more spices such as cinnamon, allspice, cardamom, cloves, fennel, ginger, yellow mustard, mace, and black or white pepper.

Curry powder is the handiest kind of seasoning for many American standbys. It gives exciting flavor to meats, fish, fowl, vegetables, salad dressings, and soups. This doesn't mean you must try for an Indian-type curried dish. Rather you "appropriate" the national spice of India into your Yankee kitchen and recipe, using just enough to enhance the natural flavors of the food.

For instance, add a teaspoon of curry powder to a can of green pea soup. Or, to a can of cream of mushroom soup and a 7-ounce can of tuna fish to be served over toast or in patty cases. For delicious flavor, cook a cup of rice in 2 cups chicken stock and season with 2 teaspoons curry powder and a tablespoon of instant minced onion. Add a teaspoon of curry powder to the mayonnaise for an egg, seafood, or potato salad.

The following recipe is one of the most exciting recipes I have found for curry. It is delightful at any season of the year and extremely compatible for dinner parties since it has an ostentatious nature.

Bombay Turkey in Clay

Roasting turkey
Salt and pepper
Curry powder
Salad oil
2 tablespoons minced prepared onion
12 pounds gray moist pottery clay
(approximately)
Worcestershire powder

Select an average-sized roasting turkey and season the cavity and outside with salt, pepper, curry powder and Worcestershire powder; rub the surface lightly with salad oil. Into the cavity place the minced prepared onion. Wrap the turkey securely in foil, placing the shiny surface toward the turkey. Using approximately 12 pounds of gray moist pottery clay, completely cover the turkey that has been wrapped in foil with a 1/4-inch layer of the clay.

Be sure that the bird is completely sealed, leaving no open places, and place — encased in the clay — into an open roasting pan. (Do not cover the roasting pan with a lid.) Place pan into a preheated oven at 400 degrees and cook about 12 to 14 minutes per pound. When roasting time is completed, break the clay away and remove the turkey from the foil.

BOUILLABAISSE

It takes only the sketchiest knowledge of French to realize that most of the culinary terms of the Western World are of that language. The words *cuisine, chef, sauté, souffle, fricassee* and *parfait* just start this list.

Unless we have eaten our way across France, we are familiar only with the haute cuisine as served in big hotels and restaurants all over the world. But there's great fun in discovering that most Frenchmen eat the *cuisine de famille,* home cooking — "like mama cooks." And then there is *cuisine du paysan* or peasant cooking to be found in rural areas.

French cooking differs according to regions. Seasonings can give us a clue in the most flavorful sort of way. Samples of provincial cooking can be found in the many big and little restaurants of Paris, so let's note the spicing and seasoning techniques of some typical provinces.

Alsace-Lorraine is famous for marvelous sausages, spiced as they are across the Rhine in Germany. Sauer-kraut is cooked with onion, clove and an herb bunch. Cheese is studded with anise, fennel or caraway seeds.

Burgundy demands lusty, well-spiced sauces and in this province we find Dijon, world-famous for mustards and fancy gingerbreads. Provence, on the Mediterranean, means Marsaille and bouillabaisse, that omnium-gatherum of seafood and spices. Provence cooks with a wide variety of highly aromatic herbs: thyme, sage, bay leaf, tarragon. Garlic has been called "the truffle of Provence." In Nice, at the eastern border of Provence, cooks swap recipes with neighboring Italians.

Westward from Provence lies the province of Languedoc. One of its most interesting cities is Montpellier, a seaport which was very active in the spice trading in the Middle Ages. The name of the city is significant, a simplified name which once meant "Mount of the Spice Merchants." As might be expected, foods are bravely seasoned in this region.

Southwestern France borders on Spain, so in Roussillon we find a generous use of garlic, saffron and red pepper, seasoning resembling that of Spanish dishes.

Bordeaux, which lies along the Atlantic is one more proof of the saying that, in France, the best cooking is to be found in the best wine country. Thyme, bay leaf, parsley, rosemary, nutmeg and cloves are among their pet aromatics, along with ever-present wine.

Normandy, on the English Channel, is cream and apple country, with a wide use of cider and apple brandy. In Triple a la Mode de Caen the famous bouquet garni is used, in this case combining thyme, tarragon, celery, parsley and bay leaf.

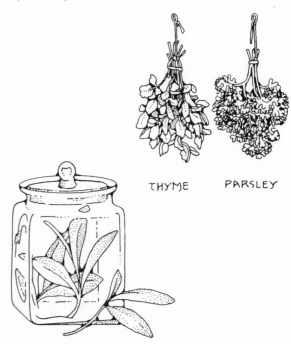

THYME   PARSLEY

Bouillabaisse

$^{1}/_{4}$ cup olive oil
1   rib celery, chopped
1   medium onion, chopped
1   clove garlic, finely chopped
1   leek, diced
$^{1}/_{2}$ teaspoon thyme
$^{1}/_{2}$ bay leaf
2   cups crushed tomatoes
1   cup bottled clam juice
1   cup dry white wine
$^{1}/_{4}$ fennel, chopped, or 1/2 teaspoon crushed
        fennel seeds
      Pinch of saffron
2   tablespoons chopped parsley
1   small lobster, cut into pieces
12   mussels, well scrubbed and debearded
12   raw shrimp, shelled and deveined
12   scallops
1   pound red snapper or cod, cut into
        serving pieces

In a large kettle heat the oil, add the celery, onion, garlic, leek, thyme and bay leaf and cook 5 minutes. Remove bay leaf and add the tomatoes, clam juice, wine, fennel, saffron and parsley and simmer 15 minutes. Add the seafood and cook 15 minutes longer. Yield 6 servings.

BRUSSEL SPROUTS A LA GRACIE ALLEN

My television program, "The Gourmet," now seen in numerous cities across the country, had its beginning in Hollywood. Each week following the telecast I would accompany the director and other members of the crew in a light repast at the famous Hollywood Brown Derby Restaurant. We usually discussed our glaring mistakes and enjoyed this period as a stage to unwind from the terrible tension. I wouldn't really say that I was afraid of television in those days, I was terrified!

The timing of our little get-together each week at the Derby paralleled the visit of that wonderful lady of show business, the late Gracie Allen. Gracie, along with her husband, George Burns, frequented the Derby just prior to the production of their celebrated network television show. I noticed that Miss Allen never ordered from the menu and always was served the same interesting entremets. She chose to dine lightly before an evening at the studio. Finally, I prevailed upon the captain of service at the Derby to effect the recipe for me and the very first taste haunted my hungry moments for weeks to come. Obviously, I added this superb recipe to my repertoire of

fine recipes and have savored and enjoyed it through the years.

I would like to share this delight with you, and this is the blueprint:

Brussel Sprouts with Imperial Sauce

$1^{1}/_{2}$ pounds fresh brussel sprouts
       Water
       Salt
2   cups heavy cream
1   cup Parmesan cheese
       White pepper

Peel away the exterior surface leaves of the brussel sprouts. Place the sprouts into boiling water and add just a hint of salt. Simmer the brussel sprouts slowly until barely tender. Be careful not to overcook the vegetable. Drain the water from the brussel sprouts and place on a heated serving dish. Place the heavy cream into a double boiler and add the Parmesan cheese. Heat slowly until the cheese has melted. Dash into the sauce a suspicion of white pepper. Top the brussel sprouts with the sauce and serve hot. Recipes serves 4.

ORIGINAL CAESAR SALAD

In a little restaurant in Tijuana, Mexico, the Cardini family, owners and operators, combined a love of fine food with an atmosphere of gourmet wisdom. Here, they created a salad which was to become a hallmark among epicurean recipes. They named it Caesar after the name of their food establishment — Caesar's Restaurant.

The Cardini family has since moved on to Mexico City where they have a fine restaurant, and the Caesar Salad has moved on and up, too. Volumes have been written by various restaurants seeking credit for the origination of the Salad Caesar. But, really, they have only appreciated and appropriated it to the delight of both the Cardinis and gourmets everywhere.

Young Alex Cardini is a good friend of mine. He still champions the colors for his famous food family in Mexico City. Working with him, I have learned to appreciate the simplicity of a good salad, but like many simple things there is much to know and learn, and unlearn, before pure simplicity is turned into great salad making.

First, due attention must be paid to the green groceries which make up a salad. They should be carefully selected, gently washed and rinsed, and even more carefully torn apart. Never cut salad greens. A French salad basket is perfect for drying greens, but a good substitute is a clean, dry towel — place greens inside and gently swing or shake dry without touching them. (When bruised, salad greens deteriorate rapidly, losing their fresh, crispy flavor.) Now place greens into the refrigerator to cool and crisp.

Alex Cardini's cardinal rule for salad making is, "A salad should never be overdone." Always remember this, too: the dressing is secondary to the green leaves. Yes, I know it's the dressing which provides the delicious taste you love. Nevertheless, a dressing should be used sparingly, tossed with the greens — again very gently — to coat all the salad bowl contents, and never used to excess.

Perhaps you have already discovered one or more reasons why your salads do not measure up to those of a fine restaurant. Simple? Yes. But if these rules are abandoned your salads will be taste-starved, chopped-up nothings instead of creative green springtime itself. Try this original recipe for Caesar Salad and note the difference. And *viva la différence!*

Original Caesar Salad

You will need a wooden salad bowl which has been oiled. This wooden, oiled bowl should never be washed with soap; only rinsed and dried.

> **Romaine leaves, whole**
> **Salt**
> **Freshly ground black pepper**
> **Olive oil**
> **Parmesan cheese**
> **Croutons**
> **Garlic**
> **Anchovy paste**
> **Eggs**
> **Worcestershire powder**
> **Lime juice**

Into the wooden bowl place whole romaine leaves (8 per serving). Sprinkle with salt, and freshly ground black pepper to taste. Coat with olive oil (4 ounces per serving). Sprinkle Parmesan cheese ($2^{1}/_{2}$ tablespoons per serving) over the romaine. Add croutons that have been seasoned with garlic and anchovy paste (4 per person) over greens and toss lightly. Break coddled egg (coddled 1 minute, using 1 per person) onto greens and toss again lightly. Always toss in the same direction. Sprinkle on Worcestershire powder and lime juice and again toss lightly.

CANTON CHOW MEIN

My advice to aficionados of the kitchen is to make an imaginative trip around the world and select a food specialty from another country. Make that specialty your own, and you will be traveling the surest route I know to becoming "known" as an exceptional cook and an exciting host or hostess. In these fast-paced days few have time to master many international favorites, but each can major in one.

If you select Chinese cuisine you won't be disappointed. It is easy to learn, different, economical and really quite fascinating to execute. Chinese cookery is an education in an ancient and venerable culture, too.

Many people think there is little difference in Chinese, Japanese, and Polynesian foods, because, as one man said to me, "the food is all chopped up and mixed together." Well, the sage Confucius, himself, would rise up and call that man a culinary oaf. Not only are the Chinese the originators of all forms of oriental cuisine, but they prepare food with great respect, tender care, and think long and lovingly as to proper flavoring and spices, exact cooking times, and serve each dish with understandable pride. Far from being "chopped up and mixed together," their recipes are the ultimate in balance and harmony.

First, we should establish that there is no broad classification labeled "Chinese" either. There are eight separate and distinct provincial systems that constitute Chinese cuisine, such as Shanghai, Peking, and Cantonese. Cantonese is most popular with Westerners.

"The longest journey begins with the first step," said the aforementioned Confucius, so take the first step into the world of Chinese cooking with Canton Chow Mein.

Canton Chow Mein

¹/₂ **pound chopped veal**
¹/₂ **pound chopped pork**
¹/₂ **pound chopped beef**
4   **tablespoons fat**
6   **tablespoons soy sauce**
1   **cup water**
1   **cup diced celery**
1   **onion, finely diced**
1   **teaspoon MSG powder**
1   **tablespoon Worcestershire powder**
     Salt and pepper to taste
2   **tablespoons cornstarch**
1   **10-ounce can water chestnuts**
1   **large can bean sprouts, drained (about 2**
       cups)
1   **small can mushrooms**
     Cooked rice or noodles

Brown all meats in the hot fat in a large skillet; then add soy sauce, water, celery, onion, MSG powder, Worcestershire powder, and salt and pepper. Simmer for 1¹/₂ hours. Blend in cornstarch, water chestnuts, bean sprouts, and mushrooms; heat through. Serve over cooked rice or noodles. Serves 6.

CARIBBEAN BLACK BOTTOM PIE

Columbus discovered Puerto Rico in 1493, and Americans have been rediscovering it ever since that time. The exotic islands of the Caribbean are many and Puerto Rico ranks very high on the top ten. The colorful isle is only 100 miles long and about thirty-five miles wide, but 'tis enough. Shining beaches and sunny days, Puerto Rico is a panorama of island life at its best. Leisurely you have time to sun, to shop, to sit, to enjoy and of course, to dine.

Greater San Juan, where you will no doubt be stationed, is a large city, but Puertoriquenos, translated "out of San Juan" or "out on the island," offers a variety of scenes which, if you are not too occupied with sunning, shopping, sitting, enjoying and dining, certainly compels you to go adventuring. Durado Beach, for instance, is about twenty-three miles to the west of San Juan. The highway number is Route 2. Here there is a Hilton and you can count on a comida puertoriquena — this is a full-course Puerto Rican dinner.

Beginning here at Durado Beach or Las Croabas, or Ponce, you can island hop by launch or plane, or you can restaurant hop (an activity which has more appeal to gourmets) to your heart's content. During such restau-

rant hopping, I obtained one of the best pie recipes in the entire world. It is a black bottom pie, and I have never tasted another pie of the superb enchantment this recipe affords. It explodes in tastemosphere. I recommend it highly for entertaining. It cannot fail to impress your guests. Make extra copies of this recipe. They will be asking you for it.

Caribbean Black Bottom Pie

1   **10-inch baked pastry shell**
1   **envelope (1 tablespoon) unflavored**
       gelatin
¹/₂ **cup cold water**
¹/₂ **cup sugar**
2   **tablespoons cornstarch**
1³/₄ **cups milk**
4   **beaten egg yolks**
1¹/₂ **1-ounce squares unsweetened chocolate,**
       melted
1   **teaspoon vanilla**
4   **egg whites**
¹/₄ **teaspoon cream of tartar**
¹/₂ **cup sugar**
2   **teaspoons rum extract**
1   **cup heavy cream, whipped**
¹/₂ **1-ounce square unsweetened chocolate,**
       grated

Soften gelatin in cold water. In a saucepan combine sugar and cornstarch. Add milk, stirring until all the milk has been added. Cook over very low heat until mixture thickens. Stir constantly. Stir small amount of hot mixture into the beaten egg yolks. Gradually add egg mixture to remaining hot mixture. Continue cooking 3 minutes. Remove from heat. To 1 cup custard, add melted unsweetened chocolate and vanilla. Mix well and cool. Pour into a 10-inch baked pastry shell and chill in refrigerator.

Dissolve softened gelatin in remaining custard. Cool until mixture begins to thicken.

Beat egg whites and cream of tartar until foamy. Gradually add sugar, beating mixture until it is stiff. Now fold egg whites into cooled custard. Add rum extract.

As soon as chocolate custard has set, pour in rum custard mixture. Chill until firm. Top with whipped cream. Sprinkle with unsweetened grated chocolate.

CARPETBAG STEAKS

There are only eight basic recipes in the entire world. In view of this, it is a thought of astronomical and gastronomical proportions when you consider what the people of the world have invented, created, and produced with only eight recipes. To be exact, the eight recipes are actually eight different methods of cooking: broiling, roasting, stewing, baking, braising, sautéing, steaming and frying.

With this as a point of departure, the various nations have struck out on their own and given us a wonderful international world of food. From Asia to South America, from North America to Europe, from the tropical islands to the frozen North, there exists an array of gourmeting designed to overwhelm any appetite.

Food is a topic of interest to everyone. I cannot recall meeting a person who was not, at least to some extent, interested in food. I shall never forget an experience I had several years ago when I was working on a project at the United Nations. I was interviewing representatives of several governments on the African Trusteeship Council. The outcome of these meetings, which were then in progress, was of international importance. One of the key figures I wanted to interview was Sir Andrew Cowan of the United Kingdom.

I called for an appointment, went to his hotel suite, and told Sir Andrew the information I wanted to record. He replied, "Mr. Wade, Her Majesty's Government has published a full report on this and it is on display in the lobby of the United Nations Building. There is nothing I can add to Her Majesty's stated views."

Abruptly, apparently, the interview was over before it had begun. So it would not be a total loss, I asked if he was possibly familiar with the recipe for Carpetbag Steaks which I had enjoyed at his club in London. His eyes lit up like a neon sign. He was obviously pleased. "So you've had Carpetbag Steaks . . . and at my club?" I told him of my interest in food, and about my television show, "The Gourmet," and that I would like to have the recipe.

"Quite," he assured me. "I know that recipe well. Glad to give it to you." Whereupon he not only dictated the recipe but offered many interesting facts about its creation, and the difference in various chefs' versions of it in England. We talked at some length about food.

Then he said, "Now, David, what was that interview you wanted?" I hooked up the recorder and off he went with a brilliant thirty-minute discussion about the African Trusteeship.

So the language of food is a language we all speak, a subject in which we are all interested. Of all the subjects which have tempted scholars, writers, actors, businessmen, artists, as well as gourmets, none have been more prolific from their pens than the subject of food. Some take the view of philosophy, some of taste, others of economy, still others of cooking, but every man is an expert on food, because he knows what he likes, and he is bound to like something.

I want to give you that recipe for Carpetbag Steaks. See how you like Sir Andrew's club favorite.

Carpetbag Steaks

4	eye-of-round steaks about 1½ inches thick
	Salt and pepper to taste
	Paprika
½	pint oysters
2	cups sherry
¼	pound butter

Cut pockets into each of the steaks. Marinate oysters in 1 cup of sherry for 1 hour. Place 2 or 3 oysters into each steak with a little sherry. Place butter into a large skillet and melt. Add 1 cup of sherry to butter. Place the steaks into wine-butter sauce and steam on each side for 1 minute. Remove steaks from skillet and salt and pepper to taste. Sprinkle paprika on steaks and place in preheated broiler. Broil desired amount of time, then baste with wine and butter sauce.

CHICKEN DIVAN

One of the questions asked me most often is "what is the single most important talent for a cook to have?" The first time I answered impetuously, but I've given a lot of thought to the question since and have not changed my mind. The art of saucery will do more for a cook's reputation than any other one thing.

Learn to make a good basic brown sauce and a good basic white sauce. Get acquainted with their versatility and their almost infinite variations, and you'll never serve a monotonous meal again; even when the end of the money comes before the end of the month or you are snowed in with a shelf full of nothing but tuna fish.

I think the greatest thing about sauces is that they are actually fun. The basic sauces are so simple and easy to make, and then it is only a short step to something absolutely exotic — to a finishing touch that makes the difference between eating and dining.

Every country has its own sauces, but it is to France that we owe a large debt of gratitude. At the wonderful restaurants of Paris, the most famous in all the world, the saucier is second in rank only to the head chef. The success of many of the most elaborate dishes in French cuisine depend on his skill, to say nothing of the success of the restaurant.

The saucier's day begins with the making of the "basic" or "mother" sauces. From these he goes on a veritable whirl of creativity. He adds onion to Bechamel (a basic white sauce) for Sauce Soubise, one of the most versatile of sauces which is good with lamb, veal, vegetables and poultry. Mornay is white sauce with grated cheese, usually Gruyere or Parmesan, or a combination. Bordeaux wine added to Sauce Espagnole (basic brown sauce) and the saucier has Bordelaise. Chasseur, great with veal, is Espagnole with tomatoes, garlic and herbs. Madeira wine and truffles added to Espagnole produce Periqueux, which adds the gourmet flair to eggs, veal and ham as well as the elegant filet of beef. The flavorsome Sauce Robert, so popular with both pork and beef, is simply Sauce Espagnole with a touch of mustard.

One of the first things you should learn to make is Sauce Espagnole. You will probably find a number of recipes in your basic cookbooks. The very best, I believe, starts with a good strong beef stock. It takes a little planning but very little time, and it is certainly worthwhile. Not the least of its virtues are the wonderful memories it will recall of the redolent soup pot bubbling on the back of Grandma's stove. She added cracked bones and bits of meat (about 1/3 bones to 2/3 meat), vegetables and seasonings and simmered for hours (maybe even days!). After straining and removing the fat, she had a base par excellence for soups and gravies as well as sauces.

Often a recipe will call for a roux, which, despite the elegant-sounding name, is simply a mixture of butter and flour for thickening. There are white rouxs and blond and brown. Each has a distinctive flavor and color achieved by the degree of browning of the flour.

Hollandaise Sauce is one of the most popular in our country and one that many people find a little scary. There is no reason to avoid it. It is really quite simple to make. It does require you to keep a hawk's eye on the measuring and the cooking temperature, but just follow the instructions as I have outlined them in the recipe and you should have no trouble at all.

Chicken Divan

1	**5-pound stewing chicken**
5	**cups water**
2	**teaspoons salt**
1	**large bunch broccoli**
1	**cup grated Parmesan cheese**
2	**cups White Sauce**
$^1/_2$	**cup Hollandaise Sauce**
$^1/_2$	**cup heavy cream, whipped**
3	**tablespoons sherry**
1	**teaspoon Worcestershire powder**

Place the chicken on a rack in a large kettle. Add about 5 cups boiling water and the salt. Bring to a boil, lower heat, cover and simmer until tender, about 3 hours. Cool the chicken in the broth.

When the chicken has cooled, remove the skin and slice the breast and leg meat. Reserve the remainder of the chicken and the broth for another purpose.

Cook the broccoli in salted water until tender, drain and arrange on a deep heatproof serving platter. Sprinkle lightly with some of the cheese. Arrange the sliced chicken meat on the broccoli.

Combine the White Sauce with the Hollandaise Sauce. Add the whipped cream, sherry and Worcestershire powder. Pour the sauce over the chicken and broccoli and sprinkle with the remaining cheese.

Place about 5 inches below high heat in a preheated broiler and broil until browned and bubbly.

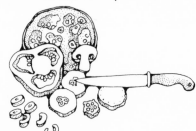

WHITE SAUCE

$^1/_2$	**cup butter**
3	**tablespoons flour**
3	**cups milk**
$^1/_2$	**teaspoon nutmeg**

Melt the butter in a saucepan. Add the flour and stir with a wire whisk until blended. Bring the milk to a boil and add all at once to the butter-flour mixture, stirring vigorously with the whisk until the sauce is thickened and smooth. Stir in the nutmeg. Keep hot.

HOLLANDAISE SAUCE

3	**egg yolks**
1	**tablespoon cold water**
$^1/_2$	**cup soft butter**
$^1/_4$	**teaspoon salt**
$^1/_2$	**teaspoon lemon juice, or to taste**

Combine the egg yolks and water in the top of a double boiler and beat with a wire whisk over hot (not boiling) water until fluffy.

Add a few pats of butter to the mixture and beat continually until the butter has melted and the sauce starts to thicken. Care should be taken that the water in the bottom of the boiler never boils. Continue adding the butter bit by bit, stirring constantly.

Add the salt and the lemon juice. If a lighter texture is desired, beat in a tablespoon of hot water.

CHICKEN ENCHILADAS

Climb aboard our flight into the land below the Rio Grande. We'll go adventuring and seeking the pleasures of the table of Old Mexico.

We are bid welcome with a hearty *¡bienvenido!* as we board. One brief stop at San Antonio, the Air-Port-of-Entry for Mexico, and we are winging southward toward Mexico City.

Night time now. As we approach, the spectacular lights of the National Palace and the Cathedral of Mexico flicker a welcome too. The Palace of Montezuma once occupied that spot, later Cortes built himself a palace there, still later Maximilian redesigned it. Ah, here is history, down in Mexico City, and you are hungry for some good authentic Mexican food.

Occupying Mexico on your own two feet now, you go through customs, get comfortably settled in your hotel, and inquire about the dining room. You scan the menu. Nothing there that you recognize as a favorite Mexican food. The waiter politely refers the señor to *chicken molé* listed on the menu — the national dish of Mexico. You nod affirmatively, and the molé is served. It is good, very good, but not exactly what you were expecting. Oh, well, *mañana, mañana.*

Mañana comes, and with it sightseeing. Popocatépetl, the National Palace, the Cathedral, shopping on the famous Paseo de la Reforma (Reforma Boulevard — the Champs Elysees of Mexico City), where you dine on *paella valenciana,* a popular dish in Mexico, but it comes from Spain (Spanish rice with pork and shrimp), then in the evening you will be entertained by Mexican guitars which set a fiesta mood, and flamenco singers and dancers. Here, along with your *tequila cocteles* you'll be served, oh, perhaps, *carnitas* (little meat pieces, baked), or *empanaditas* (tiny Mexican pastry turnovers), or with your café you may be served *quemada* (burnt sugar candy), or *bizcochitos con nueces* (little nut cookies).

You ask señor guide where you can get some really authentic Mexican food. He knows the very place. Their specialty is *pescado relleno* (large fish stuffed with small shellfish and seasoned with butter, lemon, and capers). Good? Couldn't be better! Delicious! But about that really authentic Mexican food — ? As you drift dreamily off to sleep you wonder if perhaps — *mañana*?

Ai, Chihuahua, amigo, you are forever doomed to disappointment. You have been enjoying the typical cuisine of Old Mexico. The kind of Mexican food you are thinking of you left in your own backyard — in the United States. You will find nothing like that in Mexico.

The recipe I am chronicling for you now is a genuine blend of native tortillas and chili sauce, with the refinements of a sauce, which a Spanish-speaking French chef gave to me on one of my food adventures to Mexico.

Chicken Enchiladas Capistrano

	Pancake recipe or mix
2	**8-ounce cans tomato sauce**
1	**medium onion, minced fine**
1	**cup Cheddar cheese, grated**
5	**drops Tabasco**
$1/2$	**teaspoon garlic salt**
$1/2$	**teaspoon black pepper**
$1/2$	**teaspoon salt**
$1/4$	**teaspoon chili powder**
2	**cups chopped cooked chicken**
1	**cup cooked, drained red kidney beans, sieved**

Using favorite pancake recipe or mix, make 6 very thin, large pancakes. Into a saucepan, place tomato sauce, onion, and cheese. Heat until cheese melts. Add 5 drops Tabasco, garlic salt, pepper, salt, and chili powder. Mix well. Then add the chicken, mixing thoroughly with sauce, and allow to heat through. Add red kidney beans that have been forced through a sieve. Mix thoroughly and continue heating. Lay each of the 6 pancakes out and top with chicken sauce. Roll the pancakes over and top with a little more sauce and grated cheese. Place rolled chicken enchiladas into a greased baking dish and heat in a 350-degree oven until cheese has begun to melt. Serve hot. Serves 6.

CHICKEN IMPERIAL

When the family arrives home in the evening they ask, "What's for dinner?" They are talking about the main dish, of course. When you dine in a fine restaurant you may enjoy all of the courses, but it is the entrée — actually what you ordered — that makes the meal a success or not. When you entertain you will be remembered for the main dish you serve. Even if the salad is delicious and the soup a thing to remember and the dessert quite glamorous, if the climactic part of the meal is not superb then your dinner lacks authority.

Avoid, by all means, the inclination to serve your guests a new dish which you have not done before. You should make very sure that your entrée is your *piece de résistance.* To do this you may have to have a few dress rehearsals. Perfection will be the result and give to your dinner rave reviews. No actor would go on stage for a part he had not rehearsed. They do their play, and your dinner is just as much a production, scene by scene, and over and over.

When your main dish is perfected, then take each one of the courses, scene by scene — the salad, the soup, the vegetables, the bread, the dessert, and do each one well. If necessary, improve and re-do. This is like an out-of-town tryout of a play. No producer would want to invite his friends, the public, or especially his enemies, the critics, to a drama with the possibility of a flop inherent in it.

For those rave reviews I mentioned earlier I can recommend Chicken Imperial. The first time you run through this recipe I believe you will agree with me that this is an entrée with that deliciously dramatic touch.

To prepare Chicken Imperial you must have the following items:

Chicken Imperial

2	cups sherry
12	pieces chicken (breasts, wishbone, thighs)
6	teaspoons salt
2½	cups Parmesan cheese
3	cloves garlic, crushed
1½	cups chopped, blanched almonds
2	teaspoons flaked parsley
6	cups bread crumbs
³/₈	teaspoon pepper
3	sticks melted butter

Soak chicken in sherry for 2 hours. Mix well the bread crumbs, cheese, garlic, pepper, salt, parsley and almonds. Dip chicken in melted butter, then roll well in the mixture. Place chicken in an open metal pan. Put small amount of butter on each piece of chicken. Bake for 1½ hours in 350-degree oven.

CHICKEN MOLÉ

Chicken Molé is a dish created out of necessity. Many years ago in Puebla, Mexico, the mother superior surveyed the stocks of her meager convent kitchen. Surrounded by the nuns, anxiously, nervously, awaiting orders. The problem? Preparing an appropriate menu for the visiting bishop. The food of the convent was simple fare, but for the bishop, on his tour of duty, they understandably wished to offer him something above and beyond usual convent fare.

There existed no "budget" for entertaining — not even for entertaining bishops. "We shall simply have to use what we have, and our wits," announced the mother superior. They went to work hurriedly searching the cupboards. One nun came forth with tomatoes and onions; another with raisins and almonds; still another with spices . . . cinnamon . . . cloves . . . garlic . . . red peppers. As the mother superior looked upon the materials

assembled before her, a light came into her eyes. "Chickens, we always have the chickens, and the tortillas. It is enough!"

She set them to work. Sisters divided the duties — one cooking the chicken, another preparing tomato sauce, another chopping raisins, almonds, onions, and still another grinding the red peppers on the metate, then grinding in the cinnamon, and the cloves, and the garlic. Tortillas any of them could make — blindfolded!

The mother superior went away to attend to other duties relating to the visit of the bishop, and when she returned to the kitchen, the nuns had finished their work, except for the spice-grinding nun, who was still grinding, grinding on the metate. In Spanish, moler means "to grind," and so they called the dish Chicken Molé.

Blending Chicken Molé with the zeal of necessity, plus spiritual mission, the nuns presented the dish to the bishop, who, no doubt, enjoyed it. They say that word of mouth is the best advertising, and so it must have been in Mexico, because wherever the bishop went he extolled the talents of the cooking nuns of the convent in Puebla and their Chicken Molé — so much so that it in time became the national dish of Mexico.

This is my favorite recipe for Chicken Molé:

Chicken Molé

1	5-pound chicken, disjointed
3	cups water
	Salt to taste
6	tablespoons shortening
1	medium onion, minced
1	clove garlic, crushed
2	tablespoons flour
3	8-ounce cans tomato sauce
1	cup chicken broth
12	seedless raisins
12	blanched almonds, shredded
1	tablespoon sesame seeds
¼	cup chili powder
1	teaspoon cinnamon
⅛	teaspoon cloves
	Salt to taste
	Tortillas

In a large saucepan, place the disjointed chicken, salted to taste, in about 3 cups of water. Cook over medium heat for 1 hour, or until very tender. Remove from heat. Cool in the broth; then remove meat from bones. In a large skillet, melt shortening over low heat; add onions, garlic and flour. Cook until yellow; then add tomato sauce and chicken broth. Allow to thicken. Now add the raisins, almonds, sesame seeds, chili powder, cinnamon, and cloves. Salt once again and cook for 5 to 10 minutes.

One hour before serving time, place pieces of boned chicken onto tortillas. Form into rolls. Place in an oblong baking dish and pour molé sauce over the chicken-tortilla rolls. Bake in a moderate oven, about 375 degrees, until thoroughly heated. Serve hot. Makes 6 servings.

CHICKEN SOUFFLÉ

The awe-inspiring soufflé is one of the creations of French haute cuisine. It is, in reality, nothing more than a simple airy mixture of eggs, butter, flour, and a purée of vegetables, meat, fish, or fowl. These purées are unexciting and unpretentious and, very often, left-overs.

Try the soufflé as a perfect beginning to a meal, whether it be a simple cheese affair (try a combination of Gruyere and Parmesan), a concoction of fish or shellfish, or one made with a well-seasoned base of puréed vegetables (endive, onion, or mushroom and cheese).

Savory soufflés also make light-as-air entrées of distinction for luncheon or supper parties, and there you can always let your imagination run riot. You will find that soufflés are quite easy to make if a few basic rules are followed. First and foremost: a soufflé must be eaten when ready. A soufflé will not wait for your guests. Your guests must wait for this delicate and sometimes temperamental dish. A rich, smooth sauce is the base of all soufflés. Many French soufflé recipes simply require a thick well-flavored Bechamel sauce. The egg yolks and egg whites must be beaten separately; the yolks until thick and lemon-colored, the whites until stiff but not dry. In separating the eggs, be sure there is no speck of yolk left in the whites. Otherwise, you will not be able to beat your whites stiff. Use an unbuttered soufflé dish for your first attempts so that the soufflé can cling to the sides of the dish and rise to its full height. For added flavor, when you butter the dish, sprinkle the buttered surface with fresh bread crumbs or a little finely grated Parmesan cheese. A slow to medium oven, 325 degrees to 350 degrees, is essential. If your oven is too hot, the soufflé will be well-cooked on top and undercooked inside. As long as it remains in a warm oven, a soufflé is pretty sturdy. The best way to determine when a soufflé is done is to open the door of the oven after 20 or 25 minutes and give the dish a slight shove. If the top crust moves only very slightly, the soufflé is done. However, if it really trembles, leave it in for a few more minutes.

Chicken Soufflé

¼ **cup butter**
¼ **cup flour**
1¼ **cups hot milk**
2 **tablespoons Cognac**
Salt and freshly ground white pepper
Dry mustard
5 **egg yolks**
½ **pound ground cooked chicken**
6 **egg whites, beaten stiff**

Melt butter in a double boiler, blend in flour. Add hot milk and stir over fire until mixture comes to a boil. Remove from fire and add Cognac. Season with salt, white pepper, and a pinch of dry mustard. Beat in egg yolks, one at a time. Add purée of cooked chicken. Fold the beaten egg whites into chicken mixture. Butter an 8-inch soufflé dish and tie a band of buttered wax paper completely around the outside. Fill about three quarters full with soufflé mixture and bake for 40 minutes in a preheated oven 350 degrees or until top is slightly browned and soufflé feels firm to the touch. Remove from oven, take off paper, and serve immediately. Recipe serves 4.

CHICKEN TETRAZZINI

The late Francis X. Bushman was a good friend of mine. We had long conversations about gourmet foods, and while he and his charming wife were visiting me in Dallas a few years ago, he demonstrated the proper way to blend Chicken Tetrazzini. This recipe was named for the great opera star, Tetrazzini, and was a great favorite of Francis'.

Francis X. Bushman was the first motion picture actor to receive star billing. In the early days of movie making only titles were advertised. So new and novel were these images on the screen that audiences were fascinated just watching actors go through dramatic motions. Increasingly, however, one actor was catching the eye of the women. They wanted to know his name. Fan mail poured into the studio asking one question: "Who was this magnificent young man?"

Thereafter, under the title of the movie there appeared: "Starring Francis X. Bushman." Thus, a kudo of the industry was born — star billing.

And thus, fame and fortune came to Francis, and with it came a life of princely living. Indeed, movie stars of that early period lived more like kings than kings did. One of his interests grew quickly — his delight in providing the best cuisine in the world for guests at his Hollywood mansion. In order to do that, he told me, he had to know how really good food was prepared, and so he learned to cook.

He felt, as I do, that the harmonious blending of ingredients was the success of a gourmet recipe. We discussed this as he negotiated the Chicken Tetrazzini. A recipe is great when none of the flavors of the single ingredients can be identified. The taste that haunts your hungry moments for weeks to come is the one you are curious about, because you can't say for sure what it contains. "What is that delicious flavor?" you ask yourself. "Wonder what they put in that recipe?" One rule of achieving this harmonious blend is by stirring well and carefully after each addition to the cooking pot. The more ingredients a recipe has, the more this rule should be applied, whether or not the directions call for stirring after each addition.

You will need these ingredients:

Chicken Tetrazzini

1	**six-pound hen**
1	**pound Italian-style thin spaghetti**
2	**cans sliced mushrooms**
$3/4$	**cup Parmesan cheese**
1	**clove garlic**
$1/2$	**cup sherry**
1	**cup finely chopped almonds**
$1/4$	**pound butter**
5	**tablespoons flour**
	Chicken broth
2	**teaspoons salt**
$1/2$	**teaspoon pepper**
2	**cans mushroom soup**
1	**teaspoon Worcestershire powder**
2	**medium green bell peppers**
$1/4$	**teaspoon garlic salt**
6	**cups American cheese, grated**
2	**small jars pimiento, chopped**
2	**cups milk**
1	**can whole mushrooms**

Cover hen with water. Add salt and pepper. Cook slowly 3 hours, or until meat loosens from the bones. Remove meat from bones and dice into small pieces. Cook spaghetti in boiling chicken broth until tender. Drain and rinse. Melt butter over low flame in a skillet and add finely chopped green bell peppers. Cook peppers until tender.

Add flour, milk, mushroom soup, chopped pimientos, garlic salt, garlic, Worcestershire powder, cooking sherry, mushroom slices, diced chicken, 4 cups of the grated American cheese, and the Parmesan cheese.

Cook slowly 10 minutes. Place layer of spaghetti in pyrex

dish. Cover with sauce. Continue the process until the dish is nearly filled. Sprinkle finely chopped almonds and grated American cheese (which remains) on top. Place whole mushrooms on top of the cheese. Place dish in preheated oven at 350 degrees. Cook 10 minutes. Serve while hot.

CHILI COCKTAIL CHEESE POT

October's a busy, busy month. Not only Halloween with its horripilated cats and air-borne witches, but numerous special holidays. There is, for instance, State Fair Day in Texas. Also Missouri Day; Oklahoma Day; Alaska Day or Pulaski Day (in Nebraska). In the Virgin Islands they celebrate Thanksgiving Day in October because it's the end of the hurricane season.

October is also Chili Con Carne Month and brings us Child Health Day, Poetry Day and Columbus Day. So, in honor of Chili Con Carne Month, Child Health and Poetry Day, here's a home-made jingle:

> "I'm hungry, Maw!" cried little Willie,
> "Please let me have a bowl of Chili!"

It's good "little Willie" rhymes with "bowl of Chili" because youngsters love chili con carne. (So do their elders, for that matter.)

It's also very appropriate that Columbus Day should come during Chili Con Carne Month because, of course, chili peppers and all the many other kinds of capsicum (cap-si-cum) peppers were some of the most valuable treasures discovered in the New World. While other American plants, such as potatoes and tomatoes, were ignored at first, Spanish explorers loved the nippy, red-podded capsicum peppers immediately. As early as 1493, historian Peter Martyr wrote that Columbus had found "pepper more pungent than that from Caucasus."

So popular were these capsicums that they were soon being grown in many parts of the known world. In India, for instance, where they quickly got into the habit of adding a few red peppers to their traditional curry dishes. Since the early sixteenth century, all Indian curries have contained capsicums.

It was an Englishman from India who created the first chili powder, so the story goes. This man had loved curry dishes in India. Once he'd reached Texas, in far-off America, he kept longing for curry. Chili peppers and oregano were easy to come by. So were cumin seeds, garlic and salt. One day — if we may believe the legend — he ground these ingredients together. It wasn't curry powder, for certain spices were missing, but it was just as richly flavorful. It was a completely right spice blend for beef and beans, for dishes starting with corn and cornmeal. Just as curry powder was made to simulate the typical flavor of Indian curries, chili powder produced the flavor of Mexican dishes.

Chili powder is very aromatic, but not necessarily "hot." It's a convenient and pleasing spice blend for all kinds of everyday dishes. Add it to stews of all kinds; beef, chicken, seafood. Add it to taste during the last few minutes of cooking. It's a delightful addition to canned soups: pea soup and tomato soup, mixed. Or in bean-and-bacon soup. Or pepper-pot. Not too much — just enough to give it a tingle of flavor. Then try chili in salad dressings — especially if it's to be mixed with fish or meat salads. One of the best and easiest sauces for broiled fish or vegetables such as asparagus, green beans or corn is chili butter. Simply add 1/2 teaspoon chili powder to 1/4 cup butter or margarine and melt.

This is a great party recipe:

Chili Cocktail Cheese Pot

$^1/_4$	cup crumbled Roquefort cheese
$^1/_2$	cup grated mild Cheddar or Monterey Jack cheese
2	packages (6 ounces) cream cheese
$^1/_4$	teaspoon onion powder
$^1/_{16}$	teaspoon garlic powder
$1^3/_4$	teaspoons chili powder
1	teaspoon Worcestershire powder

1. Mix all cheeses together until well blended.
2. Blend in remaining ingredients.
3. Serve in a crockery cheese jar or in a small bowl as a spread for crackers, cucumber slices or black bread.

Yield 1 cup.

CHILI CON CARNE

When traveling about the country, I am often quizzed as to what contribution the state of Texas has made to the exceptional food repertoire of America. When I answer the name of the food, Lone Star gourmets' thoughts naturally turn to when the first winter winds blow down the Texas plains, or the first chilly raindrops find their way into our Texas autumn — chili. This phase of Texas food preparation is unexcelled anywhere in the world.

Texas-style chili is not like any other. And although I can recommend some of the best of the Mexican food found in different parts of the nation, the finest Mexican cuisine is still found where it had its origin, in Texas.

If you have been to Mexico you were, perhaps, surprised when you sampled their native Mexican food. It is very different from Texas-Mexican food. Contrary to popular opinion, the real Mexican cookery, as we know it today,

did not find its way into the chapters of famous cookbooks by route of Mexico, but rather Texas. But, of course, the influence of old Mexico is unmistakable.

Texas beef and Mexican seasonings are what this marriage of ingredients and flavors combines. (Chili is really a pepper plant.) Add a couple or three (with beans), native vegetables, a Texas-size culinary imagination, and you have what the ranchers and cowboys call "A Bowl of Red."

Here is my favorite recipe for chili con carne. The astringency of most Mexican foods can be subtly subdued by just a hint of chocolate.

To make chili con carne you should commandeer the following ingredients:

David Wade's Chili con Carne

3	pounds ground round steak
2	cloves garlic, crushed
1	large white onion, diced fine
3	tablespoons chili powder
1	teaspoon oregano
1	teaspoon salt
2	teaspoons cumin powder
1	teaspoon coriander
2	15-ounce cans tomato sauce
1	15-ounce can water
1	small block bitter-sweet chocolate
$^2/_3$	cup masa harina (masa flour)
2	cups water
2	15-ounce cans pinto beans (drained)

Place meat, garlic and onion into a large kettle. Brown meat, stirring until meat is brown (gray color) and garlic and onion are soft. Drain mixture in a colander until excess fat is removed.

Wipe out kettle with paper towel and return mixture. Heat, stirring while adding chili powder, oregano, salt, cumin powder and coriander. Continue cooking until seasoning is well blended and dissolved with the meat. Add tomato sauce and water and continue cooking until rawness is cooked away from tomatoes. Add chocolate and cook until dissolved.

Using a bowl, combine masa harina and water (2 cups). Slur with a wire whisk or until mixture is smooth. Add to cooking mixture and continue cooking while stirring until recipe starts to thicken.

Add beans and cook for 4 more minutes. Remove chili from heat and permit to stand for at least 30 minutes before serving.

Yields $2^1/_2$ quarts.

CHILI RELLENOS, EL FENIX

Go where you will in Texas and there is not a town worth stopping in that doesn't have a Mexican restaurant. Cities like San Antonio, Houston, and Dallas provide the diner with an overwhelming choice of fine Mexican restaurants. It is, therefore, no small accomplishment to achieve what the Martinez family has achieved in Dallas — to wit, the best Mexican food you will find anywhere.

How did it all begin?

First, let us go back, back, back to those thrilling days of yester-year when Texans-to-be were swarming into the state. They came from the South, mostly, and from South of the Border. Here in Texas, the impact of their cultures met head-on. Who would have thought that those Southern-fried-chicken-eaters and tamales would ever be so happy together? No one. But miracles are always happening, and a food taste happened then. This taste of Mexico was enough to make them forget the Alamo!

Now to this background of history enters on the Dallas scene, Mike Martinez. The time is 1918, the place is McKinney and Griffin near downtown Dallas, the facility is one room turned into a restaurant. Ah, but the real success formula Mike Martinez possessed was a philosophy which has been proved by the test of time — his knowledge of the right way to cook Mexican food, his belief in very hard work, and his family.

You know, there are almost as many types of Mexican food as there are Mexican cooks, but to combine the best of all and reach that happy medium that pleases the taste of everyone is genius indeed. El Fenix does this superbly.

The pace of hard work is an example set by Mike Martinez that the sons and daughters still apply to their grown-up and still growing operation. "Work! Work! and Stay With It!" is their theme and their strength.

The sons, Alfred, Gilbert, Henry and Rueben, and two sisters, Irene Garcia and Tina McDonald, carry on the El Fenix tradition as a family enterprise. They have been joined by in-laws, aunts and uncles, and cousins to bring the best in Mexican food to all who go in at the door under the sign of El Fenix.

From the little one room where the Martinez family began, they have come a long way, growing with Dallas, and even out of Dallas. This growing success is evident in their spacious new headquarters building in the industrial area, and their new restaurants in Fort Worth, Houston, Richardson and Longview.

Here is a little bit of El Fenix you can take to your own kitchen and serve in the best tradition of Texas-Mexican cuisine — El Fenix Chili Rellenos.

Chili Rellenos, El Fenix

1/2	cup oil
1	onion, finely diced
3/4	cup flour
4	cups tomato juice
1 1/2	teaspoons salt
1/8	teaspoon cumin
1/2	teaspoon white pepper
1	small clove garlic, crushed
1	pound ground round
1	large potato, finely diced
2	tomatoes, peeled and diced
1	onion, finely diced
1 1/2	teaspoons salt
1/4	teaspoon cumin
1/2	teaspoon white pepper
1	small clove garlic, crushed
2	tablespoons chopped pimiento
6	tablespoons finely chopped almonds, if desired
1/2	cup chopped raisins, if desired
2	cups oil
6	large chilis poblano
4	egg whites
4	egg yolks

Heat oil in skillet over medium heat, add onion and sauté until tender. Add flour and cook until lightly browned, then add tomato juice gradually and cook until thickened. Add salt, cumin, white pepper and garlic and simmer over low heat 15 minutes.

Keep sauce warm over low heat. Fry ground round in skillet over medium heat until medium done, then add potato and cook until done.

Reduce heat to low temperature, add tomatoes, onion, salt, cumin, white pepper, garlic, pimiento, almonds and raisins and simmer 15 minutes. Remove from heat.

Heat oil in skillet over medium heat and cook chilis poblano until skins look white. Remove from oil and drain. Wrap in moistened cloth. Peel, dipping in water to help loosen skin. Slit and remove veins. Fill with beef mixture. Sprinkle a little flour over filling. Beat egg whites until soft peaks form. Fold in egg yolks and beat until fluffy.

Dip stuffed chilis in egg mixture. Fry in hot oil over medium heat until golden brown. Remove from oil and place in warm tomato sauce. Heat over very low temperature 5 minutes.

Garnish with parsley. Makes 6 servings.

NOTE: Chilis may be stuffed with pasteurized process cheese instead of meat filling if you prefer. Use 1/4 pound cheese to stuff each chili.

CHOCOLATE CHIFFON CREAM

Can you guess the name of the spice that tastes like a blend of cinnamon, nutmeg, and cloves? In fact, its name sounds as though it is a blend of spices. It looks like a plump peppercorn. It is available whole or ground. It is great for baking, delicious with meats and vegetables. It's the only real spice native to the Americas, specifically to the island of Jamaica. By now you have probably guessed — allspice.

Pungent and aromatic, allspice is the only single spice in which nature combines three flavors in one berry. It is sometimes called the All-American spice because its commercial production is limited to the Americas.

Allspice is a relatively new spice. All the other true spices such as pepper, cinnamon, ginger, and cloves, originated in Southeastern Asia or the East Indies and often have exciting family histories which go back to the beginning of the written word. The Bible tells how the Queen of Sheba brought King Solomon spices as a tribute to his great wisdom. Spices then were worth their weight in gold. It was the discovery of a westward route to the spice islands that Columbus sought when he landed on an island in the West Indies. Had Columbus been a botanist or a spice trader he would have realized that he was walking right by the very thing he had come to find.

When later Spanish explorers finally realized that the allspice berry had tempting aroma, noting its resemblance to the peppercorn, they named it "pimiento," their word for pepper. The tree itself, one of the myrtle family, is called "pimenta" to this day. Other names for allspice are pimiento and Jamaica pepper. Allspice is the most common tree on the island and is seldom found growing singly. Each tree annually produces an average of 25 to 100 pounds of the spice.

Allspice is very popular for flavoring sauces, pickles, sausages, and soups. It blends well with tomatoes and sweet potatoes; it's used in spice cakes and with chocolate. Add it to a glaze for baked ham. It's indispensable in mincemeat. Here's a little cooking tip. Because the clove flavor dominates allspice, the whole berries will give their best effect when tied in a cheesecloth bag and used in long cooking, such as pot roast, or in long soaking, such as pickling liquid and in marinades.

The following recipe is a hallmark example of how allspice teases the palate along with chocolate in a dessert recipe.

Chocolate Chiffon Cream

1 1/2	cups milk, scalded
3	eggs, separated
1/2	cup sugar
2	teaspoons flour
1/2	teaspoon ground allspice
1/8	teaspoon salt
2	squares semi-sweet chocolate, melted
1	tablespoon strong cold coffee
1/2	teaspoon pure vanilla extract
	Ladyfingers

Combine 2 to 3 tablespoons of the scaled milk with egg yolks, 1/4 cup of the sugar, flour, allspice, and salt. Mix well. Add to remaining milk and cook over low heat or hot water until custard coats a metal spoon, stirring constantly. Remove from heat. Add chocolate, coffee, and vanilla to custard. Cool. Beat egg whites until they form soft peaks. Add remaining 1/4 cup sugar gradually, beating until eggs are stiff but not dry. Fold into chocolate custard. Chill. Serve in sherbet glasses, lined with ladyfingers. Garnish with whipped cream, if desired. Recipe serves 4.

CHUCK WAGON BEANS, *OLÉ!*

After riding all morning, hot, tired, dusty, the ranch hands turn toward the chuck wagon and the food they know will be waiting for them. The chuck wagon has meanwhile located itself in the middle of a vast sea of grass, rocks, and sand. Perhaps a mountain overlooks the lunch site, or a river or stream winds along the way. But whatever the scenery, the boys can be sure of one thing for lunch — and that's beans.

The lowly bean is not, of course, absolutely synonymous with the West. Boston Baked Beans testify to the mutual claim of the East on the bean. But the pinto bean is the bean of the West and the Southwest, having formed the basic diet of the Indians and Mexicans for centuries. The bean recipe which awaits our cowboys may be good, bad, or indifferent, but the chuck wagon cook, so much maligned but sometimes praised, just may have been an epicure. The cowboy chef who invented the recipe I am giving you today was. Recipes, like the men of that early time, had to be the best to survive. And like those violent men of the West, this Chuck Wagon Bean recipe is colorful, spicy, and hot, hot, hot!

Chuck Wagon Beans, *Olé!*

1   pound salt pork (better with strips of lean)
**3   or 4 chilis, depending on size (these are
        small, hot green peppers)**
1   pound pinto beans
1   No. 2 can tomatoes
4   cloves garlic
1   tablespoon peppercorns

Soak the beans overnight. Cook them until they are tender. Cube the salt pork in pieces about 1/2 inch and fry them until they are golden brown. Add salt pork cubes to the beans, and also every speck of the grease. (Do not add salt until after the pork has cooked in the beans for a time. The salt cooks out of the pork and into the beans usually providing a sufficient amount of salt for flavor.)

Open the tomatoes and place into a bowl. Use your hands to make a purée of them removing any pieces of skin or core that might be in them. Crush the garlic, chilis and peppercorns and add them to the tomatoes. Mix thoroughly and add these ingredients to the bean pot which has been simmering.

Again mix thoroughly and continue to simmer for several minutes. Let stand for a while to let the flavors blend to perfection. *Olé!*

A Mexican bean pot for cooking the pintos will add much to the flavor and can be used as an attractive, authentic serving piece.

Serve toasted tortillas with these beans. They handsomely complement the flavor.

CINNAMON DEEP-DISH APPLE PIE

Today we can trundle our shopping carts past the spice shelves at the supermarket and think nothing of dropping in a container of cinnamon: Lined up neatly behind the one we reach for are dozens more just like it. But there was a time when cinnamon was as difficult to reach as the Golden Fleece of mythology.

Cinnamon is the world's greatest sweet spice and has been a precious commodity throughout the ages. It has been used not only as a flavoring for foods, but as medicine, as perfume and quite often in love charms.

The Chinese, forty centuries ago, believed that cinnamon was the sacred Tree of Life which grew high up in Paradise, up in the Tibetan Mountains. Anyone who ate even a small bit of this tree or its fruit, they believed, would live forever.

At the time of the Crusades — a thousand years ago — many people in Europe thought spices, such as cinnamon, came from the Garden of Eden. Eden, they'd been told, was a "place of delight, full of beautiful trees and fragrant perfumes." These spices were carried out of Eden by the Ganges River and the Tigris. This would have seemed likely to them, for the Garden of Eden was somewhere in the East and cinnamon came from that direction, brought by spice traders from Arabia.

The Romans used cinnamon in their religious ceremonies — even by the reprobate Nero. After he'd kicked his wife Poppaea to death, he ordered the annual cinnamon supply of the entire city of Rome burned at her funeral!

Naturally, the Arab spice traders knew where cinnamon came from, but they were too smart to say. To keep competition out of cinnamon country they told frightening tales of weird dangers: That cinnamon came from deep glens filled with deadly snakes. That cinnamon thickets were guarded by ferocious birds. That only priests were allowed to collet cinnamon and that the sun god claimed the first bundle for his own, igniting it with a spark of divine fire.

Cinnamon is the bark of an evergreen tree. It is native to the Far East and today we get it from Indonesia and South Vietnam. The bark is first split, then peeled off the tree. As it dries it is rolled into tight quills or sticks. These are cut into lengths of from two to three feet and then shipped that way to the United States. Here we either grind the sticks into a fine powder or cut them into pieces three or four inches long for sale as cinnamon sticks.

Cinnamon gives delightful aroma to hundreds of dishes. For instance: Add a teaspoon of ground cinnamon to a graham cracker crust for pies.

When making rolled out cookies, sift together confectioners' sugar and cinnamon and sprinkle over the pastry board in place of flour.

Add a teaspoon of ground cinnamon to the dry ingredients of a chocolate pudding mix.

Tuck one-inch piece of stick cinnamon in the water when cooking carrots which are to be candied. Or dust ground cinnamon over candied sweet potatoes.

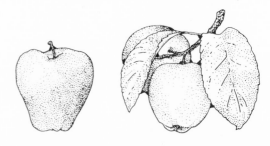

Cinnamon Deep-Dish Apple Pie

5   **cups (5 medium) sliced cooking apples**
2   **sticks cinnamon, 2 inches long**
³/₄   **cup sugar**
¹/₂   **teaspoon salt**
1¹/₂   **tablespoons quick-setting tapioca**
2   **tablespoons butter or margarine**
      Pastry, using 1 cup flour

1. Place apples in an 8x8x2-inch pan.
2. Add cinnamon.
3. Mix sugar, salt and tapioca. Sprinkle over apples.
4. Dot with butter or margarine.
5. Cover with pastry rolled 1/8-inch thick.
6. Trim, turn under and flute edge.
7. Cut a gash in pastry to allow for escape of steam.
8. Bake in a preheated very hot oven (450 degrees) 10 minutes.
9. Reduce heat to moderate (350 degrees) and bake 40 minutes or until apples are tender.

Yield 8 servings.

CLAM CHOWDER

Are you a fan of the clam chowder? If you are, I know from past experience that you are going to be decidedly in favor of one of these recipes and decidedly against the other. Public food opinion usually divides right down the middle like the preference for one or the other of the two major political parties.

It is not as simple as New York casting its votes for Manhattan Chowder, and New England casting its block of votes for New England (sometimes called Maine Chowder). A Democrat from California may vote for New England Clam Chowder, and a Republican from Connecticut may vote for Manhattan. Since there is no way to measure support for or against (someone should really do a national survey on this!) I play no favorites. I give two recipes, and since I am of the "both-of-them-are-good-school," that makes me an Independent of the Gourmet Party.

What both recipes have in common are clams, as well as potatoes and onions. There the similarity ends. Manhattan has tomatoes and New England doesn't; New England has milk and Manhattan doesn't. The clams may come from the same ocean, but our forefathers were highly individual and did with clams what they pleased.

A chowder is not technically a soup, nor is it a stew. It is somewhere in between, related in recipe format to the bouillabaisse and the gumbo. The name comes from France, where fishermen along the coast cooked some of their catch in a large "chaudiere" which means caldron. Somewhere along the way the Early Americans developed their own chaudiere and it got to be called chowder. Eschewing other fishes of the sea, they cast their votes for clams.

Chowder is a meal in itself and can be, should be, for special occasions.

Happy chowder-time, good living and *bon appétit!*

New England Clam Chowder

3   **dozen soft-shell clams, shucked**
2   **ounces salt pork**
1   **cup sliced onion**
¹/₂   **cup sliced leeks**
6   **cups diced potatoes**
1   **teaspoon salt**
3   **cups water**
      Clam liquor
4   **cups milk, scalded**
2   **cups light cream, scalded**
3   **tablespoons butter**
2   **tablespoons flour**
2   **small bay leaves**
      Dash black pepper

Drain clams, reserving liquor. Keeping separate, finely chop hard part of clams, coarsely chop soft part. Sauté diced salt pork in deep kettle until golden brown. Add finely chopped clams, sliced onion, sliced leeks, diced potatoes, bay leaves, salt, pepper and 3 cups of water. Add enough water to clam liquor to make 3 cups liquid. Add to mixture with remaining ingredients of coarsely chopped clams, scalded milk, scalded light cream and butter blended with flour. Continue cooking over low heat for 20 minutes. Remove bay leaves. Serves 6.

Manhattan Clam Chowder

6   strips bacon
4   carrots, diced
2   tablespoons chopped fresh parsley
2   teaspoons thyme
1   tablespoon Worcestershire powder
    Salt and pepper to taste (suggest cracked
      black pepper)
4   medium onions, diced
1   small rib celery
1   12-ounce can tomatoes
1   bay leaf
3   medium potatoes
1   pint clams (2 cans minced clams may be
      used, 10^1/$_2$-ounce size)

Cut bacon into small pieces and fry in a large kettle until brown, but not crisp. Add diced onions and sauté until soft. Next add finely diced carrots, celery and chopped parsley. Simmer slowly for about 4 minutes while stirring. Drain clams and tomatoes, placing the liquid into a measuring container. Add enough water to make about 1^1/$_2$ quarts of liquid. Add tomatoes and liquid to the pot and bring to a boil. Season with salt and pepper, bay leaf, thyme, and Worcestershire powder. Reduce heat and simmer for 45 minutes. Remove bay leaf. Add finely diced potatoes and simmer for 20 minutes more. Last, add the clams and simmer gently for 10 more minutes. Recipe makes about 3 quarts.

COCONUT RICE PUDDING

Look at a map of the Caribbean Sea and you'll realize there are dozens of islands, some big, most of them mere dots on the map. They pop up here and there through three-quarter million square miles of beautiful blue water.

The ancestors of the people who live on these islands came from Spain, France, Great Britain, Denmark, India, Africa, China, and many other places around the globe. Like people in other regions, they eat what is most easily available. The waters of tropical America are rich with 1,300 varieties of fish. Fruits and vegetables of many kinds grow profusely in tropical gardens and orchards.

Allspice, nutmeg, mace, ginger, turmeric and chili peppers are produced in commercial amounts — one of our good sources of these spices. As may be expected, Caribbean cooks use these spices daily in preparing regional dishes.

Remember Ponce de Leon who came to the Caribbean seeking the Fountain of Youth? We almost never hear of his wife, Doña Inez. She brought European herbs and vegetables to their garden in Puerto Rico. She not only showed the Indian women how to use these new flavoring ingredients but, in turn, became acquainted with the use of native foods and seasonings. She serves as a for-instance of early homemakers and mixed-and-matched cooking skills and recipes with the native peoples.

There are variations in cooking and seasoning, but popular in most of the Caribbean are rice, beans, sweet potatoes, corn, cassava, black-eyed peas, cooking bananas, breadfruit, okra, eggplant and many, many peppers. With these rather starchy foods they like lemon and sour orange juice, garlic, onions, pepper, cinnamon, cloves, ginger. Green coriander leaves, called cilantro, and oregano are important herbs. This is mortar and pestle country for they like to grind together mixtures of seasonings.

Sofrito is a spiced sauce made of salt pork, ground ham and such spices as onions, garlic, peppers, and oregano for flavor. The islanders also add coriander leaves and achiote (ah-she-oaty) seeds for red color. But coriander seeds and paprika may be used instead. This sauce is made up in quantity and a few tablespoons are used to flavor soups, meats, vegetables.

As we get down to islands nearer the South American coast, meals become lighter, less rich because of the heat. More spiced cold dishes and iced beverages are served to excite the appetite. Hospitality is charming, without ceremony, but guests are genuinely welcomed by their generous hosts.

As a little taste of what one might eat at a Caribbean dinner table, do try this recipe:

Coconut Rice Pudding

In a small saucepan combine:

1^1/$_2$ cups milk
1   can (4 ounces) shredded coconut

Bring to boiling point. Remove from heat and cool.

In a medium saucepan bring to boiling point:

2^1/$_2$ cups milk

Stir in:

1   cup raw regular cooking rice

Reduce heat; cover and simmer 25 minutes or until rice is tender. Meanwhile, squeeze milk from coconut through a fine sieve or cheesecloth; set milk aside. Sprinkle coconut on a baking sheet. Toast under hot broiler until lightly browned; set aside.

Stir into cooked rice:

Reserved coconut milk
1/2 **cup sugar**
2 **egg yolks, beaten lightly**
1 **teaspoon ground cinnamon**

Cook 5 minutes, stirring constantly. Turn into serving dish. Chill thoroughly. Garnish with reserved toasted coconut. Yield 6 portions.

COLD HAM MOUSSE

It's strange, the roundabout way in which modern words have acquired their meanings. Take the word "garnish," for instance. First this meant "to warn," then it was extended to include battle equipment and armor. Armor was often very beautifully adorned. So, eventually garniture or garnishing meant anything handsomely decked out and that included things to eat. To the present-day American cook, a garnish has come to mean, first of all, a dash of gay red paprika!

Great-grandmother — if she lived in America — probably never used paprika in the course of her lifetime. Today, however, we use about twelve million pounds of this brilliant spice. Paprika is right up there among the first five of America's favorite spices.

Paprika does for dozens and dozens of dishes what rosy cheeks do for a tree-top apple — makes food look good enough to eat. We should be able to enjoy our food with all of our senses: its color, shape and arrangement should delight the eye. Crispness, smoothness please the sense of touch. Fragrance excites the appetite almost as much as does the taste.

Keep paprika close at hand; you can use it to garnish foods for every meal. Dash some on the breakfast scrambled eggs. At lunch time send a cheese rarebit to the table with a rosy-red cast of paprika. Shake up a tomato juice cocktail with a little paprika to intensify the tomato color and increase the tang of the tomato. Pork and beans, salad dressings, meat, fish, chicken, potatoes, noodles, macaroni and a long list of creamed dishes all look more attractive, more appetizing if you'll remember to reach for your container of paprika.

Cold Ham Mousse

1/2 **teaspoon powdered mustard**
1/2 **teaspoon warm water**
2 **packages unflavored gelatin**
2 **egg yolks, beaten lightly**
1/2 **teaspoon salt**
1/2 **teaspoon instant minced onion**
   Dash ground black pepper
1 **cup milk**
1 **chicken bouillon cube**
2 **cups chopped cooked ham**
1 **teaspoon paprika**
1 **teaspoon parsley flakes**
1/2 **cup heavy cream, whipped**

Blend mustard and water; let stand 10 minutes for flavor to develop. Soften gelatin in 1/2 cup cold water and set aside. Combine mustard egg yolks, salt, minced onion and black pepper in top of double boiler. Gradually stir in milk, 1 cup water and bouillon cube. Cook over hot water 15 minutes or until thickened, stirring constantly. Stir in softened gelatin, ham, paprika, parsley flakes and vinegar. Chill until mixture begins to thicken. Fold in whipped cream. Turn into a 6-cup ring mold which has been rinsed in cold water. Chill until firm. Just before serving, unmold on serving plate. Serve with watercress and mayonnaise, if desired.

Yield 8 servings.

COLUMBIAN CUCHUCO
(Barley Soup)

All the South American countries naturally have their own characteristic dishes, according to their produce and to their climate conditions. But if you tried to discover where their overall ideas in gastronomy were derived, you would find a definite Spanish trait.

From Argentina, the land of the beef, comes some very interesting and highly flavored meat dishes, like the *puchero*. The other fascinating dish from the same country is the Argentine *carbonado*, an exotic mixture of sweet and savory flavors. It seems to me that in the land of plenty of Argentine beef, they are inordinately fond of mixing fruit and meat in their cookery; probably because "just steak" is such an everyday occurrence that good cooks hardly give their thoughts to it. I am told that until quite recently the Argentines served steak with every meal, in much the same way we get bread on the table without ordering it separately.

The Bolivians, too, are very partial to highly seasoned food, but the Bolivian recipes can be served without risk of offending the most sensitive palates. Their stuffed avocados will lend style and elegance to any dinner table and will start off a dinner party on a high note of gastronomic finesse.

From Venezuela, the land of contrast and exotic, unexplored jungles, comes a real work of art in the shape of meat pies: Venezuela *hallacas*. In spite of the fact that these meat pies contain no outlandish ingredients, they are a real gourmet's joy. What I like about them is their mundane and ordinary outer appearance coupled with their most luscious filling. It is always fun to watch your guests lift up an ordinary-looking meat pie and go into raptures of praise after the first bite.

From Columbia comes a very filling and satisfying soup called Columbian Cuchuco, a very palatable soup without any sharp or spicy ingredients.

Columbian Cuchuco

1	**pound soup bones**
4	**pints water**
1	**bay leaf**
3	**peppercorns**
1	**large onion, chopped**
1	**pound barley**
	Water to cover
8	**ounces fresh green peas**
8	**ounces cabbage, finely chopped**
2	**teaspoons salt**
1/2	**teaspoon pepper**
1	**teaspoon Worcestershire powder**

Place the bones in the 4 pints water, then add onion, bay leaf and peppercorns. Simmer in a covered container for 2 hours. Wash the barley and place in another container, cover with water, and bring to boil. Strain the barley and recover with water and cook for 3 additional minutes. Strain this mixture and add to the strained bone stock when cooked. Bring this mixture to a boil and add vegetables and seasonings. Gently simmer until the soup thickens and the barley is cooked.

COQUILLES ST. JACQUES

The gourmet's richest rewards are found in the haute cuisine of France. Haute cuisine means, literally, "high-class cooking." Even the smallest bistro in Paris is justifiably jealous of its culinary reputation, but the haute restaurants are famous for the elegance of their creations.

Americans have always made Europe their first overseas vacation choice. France is an integral part of the *grande tour*. Naturally, Americans look forward to tasting the world famous *cuisine francaise*. They have heard of it all their lives. Now, they are in Paris — the world center of gastronomy. So what happens? We are often frightened away from really magnificent foods by the odd names on the menu.

Unless you speak, write, or understand French (gourmet French, too, please), it can be disturbing to see *Le Pigeonneau Roti le Riz Sauvage Americain,* staring back at you from a *cafe programme.* The best we are apt to come up with, lacking a knowledge of the language, is something like "American Pigeon." This is not very appetizing. Indeed, it makes us downright uncomfortable. But, *Le Pigeonneau Roti le Riz Sauvage Americain* is only roasted squab, with wild rice, American style.

If we are going to enjoy French cooking abroad, or at home, we'll just have to "take a chance" and experiment a little. Keep in mind that this style of cooking has been popular for centuries. Only the best survives that long on a worldwide basis. Usually, your reward is a happy new taste thrill. Another clue for ordering in French: When in doubt, order *Specialities de la Maison*. This is always a safe choice, because the specialty of the house is the dish, or dishes, they are proudest of, think they prepare best, and so recommend to one and all.

I have never known anyone to return from Europe without "discovering" a new recipe about which they went into exclamations of praise. They could, of course, have enjoyed those same foods right here in America. But in Europe they discover that they were really gourmets at heart all the time.

Transplanted among foreign people who are savoring these strange morsels with gusto; seeing different sights; listening to another language; surrounded by an atmosphere that is exciting and stimulating, the scene is set for a new food experience. Add to this the important fact that they can't get what they are "always accustomed to eating" at home. *Voilá!* A gourmet is born.

It is unnecessary to go abroad to enjoy haute cuisine. America abounds with superb restaurants serving haute style. We can create *cuisine francaise* in our own kitchen anytime we please. The longest trip you'll have to make is to your supermarket.

I captured this recipe for Coquilles St. Jacques (they are only scallops!) from a very haute restaurant near the Montmartre section of Paris several years ago. It has been a favorite of mine ever since I first tasted its enchanting flavor.

Coquilles St. Jacques

8 scallops
1 large tomato, peeled and sliced
1 small onion, finely chopped
1 can (4 ounces) finely sliced mushrooms
 Salt and pepper to taste
$^1/_4$ cup butter or margarine
$^1/_4$ cup Bechamel Sauce (white or cream
  sauce)
 Parsley, garnish

Wash the scallops, and cover with cold, salted water, and cook over medium heat. Bring them to a boil. (This takes about 8 minutes to cook until soft). Drain and chop the white and red parts together. Mix with tomato, onion, mushrooms, and salt and pepper.

Now we intensify these flavors by melting the butter in a skillet and adding the scallop mixture. Cook 3 to 5 minutes. Add the Bechamel (white or cream) sauce. Stir well. Spoon the entire mixture into 4 scallop shells. Brown them in your broiling compartment about 3 inches away from the heat. Garnish with parsley before serving. Recipe will serve 4 people.

Coquilles St. Jacques is the epitome of haute cuisine, yet it is not difficult to prepare.

CRAZY BEAN CASSEROLE

Obviously the tastemakers have been busy sniffing and sampling their way along the American spice shelf looking for new flavor effects. Spice import figures show a sharp increase in black and white pepper and cinnamon, and a jump in the quantity of celery and anise seeds and sage leaves which entered the country.

While thousands of tons of stalk on salad celery is grown in this country, the celery seed for the spice shelf must all be imported from India, France and Indonesia, a total of some 10,116,000 pounds.

The botanical name is the same — *Apium graveolens* — but there is a distinct difference in flavor. Celery seed is the fruit of wild celery or smallage, harvested for many centuries for its medicinal properties: "The disease then to celery yields, conquered by the remedy." Then, as now, only the seeds had appetizing aroma, for the rest of the plant was unpleasantly bitter. "Ungrateful" they would have called it several centuries ago. It took centuries of taming to develop the much sweeter plant which puts celery flakes and diced celery on our spice shelves.

The flavor fillip of the tiny brown celery seed is available whole or as celery salt, which is a mixture of ground celery seed and table salt. Celery seed is one of the impor-

tant pickling spices. It is excellent, too, in chowders and fish soups; in egg dishes; and with seafood and salads of different kinds.

Crazy Bean Casserole

1 package (10 ounces) frozen lima beans
$^1/_2$ pound frankfurters
2 tablespoons butter or margarine
1 medium onion, chopped
1 clove garlic, minced
1 can (1 pound) kidney beans, drained
1 jar (1 pound 6 ounce) baked beans
$^1/_4$ teaspoon celery seed
1 teaspoon mustard (prepared)
1 tablespoon brown sugar
$^1/_2$ cup catsup
$^1/_2$ cup dry red wine
$^1/_2$ teaspoon salt
 Dash pepper
$^1/_2$ cup crushed corn or potato chips

1. Cook lima beans according to package directions; drain.
2. Preheat oven to 350 degrees.
3. Slice frankfurters.
4. Heat butter in large skillet, and sauté frankfurter slices, onion, and garlic, stirring occasionally.
5. When onion is tender, stir in lima beans and all remaining ingredients except chips.
6. Spoon mixture into a 2-quart casserole and top with chips.
7. Bake 30 minutes.
Makes 8 servings.

CREAMED MUSHROOMS AND ONIONS A LA ROMANO

Walk into a well-stocked housewares department and there seem to be pots, pans and cookers for all kinds of foods — special egg poachers, fish poachers, potato bakers, asparagus cookers, soufflé dishes and many more. This may seem like over-specialization, yet 2,000 years ago the Romans had a special pan for cooking mushrooms. They called mushrooms *boleti* and the mushroom cooking vessels were *boletaria*. They were to be used only for mushrooms, never lesser foods.

There must have been instances when other foods were cooked in the *boletaria*. At least the Roman writer, Martial, depicts an unhappy mushroom vessel bewailing its comedown in a carelessly run Roman kitchen. Said this mushroom pot, "Although *boleti* have given me so noble a name, I am now used, I am ashamed to say, for Brussels sprouts."

Creamed Mushrooms and Onions a la Romano

$1/2$	pound fresh mushrooms or 1 can (6 to 8 ounces) sliced mushrooms
1	package (2 ounces) white sauce mix
$1/2$	teaspoon Italian seasoning
$1/8$	teaspoon ground black pepper
1	can ($15^1/_2$ ounces) small white onions
$1/3$	cup grated Romano or Parmesan cheese

Slice fresh mushrooms (makes $2^1/_2$ cups) or drain canned mushrooms. Prepare white sauce according to package directions. Season with Italian seasoning and black pepper. Place mushrooms and onions in buttered 1-quart casserole. Pour over all. Sprinkle with cheese. Bake in preheated moderate oven 30 minutes. Yield 4 portions.

CREOLE STUFFED GREEN PEPPERS

When the spice-seeking Spaniards sailed west to accidentally discover the New World, they didn't find the spices of India, but they did find many new taste thrills. They must have been particularly fascinated with the Capsicum family. Not only were the fruits of the pod pepper plant pleasing to the taste, but the plants themselves were a joy to behold, with their glassy green leaves and colorful fruit.

There are hundreds of varieties of the Capsicum family; its fruits vary in size and shape as well as flavor, and they come in a myriad of colors. Some peppers are green at maturity, others are red. Some are yellow, violet, white or brown.

The pod pepper plant is, in fact, so pretty that many gardeners plant it in the flower garden right along with other ornamental plants, and it is a particular favorite with kitchen-window gardeners. See for yourself — plant a few seeds in coffee cans in the fall and by Christmas, with very little investment of time or money, you will have wonderful remembrances for your gourmet friends.

In general, the Capsicum family can be divided into two categories — the hot, especially beloved south of the border, and the mild, sweet-flavored bell or bull-nosed pepper, most popular in the United States where a whopping 485 million pounds reach the markets annually.

Most popular of these sweet-flavored peppers are the California Wonder, which has a large, smooth fruit, dark green at maturity, but turning red as it continues to ripen; the Chinese Giant, which is short, chunky and a brilliant scarlet in color; the long, thin, bright-red Ruby King; and the Sunnybrook, which looks a bit like a flattened tomato. The pimiento, which is so widely used in

its canned version, is also a member of the group.

Let your eye be your guide when selecting peppers. A good pepper looks like a good one! You will avoid blemished and wrinkled fruit, of course, and remember that a pale color denotes immaturity. A good quality pepper is bright-colored, whether red or green, fresh and crisp-looking and well shaped.

There may well be as many recipes for stuffed peppers as there are varieties of pepper, but remember this — just as the same eighty-eight notes can be arranged to produce a delightful melody, so can a basic recipe become a work of art!

The following recipe is in that category — simple enough to serve again and again to your family and grand enough to serve on any occasion.

Creole Stuffed Green Peppers

4	large green bell peppers
1	cup boiling water
	Salt
1	pound ground chuck
$1/2$	cup minced onion
$1/2$	cup minced celery
$1/4$	cup minced green pepper (optional)
1	egg, unbeaten
$1/2$	cup light cream or evaporated milk
1	one-pound 4-ounce can tomatoes ($2^1/_2$ cups)
1	tablespoon sugar
$1/4$	teaspoon cinnamon
6	whole cloves
1	tablespoon flour
$1/4$	cup cold water

Wash 4 green bell peppers; cut thin slice from stem end of each; remove seeds. Boil peppers in boiling water with $1^1/_4$ teaspoons salt; tightly covered, 5 minutes.

Meanwhile, combine meat, $1/4$ cup onion, celery, 1 teaspoon salt, $1/4$ cup minced green pepper, egg, cream. Drain boiled peppers; stuff with meat mixture. Place in 8x8x2 baking dish.

Start heating oven to 350 degrees. In saucepan, combine tomatoes, $1/4$ cup onion, $1/2$ teaspoon salt, sugar, cinnamon, cloves; simmer, uncovered, 10 minutes; then strain, reserving liquid. Stir flour and cold water until smooth; add to strained liquid; cook, stirring until slightly thickened; pour over peppers. Bake 45 to 50 minutes. Makes 4 servings.

CREPES D'ORANGE, FRENCH PANCAKES

Let's take a page from the cookbook of France for a fancy holiday recipe. This is a versatile recipe, for you can serve it as a dessert, as a holiday breakfast, or make a perfect brunch for entertaining.

Crepes are light, small pancakes, with a filling, which are rolled up into a compact serving package. The most famous, I am sure, of the crepes is Crepes Suzette. These crepes were named for an actress who played in the Comedie Francaise about 1900. The role she played had a direct connection with the recipe named for her. Her part in the play was that of a maid, and she had to serve the crepes to a group of characters meeting for an intimate supper.

However, the actors in this play were gourmets, and the crepes which were sent into the theater as props were cold before they reached the discriminating taste buds of the gourmet actors. They decided to make a deal with the chef to devise some way of getting hot crepes to them. They simply would not tolerate such unappetizing fare as cold crepes.

The chef, Joseph by name, was inspired. The idea he created was pure inspiration — prepare the crepes beforehand, but reheat them at the table on the stage by flaming them. *Voilá!* A new recipe and a new flair in French cooking had been born. Of course, he appropriately named them for the actress who played the part of the maid and served the crepes. But the demands of the gourmet actors were really responsible for this recipe, as so often happens when people are not satisfied with less than the best.

To this day Crepes Suzette are served at the table and flamed before the interested eyes of the diners. And so you may do with Crepes d'Orange if you wish. You too can prepare the little, petite pancakes in advance, then bring them to the table with the sauce all ready, combine them there and flame them. For a large party they can be made up as eaten, so be sure you have enough batter to keep the crepes coming to the tables. Seconds, thirds and even fourths will be demanded.

Crepes d'Orange, French Pancakes

1	cup sifted flour
6	tablespoons confectioners' sugar
1/2	teaspoon salt
1	cup milk
2	eggs
	Cointreau

Sift flour, confectioners' sugar, and salt together. Add milk and stir until perfectly smooth. Add eggs and beat thoroughly. Pour batter from pitcher or large spoon onto lightly greased hot griddle. When pancakes are puffed and full of bubbles, after 1 or 2 minutes, turn and cook about 1 minute on second side. Spread crepes with Orange Hard Sauce, roll, and pour Cointreau over crepes.

FOR ORANGE HARD SAUCE:

1/2	cup butter
1	package superfine sugar
	Grated rind of 3 oranges
1/2	teaspoon salt
	Juice of 3 oranges

Combine butter, sugar, orange rind, and salt. Beat well. Add orange juice gradually and blend thoroughly.

DOLLY MADISON POUND CAKE

In 1779, General George Washington, writing from West Point to a friend, commented about food, as he so often did. "The cook has had the sagacity to discover that apples will make pies." Adding that he wondered how his guests would accept an apple pie alongside a beef-steak pie the following evening when he was entertaining at a somewhat (as much as the war allowed) formal dinner. Then he mentioned other items on the menu. But my mind goes back to the picture of those guests tasting the surprising apple pie for the first time. Of course, Washington needn't have wondered about his guests' approval of the pie. Anything the man who was becoming first in war, first in peace, and first in the hearts of his countrymen, and who, even before that shot was fired at Lexington, was known to be a very proper gentleman, served at the table was correct.

Actually, I imagine the guests went home to tell their cooks to cook up a pie "with apples in it." A new pie was presented to a new nation that night. "As American as apple pie" the saying goes, and that pie is as American as George Washington.

The father of our country was not the only Early American Gourmet. He was, indeed, far surpassed by the eminent author of liberty, Thomas Jefferson. The same hand that penned those immortal words, ". . . we hold these truths to be self-evident . . ." also spent much time penning good "receipts" as they were called. Jefferson was such a great epicure and had such a profound fondness of the intricately prepared dishes of France that Patrick Henry critically remarked that Jefferson was a man "who abjured his native victuals." Henry's preference was for that Virginia menu he had learned to love, to wit: Virginia Ham, batter bread, Brunswick stew, and pound cake.

Jefferson urged his daughter (he was widowed early in life) to collect good receipts and perfect the finer culinary arts. She did and later ran his Monticello home. At Monticello it was not unusual to sit down to dinner with fifty guests, and never fewer than fifteen guests, any evening. The grocery lists which appear in Jefferson's account books attest to his epicurean fancies:

two pipes Marsalla; two casks of Bucellas; five casks porter; 40 beef tongues; 100 ham of Colonel Mason; 4 kegs tomp and sounds; 40 lbs. crackers; 5 bottles anchovies; 3 dozen pickles; 10 lbs. almonds; 2 ounces cinnamon; 2 ounces nutmeg; 1 lb. all-spice; 1 lb. pepper; 6 bottles mustard; 6 lbs. chocolate; 6 lbs. sugars; 20$^1/_2$ lbs. good cheese; 11$^3/_4$ lbs. cheese, ordinary; 40 lbs. coffee; 10 lbs. rice; 25 lbs. raisins.

Like Washington at Mount Vernon, Jefferson found he was running an Inn at Monticello. Eventually, all of this Southern hospitality veered him toward bankruptcy, but he never scrimped on setting a fine table. He introduced macaroni into this country, and vanilla, new wines and the first receipt for ice cream.

Dolly Madison was also famous for her desserts. This cake is an example:

Dolly Madison Pound Cake

1	**pound butter**
1	**pound granulated sugar**
$^1/_2$	**pound pitted dates**
6	**tablespoons honey**
12	**eggs, separated and beaten**
1	**pound flour, sifted twice**
12	**almonds, skinned**

Cream your butter and sugar together and add well-beaten egg yolks, and stiffly beaten egg whites. Add flour alternately with the eggs to the creamed sugar-butter mixture. Beat. When very light, pour into a well-greased and floured round pan. The pan should be large enough to hold the entire mixture plus an inch or more at the top of the pan. Bake in a moderate oven (350 degrees) until golden brown. Baking should be slow and watched carefully. Allow to cool while in the pan. When cooled, remove from pan and decorate with dates and almonds. Pour honey over the top for glaze.

DOVES EPICUREAN

The crackle of leaves, the bracing, nippy air, signals the fall of the year and turns a shooting man's heart to thoughts of the great outdoors, and a meticulous search for a very delectable little bird — the dove. A small bird, the dove, but many hunters think it all the more challenging to the sportsman and one of the highest-class pleasures of the table. A dove dinner, cooked to a hunting man's discriminating taste, is a gourmet food concerto.

After the partaking of these fine-feathered birds done to such intoxicating perfection, the sportsman can say with the epicure, "Fate cannot harm me, I have dined today."

Many years ago I began testing recipes and sampling foods around the world. Surveying people's tastes for certain flavors and combinations of flavors, noting what they most enjoyed and the recipes most often and consistently requested from my television show, shown across the country. I encountered the plain fact that Americans are cautious about eating game, and won't include it in their menus. Except for the sportsman, who understands game, and takes precautions to keep it fresh and properly dressed, most cooks — even those with the best cooking credentials — avoid it. A great shame. They don't know what they're missing. However, dove is a bird you need have absolutely no worry about eating. You can serve it with safety, and if you use Dove Epicurean as your recipe you will eat it with exclamations of praise. It is a wedding of flavors — tender little birds companioned with a delicate haunting sauce.

These are the ingredients you will need:

Doves Epicurean

8	**doves, cleaned and dressed**
$^2/_3$	**cup brandy**
1	**cup butter (or margarine)**
1	**tablespoon Worcestershire powder**
1	**teaspoon garlic salt**
$^1/_2$	**cup chopped truffles**
$^1/_2$	**teaspoon nutmeg**
$^1/_2$	**cup sliced carrots**
1	**cup yellow or green seedless grapes**
	Salt to taste
	Pepper to taste
$^1/_3$	**cup flour**
	Toast

Place doves into brandy and let stand 30 minutes. Melt butter in a skillet, slowly, over low heat. Add doves to melted butter and cook slowly until lightly browned.

Add Worcestershire powder, garlic salt, truffles, nutmeg, carrots, grapes, salt and pepper to the dictates of your own taste. Cook, covered, over low heat 15 to 20 minutes.

Remove doves. Add flour to skillet mixture, stirring constantly, until thickened. Place doves onto slices of toast. Cover with the sauce in the skillet. Garnish with parsley. This recipe serves 4 sportsmen-epicureans.

DUTCH CARROT BREAD

In the beautiful gardens of King Meroldad-Baladan, in ancient Babylon, a lacy-leaf ornamental plant grew among the scented herbs. In Elizabethan England, ladies wore the same wispy leaves to adorn their hair.

We don't know whether King Meroldad-Baladan ever realized that his pretty plant had such a delicious root, but we do know that the carrot has been cultivated as a much-loved food for centuries.

Carrots, in addition to their many other virtues, are among our most accommodating foods. They are easily grown and they store well; they can become a salad, a vegetable, or a dessert, and they combine well with other foods to become a main dish.

Little girls eat carrots to make their hair curly, pilots eat them to make their eyes sharper, and the diet-conscious find them low in calories and high in taste appeal. I can't offer any documented evidence to show that carrots do make little girls' hair curly (they haven't done much for mine!) but they are very high in vitamin A, which is necessary for good eyesight.

By the way, while preparing the delectable delight I'll give you later, take just a moment for this little adventure — you'll see what it was that King Meroldad-Baladan and the Elizabethan ladies found so appealing. Select a particularly likely-looking carrot top, slice off about 1/2 inch and place it in a saucer of water on your window sill. Before long, you will be rewarded with an exquisite miniature fern!

I often feel that carrots are a very much misunderstood vegetable. Countless adults are certain they "don't like carrots" when in fact, they may never have tasted them properly cooked. Old-time cooking methods that left the carrots devoid of flavor (the flavor having been dumped down the drain with the over-abundant cooking water) were the culprit. Properly cooked carrots are full of flavor, and vitamins as well.

If you have never tried carrots in baking, I urge you to do so now. They add such a delightful flavor and wonderfully moist texture!

The following recipe is one I know you'll want to create over and over. This Dutch Carrot Loaf stores well — great to have on hand to serve with coffee when unexpected guests appear, and if you have any lunch box carriers in your household, it will be doubly appreciated. Perhaps I shouldn't even mention nutrition — but then surely none of my readers would be so devious as to allow a child to eat his vegetables when he thinks he is eating cake!

Dutch Carrot Bread

2	cups sifted flour
2	teaspoons soda
1/2	teaspoon salt
2	teaspoons cinnamon
2	cups grated carrots
1 1/2	cups oil
1 1/2	cups sugar
2	tablespoons vanilla
3	eggs

Sift dry ingredients into large mixing bowl. Push to sides of bowl and add all other ingredients except carrots. Beat on medium speed until well blended. Fold in carrots. Turn into greased and floured loaf pans. Cook at 300 degrees for 1 hour. Dust with confectioners' sugar if desired. Makes 2 loaves.

EGGPLANT PARMESAN

Cheese is certainly one of the most versatile foods in the world as it can turn up at any point during a meal. It is served more than any other product as an appetizer, provides a perfect topping on soup, excites our appetites in salads, and is the most popular ingredient for casseroles. There must be thousands of variations of the cheese sauce and more and more this hallmark dairy product is being used as a dessert. "A meal without it," according to Brillat-Savarin, "is like a beautiful woman with one eye missing."

Like its classic champions, bread and wine, cheese is made by the process of fermentation, which can transform one substance, at the point it is about to spoil, into something far superior to what it was in the first place. Legend provides the story that cheese was discovered by an Arab merchant who put milk into a pouch made of the stomach of a suckling calf. When he went to drink the milk he found curds of cheese. This metamorphosis had been accomplished by an enzyme called rennet in the calf's stomach. Cheese-making was the earliest manner of preserving milk, and soon became popular as a special product. Cheese soon gained such status that Viking sailors were sometimes paid in cheese rather than money at the end of a voyage. There is even a story which gives cheese a place in history; supposedly the Montevidean Navy once defeated the Buenos Aires Navy by using cheeses as cannon balls.

From its accidental beginnings cheese-making developed into a fine skill. In the southern part of France is a small town called Roquefort. Surrounding Roquefort is a range of hills that are interlaced with limestone caves. Around 1000 A.D., monks near the town of Roquefort discovered that milk left in these local cool, humid limestone caverns would, in a matter of months, transform into a delicious cheese veined with blue mold. Soon other monasteries throughout Europe began developing varieties of cheese as a source of income. Today, there are over 500 kinds of cheese, most of them of European origin, although cream and cottage cheeses and Liederkranz are native to America.

While cheese can be a feature attraction at any table, it has become a cardinal trapping in many recipes for great cuisine. The following recipe demonstrates the compatibility of cheese with a garden product.

Eggplant Parmesan

1	eggplant
4	cups dry bread crumbs
1	egg
	Olive oil or shortening for frying
1	onion, chopped
$1/2$	green bell pepper, chopped
$2^1/_2$	cups canned or fresh tomatoes
1	teaspoon salt
$1/_8$	teaspoon pepper
1	teaspoon sugar
1	cup Parmesan cheese

Slice the eggplant in $1/_4$-inch slices, peel, dip in bread crumbs, then egg (slightly beaten and mixed with $1/_2$ cup water), and again in the crumbs. Fry in oil or shortening until brown. Sauté the onion and green bell pepper until soft; add tomatoes, salt, pepper, and sugar and cook until well blended. Place the eggplant in a casserole in alternate layers with cheese and the sauce, having the top layer end with cheese. Bake covered at 350 degrees for 15 minutes. Remove cover and continue baking until crusty and brown.

ELEPHANT'S FEET

For several years I enjoyed the good fortune of working with the personable and famous television and motion picture star, Dick Van Dyke. We shared the microphone on the network radio program, "Flair," originating in New York. Dick performed as the emcee on the daily broadcast while I delivered a daily feature on food. Believe it or not, Boris Karloff gave advice on children and Arlene Francis occupied a more compatible role as beauty consultant. After Dick launched his celebrated television series, "The Dick Van Dyke Show," it was necessary for us to meet in Hollywood for recording. One day, during a coffee break, Dick, in a teasing mood, inquired if I had a recipe for "Elephant's Feet." I immediately responded with a recipe that I commandeered

while traveling in India. While Dick stared in disbelief, I chronicled the following directions. First, you marinate a mess of elephant's feet overnight in olive oil and lemon juice. Next you go outside and dig a hole in the ground four feet deep by two feet in width. Place several wooden logs in the bottom of the pit and set ablaze. After several hours, when the wood has burned almost completely down and remains only as smoldering embers, you cover with a thin layer of sand. Next, you place a layer of straw matting over the sand then fill the remainder of the hole with sand. You allow the elephant's feet to roast slowly on the retained, stored heat in the ground for 48 hours.

At this point, I described to Mr. Van Dyke the technique of carefully removing the cooked elephant's feet and he exclaimed that never in his life had he tasted such succulent, intrinsic-flavored elephant's feet. Dick, looking a bit green of face, said, "David, how many persons will this recipe serve?" I quickly answered that the recipe would satisfy approximately fifty hungry appetites. Dick then observed that if most people were like him it would serve 50,000!

Good living and *bon appétit!*

"EN GUETE" FONDUE

A gift shop owner friend of mine asked me to help him solve a merchandising problem. His business had taken an unusual turn on one special item. "Several years ago," he said, "I'd sell about one to two fondue dishes in a year. Now I'm selling a couple dozen of them. But the funny thing is I sell all of them in September. Can you figure that one out?"

No. I couldn't. But I kept working on it. Let's see now, what goes on in September? School starts. Football games. Autumn. Cooler. More entertaining; but surely hosts were not serving fondue only in September. Too early for Christmas buying.

I attacked the problem from another angle: the fondue itself. It is almost the national dish of Switzerland, but also popular in other European countries. Then I thought of the exodus of tourists to Europe. They were discovering fondue.

I further tested my solution by calling a Swiss chef. "Ah, yes," he said, "we get many calls for fondue in the fall. It is a little joke for us. A customer orders fondue — we say they've been to the Old Country. We have it on our menu, of course, but you know it is really a party food — for fun."

The Swiss say you only invite a special kind of person for fondue — good friends and jolly fellows, food lovers and companionable companions. A friend of mine calls this "Drunken Cheese Sauce" but the fondue itself is not the cause of levity as the alcohol in it evaporates when cooked, leaving only flavor. It is the *esprit de corps* of fondue guests which makes for fun and games.

As a matter of actual fact, in Switzerland they really do make a game of fondue. A forfeit has to be paid by anyone who loses a piece of the crusty bread in the sauce. For men the forfeit is either a bottle of wine or they pay for the next fondue; for women the forfeit is a kiss.

It is not necessary to have a special fondue dish. A chafing dish will do. In Switzerland they use an earthenware dish and keep it hot over what they call a spirit-fire — sterno to you Americans.

For serving 4 you will assemble the following:

"En Guete" Fondue

1	**pound Swiss cheese, grated**
3	**tablespoons flour**
1	**clove garlic, cut**
1	**cup white, dry wine**
$^1/_2$	**teaspoon salt**
	Dash of pepper
	Dash of nutmeg
$^1/_4$	**cup Kirsch**
	Abundance of bite-size pieces of French or Italian crusty bread

Grate the Swiss cheese and set aside. Rub around the inside of your fondue dish with garlic, vigorously. Heat the wine but do not let it boil. Add the cheese gradually, stirring constantly. Do not add more cheese until the first addition is melted. When all cheese is melted add salt, pepper and nutmeg. When the mixture starts to cook, stir in Kirsch in which you have dissolved the flour. Cook and stir until a smooth consistency is reached. Taste. All right? If not, adjust your seasonings to taste, and serve to your guests wishing them *En Guete*. Each person spears a piece of bread and swishes it around once or twice in the fondue and then pops the tasty morsel into the mouth and repeat, and repeat, and repeat.

En Guete wishes you good appetite as I wish you good living and *bon appétit!*

FARMER'S MARKET SALAD

In the heart of the film capital of the world there is a very unique establishment — the Farmer's Market. If you have visited Los Angeles, I'm quite sure you have also visited the fabulous Farmer's Market. It is a melange of food booths, gift shops, produce markets, specialty stores where you may purchase meat, cheeses, nuts, candy, fruits, groceries — and an eater's paradise!

International dining patio might be an appropriate description because you may choose from Turkish, Chinese, French, Italian; seafood, barbecue, ice creams, candies, pies, hamburgers; and others too numerous to sample on one vacation, even if you go there every day.

California is a salad-eating state and Californians are very salad-conscious. I have seen many film stars at the Market strolling from food stall to food stall hungrily eyeing the luscious offerings and then automatically turn to the salad bar. Here they have a good and nutritious luncheon — tasty, satisfying, and still hold the line on calories which cameras are so expert at detecting and emphasizing. They have their glamour image to consider, of course, but to do it with a Farmer's Market Salad is no sacrifice.

When you have made your selection you find a table under a colorful umbrella and dine in the sunshine — well, there used to be sunshine, and blue skies too, but that was B.S. — before smog! Well, you can enjoy the open air and warmth of California living while you savor a Farmer's Market Salad.

Select with care, the freshest, best looking green groceries you can find:

Farmer's Market Salad

1	**head romaine lettuce**
1	**head iceberg lettuce**
3	**tomatoes**
4	**hard-boiled eggs**
1	**large can English peas (drained)**

Shred romaine and iceberg lettuce. Section tomatoes and hard-boiled eggs and place in with lettuce. Place English peas into recipe and toss with the following dressing recipe.

FARMER'S MARKET SALAD DRESSING:

2	**tablespoons chopped green onions**
1	**garlic clove, crushed**
$^1/_4$	**cup chopped parsley**
1	**cup mayonnaise**
	Salt to taste
1	**tablespoon lemon juice**
$^1/_4$	**cup vinegar**
$^1/_4$	**cup (2 ounces) Blue Cheese, crumbled**
$^1/_2$	**cup thick sour cream**
	Pepper, freshly ground

Combine all ingredients well. Chill. Makes $2^1/_4$ cups.

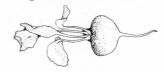

FIESTA TACOS

Mexico — colorful Latin land to the south of us — offers food for the gourmet as different from our regular American diet as the people are different from us. This big and happy contrast gives Mexican food an atmosphere of party-time. Mexican food is fun food, a change of pace-taste, and there is something of the fiesta in all of their dishes for they are snappy, smellful, tasteful, and their Spanish names also impart an other-worldliness to the menu. When served with Mexican pottery, bright native accoutrements, piñatas, and all the easily obtainable decorative pieces, you can transport your guests into a world of Latin entertainment. All of this for a very economical cost — in fact, Mexican food is probably less expensive to prepare and serve to large groups than any other.

It is among the Indians that these basic Mexican foods were invented, and they are still the regular diet of the people on the land, and in the tiny villages, where the corn is cultivated and prepared on the stone metate into masa — the dough of tortillas. Corn is to Mexico what wheat is to America — their staff of life. In past days they worshiped the god of corn for the whole nation was dependent on it for life. In some ways, agriculturally, for instance, Latin Americans had a civilization comparable to European standards when Cortés arrived. Unfortunately, for them, they had not advanced in modern weapons and warfare. They had settled down to grow corn. This is when their civilization began. Not only did they grow corn, but potatoes, tomatoes, squashes, avocados, papayas, pineapples, vanilla beans, and peanuts. None of these foods were known to the Spanish when they arrived.

It was a collision of two worlds. The Spanish took the new foods home, and thereby lies the misconception of many that Mexican and Spanish foods are alike. They are no more the same than American and English foods.

The hotness of Mexican food can be controlled in your own kitchen, although many aficionados of this cuisine like it hot. The chiles (peppers to Norteamericanos), come in many sizes, colors, and tastes — but they are all hot. The Latins claim wonderful things for the chiles. These claims range all the way from their belief that they "air-condition" the body (by making the inside hotter than the outside!), to prevention of dangerous fevers — even malaria; from aiding digestion by stimulating gastric juices to intensifying romance!

Today's recipe is really the Mexican's sandwich — tacos. Tacos are easy to prepare, delicious, inexpensive, adaptable to all manner of dining. No genuine Mexican meal will be complete without tacos.

Fiesta Tacos

3 **pounds chuck roast**
1 **large onion**
2 **to 3 tablespoons water**
   Salt
1 **tablespoon Mole spice**
2 **tablespoons taco spices**
   Vegetable oil
   Tortillas
   Shredded lettuce
   Diced tomatoes
   Hot Sauce

Trim chuck roast and cut into 2-inch cubes. Place meat cubes, onion, and water in pressure saucepan. Add salt, Mole spice, and taco spices. Cover saucepan, adjust cover, and place over full heat. Allow steam to escape according to manufacturer's directions. Cook at 15 pounds pressure for 30 minutes. Remove from heat and reduce pressure immediately. Remove meat and onion, and put through food chopper. Add broth from cooker until meat is moist and no longer crumbly. Add additional salt and taco spices to taste.

Heat vegetable oil in a heavy skillet. Place a heaping spoon of meat mixture in center of soft tortilla. Fold tortilla and fry in hot fat until golden brown on each side.

Drain on paper towel. Serve with bowl of shredded lettuce, diced tomatoes and hot sauce.

FILET GOURMET BURGERS

A centuries-old saying is that "when in Rome you do as the Romans do," and it is good etiquette no matter what country it is practiced in.

As far as good goes, however, we find some pretty puzzling circumstances: In Mexico you order chili and you get a bowl of very hot peppers; in Spain there is no such taste delight as Spanish Rice; if you venture into Hong Kong there is no chop suey — that is the invention of an American-Chinese; and in England I can absolutely testify that they do not even know what English muffins are. I spent a great deal of time asking, because I wanted to taste the real thing in the country of its origin.

At the Selsdon Park in Surrey, where we were staying, I talked to the maitre d'. He was very polite, tried very hard to figure what it was. Finally, I thought I (knowing full well what an English muffin really was) would help him. "Perhaps it is a kind of biscuit." "Yes," he said, "that's it." He was obviously relieved that "we" had solved the problem.

But the most outrageous food faux pas you can commit

in Germany is to order a hamburger in Hamburg. Indignantly the waiter replies, *Ich bin ein Hamburger!&?* Rough translation: "We are all Hamburgers in this city." Moral is, unless you want to be thought cannibalistic, never order a hamburger in Hamburg.

You may have wondered why hamburger is called hamburger since it has no ham in it. The reason is Hamburg, Germany, the city of its invention. There they created a new meat product from inexpensive cuts and trimmings. Originally, it was any ground up meat. Could be lamb, veal, mutton, pork, beef, or ham, as well as some of the organ meats such as heart, kidney, or liver. Or it was sometimes a combination of several of these. Grinding tenderizes the cheaper cuts of meat. These meat-mixtures were found to be very versatile, too.

Even though we don't get our hamburger from Hamburg, the word is one which always transitions with the product, and no doubt, will never change just to accommodate semantics. Americans are primarily beef eaters. Hamburger to us is ground beef.

Meanwhile, at home on your patio where hamburgers are not people try Filet Gourmet Burgers, which are not just hamburger, either.

Filet Gourmet Burgers

1½	pound ground hamburger
2	onions, diced fine
1	teaspoon garlic salt
	Dash Tabasco
¼	teaspoon chili powder
	Paprika
	Dash Worcestershire powder
½	pound bacon
	Salt and pepper
1	small can button mushrooms, drained

Mix all above ingredients together except bacon and paprika. Form into large, flat patties. Strip all the way around the edges with bacon. (Use two slices if one will not surround.) Secure bacon with toothpicks. Sprinkle paprika on both sides and broil to taste. Recipe makes 6 generous servings.

FRESH BROCCOLI SICILIAN STYLE

"Of such are we — let us live while we may!" This was the philosophy of Trimalchio, one of the richest and most famous of the gourmands of Imperial Rome. Trimalchio wasn't the only one to give or attend the memorable Roman banquets. Heliogabalus was another rich Roman, famous for unbridled luxury. He served peas and lentils garnished with gold nuggets and precious stones to 600 guests.

Lucullus, Nero, Vitellus, Commodus, and Caracalla also wasted the resources of conquered peoples in the banquet hall. One of the most famous of these Roman eaters was Apicius, that Apicius who gave his name to the world's first cookbook, one on Roman cookery.

Today, we wouldn't eat many of those Roman banquet foods on a dare! We do, however, share with these ancients a keen appetite for broccoli. In fact, there are four or five ways of cooking "sprouting broccoli" in the Apicius cookbook. Broccoli was seasoned with pepper, chopped onion, cumin, and coriander and a little oil and "sun-made wine." One of his broccoli recipes was prepared with raisins and nuts; still another called for green olives.

It required almost 2,000 years for broccoli to become popular in this country, however. Today, in almost every region of the country, it is a table habit food. There are two distinct forms of broccoli. There is the familiar Italian or sprouting broccoli. It looks like a green bouquet. That's really what it is — a bouquet of buds; if not harvested, it would burst into yellow blossoms. Then there is "heading" or "cauliflower broccoli." This forms a white "curd" which looks like cauliflower, and, in fact, the winter cauliflowers we see are actually the slower growing, "heading" broccoli. This is so much like true cauliflower that most of us couldn't distinguish between them. Strangely enough, all three of these have the same botanical name and are highly developed forms of the cabbage family. All are what Mark Twain once called, "cabbage with a college education."

I personally feel that any college in the country would give this recipe a master's degree of elegance:

Fresh Broccoli Sicilian Style

2	tablespoons olive oil
1	medium onion, thinly sliced
1	clove fresh garlic, sliced
1½	tablespoons flour
1	cup chicken stock or chicken bouillon cube
1	cup water
4	anchovies, chopped
½	cup sliced black olives
⅛	teaspoon ground black pepper
2	cups shredded Mozzarella or American cheese
1	large bunch (1¾ pounds) fresh broccoli, cooked

Heat the olive oil in a 1-quart saucepan. Add onion and garlic and sauté 1 to 2 minutes or until limp. Blend in the flour. Add chicken stock or chicken bouillon cube, dissolved in 1 cup boiling water. Stir and cook until medium thickness, 5 to 6 minutes. Add anchovies, olives, ground black pepper and cheese. Mix well and serve over hot, cooked broccoli. Recipe serves 6.

FRESH PINEAPPLE, LUAU STYLE

Some of our most popular fruits such as grapes, apples and oranges have been known for many, many centuries and it is natural that there should have been paeans in recognition of their obvious delights. The pineapple, however, was one of the New World's gifts. But in less than 500 years it has collected the most extravagant compliments from the world's epicures.

The sailors of Columbus found pineapples growing on the island of Guadulupe in 1493. This was in the course of the second of Columbus's journeys to the New World. He and his men might have missed this fragrant fruit if they hadn't wandered off into the dense tropical forests and been lost for several days. While they were trying to find their way back to the ship, they found and gathered as many pineapples as they could carry. Peter Martyr, historian of the expedition, records the excitement of tasting these first pineapples.

Pineapples were found in many other parts of tropical America. On different islands in the Caribbean; in Mexico; Central America; Brazil. Its discoverers were always astonished and delighted with the new fruit. Just how delighted we can judge from some of these records from the sixteenth and seventeenth centuries:

We might start with Sir Walter Raleigh. He wasn't the first, but his name is most familiar. He wrote "Pines, the princess of fruits, that grown under the sun, especially those of Guiana."

Then there was explorer Acosta who noted, "Pineapples have an excellent smell, and it is very pleasant and delightful to taste, it is full of juice, and of a sweet and sharp taste." Early missionaries loved it, too. One, Father Oviedo, wrote, "It — the pineapple — restores a healthy appetite and stimulates people to eat."

One of the most glowing accounts was given by another missionary, Father White, who discovered pineapples in the Barbados. He said: "The rarest of all others that I think is in the world, is the pineapple, of the color of gold, mixed with an orient green. It is not hard to peel, but of soft and thin skin, of delicious taste, not having one membrane or kernel, but all clean through, equally dainty to taste. It is the queen of all meat fruits without exception. The taste, as near as I can express it, is an aromatical compound of wine and strawberries."

When selecting your pineapple, remember these signs of a fine fruit: It will have a pleasing fragrance; also, if you tug at one of the stiff spiky leaves in its top-knot, it will loosen readily. The Spanish Red Pineapple is the best known variety. Its color will be red-gold when ripe. The other common variety called "Sugar Loaf" remains a dark green, even when completely and sweetly ripe.

I have received many requests from my readers to blueprint the directions for serving a luau style fresh pineapple. While it might appear difficult, it is really very simple if you follow these simple directions.

Fresh Pineapple, Luau Style

Cut a thick slice from the top and bottom of a fresh, ripe pineapple, saving the bottom slice. Run a sharp, thin, long knife blade around the pineapple between the rind and meat, leaving a shell, 3/8-inch thick, intact. To do this, cut the pineapple from either end to the halfway point, keeping the knife blade pointed toward the rind. Push the pineapple cylinder out the big end by pressing from the small end. Cut the cylinder in half, lengthwise, then cut each half into quarters. Cut away and discard core from each quarter. Cut quarters into lengthwise strips. Place the bottom that was cut from the pineapple on a plate, over which rests the pineapple shell. Fill the shell with pineapple strips.

GAZPACHO GRANADA

From sunny Spain we have a salad soup which is a wonderful blend of many raw vegetables. Typically Spanish, it has the calm of the Mediterranean's blue waters in its velvet smoothness; the snappiness of Spanish castanets as they set the rhythm of Spain's thrilling dances — the fandango, the bolero, and the flamenco. And yet the adventurous touch of the Spanish explorers De Soto and Balboa; the colorful tradition of the bullfighters.

Although España is responsible for this recipe, it could never have been evolved without the help of South America. Here was where the tomato was found in cultivation by the conquistadors. They brought it back to Spain. As you will see, the tomato is basic to gazpacho. Gazpacho is versatile, too. Makes a wonderful appetizer served in cups before dinner, it goes as well as an early course of a dinner, and is also appropriate for a light luncheon.

Appreciators of this soup often indulge in heated arguments as to whether the best method of preparation is blending, puréeing, or chopping (finely). At other times they will disagree as to the proper base to be used — water, white wine, beef stock, or tomato juice. My gazpacho I have named for Granada, perhaps the most colorful city of Spain even in its decline. It still has the atmosphere of that time when Spain was the most powerful of European countries, and these traditions have been kept intact in Granada. So it is a fitting name combination — gazpacho and Granada — both showing the character and the glory that was Spain.

You will need these ingredients:

Gazpacho Granada

1	clove garlic, peeled and mashed
1	large green bell pepper, seeded and chopped
2	cucumbers, peeled, chopped and seeded
$1/4$	cup olive oil
$1^1/_2$	cups cold tomato juice
8	ripe tomatoes, peeled and mashed
1	small, milk onion, peeled and chopped
3	teaspoons salt
$1^1/_2$	teaspoons paprika
9	tablespoons wine vinegar

Combine about half of the vegetables with salt and paprika. Place into a liquefier or chop well and finely. Mix the oil, vinegar, and tomato juice. Put half in the liquefier and run the liquefier until vegetables are smoothly blended.

Repeat the process with the remaining chopped vegetables and remaining liquid. Combine the two batches. Chill until very cold, but not so cold that the oil hardens. Taste for seasoning and correct by adding more if desired. Pour into chilled bouillon cups.

At table, offer toasted croutons, chopped cucumbers, chopped scallions, and chopped green bell pepper.

GERMAN CHOCOLATE PIE

There never has developed a strictly American style of cooking. Not, that is, compared with the French way of cooking, or the Chinese, or the Italian. This is because America has taken all of the foods of other nations into its kitchen. They say we are a nation of immigrants; so, like a colossal tasting bee we sample from every country's cuisine which has immigrated to this nation with its people.

Such is the story of the most popular food flavor in the United States — chocolate. We import 650 million pounds of the cacao bean, from which chocolate is made, every year. We consume more chocolate than any other nation in the world. We consider it as American as Valley Forge, hardly stopping to think that it is an immigrant food.

It is interesting to trace the evolution of chocolate on its way to us. Columbus had to discover the New World. The Spanish explorers had to go to Mexico, there discovering the cacao tree and its raw beans which the Indians used for brewing a strange new beverage. Cortés had to return, with the secret brew, to Spain where the new "chocotal" became immediately popular. Its fame spread throughout the continent; then on to America. And all the while, had we but known it, just across our own borders the Mexicans had been cooking with chocolate for centuries. They call it "the food for the gods."

German Chocolate Pie is a pie "for the gods." This is the most popular recipe ever featured on my television show, "The Gourmet." The number of copies I have sent out number into the thousands by now.

But the recipe is not complicated — just delectable. It is not extremely unusual — just a combination of flavors that makes it a winner. It has a touch of the everyday and a touch of the gourmet.

German Chocolate Pie

1	9-inch baked pie shell
$1/2$	pound marshmallows
$3/4$	cup milk
$1/4$	teaspoon salt
$1/2$	bar German sweet chocolate
1	teaspoon vanilla
$1/2$	pint whipping cream

Combine marshmallows, milk, salt and German sweet chocolate in top of a double boiler. When melted and completely blended, set aside and let cool. Add vanilla. Now whip the cream and fold it into the chocolate mixture and pour the mixture into a 9-inch pie shell. Place in your refrigerator.

Both pie and crust will taste better if removed from the refrigerator about 20 minutes before serving.

If you wish you may top German Chocolate Pie with more whipped cream. This is strictly optional, however, as it is deliciously rich without a topping.

GRECIAN DOLMADES

There is a phrase well-known throughout the world, "the French have a word for it," and by comparison, it may be said that "the Greeks have a god, or goddess, for it." Mythological gods abound in Greece. Amid Athens's modern traffic patterns, little English Fords drive past the unforgettable, and almost unbelievable, Acropolis with its Parthenon, which was the temple of Athena, by the Temple of Zenus. Streets are often named for gods, and businesses reside side by side with the temples of the ancients. Likewise, you will find the Rent-A-Car Office opposite the Temple of Jupiter. On first hearing this, it gives one pause, but it is a good picture of today's Greece. The very, very old and the new thrive together harmoniously.

In spite of the multitude of gods and goddesses, I cannot find the results of a goddess of gourmet cooking. The ancient Athenians were obviously more interested in ideas, art, literature, in thinking and discoursing at length than in spending more time in the kitchen gourmeting their menus. Not that the native dishes are not good, satisfying, hearty fare, but American and Greek tastes are, well, worlds apart. If you already like Greek food you are in luck. That is about all you will get, except in the few large hotels which cater to American, English, and French. Even here the cuisine seems to miss the good intention. It is as if the cook developed a case of stage fright when straying from the traditional Old World ways of cooking.

Although elegance of menu and decor are rarities in Greece, the whole country abounds in culture, architecture, statuary, literature, theater (here is where theater began; the Theater of Dionysius is still there), Western philosophy, and so many intellectual and artistic accomplishments that it would be almost too much if they had originated gourmet food as well.

When you can dine in a little tavern at the foot of the hill of the Acropolis, who could ask for more elegance? To look up and see the Acropolis and Parthenon as it is lighted softly at night, guarding over the city as in the days of old, the epitome of beauty and grace.

Fruits are plentiful and good, fish is fresh from the Mediterranean, vegetables are large, wholesome and tasty, and grape leaves are much used in preparation of a national favorite called Dolmades. These are tasty little tidbits of meat and seasonings enveloped in grape leaves. They can be, and are, great hors d'oeuvres. (In fact, Dolmades really are considered the Hors d'Oeuvres of Greece). These versatile little Grecians can also be a whole meal, the main event. They can be a side dish with a larger meat course. Dolmades are a favorite of tourists, and a recipe easily duplicated once you are home again. One thing: find a specialty (or Greek) food store where you can buy grape leaves, canned, ready for the making of Dolmades.

Grecian Dolmades

1	**can grape leaves**
1	**pound ground beef**
1	**cup cooked rice, underdone**
$^1/_2$	**cup green onions, finely chopped**
$^1/_2$	**cup chopped parsley**
2	**tablespoons butter or margarine, melted**
$1^1/_2$	**teaspoons salt**
$^1/_2$	**teaspoon fresh ground black pepper**
$^1/_2$	**teaspoon cinnamon**
	Juice of $^1/_2$ lemon
2	**cups beef broth**
2	**tablespoons tomato catsup**

A can of grape leaves will contain about 50 to 60. Reserve 10 to 15 leaves to line the bottom of cooking pan. Use the remainder for wrapping around the meat stuffing. Pour hot water over the grape leaves when they are removed from the can. Drain and spread on a towel to dry. Remove rough stems.

To mix the stuffing: Blend together ground beef, rice, onions, parsley, and butter. Add seasonings: salt, pepper, and cinnamon. Mix lightly.

Place a tablespoon of the meat stuffing in the center of a grape leaf. Fold left and right ends toward the middle, then roll like a sausage. When all the stuffing is used, prepare your cooking pan by lining bottom with leaves. Then place little envelopes of meat mixture all around, stacking them on top of each other until all are in the pan. Pour over the leaves a mixture of lemon juice, broth, and tomato catsup. Cover pan and cook on low heat for an hour. If Dolmades are not very tender, cook for an additional 15 to 20 minutes.

The Greeks like to serve yogurt with this dish. Sometimes it is served with a lemon slice. To obtain a tart flavor, squeeze juice over Dolmades. This should serve about 8 people.

GREEK TAVERNA MOUSSAKA

The place to find native Greek food, and fun, at its best, is in the taberna. These are (usually) small bistro-like eateries where the Greeks like to congregate to enjoy their favorite foods, each other, and themselves. Here are Grecian dishes, native wine and local beer, plus music, sometimes dancing, atmosphere, and a true personality portrait of the Greeks, as they live their daily lives. Hospitable, gracious, and thoroughly likeable (and they like Americans, too!) these people love to be entertained while they dine. There must be a belief that ear-pounding music aids the appetite because the strains of *Zorba, the Greek, Never On Sunday* and native folk songs bring the roof down, and could be the beginning of acute deafness. And then there is the bouzouki dance (also seen in *Never on Sunday*) wherein they break pottery and other assorted tableware, during this terpsichorean art (named incidentally after Terpsichore, the mythological Greek muse of dancing).

Some tavernas feature only one or two specialty items, most offer a large variety of Greek dishes. Unless the menu has a very limited repertoire, you will find moussaka. Moussaka combines two of Greece's more plentiful and popular foods, lamb and eggplant. Beloved by the natives, most visitors who sample this classic Greek cuisine like it heartily. It has authority and is a nutritious and pleasant new taste experience. This recipe features moussaka a la casserole in the Old World tradition:

Greek Taverna Moussaka

2	medium-sized eggplants
1½	sticks butter
3½	teaspoons salt
1½	cups onions, chopped
1½	pounds ground lamb, lean
2	tablespoons tomato catsup
⅓	cup dry red wine
½	teaspoon black pepper, freshly ground
¼	teaspoon cinnamon
¼	cup chopped parsley
3	tablespoons flour
2	cups hot milk
1	cup cottage cheese, drained and dry
2	eggs, beaten
⅛	teaspoon nutmeg
¾	cup soda crackers, finely crumbled into meal
¾	cup Parmesan cheese, grated

Peel eggplant, and cut into thin slices. Brown in melted butter (using about 4 tablespoonsful). Brown eggplant on both sides. Remove and season with 1 teaspoon of salt.

In the same skillet, melt 4 more tablespoons of butter, and sauté the onions for about 7 minutes, until soft. Add the lamb and cook for 15 minutes, stirring often. Add tomato catsup, wine, pepper, cinnamon, parsley, and 1½ teaspoons of the salt. Cook over low heat until nearly dry, making sure all ingredients are well blended. Cool and sample for seasoning. Add more salt and pepper to taste, if necessary.

Take the remaining butter, place in a saucepan, and melt. Stir in flour and the remaining 1 teaspoon of salt. Stir in milk, constantly agitating ingredients. Bring to

point of boiling and cook an additional 6 or 7 minutes before removing from the heat. Allow to cool for a few minutes; then add cottage cheese, eggs, and nutmeg.

Grease an 8x12-inch baking dish, and dust lightly with flour. Cover the bottom of the baking dish with eggplant slices; then add a layer of lamb mixture and sprinkle with cracker meal and Parmesan cheese. Repeat layers of eggplant, lamb mixture, cracker meal, and Parmesan cheese, ending with eggplant for the top layer. Pour sauce over the top, and bake in a preheated 375-degree oven for 1 hour, or until the top is custard-firm and golden-colored. Let cool to warm before serving. Serve by cutting into large squares. This recipe will serve 6 generously.

GREEN BEANS WITH HOT MUSTARD SAUCE

It was Alexander Dumas, the elder, who may be considered the granddaddy of cloak-and-dagger fiction. D'Artagnan leaps to mind, sword in hand, as do Porthos, Athos, and Aramis. The Count of Monte Cristo, the Chevalier of Maison Rouge (or red house), and a whole parade of fearless men and beautiful women, were Dumas products. Yet, how many know that in addition to more than 400 volumes of fiction, he made time for a dictionary of cuisine. Father Dumas was a great trencherman.

In the original edition of this dictionary, there appeared an advertisement for mustard. The copy for this ad runs to about 3,000 words and is signed by Dumas. No modern Madison Avenue copywriter would have the slightest little hope of getting such an ad in print, even if he had the energy to write. But, Dumas's mustard copy is very interesting indeed.

Dumas begins his mustard ad with the ancient history of the spice. Both the Greeks and Romans called it, "sinapis" (si-NAH-pis), which is still its botanical name. The Romans in the days of the Caesars did not, however, use it in "its primitive simplicity." They made a sort of suspicious mess called garum (GAH-rum), which started with a little mustard. To this were added the spare parts of anchovies, mackerel, dolphin, mushrooms, and a number of other seasonings.

Dumas did not write his mustard ad for the man who reads as he runs. He mentions the names of forgotten Greeks and Romans who had anything to say about mustard and tells how they used it. He tells us that Charlemagne and his Court, in the ninth century, sat down to dine at 9:00 A.M., but apparently never used mustard. Some 500 years later, when the Duke of Burgundy entertained King Phillip of France, 100 gallons of mustard were used at a single meal. Another big mustard eater was King Louis XI in the fifteenth century. He used to drop in on his noble friends, just to see what they were up to. On all of these surprise visits he carried his own pot of mustard, says Dumas.

There have been twenty-three Catholic Popes named John. Pope John XXII lived almost 600 years ago. Dumas tells us he loved mustard and good food. When this Pope had to find a post for an untalented nephew he named him, "Chief Mustard Maker." It isn't likely that the nephew actually had much to do with the mixing of the papal mustard, for Dumas reminds us the expression "Chief Mustard Maker to the Pope" applied to a stupid and vain person.

Louis XIV was so fond of the nippy flavor of mustard that he granted a coat of arms to the spice. In the eighteenth century, mustard making had become one of the esteemed arts. One mustard maker, Maille, won for himself the title of Purveyor of Mustard to Madame Pompadour and Vinegar Distiller and Mustard Maker to the King of France and the Emperors of Germany and Russia. He made twenty-four kinds of mustards. One of his rivals invented forty different mustard mixtures.

To bring Dumas up to date, mustard comes to us in three forms. The whole seeds are used for pickles, with boiled beets and as a garnish on salads. Then there is powdered mustard, which is also sometimes called, "dry mustard," or "ground mustard" or "mustard flour." This is one of our important spices. The familiar prepared mustard, which is a mixture of ground mustard with salt, vinegar, and other spices, is a condiment. There are hundreds of variations of this spread, although all team famously with the mighty frankfurter.

Green Beans with Hot Mustard Sauce

$1/2$	teaspoon powdered mustard
$1/2$	teaspoon water
1	tablespoon butter or margarine
1	teaspoon flour
$1/8$	teaspoon salt
$1/8$	teaspoon ground black pepper
2	large egg yolks, beaten
$3/4$	cup milk
2	teaspoons fresh lemon juice
1	pound (3 cups) hot cooked green beans
	Chopped pimiento

Combine powdered mustard and water; let stand 10 minutes for flavor to develop. Melt butter or margarine. Stir in flour, mustard, salt and ground black pepper; blend well. Mix egg yolks with milk and stir into the mixture. Cook until slightly thickened, stirring constantly. Do not boil. Add lemon juice and pour over beans. Garnish with chopped pimiento. Recipe serves 6.

GRILLED SALISBURY STEAK BELMONT

If I were to walk into your kitchen and look over your spice cabinet I wonder what I would find. Salt and pepper, of course. Paprika and cinnamon and vanilla probably, maybe some Worcestershire sauce and an old bottle of garlic salt left over from last summer when Dad barbecued steaks out on the patio.

If your spice cabinet reads thusly, then you are not cooking on all cylinders. The wonderful world of herbs and spices awaits your experimentation, and they are at your grocer's now.

In former times the value of spices was beyond our comprehension. A cargo of cloves in the 1700s was worth more than the ship which carried it. Columbus discovered the New World searching for a route to the Spice Islands where these precious foodstuffs were to be found. He didn't find the Spice Islands, but he did discover some new herbs and spices which enlivened the taste buds of Europeans when he returned home with them.

In the same way you learned to season food with salt and pepper you can learn to use *fines herbes*. Begin with a small amount at a time, experimenting with this one and that one until a satisfying blend is obtained. When following recipes use "scant" measurements, so as not to overdo. Take it easy. Also be sure your condiments are fresh — most keep well for about three months and then begin to deteriorate.

Let's begin your "spicing" career with Grilled Salisbury Steak Belmont:

Grilled Salisbury Steak Belmont

$1^3/4$	pounds finely ground lean chuck beef
2	tablespoons grated onion
2	tablespoons grated raw green bell pepper
1	clove garlic, mashed
$1^1/2$	tablespoons finely chopped chives
1	tablespoon finely chopped parsley
	Salt and pepper
	Paprika
$1/4$	teaspoon powdered thyme
	Flour
	Olive oil
3	tablespoons butter
$1/3$	cup tomato catsup
1	tablespoon lemon juice
1	teaspoon Worcestershire powder
	Dash Tabasco
1	teaspoon prepared mustard
	Salt and pepper
	Mace to taste
2	tablespoons sherry

To the finely ground lean chuck beef add onion, green bell pepper, garlic, chives, and parsley. Season with salt, pepper, paprika, and thyme. Shape the meat mixture into 6 individual steaks about ³/₄-inch thick; sprinkle lightly with flour and brush with olive oil. Place them on the broiler rack about 3 inches below the flame and broil for 5 to 6 minutes or more on each side, depending on the degree of doneness desired. While the steaks are broiling, prepare the sauce by melting butter in a saucepan with tomato catsup, lemon juice, Worcestershire powder, a generous dash of Tabasco sauce, prepared mustard, salt and pepper and a little mace to taste. Blend these ingredients well; stir in sherry and bring almost to the boiling point. Arrange the steaks on a hot platter and pour the sauce over them. Serves 6.

GOURMET DESSERTS

John Jacob Astor once remarked that, "A man with a million dollars is as well off as a man who is rich!" Well, those must have been the "good ole days" people are always talking about. But today, anyone of us can enjoy food which only the high and the mighty could afford in days gone by.

People often complain to me that they cannot afford to serve gourmet-type food, because it is too expensive. I won't argue the cost of prime rib or lobster flown from Maine, but I will suggest that you stop and look around the next time you are shopping in your supermarket. The very shelves cry out to you with their wares from every part of your country and from around the world, packaged for convenience and economy. Never have so many enjoyed so much for so little.

I believe the misunderstanding comes from a misconception of what gourmet food is. Gourmethood is achieved by what is done to the food not the groceries per se. A recipe which boasts a flair for seasoning and serving, creativity, rightness to the occasion, tender attention to the component parts, and execution of small details lifts the ordinary into the extraordinary.

So I insist that you can enjoy gourmet food with nothing more expensive than using your wits to gourmet advantage. It is a matter of attitude, feeling, appreciation of food, a willingness to experiment, and not the fatness of the purse which is important.

When a recipe with the qualities described above meets a household chef with the qualities of mind and hand just mentioned, culinary miracles come forth.

To prove my point I'm giving you, not one, but two dessert recipes which I consider gourmet, yet they are not budget-busters.

Charlotte Russe Economi

1   box frozen strawberries
1¹/₂   pints sour cream
    Brown sugar

Place frozen strawberries, thawed and drained, into a baking dish. Cover strawberries with 1¹/₂ pints sour cream. Cover this mixture thoroughly with brown sugar. Place into a preheated oven at 350 degrees and bake until bubbling (20 to 25 minutes). Serve in dessert glasses, either hot or cold.

Trader Doug

1   fresh pineapple
    Honey

Divide fresh pineapple into four sections, slicing lengthwise and leaving leafy tops. With a sharp knife loosen fruit from the peel, score into chunks. Brush honey over the pineapple. Place under hot broiler and heat just long enough to glaze the fruit. Serve with small forks. Four servings per pineapple.

GUACAMOLE SALAD DRESSING

Have you ever wondered how some of our slang expressions came into being? For instance, "He knows his onions!" Who said it first? And when? And why? It's possible we started "knowing our onions" the year the thirteen-volume *Oxford English Dictionary* was published. There are 15,487 pages altogether. Work was started in 1879 and was completed fifty-four years later, in 1933. There were four editors in those fifty-four years. The latest was a Mr. Onions. (Some pronounce his name "oh-NIGH-uns" instead of "onions.") At any rate those who used this thumping big dictionary must be absorbing the wisdom of Mr. Charles T. Onions. They knew their onions. They were smart.

If you know your onions, you know that the very latest thing in onions is dehydration. While drying is probably the oldest means of food preservation known to man, it wasn't until 1931 that the first of the dehydrated onion products became commercially successful. Since then, other forms have been added. Now instant minced onion, instant onion powder, onion salt and onion flakes are sold nationally.

There are several reasons why the use of dehydrated onions has increased tenfold in ten years. They have no-fuss, no-muss convenience; they're ever-ready right on the spice shelf. In finely minced or powdered state, the onion flavor is distributed evenly through mixtures. In this time of high prices, dehydrated onion products cost less than they did ten years ago. One other quality we mustn't overlook: Dehydrated onions have dependable, uniform flavor. They are never too strong or too mild.

There are some 500 known varieties of onions. They differ in color, shape and moisture content. They can also differ enormously in pungency. Chemists have a chemical test for onion juice which turns the juice pink, pinker, pinkest, depending on the strength of the aroma of the particular onion. California grows the onions best suited to drying. As might be expected they are comparatively low in moisture and high in flavor particles.

Onions have been a favorite seasoning for many centuries and in many lands. Builders of the Egyptian pyramids consumed enormous amounts of onions, according to the Greek historian, Herodotus. We know from the Holy Bible that the children of Israel developed a great yen for onions when they were crossing the wilderness. Alexander the Great urged his soldiers to eat plenty of onions. This was supposed to make them brave. A couple of thousand years later, General Grant must have believed the same thing. At one point, when his troops were minus onions, he warned the War Department at Washington: "I will not move my army without onions."

Onions were not only in demand as food and flavoring, but played a great role in medicine and magic. Egyptians thought the onion sacred, a symbol of the universe. When necessary to take an oath, the ancient Egyptian would rest his hand on an onion. Among the Greeks, the onion was supposed to contribute to wedded bliss. So, wedding gifts would include a jar of snow, a jar of lentils, a jar of onions.

English girls once thought it possible to tell fortunes with onions. Also, when buying onions, they used to think it bad luck to enter and exit from the same door; it was wise to shop in a market with two doors. While young girls tucked an onion under their pillows to dream of future husbands, once they had married it was considered bad luck to dream of eating onions. This was sure to bring on a family fight.

As a practical bit of advice to wives, if an argument with friend husband seems in the offing, cook something very good, with lots of dehydrated onion in it. This will get him in a darling mood, one might hope.

For inspiration, do try this recipe:

Guacamole Salad Dressing

1	medium-size ripe avocado
1	tablespoon lemon juice
$^1/_4$	cup finely chopped tomato
1	teaspoon instant minced onion
$^1/_2$	teaspoon salt
$^1/_{16}$	teaspoon ground black pepper
$^1/_{16}$	teaspoon instant garlic powder

Cut avocado in half, remove seed and skin. Dice and combine with lemon juice. Mash and put through sieve or blend in electric blender. Add tomato, instant onion, salt, pepper and garlic powder. Chill until ready to serve. Serve over cooked or raw vegetable salads.

Yield 1 cup.

GULFPORT BAKED RED SNAPPER

There is a saying that some people eat to live and others live to eat. Although living to eat may be too extreme to be completely desirable, I can't help thinking that it is a great mistake eating only to live. You miss so much.

I have never understood those people who say they pay no attention to what they are eating. I'm amazed when a person replies, "I don't remember whether or not I had lunch." To one who is enthusiastic about fine food these seem as aliens in a lavish land, only tourists who disdain to take up residence at the epicure's table and will hardly allow themselves to look upon the infinite variety available to them in gourmetland. I want to say, "Stop. Look. Smell. Taste. Make a new discovery."

Jean Anthelme Brillat-Savarin, that great connoisseur and philosopher of gastronomy, once said this: "The discovery of a new dish does more for the happiness when a new star is discovered? Nothing, unless you are an astronomer. But suppose you have a proclivity for fish? Suppose you hear about a new fish dish? Suppose this is a recipe for your favorite fish? Ah, now here is a great addition to your happiness — to be enjoyed over and over again, to be shared with good friends."

I believe Brillat-Savarin was right, and I hope Gulfport Baked Red Snapper will be a happy new discovery for your dossier of fine fish recipes.

The materials needed to create this recipe are:

Gulfport Baked Red Snapper

1   (4-pound) red snapper
1   teaspoon salt
$^1/_4$ teaspoon freshly ground black pepper
$^2/_3$ cup butter or margarine
1   small onion, chopped
4   cups fine, stale bread crumbs
1   cup chopped cucumber
2   teaspoons capers or chopped sour pickle
$^3/_4$ teaspoon powdered sage
$^1/_2$ cup white wine
    Salt pork or bacon slices

Construction of this recipe:

Sprinkle inside of fish with salt and pepper. Melt $^1/_3$ cup of butter in skillet over medium heat. Add onion and cook until lightly browned. Add the crumbs, cucumber, capers, sage and half of the wine, mixing well.

Stuff the red snapper with this mixture and close with skewers and string. Line a shallow pan with foil and grease it well. Place the fish in the pan and cut gashes measured to individual servings. Into these gashes place pieces of salt pork or slices of bacon. Brush with remaining butter and pour remaining wine over the top. Bake in a hot oven (400 degrees) 50 minutes or until fish flakes easily when tested with fork. Baste frequently with pan drippings, or additional butter and white wine. This recipe will serve 6.

HAUTE CUISINE

The man in France to equal our Mr. Webster, of the dictionary Websters, that is, is Monsieur Larousse. In his word bible of the French language he identifies haute cuisine as "high-class cooking." Haute cuisine is the best, the very highest class cooking in and from France. It is no secret to you, I know, that the French are renowned for the food they cook. So renowned that other countries borrow from them, but this has never diminished their cooking quality, nor their reputation.

The very language of France adds its blessing to their famous dishes. When you see on a menu: *Les Fromages Varies* you must be impressed. But what is it? It is what the French call "cheese board" or what we call "assorted cheese." Or this menu item: *Le Pigeonneau Roti Le Riz Sauvage Americain.* How about that? "Squab with wild rice."

So don't let an albeit impressive name keep you from enjoying haute cuisine for herein lies the gourmet's richest rewards.

Historic Les Halles Market District of Paris (unfortunately being torn down now) has always been the proper place to find the world's truly great recipes for French Onion Soup. This market district came to life at midnight and until about six in the morning, was the busiest section in all Paris. Beginning at midnight, small sidewalk cafes commence serving their specialty — French Onion Soup. The recipe for French Onion Soup Escoffier was given to me by the maitre d' Am Fried de Cochon.

To make French Onion Soup Escoffier you will need:

French Onion Soup Escoffier

$^1/_4$ pound butter
$2^1/_2$ pounds onion, sliced
1   quart beef stock
1   quart chicken stock
1   tablespoon Worcestershire powder
1   bay leaf
$1^1/_2$ teaspoons celery salt
1   teaspoon black pepper or 12
    peppercorns, crushed
1   cup Parmesan cheese

Heat butter in heavy kettle. Add sliced onions and brown well, stirring constantly. Add beef and chicken stock, Worcestershire powder, bay leaf, celery salt and pepper. Allow to simmer for 40 minutes. Remove bay leaf and salt to taste. Serve soup at once in heated tureen and float croutons and sprinkle generously with cheese.

HEAVENLY FRUIT DESSERT

Coriander seed rates among the most venerable of spices. It grew in the hanging gardens of Babylon, resembling the manna which sustained the children of Israel on their long trek across the desert. It was known and loved by Romans and is still used in some of the world's most famous dishes.

While 2,742,000 pounds of coriander were imported last year, principally from Morocco and Rumania, most of this was used in mixed pickling spices, curry powder or in the zillions of frankfurters consumed in the United States.

Coriander can be grown in this country easily enough, but it is hard to harvest, for it must be completely ripe to taste good and then the seeds fall to the ground at the slightest touch. Most of the coriander grown domestically ends up in gin bottles or other liquors as a flavoring.

Incidentally, green leaves of *Corindrum sativum L.* are widely used in Latin-American cookery and are called "cilantro." They are also called "Chinese parsley."

Coriander is a fragrant but mild spice with a hint of orange about it. You would use several times as much coriander as of most sweet spices. An old-fashioned coriander cookie made with two cups flour requires four or five teaspoons ground coriander.

Coriander is available whole or ground. Use it only in breads, cakes, candies and cookies, but try it also in pea or mushroom soup. Ground coriander butter is excellent with artichokes or mushrooms. Or, use coriander in this recipe for a simple but great dessert:

Heavenly Fruit Dessert

1   **can (8¹/₄ ounces) crushed pineapple**
1   **package (3³/₄ ounces) deluxe whipped vanilla dessert mix**
2¹/₂ **teaspoons ground coriander**
1   **teaspoon pure vanilla extract**
¹/₂ **cup diced maraschino cherries**

Drain pineapple, reserving liquid; set aside. Prepare dessert mix according to package directions using reserved pineapple liquid in place of water called for in directions. Stir in coriander and vanilla extract. Fold in reserved crushed pineapple and cherries. Turn into a 2-cup mold or 6 individual dessert dishes. Garnish with whipped cream, if desired.

Yield 6 portions.

HOLLANDAISE SAUCE

The art of genuine gourmet cooking may be said to begin with the mastering of sauce. No less an authority than the greatest gourmet-chef who ever lived — Escoffier — said it himself. He said that if a culinary craftsman could command five basic French sauces, then he was pretty much in business as a chef.

During Escoffier's lifetime a master chef had to be inventive and resourceful. Negotiations of these fundamental sauces — Espagnole, Veloute, Bechamel, Tomato, and Hollandaise — spelled the difference between a mundane food and one that brought exclamations of praise. Often sauces disguised slightly spoiled foods, camouflaging them with a sauce more flavorful than the food they covered. Refrigeration was not available, and other methods of preservation were not dependable.

These sauces were developed for specific groups of foods, such as meats, fish, fowl, vegetables, etc. As the Frenchmen chefs' reputations and repertoires expanded, hundreds of variations of these five basic sauces appeared on the gourmet's plate.

For instance, mayonnaise was a sauce developed espe-

cially for fish. Today, we use it for everything else, and its origin has been all but forgotten.

Let's take one of these sauces — one which I feel is popular on the American scene, but one which many cooks shy away from and, therefore, deny themselves the delicious enjoyment Hollandaise gives by enhancing vegetables. It is not so much that actualizing Hollandaise is difficult. It does require whole-hearted, undivided attention, though. Also careful following of directions. Soon you will get "a feel" when it is coming along right. All right, let's try it.

Hollandaise Sauce

¹/₄ **pound butter (divided into three parts)**
4   **egg yolks**
2   **teaspoons lemon juice**
    Dash of white pepper
    Salt

Place one part of the butter into the top part of a glass double boiler over water. (I think it is best to use a glass double boiler for this sauce. Aluminum may discolor it.) Allow the butter to melt slowly, and add egg yolks. Keep heat low. Stir with a wooden spoon until creamy; then add the second part of the butter and stir. (Do not allow the water in the double boiler to boil.) After the second part of the butter is melted and blended into recipe, add the third part. Continue to stir until well mixed; then add lemon juice, salt, and pepper. Remove from flame and stir. Hollandaise sauce should not be served hot, but rather just warm.

There are several points to be especially careful about for a successful sauce. Egg yolks, which are the base of the sauce, can be overcooked quite quickly, which causes curdling. To prevent this trouble, make sure the sauce does not get too hot. If the sauce starts to curdle, stop stirring and remove immediately from the heat. Cool it in a pan of cold water, and stir it gently to reconstitute smoothness. The sauce will "hold" — stay as it should be served — for about 30 minutes if you will place the top part of the double boiler in a shallow pan of warm water. However, it is a sauce best savored when served at once.

Try this recipe for Hollandaise Sauce and serve it as follows for an ideal dish.

BROCCOLI BENEDICT:

Toast
Sliced fried ham
Drained, cooked broccoli

Arrange toast on a plate. Then on the toast place one slice of fried ham. Place drained, cooked broccoli on the ham; then top with Hollandaise Sauce.

HONG KONG SAUTÉ PEAS

The spotlight is on Chinatown, San Francisco, U.S.A. Three weeks of preparation, a brigade of cooks, and most of the stocks of Chinese markets, culminate in the famous, annual Chinese Sportsmen's Banquet guesting and honoring San Francisco's finest. Although famous, this elaborate food festival is not much advertised as it is by invitation only. Sportsmen, financiers, business and professional men, society big-wigs, athletes and gourmets value an invitation to Chinatown on this special night for this honorable event.

If you have ever had a full-course Chinese dinner you know how many different foods are offered one after another. But a Chinese banquet! It would take the linguistic skill of all the Chinese dialects to describe to you the exotic eye-smell-taste experience of that evening in Chinatown.

The exquisite food delicacies were expectantly sampled in Chinese style — everyone takes one small portion of each recipe since there are so many foods to partake of. However, it is not improper to ask for another bite of a particularly taste-pleasing item. As this many-splendored bite-by-bite ceremony progressed an interesting thing captured my attention. Several men asked for a second portion of a dish, the main ingredient of which was peas, almost exactly like our well-known English green peas. Peas are definitely not a man's favorite vegetable by any stretch of the culinary imagination. I wondered about this small miracle when Hong Kong Sauté Peas arrived in front of me. Then I knew! Now I wanted this recipe.

But here I was a guest, and anyway the Chinese won't give away their ancient, honorable, and treasured cooking secrets. They have, in fact, developed a confounding way of politely refusing to do so. Suddenly, third, fourth, and fifth generation American-Chinese can cook only in their ancestral tongue. They will give you the instructions in Chinese!

However, I really wanted that recipe, and I had an inspiration. My dinner companion for the evening was a gentleman on the San Francisco staff of the FBI. I asked him to ask them. There is something very authoritative about those three letters F, B, and I, because here is the recipe for Hong Kong Sauté Peas, and in Americanese.

I have simplified the recipe into standard ingredients and sizes but follow directions just so:

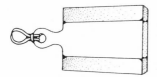

Hong Kong Sauté Peas

- $^1/_2$ **pound bacon sliced**
- 1   **onion, finely diced**
- $^1/_2$ **green bell pepper, finely diced**
- 1   **small can sliced mushrooms**
- 1   **tablespoon garlic salt**
- 1   **teaspoon Worcestershire powder**
- 6   **drops Tabasco**
- 1   **teaspoon MSG powder**
- 1   **large can English green peas with liquid in the can**

Place bacon slices into skillet and fry until softly and lightly browned. Remove bacon, leaving the bacon fat. Place onion, bell pepper and mushrooms into the bacon fat. Sauté until items begin to soften. Add garlic salt, Worcestershire powder, Tabasco and MSG powder, and simmer slowly for 3 more minutes. Now add the English green peas, with the liquid in the can. Cover skillet and simmer slowly until peas have a wilted look. Hong Kong Sauté Peas are ready to serve. They should be moist, but should not have excessive liquid.

HOPKINS COUNTRY STEW

In the northeast corner of the state of Texas there is a county famous for its stew — Hopkins County. Everyone came to town to the county seat on Saturday for shopping and sociality. Soon it became a custom for each family to bring a victual or two to contribute to the big cast-iron kettle set up at the courthouse square for a genuine Hopkins County Stew. In those days an old-timer would start a hardwood, hot coal fire early in the morning. As the county folk began to arrive the first thing that went into the huge kettle which had been placed on top of the fire was bacon — a few slices to begin the sizzling goodness. Then came chickens (plentiful in the county), squirrel, quail, perhaps beef or pork. Then the potatoes and onions, beans, or peas, and corn, tomatoes and proper seasonings.

A long-handled ladle kept the stew moving around for hours and hours. Self-appointed Hopkins County Stew experts volunteered for this job. Then, by late afternoon a picnic — Hopkins County style — was well under way. The giant cauldron (twenty to thirty gallons) made enough stew to feed them all. And a very, very good stew it was too.

This is still a wonderful way to entertain. Perfect for outside "feeding" — and if the weather plays tricks this stew can be accomplished inside. You need a large iron kettle, and a long-handled ladle. Inform guests to bring something for the party stew. As they arrive ask them to prepare and donate their offerings to the chuckling kettle. Cooking is part of the fun, and oddly enough, this nearly always turns out to be a wonderful stew. To prevent too many cooks from spoiling the broth the host or hostess should be in charge of stirring, and adjusting seasonings.

I have "modernized" this recipe so you may reproduce it in advance if you wish to do it all yourself.

Hopkins County Stew

1	**2-pound chicken**
1	**bay leaf**
	Pinch thyme
2	**sprigs celery tops**
6	**sprigs parsley**
	Salt and pepper to taste
2	**cups diced potatoes**
1	**cup frozen cut green beans**
$^1/_4$	**pound butter (or margarine)**
2	**medium onions, chopped fine**
3	**small pods garlic, minced**
1	**16-ounce can tomatoes**
1	**cup whole kernel corn**
1	**cup frozen peas**
12	**whole onions**

Cover chicken with water in a large kettle. Add salt and pepper, and begin cooking over low heat. Prepare a bouquet garni by placing in a loosely woven cloth 1 bay leaf, thyme, 2 sprigs celery tops, sprigs of parsley, salt and pepper. Secure spices by tying package with string. Submerge into water where banquet garni imparts a spicy flavor and leaves a suspicion of taste when chicken is done. Bring chicken to a boil and cook until tender. Remove chicken from broth. Bone and dice chicken. Remove bouquet garni, and reserve the broth.

Cook potatoes and green beans together until tender. Fry the chopped onions and garlic in butter or margarine until brown. Add tomatoes. Cook 5 minutes. Now add this to chicken broth. Add corn, frozen peas, 12 whole onions, cooked potatoes and green beans. Return the diced chicken to broth. Stir well; bring to boil; reduce heat to simmer and cook 40 minutes longer.

Serve in individual iron pots, heated well.

HUNTER'S SAUTÉED QUAIL

The skies of our country were once darkened with immense flocks of wild birds. Then came the hunter with his taste for game and his need to supply his family table. With his arrow, guns, and dogs, birds were killed and soon whole species had all but vanished. The farmer came and, with his plow, ripped up vast natural breeding grounds. Since that time we have launched an intelligent conservation policy and the adaptability of these wild birds themselves have restocked the skies. During any normal hunting season, hunters can now bring home millions of assorted fowl.

All game birds have a special intrinsic flavor, something apart from the natural taste of their flesh. For any sportsman, a bite of a bird that he has bagged will bring back fond moments he likes to remember — the sudden flush of a grouse from cover, the hoarse whistle of ducks coming in, the shuffling flight of a woodcock. The faint taste of gaminess will, for a moment, transport anyone to the hills, fields, and marshes, and the days when men hunted to live.

The flavor of game birds varies considerably, much more than domestic fowl. Some birds, like woodcock and rail, possess a cogent wild flavor. Other white meat species such as pheasant, quail and grouse, have a more sanguine taste factor. Wild ducks vary considerably in taste, depending on the time of the year and the area from which they come. Their taste depends, for the most part, on what they have been eating. An esculent mallard bagged in the Midwest where it has been eating grain, might be most undesirable in the deep South where it has been feeding in the swamps.

During each hunting season I receive hundreds of phone calls and letters requesting recipes and kudos for the proper presentation of game birds. The trenchant gourmet prefers the natural game flavor while the average cook desires a more subtle approach. I have observed, through experience, that the length of time the birds are hung is an important factor in their taste. Quail, for example, needs little or no hanging and can be eaten the day they are shot. Other birds, like pheasant, improve in flavor if they are hung for awhile in a cool, airy place. Depending, of course, on the weather, a pheasant may be hung from two days to two weeks.

I have found, likewise, that the cardinal rule of not roasting older birds is one to follow. An old bird should be cut up and braised or prepared casserole style. Some game birds, including pheasant and partridge, have a dry flesh and should be larded or cooked covered with strips of bacon. A goose or a duck, on the other hand, normally has excess fat and does not require this attention. I suggest, also, that when cooking wild game birds that fresh or canned juniper berries be added to the container. This trapping removes a large percentage of the wild taste. The following recipe is my favorite for quail.

Hunter's Sautéed Quail

6 quail, split
6 club rolls
³/₄ cup butter
1 teaspoon salt
   Freshly ground black pepper
   Fruit sauce

Split rolls in half and hollow out centers. Toast in a low oven (325 degrees) until brown. Melt ¹/₄ butter and brush the rolls with the butter. Sauté the quail over high heat in the remaining ¹/₂ cup of butter for 10 minutes or until golden brown. Sprinkle them with salt and pepper. Arrange quail on rolls and serve with fruit sauce.

Serves 6.

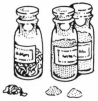

FRUIT SAUCE

1 cup seedless white grapes
4 tablespoons butter
¹/₂ cup port wine
¹/₈ teaspoon ground cloves
¹/₂ teaspoon ginger
2 tablespoons finely chopped mushrooms
¹/₂ cup finely chopped hazelnuts

Bring grapes and 1 cup of water to a boil. Cover, reduce heat and simmer for 5 minutes. Drain off water. Add butter, wine, cloves, and ginger. Cover and simmer for 5 minutes. Stir in mushrooms and simmer for 5 minutes. Add hazelnuts and serve immediately. Makes about 2¹/₂ cups.

HUNTER'S VENISON

I hear it every year: How do I cook the game the hunter brings in? I, myself, am no hunter — the last deer hunt I "attended" someone calculated my score: it was fifteen Pommac bottles, twenty-two beer cans, and the bark off seven trees, suggesting that I content myself with adding to the compendium of cookery of wild creatures and give up "attending" deer hunts.

But I have come to your rescue with a recipe for venison. Give your full attention to preparing Hunter's Venison. Cook it with carefulness and as well as you can. Then invite friends over to experience the taste of really well-cooked venison.

You have the venison roast. This recipe is for a five-pound roast. In addition to that you will need the following:

Hunter's Venison

2 cups Cognac
¹/₄ cup melted butter
¹/₄ cup olive oil
1 clove garlic, chopped fine
3 tablespoons finely chopped parsley
   Salt and pepper to taste
1 cup red currant jelly
3 tablespoons Cognac
1 teaspoon horseradish

If roast is lean and somewhat dry, lard it through with a little pork fat or butter. It may be roasted in oiled paper to supplement fat content. Venison roast should be marinated for 6 hours in Cognac. Refrigerate while marinating.

Mix melted butter and olive oil in a skillet and heat. Sauté garlic and parsley until soft and add roast for browning. Brown quickly on both sides over high heat and place into roast pan. Roast in a moderate oven until tender. (A longer roasting period is necessary for older venison.) Using skillet that roast was browned in, add the 3 tablespoons Cognac and deglaze over flame. Mix in red currant jelly and horseradish and blend. Serve this sauce over the venison roast and garnish with steamed onions. Serves 6.

ITALIAN TUFOLI IMBOTTITE

Escoffier, the King of Cooks and the Cook of Kings, once said that no one could hope to become a really great cook unless he had a "passionate love of garlic." The great Escoffier used garlic with artistic and subtle discretion, and he taught his many disciples to do the same.

But next door to the famous Frenchman the Italian chefs were loving garlic even more passionately than Escoffier and his crew. Italians know how to cook with garlic! Furthermore, when the other basics of Italian cuisine — pasta, tomato, and olive oil — are combined with garlic an intrinsic blend is created.

This marriage of flavors is productive of many "children." This basic four-ingredient formula is the Italian aura. The addition of a variety of in-law, cousin, aunt and uncle ingredients accounts for the infinite selection of dishes which await you in any Italian restaurant, home or cookbook. None are exactly the same just as in the human family of children, still all bear the stamp of the clan Italia.

Tufoli is a less known, but interesting member of the pastas. It has a tube-like shape for it is a pasta shell for stuffing. It can be purchased in many supermarkets, and in any specialty food store.

This recipe is divided into two ingredient lists — one for the sauce and one for the stuffing. There are three sections of instructions. One for the sauce; one for the stuffing; and one for cooking and preparation of the tufoli.

Italian Tufoli Imbottite

SAUCE:

1/4	cup olive oil
1	large chopped onion
1	chopped clove of garlic
3/4	pound ground beef
1/4	pound ground pork
1	large can peeled tomatoes
2	small cans tomato paste
2	cups water
1	cup chopped, cooked mushrooms

FILLING:

4	ounces mozzarella cheese, diced
4	soft scrambled eggs
1	pound ricotta cheese (or cottage cheese)
1	teaspoon chopped parsley
	Salt to taste
	Pepper to taste
1	pound tufoli
	Parmesan cheese

To make the sauce, first heat oil in saucepan; add onion and garlic and sauté until golden brown; add meat and stir until brown. Add tomatoes, paste, and water. Season to taste with salt and pepper. Simmer this mixture for 3 hours (the longer it cooks the better the flavor). Now add the mushrooms.

While the sauce is simmering, prepare the filling. Blend mozzarella cheese with warm scrambled eggs (this will melt the cheese); add the ricotta (or cottage cheese), parsley, and salt and pepper to taste. Beat with fork until light and fluffy (or mix with hands as in making meat balls).

Cook 1 pound of tufoli in a large pot of boiling water for 15 minutes. Drain. Run cold water over them to prevent sticking and to cool for handling. Stuff them with the already-prepared filling. Cover the bottom of a baking pan with the sauce. Line the stuffed tufoli in this; then add more sauce. Repeat this process until all tufoli are used. Cover and put into a 350-degree oven for about 30 to 40 minutes. Serve hot with Parmesan cheese and extra meat sauce. Recipe serves 6.

KAHLUA CHIFFON PIE

At its best, coffee is everything good that can happen to man. Compounded with spirits, it becomes even more. It becomes an art object known as coffee liqueur.

Spanish dons and Jamaica planters were probably the first to experiment with coffee liqueur, but their early products were often unstable since the coffee used quickly separated from the spirits with which it had been compounded.

When coffee moved to the New World to be married with an already developed native distilling art, it started a trend. In Mexico the makers of Kahlua have long enjoyed a reputation for their fine product. But in the United States, where rum and corn and bourbon were each so long king, coffee liqueur was all but unknown until 15 years ago.

Then Jules Berman, an enterprising California entrepreneur, entered into the scene and recognized that Kahlua could be the leader of a major move to lighter drinks. He purchased the Kahlua plant in Mexico and became its exclusive U.S. distributor.

In 1951 Kahlua sold only 2,000 cases in the United States. Today its worldwide distribution is eighty times that. In 1960 Berman consummated a deal with Peter Heering Company of Copenhagen, which gave Heering the right to produce and distribute Kahlua in Europe, Asia and Africa. This marked the first time in 150 years that the makers of Cherry Heering had ever added another product to its line.

The increasing popularity of liqueurs in general, and Kahlua in particular, has been due, partly at least, to Berman's efforts in spearheading the development of many intriguing cocktails using Kahlua. For example, there is the famous Black Russian (one part Kahlua, two parts Vodka), the Kahlua Sour (Kahlua with lemon juice), the Highland Fling (Kahlua with Scotch) and even Kahlua Irish Coffee.

Kahlua has also become a favorite with gourmets. It can transform a pudding or sauce into a food fit for kings. It does delicious things to ice cream. Many famous restaurants throughout the world feature exotic desserts in which Kahlua is an essential ingredient.

As long as the coffee flavor remains a standard among the palate pleasers, Kahlua will continue to reign supreme. The following Kahlua Chiffon Pie recipe is an example of how to incorporate this coffee liqueur into an epicurean recipe.

Kahlua Chiffon Pie

1 envelope unflavored gelatin
$1/4$ cup cold water
4 egg yolks
$1/4$ teaspoon salt
$1/2$ cup Kahlua
4 egg whites, stiffly beaten
$1/8$ teaspoon salt
$1/4$ cup sugar
1 baked pie shell
Pecan halves

Combine gelatin and cold water. In top of double boiler combine egg yolks, salt, and Kahlua. Stir. Cook in double boiler until mixture coats spoon. Add gelatin. While mixture is still warm, fold into meringue with egg whites, stiffly beaten, salt, and sugar. Fill pie shell and decorate top with pecan halves. Chill and serve.

KIDNEY BEAN TUNA SALAD

Anyone who has read the epics of the ancient Greek, Homer, or loves the tales of Greek mythology may know about that fabulous herb, moly. (Moly rhymes with holy.) This herb has never been identified exactly, but has been regarded historically as "a sort of garlic" with occult powers. Odysseus, who spent years trying to get home after the Trojan War, would never have returned to Penelope if it hadn't been for the moly which the God, Hermes, had given him.

Remember that Queen Calypso induced him to bite into the apple of immortality which should have killed Odysseus — but he ate the yellow flowered garlic at the same time, so Calypso could do him no harm.

Odysseus met all manner of charming, but deadly females. There was Queen Circe, who turned men into pigs just for fun. The white goddess, Ino, who disguised herself as a mermaid and tried to pull him down to her deep-sea tavern. He escaped, too, from the Island of Sirens and the Island of Dogs. None of these wicked beauties were able to harm Odysseus because he kept gnawing away at the garlic-like moly.

To the Romans garlic was not only a cure-all, but a source of great strength. Supposedly, it made men brave, so soldiers were supplied with garlic to make them fearless.

Garlic lost none of its reputation in medieval times, either. It was supposed to be a cure for snake bite, dog bite, and the blues. It was dropped into a sick child's stocking as a "cure" for whooping cough. In sixteenth-century Paris, they ate garlic-flavored butter in the spring to insure good health for the rest of the year. Even

today, there are parts of the world where youngsters wear a necklace of garlic as a talisman to ward off evil.

Now that we have all kinds of miracle medicines we can put the world's garlic crop to its best use: in good cooking. Of course, garlic has been used as a seasoning for many centuries and in many lands. It seems to have originated around the eastern Mediterranean. Passing caravans eventually carried it in all directions. It was taken to China and other eastern lands at a very early date.

Garlic was not native to the Americas, but Spanish, Portuguese, and French explorers brought it with them. California belonged to Spain at one time and that is probably when and how the garlic bulb got to this part of the world where it thrives so well.

Instant minced garlic is ideal in all kinds of cooked dishes, although it flavors cold mixtures, such as French Dressing, beautifully if it's allowed to stay in the mixture for about an hour or more. The following recipe is one that I feel best exemplifies the true character of instant minced garlic.

Kidney Bean Tuna Salad

2 cups (1-pound can) red kidney beans, drained
1 7-ounce can chunk-type tuna fish, drained
$1/4$ cup sliced cucumbers
6 anchovy fillets, quartered
$1/4$ cup mayonnaise
1 teaspoon vinegar
$1^1/2$ teaspoons salt
$1^1/2$ teaspoons basil leaves
$1/4$ teaspoon instant minced garlic
$1/4$ teaspoon ground black pepper
Head of lettuce
6 tomato wedges

Combine all ingredients except lettuce and tomato wedges. Mix slightly to prevent breaking tuna chunks. Chill 1 hour. Serve on lettuce and garnish with wedge of tomato. Serve as a main dish salad. Recipe serves 6.

KING CRAB

One of the best seafood treats of all is the deliciously different, delicately flavored meat of the king crab. Full of protein, vitamins, and minerals, this is truly a dish fit for a king.

King crab are caught in the Bering Sea off the coast of Alaska in huge crab pots lowered to an ocean depth of around 300 feet, from the sides of fishing vessels. Females and small males are returned to the sea for the preservation of the species, and the average size of the big male crabs which are kept is around eleven pounds. However, occasionally huge king crabs six-foot big, barnacled, and ferocious looking, are caught. It is estimated that these giants may have crawled great distances along the ocean floor for over thirty years. The crabs are kept alive and healthy in a "live" tank of circulating sea water until ready for the processing plant.

Prime meat of the king crabs is in the claws, legs and shoulders, and this is the only part used. These parts are cooked in boiling water in stainless steel tanks for eighteen to twenty-five minutes, then chilled and washed again before being trimmed, processed, inspected, packaged and quick-frozen, ready for marketing. King crab is available either fresh packed or frozen and also canned, usually in 5-, 6$\frac{1}{2}$-, and 13-ounce cans.

King Crab Salad Bowl

1   pound king crabmeat or other crabmeat, fresh or frozen or
3   cans (6$\frac{1}{2}$ or 7$\frac{1}{2}$ ounces each) crabmeat
1   quart mixed salad greens
2   tomatoes, cut into wedges
1   cup corn chips
$\frac{1}{2}$ cup sliced pitted ripe olives
$\frac{1}{4}$ cup chopped green onions
     Avocado Cream Dressing
$\frac{1}{2}$ cup shredded natural Cheddar cheese
     Whole pitted ripe olives

Thaw frozen crabmeat. Drain crabmeat. Remove any remaining shell or cartilage from crabmeat. Break crabmeat into large pieces. Combine salad greens, tomatoes, corn chips, olives, onion, and crabmeat. Add dressing and toss lightly. Sprinkle with cheese and garnish with olives. Serve immediately. Serves 6.

AVOCADO CREAM DRESSING

$\frac{1}{2}$ cup mashed avocado
$\frac{1}{3}$ cup sour cream
2   tablespoons lemon juice
$\frac{1}{2}$ teaspoon sugar
$\frac{1}{4}$ teaspoon chili powder
$\frac{1}{4}$ teaspoon salt
$\frac{1}{4}$ teaspoon liquid hot pepper sauce
1   clove garlic, crushed

Combine all ingredients and mix until smooth. Chill. Makes 1 cup dressing.

LAMB CHOPS DURBAN

Next stop, the Union of South Africa. The scene by jet arrival is not different from your arrival in any metropolis in any country. A large, modern airport, located between Johannesburg and Pretoria, cars, taxis, luggage check out, well-dressed travelers and plane greeters. If you were brought up on Tarzan and the late-night movie safari, your initial impulse may be a twinge of disappointment. No great white hunter bedecked in his safari best to greet you; not even a slithering snake outside your hotel; nor chattering monkeys in the trees. But just a few miles away . . .

Arriving by ship at Cape Town you are eyewitness to the same point of entry the very first Europeans gazed upon when they penetrated the little-known and primitive Dark Continent. That is, this is the same spot. More modern, more populated, more citified, more sophisticated. Charming, but much like other ports of entry in other countries. Again, that twinge of disappointment. Where are the sailors of those old sealore dramas, the beat of the native drums, the trumpeting of elephants? Not here, but just a few miles away . . .

The food of South Africa and the country itself are much alike. Just as your arrival did not reveal the real Africa, you will not get the authentic food of Africa in the city hotels and restaurants which are popularly frequented. In these fine establishments you will order "Continental" dishes which are the same the world over. But just a few miles away . . .

In the city cafes the magnificent South African Rock Lobster Tails are featured, the most desired seafood delicacy on the planet, along with oysters, and salmon, of highest quality. Steaks, Americans will be glad to learn, are good, popular and plentiful. Afrikaners are a meat-producing and meat-eating people. Cattle and sheep are raised on the plains in fatuous abundance. The opulence of the table includes taste-pleasing tropical fruits — pineapples, apples, peaches, tangerines, pawpaw, melons, lemons and pears.

If, however, you like to adventure palate-wise in your traveling, as well as by sight and sound, then investigate the food world of the Afrikaner. Ask for *bredee* (meat stew), and *maika* (fish stew), ask for *boerewors* (sausage), and *Kaffir* (home-brew beer), and *braaivleis* (barbecues) and *melksynsels* (milk soup). There is absolutely no need to worry about the purity of either water, milk, or fruit. All are safe.

I'm sure there is no food in South Africa which can overshadow the sight of the awesome animals (nor anywhere else in the world) but while you search out the King of the Beasts (you can't go home without seeing him) in that last Eden of the world, search out the national dishes of the Afrikaners. (Don't go home without trying some of these either.) You may have to wangle an invitation from an Afrikaner to get the full, real taste of the authentic, but it will be worth it.

Here is a good example of Afrikaner cuisine:

Lamb Chops Durban

²/₃   **cup tomato sauce**
²/₃   **cup vinegar**
2   **tablespoons Worcestershire powder**
1   **onion, grated**
1   **teaspoon dry mustard**
1   **teaspoon salt**
12   **lamb chops**

Combine the tomato sauce, vinegar, Worcestershire powder, onion, mustard, and salt in a bowl. Mix well. Marinate the chops at room temperature for 1 hour. Drain. Take the sauce and put it in a saucepan. Meanwhile, pan-fry the chops, turning them over and over until well done. Now heat the sauce until hot. Pour over the lamb chops and serve hot.

LAMB CROQUETTES

"Flair" is one of the many expressive words which we've borrowed from the French. Originally, it meant to sniff the air or follow your nose in order to find out what was "cooking" or going on. Today, "flair" means "an instinct that leads to success in following it."

Or, we might say, "a gifted cook when she has a flair with seasonings, who reaches for one of her dehydrated garlic products for seasoning a meat, fish or fowl or salad dressing." Instinctively she "just knows" as she follows her nose, that garlic will give her creation tantalizing aroma. When members of the family come in and sniff to see what smells so tempting, we're truly back to the original French use of "flair."

When we're talking about garlic another French word applies and that's *soupçon* pronounced "soups on." This means "suspicion," of course, and that's how garlic is best used in most cases — just a drifting of aroma, now-you-smell-it, now-you-don't. The easiest and most certain way of regulating garlic aroma and flavor is to use modern dehydrated garlic products, instant minced, garlic powder, or garlic salt. Easy to measure, they assure consistent results.

Just how much is a "suspicion" of garlic? It depends almost entirely on who is cooking what and for whom. As a general rule, however, approximately one-fourth teaspoon of instant minced or powdered garlic should give tempting flavor to six servings of food. Up this to one-

half teaspoon if using garlic salt since part of the mixture in this case is plain table salt. When taking a recipe from an old cookbook calling for raw garlic, replace a large clove of garlic with one-fourth teaspoon instant minced garlic or garlic powder.

If dehydrated garlic products are new to your kitchen, start by using even small amounts, stir in one-eighth teaspoon minced or powdered garlic into six portions, then taste. If it needs more to make an impression, add it. Garlic is a very ancient flavoring and medicine. Records show that it was enjoyed by workmen building the Egyptian pyramids 6,000 years ago. The Israelites became acquainted with garlic during their stay in Egypt. The Greeks loved garlic; the Romans of Caesar's day did not. However, their descendants, modern Italians do, and use garlic in some of their most famous dishes. Garlic seems to have been taken to China about 140 B.C. and its use spread throughout most of Asia and the Far East.

Garlic grows most lustily in warm climates, and so it is not too surprising to learn that the garlic fields of California supply nearly all the garlic dehydrated today.

Every day, good cooks are finding new uses for dehydrated garlic products. Here, for instance, is a new recipe for a marvelous garlic-scented dish.

Lamb Croquettes

¹/₄   **cup (¹/₂ stick) butter or margarine**
¹/₄   **cup all purpose flour**
1   **cup milk**
1   **teaspoon instant minced onion**
1¹/₂   **teaspoons salt**
¹/₄   **teaspoon instant garlic powder**
¹/₄   **teaspoon ground black pepper**
3   **cups ground cooked lamb**
     Flour
1   **egg, beaten slightly**
1   **tablespoon milk**
     Dry bread crumbs
     Salad oil or shortening

Melt butter in a saucepan, blend in flour. Remove from heat and stir in 1 cup milk and onion. Cook until very thick, stirring constantly. Add seasonings and lamb. Mix well. Chill. Shape into croquettes. Roll in flour. Dip into beaten egg mixed with the 1 tablespoon milk and then into bread crumbs. Chill again. Fry in deep fat (375 degrees) 3 to 5 minutes or until golden brown. Drain on absorbent paper. Serve hot.

Recipe yields 12 croquettes or 6 portions.

LAND OF MYSTERY — FOOD OF MYSTERY

India. Continent of mystery and intrigue. In a small village just outside Calcutta, an Englishman strolls through the bazaar stalls examining brass, jewelry, fine cloth. He stops at one stall, and the Indian merchant hands him a small piece of paper. It is a secret formula — never intended to reach alien hands. The Englishman leaves the pay-off under a piece of fine cloth, glances furtively around, then quickly, silently, disappears into the crowd.

The paper is passed along, through top-secret channels, to the home office in London. The chief rings for his assistant, hands him the formula. Puzzled, the assistant comments, "It looks like a — recipe?" "Of course, it's a recipe, old man," replies the chief. "Paid dearly for it, too — from the Maharajah's own palace householder. It's for the Commonwealth dinner. We could not possibly offend the government of India by serving an inferior curry. Tell the chef it must be perfect, exactly like this secret formula."

Well, perhaps, this is somewhat far-fetched, even in the world of Agent 007's and spies around every corner, but in India curry is as important as any national secret they possess. Maybe you have known a few people yourself who were just about this secretive with their recipes. Through the ages, many recipes have been regarded as family treasure and passed from one generation to another. Sometimes (but not as often as imagined) a big price is paid for a recipe. Amusingly, some people will give you a recipe but leave out the really important ingredient or method. It would take a spy, and possibly even torture, to pry the secret from them. Come to think of it, our spy story is not so far-fetched after all.

Seriously, Indian curry is a serious, even sacred, dish in every household, be it ever so poor and humble, or royal and affluent. The poorest home in India will have at least three or four curry blends which they use for different types of foods. The more regal palaces parade anywhere from fifteen to twenty-five different curry mixtures.

You see, curry is a blend of many spices. It is not itself a spice, but the recipe for other spices in infinite combinations. Curry shouts its presence, or subtly undertones a food. A real curry fancier will fancy only one blend for vegetables, and an entirely different one for rice, or fish, or fowl. The blends can be very simple, consisting of only seven or eight spices, or very intricate, with as many as twenty-seven different condiments. This is the great mystery of curry, and why "secret" blends so often exist. Yes, really. The balance of the different measurements would not be easy to duplicate even if the exact number and names of the spices were known.

The reason so many Americans think that curry is a spice like, say, nutmeg, is that curry powder is sold commercially. Many of these are excellent curry blends, and you won't have the bother of grinding and mixing. But, likewise, you won't have the fun of experimentation, and perhaps, discovering your own curry, your own "secret formula." If you are a food chemist at heart, curry is probably the most fascinating experiment you can conduct. You'll learn volumes about most other spices too, for curry often contains a long list of the familiar and unfamiliar: paprika, cinnamon, cloves, cayenne pepper, mustard, allspice, mace, ginger, garlic — among the familiar items; fenugreek, cumin, coriander, poppy seeds, saffron, turmeric, fennel, anise — among the not so familiar. Still others are: white pepper, dill, nutmeg, sage, bay leaf, chilies, caraway, mint, and juniper berries.

If you are not so adventurous as to create your own blend, often a curry powder, commercially bought, is used as a base for the curry flavor, then heightened by a few choice condiments of your own choosing. This makes curry blending easier, but still offers a little individuality to your curried dishes. This is the case with Maharajah Chicken Curry, which I am showcasing for you now.

I know you are wondering if this is the secret formula recipe the spy in our opening story was after, but I don't tell you that. We spies in the gourmet department must protect our sources. I will say that it is "just as good as" and so I have named it after the Maharajah.

Maharajah Chicken Curry

1/2	cup chopped onion
1	clove garlic, minced
1/4	cup salad oil
1	medium tomato, chopped
1	small bay leaf
1/2	teaspoon cinnamon
3	whole cloves
5	cups cubed, uncooked chicken (2 1/2 pounds, boned)
1 1/2	teaspoons salt
1	tablespoon curry powder
1/2	teaspoon cumin
1/2	teaspoon coriande
1	teaspoon Worcestershire powder
	Dash pepper
	Pinch powdered saffron
1 1/2	cups water
1/4	cup fresh coconut milk

In a large skillet cook onions and garlic in oil until tender, but not brown. Add tomato, bay leaf, cinnamon, and cloves; cover and cook 5 minutes. Add cubed chicken; simmer slowly uncovered till juice of chicken has steamed off (about 30 minutes). Stir in salt, curry powder, cumin, coriander, Worcestershire powder, pepper, saffron, and water. Cook slowly for 35 to 40 minutes, or until chicken is tender. Blend in coconut milk. Serve over hot Saffron Rice. Makes 6 to 8 servings.

NOTE: If you cannot obtain fresh coconut milk you can make a substitute by using the vacuum-packed shredded coconut. To make ¼ cup (as called for in this recipe) of coconut milk take ¼ cup of the dried coconut and let it stand in ½ cup cold water until it is soaked well — about 20 minutes. Then squeeze the juice through muslin cloth. Repeat the process two or three times as each time the milk becomes richer, thicker.

SAFFRON RICE

	Dash powdered saffron
½	cup hot water
¼	cup butter or margarine, melted
1½	cups uncooked rice
¼	cup chopped onion
½	teaspoon salt
2½	cups hot water

Dissolve saffron in ½ cup hot water. Combine the dissolved saffron, butter, rice, onion, salt, and 1 cup of the water in a 1½-quart casserole. Bake uncovered in hot oven (450 degrees) for 20 minutes or until rice is very dry, stirring at the end of 10 minutes. Stir in remaining 1½ cups hot water; cover and return to hot oven for 15 minutes. Uncover and cook 5 minutes longer. Fluff with fork before serving. Makes 8 to 12 servings.

You may not be entertaining a Maharajah, but curry can be an intriguing new food adventure for you into the world of spices, new taste thrills, enjoyment, and new cooking knowledge.

LETTUCE IN CREAM

Each year I conduct numerous cooking schools across America. These sessions afford me a splendid opportunity to study the table habits in the different areas. Naturally, questions arise regarding some trapping used in various recipes. I have learned that more confusion exists about types of lettuce than any other recipe aggrandizement.

There are five different types of lettuce, but it is iceberg — head lettuce — which is, by far, the most important on the produce counter. It is especially adapted to mass production in western fields. It is so familiar it needs no description. Have you ever wondered why this firm iceberg lettuce is always free of sand or similar foreign matter? It's one of nature's tricks. When a little head lettuce plant begins to grow, it starts by curling several of its larger leaves up and over the space which will shortly be filled by other growing leaves. This forms a sort of porch

which wards off blowing sand and dust. In other words, the lettuce head fills out when inner leaves grow up from the stem below.

The butterhead is the second type of lettuce. It, too, is a head, but loosely formed of leaves which are very tender so that they have a sort of satin-smooth or "buttery feeling." "Big Boston" and "White Boston" are the most common varieties. Bibb is a miniature butterhead, about twice the size of a tulip. It is much prized by the trenchant gourmet. Its flavor has been described as "distinctively lettuce with a touch of cultivated dandelion."

Cos or Romaine is almost always available, too, on produce counters. This is a long head of lettuce. The leaves are stiff and perhaps a bit coarse, but always sweet and of good quality.

Leaf or bunching lettuce is characterized by loose leaves which never form a head. It is well suited to greenhouse lettuce culture and is the most easily grown in the home garden since it endures somewhat more heat than other lettuce varieties grown commercially.

The fifth type of lettuce has an enlarged stem and no head. It may, occasionally, be encountered under the name of "celtuce."

Lettuce is not only good eating, but it is good for us. Lettuce, especially the greener types, provides a useful amount of Vitamin A and C, iron and other vitamins and minerals. It gives us desirable roughage for good digestion. With all of these values, it is very low in calories.

Lettuce in Cream

⅓	cup top milk or light cream
3	tablespoons cider vinegar
¾	teaspoon sugar
¾	teaspoon salt
⅛	teaspoon ground black pepper
1	medium head lettuce
1	cup chopped green onions (scallions)

Combine the first 5 ingredients and set aside. Wash and dry lettuce, tear into bite-sized pieces, and place in a salad bowl. Add green onions and cream mixture. Toss lightly and serve as a salad course. Recipe serves 6.

LIVER NAISH

My television viewers often accuse me of making them fat, getting them off their diets, tempting them beyond human ability to withstand rich and delicious foods. I plead guilty to taste tempting my video audience, but innocent of getting them off their diets — that, dear readers, is your own decision.

As battles rage on about this diet and that diet I do, however, find myself very much in sympathy with those who must restrict their diets and miss so much palate pleasing. As La Rochefoucauld said, "Preserving the health by too strict a regiment is a wearisome malady." Some diets I have seen are more to be feared than the disease!

A favorite story of mine is illustrative of this point. Seems a man suddenly became deaf. He took himself to a medical clinic to find out why. After examination by several doctors, his hearing apparatus was pronounced normal, so he was turned over to the staff psychiatrist who promptly diagnosed his trouble as psychosomatic. "I have cured many people of this. It is caused by over stimulation of the nervous system," said the good doctor. "I have found gambling, drinking, women, and highly seasoned, rich foods are the causes."

"So, what do I do about it?" asked the patient.

"Obviously, you will need to give up gambling, drinking, women, and highly seasoned, rich foods."

"Are you kidding, doc?" yelled the patient. "Just for a little hearing?"

That's the plight of the dieter for figure fashion or for health — are you kidding, doc? Just for a little slimness, or health? While it is true that many gourmet foods are loaded with calories, cholesterol, carbohydrate units, or whatever it is popular to watch and count nowadays, it is also true that many equally good recipes are to be found which are not. This recipe will prove that you can have gourmet food with healthfully pure ingredients, low on the calorie chart, and definitely optimum flavor.

This recipe, which in my opinion is the ultimate in liver preparation, is an original by the famous actor of radio, television, and films, J. Carrol Naish. He demonstrated his chafing dish prowess when he was a guest on my television show in Los Angeles, "The Hollywood Gourmet."

Liver Naish

1½   **pounds calf's liver, sliced into thin pieces**
4   **red onions, diced finely**
½   **pound butter**
1   **can mushrooms, drained**
½   **cup red Du Bonnet wine**
  Salt and pepper to taste
  Worcestershire powder

Melt the butter in blazer pan or chafing dish over direct heat. Add onions and mushrooms. Sauté until these items are soft. Add wine and salt and pepper and Worcestershire powder to taste. Over these onions and mush-

rooms place slices of liver. Cover blazer pan with lid and allow to simmer until liver is done. The liver will become white in color when completely cooked. Serve on heated plates.

LUAU

How would you like to escape the hurry and worry of busy modern America and take an evening's vacation to a little island of tropical delight? Relax in an atmosphere of casual elegance? Invite your favorite people to savor a feast and amaze them with your genius for entertaining? You would? Then come along with me while we construct a typical Hawaiian Luau right in your own home.

It isn't as complicated as you think, not as costly either. Step one: Get into the mood. Plan your luau decor. To begin with, a luau table can be devised by simply placing several bricks or boxes to an elevation of about one foot above floor level. Over this structure, place a piece of plyboard or several planks. Cover the entire table with an inexpensive straw matting, or green crepe paper, and cover with large leaves. Arrange tropical type fruits, such as pineapple, bananas, oranges, melons, into a centerpiece directly on the table. Island music can be piped in by means of a stereo system. Paper leis may be purchased from the five and dime store. Pillows or cushions provide comfortable floor seats for your guests. If you have large indoor plants, or rubber plants, or artificial trees, or can borrow some greenery from your garden, move them into the dining area for background. A portable screen provides an excellent backdrop for a luau if you will cut travel pictures, tropical scenery, or Hawaiian art objects from magazines and tape them to it. Now your scene is set. Step two: Food, Polynesian Chicken. Gather together the following ingredients for a luau delight everyone will remember.

Polynesian Chicken

1   **baking-sized chicken**
  Melted butter
  Salt and pepper
  Fresh peach halves
  Apple halves
  Fresh pineapple chunks
  Chard leaves or Taro leaves

Rub the surface of the chicken with melted butter, and salt and pepper the cavity. Place into the cavity of the chicken fresh peach halves, apple halves, chunks of fresh pineapple. After filling the cavity of the chicken with fresh fruit, wrap the chicken with chard leaves or taro leaves. Secure the leaves with string. Using smaller chard or taro leaves, wrap small pieces of the fresh fruit used above. Place these small fruit packages on top of the chicken and secure with additional chard or taro leaves and toothpicks. The juices of the fruit and leaves will baste the chicken.

Place the wrapped chicken into a roasting pan and then into a preheated oven at 300 degrees. Roast chicken about twenty-five minutes per pound. A small amount of water may be added to the roast pan. Polynesian Chicken is perhaps the most sympathetic recipe for chronicling an entree in leaves. Here we see that the use of superfluous items can greatly enhance the taste magic and overall eye appeal of a food creation. We do eat with our eyes to a great extent. Food presented in a pleasing and appropriate-to-the-occasion manner will always stimulate the palate.

MELON CHICKEN

For the hostess, or host, who wants to bring to the dining table a recipe enchanting, a *piece de résistance,* a supreme delight, a beautiful food fantasy, Melon Chicken is just what the gourmet ordered.

Melon Chicken is a Polynesian method of cooking and it comes to us from Hawaii. In every country there are basic food preparation procedures which are handed down from generation to generation, and which seem quite unusual to us today. But we find these tried and true recipes cannot be fundamentally changed with any appreciable improvement. They can be adapted to our available supply of green groceries, or seasonings, and also to our way of cooking. This is the reason I recommend preparation in the way of the originators of Melon Chicken, but recommend you cook it in your modern, controlled oven, even though the natives cook it in a hot coal pit. This way we get the exotic effect, the same superb taste and colorful eye appeal, and you won't have to dig up your backyard to cook native style.

A great wave of interest in Polynesian foods has developed. It is a late-comer as far as gourmet popularity is concerned, but it is making up for lost time — fast! Surely seamen, adventurers, and world travelers tasted foods like these many years ago on these enchanted isles. But news of such as this never reached the mainland.

After World War II when the soldiers came sailing home, they told of some delectable dishes served them in Hawaii and other Polynesian islands. Also the restaurant boom was on; the travel boom was on; Polynesia just had to part with some native secrets of cooking. It was love at first bite for Americans.

Those of us not fortunate enough to live on a tropical isle where the ingredients grow around the cook will have to assemble the following to create (by imitation) a mainland Melon Chicken.

Melon Chicken

1   **oval-shaped watermelon (approximately 25 pounds)**
1   **baking-sized hen**
    Selected canned sweet fruits (such as pineapple, peaches, apricots, cherries, oranges)
    Salt and pepper
    Minced onion (optional)
$1/_2$ **cup soy sauce**
$1/_2$ **cup powdered almonds**

With a very sharp knife, slice the melon lengthwise — end to end — in halves, and with a large spoon core out enough of the red melon meat and seeds to form a cavity that will hold the chicken. Core melon from both halves, leaving about $1^1/_2$ or 2 inches of ripe red fruit.

Season cavity of the chicken with salt and pepper and place a few pieces of the sweet canned fruit in the cavity. Brush a light coat of soy sauce over the outside surface of the chicken and place about 1 tablespoon of soy sauce into the cavity. A few pieces of minced onion may be added, if desired. Sprinkle a half cup of pulverized or crushed almond powder over the surface of the chicken. Place chicken into the cored-out section of one of the melon halves and cover with the other melon half. Secure the halves together with small metal skewers, and place the melon on a baking sheet or shallow pan. Place into a preheated oven at 400 degrees. Roast at this temperature for 2 hours, then lower the temperature to 300 degrees and continue roasting for approximately 5 hours.

MEXICANO STUFFED EGGPLANT

I once read, some time ago, of an Armenian cook who declared that he knew 100,000 ways of preparing eggplant. He was surely boasting; he probably didn't have more than 1,000 eggplant recipes.

One of the most famous eggplant recipes from the near East is a Turkish concoction, *Imam Baaldi.* This means, in Turkish, "The Priest" — or Imam — "has fainted." This is a stuffed eggplant which is flavored with lots of garlic and olive oil, baked slowly and served cold. The story goes that this particular Imam was so excited by the aroma of the dish as it was carried toward him that he fainted from impatience!

Eggplant is one of the oldest of all cultivated vegetables. Plant historians believe that this vegetable originated either in tropical India or in the warmer parts of China. For many centuries it was known only in southeastern Asia. Gradually, it made its way west by caravan to the

Arabian peninsula and the lands of northern Africa. The ancient Greeks and Romans must not have known eggplant for they had no name for it.

When Arabs overcame so much of southern Europe they brought along their taste for eggplant. The Spanish and Italians learned to love them. When Spanish explorers and conquistadors reached the New World, they in turn transported eggplant to the Caribbean Islands and the Central and South American mainland. Records show, for instance, that eggplant was grown in Brazil before 1650. It's a very popular vegetable throughout Latin America and the Caribbean. In Jamaica, eggplants are called "garden eggs," which is a good name for them.

There are many varieties of eggplant although we may see only the big purple ones on our produce counters. There have appeared, however, yellow, white, ash-gray, and brown eggplants. Big and little, round, oblong, pear-shaped, and cucumber-shaped. When eggplants first reached northern Europe, they were planted among oriental plants. That's what happened to the first tomatoes, too. This isn't so surprising because a couple of centuries ago, people used to eat flowers such as violets, rose petals, marigolds, and similar posies.

We can now obtain in our supermarkets fresh eggplant throughout the year, with Florida, California, and Mexico, the principal suppliers. Eggplant is often served as a substitute for meat. In fact, eggplant is often called "vegetable beef steak." Men always seem to love it especially.

Unlike the Armenian cook mentioned earlier, I only have forty or fifty excellent eggplant recipes in my own repertoire, but the following is certainly one of the best.

Mexicano Stuffed Eggplant

1	large (2 pounds) eggplant
6	tablespoons butter or margarine
1/4	teaspoon finely minced garlic
1/2	cup diced celery
1/2	cup coarsely shredded carrots
1/4	cup chopped onion
1/2	teaspoon salt
3/4	teaspoon chili powder
1/2	teaspoon oregano leaves
1/3	cup sliced stuffed olives
1	cup toasted croutons
1/2	cup chopped tomatoes

Cut a lengthwise slice from one side of the eggplant. Parboil 25 minutes. Cool. Using a grapefruit knife, scoop out pulp to within 1/4 inch of the skin and cut into cubes. Melt butter or margarine in a medium-size skillet. Add garlic, celery, carrots, and onion, and cook until onions are transparent. Blend in seasonings, diced eggplant,

and remaining ingredients. Spoon the mixture into the eggplant shell. Place in a buttered baking dish and bake in a preheated 400-degree oven for 20 minutes. Recipe serves 6.

MUSHROOM CHEESE CASSEROLE

There are certain eras of history when the very rich and privileged really lived it up. Wealthy Romans of Caesar's day made the banquet table famous. Centuries later, in France, Louis XIV, XV, and XVI, lived off the fat of the land, feasting on the choicest viands.

The mushroom serves as a symbol of the fabulous foods set before these privileged people. At one point in Ancient Rome, a reform government decided people were living too richly, eating too much meat and fish. They must eat more vegetables, and a law was passed to that effect. It didn't take some of the smarter Romans long to remember that mushrooms are vegetables. Ingenious cooks discovered more and more delicious ways of preparing mushrooms.

This passion for mushrooms was noted by the Roman orator, Cicero, who declared "These elegant eaters prepare their fungi (that is, mushrooms) and all their vegetables with such highly seasoned condiments that it is impossible to conceive anything more delicious . . ."

Historian Pliny noted that mushrooms were the only food which the "dainty voluptuaries" prepared with their own hands, using knives and silver service. The Romans went so far as to fashion sets of cooking utensils to be used only for mushrooms, never to be used for lesser foods.

Today's cultivated mushrooms are so delicately good that they can be prepared very simply. Broil or sauté in a little butter or margarine and serve them on buttered toast. Spoon sliced fresh or canned mushrooms on half an omelet before folding it. Marinate sliced mushrooms in French dressing and toss with mixed greens or add to a macaroni salad flavored with onion and oregano.

Mushrooms are a real convenience vegetable, whether fresh, canned or frozen. Wash fresh mushrooms briefly, jiggling them in clear water. Do not peel. Sauté for three to five minutes in hot fat.

Canned mushrooms should be drained carefully before sautéeing. (Save the canning liquid for a soup or sauce.)

Mushroom flavor can be varied deliciously with herbs such as thyme, tarragon or garlic powder. Oregano is so compatible with mushrooms that Italians call this "the mushroom herb."

This is one mushroom recipe that I often enjoy:

Mushroom Cheese Casserole

Sauté ¹/₂ pound sliced fresh mushrooms, or 1 can (6- or 8-ounce) mushrooms, drained, in 2 tablespoons melted butter or margarine 3 to 5 minutes. Cook 1 package (10-ounce) Brussels sprouts in ¹/₂ cup water 5 minutes. Place mushrooms, Brussels sprouts and ¹/₂ pound cooked, diced ham in layers in 1¹/₂-quart casserole. Prepare 1 package (1¹/₂-ounce) cheese sauce mix according to package directions and pour over ingredients in casserole. Mix together ¹/₄ cup dry bread crumbs, ¹/₄ teaspoon paprika and 1 tablespoon melted butter or margarine. Sprinkle over casserole. Bake in preheated hot oven (400 degrees) 10 to 12 minutes.

Yield 4 portions.

NEW SOUTH VENISON STEAK

In many of our rural areas, sportsmen still go a-hunting for the makings of a brunswick stew or a rabbit roast. For gourmets, however, most game comes from the market man. He selects it at a game farm, where animals and birds are raised in conditions closely approximating the wild state. From time to time these game farms release surplus stocks to the countryside and thus do a double service, supplying the gourmet's table and replenishing the wild species for their own sake and the sportsman's. The most popular game meat in America today is venison. Any antlered animal is venison. The most often eaten venison is deer, with elk coming in a tardy second. I have found that to insure tenderness, venison should hang from two to four weeks. Chops and steaks from a reasonably young animal may not require marinating, but they should be cooked in a generous amount of fat. Roasting cuts of venison are usually very lean and should be larded through with fat pork or some other lubricity.

Whether a sportsman bags his game or buys it, the initial preparation will probably be left to the sharp knives, skilled hands, and experience of a professional. Let him bleed the deer, skin the rabbit, and pluck the pheasant. After the proper preparation of the meat and hanging, large game, generally speaking, can be cooked like corresponding cuts of meat, and small game and game birds like poultry.

There are numerous compatible uncooked marinades for venison but the one I prefer is a blending of olive oil, vinegar, and dry white wine, seasoned with onion, carrots, parsley, salt, braised peppercorns, juniper berries, and a little thyme. The olive oil in this mixture coats the meat and prevents it from discoloring, and aids in retaining the marinade flavor. For the best flavor effect, coat the venison with this marinade in a bowl and place into the refrigerator. Allow the meat to marinate for two or three days, turning the selection once a day. When the meat is ready to cook, wipe clean with a cloth but reserve the marinade, which is often used for basting during the cooking time. The following recipe will excite any hunter's discriminating propensity for venison.

New South Venison Steak

³/₄	**cup flour**
³/₄	**teaspoon salt**
	Cayenne
	Dash of thyme
	Dash of nutmeg
	Dash of clove
	3-pound steak cut from rump of venison
2	**tablespoons melted beef suet**
3	**large onions, thinly sliced**
2	**cups fresh tomatoes, peeled and quartered, or 2 cups stewed tomatoes**
1	**tablespoon Worcestershire powder**
4	**drops Tabasco**
1¹/₂	**cups red Burgundy**
1	**clove**
¹/₂	**small clove garlic**
	Bouquet garni
	Salt and pepper to taste
1	**scant cup sautéed mushroom caps**

Sift flour with salt, a few grains of cayenne, thyme, nutmeg, and clove. Vigorously pound this seasoned flour into venison steak. Cut the steak into 1-inch cubes.

Heat melted beef suet in a heavy stew pot or Dutch oven and sear venison on both sides, adding thinly sliced onions to the pot. When meat and onions are well browned, add peeled and quartered fresh tomatoes or stewed tomatoes, Worcestershire powder, Tabasco, Burgundy, clove, garlic, and bouquet garni.

Cover pot closely, set in a moderate oven, and cook 2¹/₂ hours or until meat is tender. Add salt and pepper to taste and bring to boil over direct heat. Stir in sautéed mushroom caps and serve with wild rice and red currant jelly.

As a variation, port may be substituted for part of the Burgundy, or 2 tablespoons red currant jelly may be stirred into the sauce.

OLD ENGLISH PRIME RIB

In Germany you will be wished *Frohliche Weihnachten* and in Italy the greeting will be *Buon Natale* and in Brazil they will salute you with *Feliz Natal*. Around the world the languages differ but the meaning is the same. So it is with Christmas feasting. The national favorites differ from country to country.

Sweden loves their *lutfisk* at their *God Jul* celebration while France thinks a goose is the best serving for a *Joyeux Noel*. In jolly old England it is Prime Rib which is the order of the Christmas holiday, and in which the British take an understandably warm pride.

Last year I decided to let turkey be the star of the dining table for Thanksgiving, but for Christmas — old English Prime Rib! The English discovered this method of cooking Prime Rib long before thermostatically controlled ovens. They found that by employing rock salt — comparable to our ice cream rock salt — they could seal in the vital juices of the meat thus retaining flavor and nutrition, and weight (which means money as well). I have found through many years of using this unique procedure that there is almost one hundred percent elimination of shrinkage.

Old English Prime Rib

Prime rib or standing rib ($^1/_2$ pound per serving)
1   **teaspoon MSG powder**
    Rock salt (ice cream salt)
2   **tablespoons Worcestershire powder**
1   **teaspoon paprika**
    Salt and pepper to taste

Select choice prime rib or standing rib. Season meat with seasonings and rub into the meat. In a large, heavy pan, such as the bottom section of a roaster, pour a layer of rock salt until the bottom surface of the container is completely covered. Lightly dampen the rock salt with water until the salt is just moist. Place the prime rib onto the salt in a standing rib position. Then cover the prime rib completely with rock salt, again dampening all of the salt very lightly with water. Be certain none of the prime rib is showing. It must be completely covered. Without a cover for the roaster, place the meat, covered with salt, into a preheated oven at 500 degrees.

Allow the prime rib to roast for 12 minutes per pound. When cooking time is completed, remove the roast from the oven. The rock salt will be extremely hard and must be carefully broken away from the prime rib. This can be done with a wooden mallet (or hammer) by gently striking the surface of the salt, creating cracks. Pull the particles from the roast.

This process, which does not impart a salt flavor to the meat, traps the vital flavor juices and insures the very minimum of shrinkage.

OLD ENGLISH TRIFLE

This recipe is as unmistakably and traditionally English as the "separate tables" custom. Sitting at my "separate table" with my family at the Selsdon Park Hotel in Sussex one gray November day, I enjoyed English Trifle and became an immediate champion of this recipe.

The Selsdon Park was once a great English mansion. It is still a great English mansion, but also, now a resident hotel. Still very much as it was in the good old days of the aristocracy, it is surrounded by vast lawns, tennis courts, riding paths, and completing the picture, a vintage Rolls-Royce awaits you at the entrance for your drive to the local rail station and a train to London's Victoria Station.

In our room the down mattresses into which you sink about a foot invite late sleeping. Indescribably luxurious heavy tapestry drapes surround the turret-like, castle-like windows, and I fully expected Sherlock Holmes and Dr. Watson to step from behind them at any time in search of Professor Moriarity.

I wanted to live in the English countryside for awhile to observe the true English way of life and, at the same time, flex my taste muscles over English food. Contrary to public thinking that English cooking is dull and undeserving of praise, I have found no better food anywhere. One of my most treasured and popular recipes is Old English Prime Rib. I defy anyone to produce a better recipe. On this sojourn in Britain I accumulated many fine recipes including this one — English Trifle.

The "separate table" custom in England is an attempt to preserve privacy and to prestige each guest. In a changing world, having your own table in the dining room is a changeless security. For a visitor to a strange country, the maitre'd's instruction to the waiter, "Show Mr. Wade to his table," makes one feel welcome and at home.

Unlike American hotels, meals are not served continuously, but at specified times, which makes a mealtime anticipated and more formal. Downtown London hotels have service anytime, but heaven forbid that the English country dining room should be turned into a coffee shop! I for one, wouldn't like it.

Here at the Selsdon Park Hotel I met wonderful people, and wonderful foods. English Trifle (pronounced try-ful) was one of them. The recipe is easy to accomplish and dresses up a special dinner or a holiday entertainment with a proper finale.

Old English Trifle

1   **tablespoon cornstarch**
2   **cups eggnog**
6   **ladyfingers**
$^1/_2$ **cup raspberry jam**
6   **teaspoons sherry (1 teaspoon to each
      ramekin)**
$^1/_2$ **cup heavy cream**
6   **teaspoons slivered, blanched almonds**

Combine cornstarch and eggnog. Cook over medium heat until mixture thickens and boils (about 5 minutes), stirring constantly. Remove from heat. Cool, and stir. Chill in refrigerator for 1 hour.

Split ladyfingers lengthwise and spread them with raspberry jam. Place 2 ladyfinger halves in each of 6 ramekins with the jam side up. Sprinkle with sherry, 1 teaspoon for each ramekin. Let stand for a few minutes. Spoon the cooled custard into the ramekins. Whip the heavy cream until stiff. Fill a pastry bag, fitted with a fancy tip, with the whipped cream. Pipe rosettes of cream around the edges of each ramekin and pipe 1 rosette in the center of each. Now sprinkle with slivered, blanched almonds. Chill in the refrigerator for 30 minutes or until ready to serve. Makes 6 servings.

OMELET PARISIENNE

A volume of words has been written about the temperamental nature of the classic omelet. So much so, in fact, that otherwise daring kitchen technicians often refuse to attempt it. I find that it is much easier to actualize an omelet than it is to blueprint the production techniques.

Omelets can be infinitely varied in flavor, for no other dish so lends itself to the imagination of the cook. Once you learn to negotiate the basic omelet, its countless variations become a simple matter of inventiveness. While an omelet is simple to produce, one false move and the dish is ruined. It requires diligence to stage it properly as you must be on the job every moment during its preparation, for speed and efficiency count above all. Each omelet must be prepared to measure; allow your guests to wait for the omelet, never allow the omelet to wait for your guests.

Contrary to popular belief, small omelets are more easily accomplished than the larger ones. A four-egg omelet is the easiest to manipulate and will usually serve two or three persons. If your guest list is larger than three, I suggest that you make several omelets, for they are presented hotter at the table with a nice consistency.

For each small omelet, break four eggs into a bowl and season according to the dictates of your own particular taste with salt and pepper. Add one tablespoon of heavy cream to this mixture.

Heat the omelet pan gradually over a medium flame until it is hot enough to force butter to sizzle on contact. Beat the eggs with a fork or wire whisk just enough to mix yolks and whites. (About 30 seconds.) Add two tablespoons of butter to the heated pan and shake so that butter will coat the bottom of the pan evenly. When the butter starts to sizzle, but before it has changed in color, pour in the beaten eggs, all at once. Next quickly stir the eggs for a second or two in the pan to assure even browning as you would for scrambled eggs. Then, as the eggs start to set, lift the edges of the omelet with your fork so that the liquid on top can run under. Repeat this procedure until all of the liquid is used but the eggs are still moist and soft. You can always keep your omelet "slipping-free" by shaking the pan during the above operation. Now remove the eggs from the flame and with one movement press the handle of the pan downwards and slide the omelet towards the handle. When about one-third of the omelet has slid up the rounded edge of the pan, quickly fold this amount of the recipe toward the center with a knife. Then, very quickly, raise the handle of the pan, and slide the opposite edge of the omelet one-third up the side farthest away from the handle. Hold a heated serving dish under it and, as the rim of the omelet touches the dish, raise the handle more and more until the pan is turned upside down and your oval-shaped, lightly browned omelet rests on the dish. Rapidly "finish" the omelet by impaling a piece of butter with the tip of a knife and brushing the surface of the omelet lightly to leave a glistening finish. Garnish your omelet with fresh mint snippets of parsley and serve at once.

Although many expert cooks contend that an omelet can be produced in any pan, I champion the practice of reserving a special pan exclusively for these egg recipes. There are pans expressly designed for cooking omelets, but I have found the french skillet with slanted sides so the eggs can slide easily onto the plate when cooked to be effective. To prevent your omelet from sticking, never wash your special pan. Instead, just rub it clean with a paper towel coated with a few drops of cooking oil.

Omelet Parisienne

8   **eggs**
    Sugar
3   **tablespoons butter**
1   **tablespoon peanut oil**
3   **tablespoons Cointreau or Grand Marnier
      Orange or banana slices or diced pineapple
      Butter**
2   **teaspoons sugar**
4   **tablespoons Cognac, Armagnac or Rum**

Separate eggs; whisk yolks until frothy; whisk whites until very stiff. Fold yolks into beaten whites and add sugar to taste. Heat butter and oil in an omelet pan, and, when very hot, pour in omelet mixture. Spoon over Cointreau or Grand Marnier and cook until omelet is done but still moist. Place slices of orange, banana, or pineapple, which you have heated in a little butter, in the center of the egg mixture. Fold over. Place on a hot platter. Sprinkle with sugar and glaze under a hot grill. Flame with Cognac, Armagnac or rum and serve immediately. Recipe serves 6.

OYSTERS IN SHERRY BARCELONA

The El Presidente Hotel in Barcelona offers among the best food experiences I have ever had, in a life filled with great food experiences. Barcelona is lucky also — at least the diners there are lucky — to be on the Mediterranean where the seafood is fresh and first class. Most of the traditional Spanish recipes are seafood favorites, or they contain seafood, as for instance, the *paella* which is really a rice dish but combined with vegetables, fish, meat, and seasonings. *Paella* at El Presidente is highly recommended.

But the oysters in sherry you won't want to miss. You know that sherry is the national drink of Spain. You are offered sherry everywhere, both to drink and in most recipes, at least recipes in the haute cuisine of Spain. There it is pronounced "Hear-ez." All meals begin and end with it if you do in Spain as the Spanish do. If sherry is your favorite drink per chance, you have entered a Latin paradise.

Spanish-style dining is a whole evening's occupation. Starting late at 9:30, pushed to 3:30 in cities for tourists, the menu begins leisurely, is served leisurely, ends leisurely. At 11:30 you may be still awaiting your dessert. This is not due to poor service. Quite the contrary. The service is extraordinarily good. This is just the Spanish way of dining. Don't fight it, enjoy it. The Basques and the Catalans are the cultured cooks of Spain. Barcelona is the stronghold of the Catalans. On the outskirts of Barcelona — away from the El Presidente — you have to do a little detective work to find a good, typically Spanish restaurant. You could run out of time before you find one. The *tasca* (a tavern that serves food) is usually a good bet.

An odd thing about most of these is that they have floors covered with shrimp shells, a kind of messy-looking place, but the Spanish think not. "The more shells, the better the food," they say.

It's no good asking hotel personnel about restaurants. English-speaking is not necessarily English-understanding, neither is Spanish-speaking the same as Spanish-understanding. This is another reason for recommending El Presidente dining. Everyone knows where it is and how to get there.

As I have said, Spain's main claim to food fame is seafood, and proof of this is that all the nationally famous recipes are from coastal communities. Centuries of experience and experimenting have taught them just how to cook seafood for exclamations of praise from both natives and tourists.

Oysters in Sherry Barcelona

24	selected oysters
	Salt and pepper to taste
	Flour
	Butter
$1/_2$	cup fresh lemon juice
1	cup steak sauce
2	tablespoons Worcestershire powder
2	1-ounce jiggers sherry
3	tablespoons water
2	tablespoons flour

Salt and pepper oysters. Dredge in flour and grill on lightly buttered griddle on top of range until crisp and browned on both sides. Do not broil in oven. If no griddle is available, use heavy skillet on top of range. Sprinkle oysters with butter or cooking oil while grilling. Do this on both sides; it browns and crisps them. Heat lemon juice, steak sauce, Worcestershire powder and sherry in saucepan over low heat. Do not allow to come to boil. Blend flour and water and stir into sauce to thicken. Correct sauce seasoning to taste by addition of steak sauce if too thin or sherry if too thick.

PAPRIKA POTATOES

Paprika is known as the "cosmetic spice." It does for many foods what rouge does to a woman's cheeks — they say, it makes a "tasty-looking dish."

Getting back to the origin of words, how did paprika get that name? Looking in the dictionary, we find that "paprika" is a Hungarian word meaning "Turkish pepper." As it happened, paprika didn't originate in Turkey — any more than our Thanksgiving bird, the turkey was first found there. Both, however, were among the many marvelous new foods found in the New World by Columbus and his successors and taken back to the Old World. Eventually paprika reached Hungary and parts of eastern Europe.

During this same period in history, the Turks were invading from the east, bringing with them Turkish foods and eating habits. Soon people weren't sure which foods had come from where and the shiny red pod peppers from the New World became known as "paprika" or "Turkish pepper."

Ever since that time the "paprikash" has been Hungary's most famous kind of dish. Whether paprikash starts with meat, fowl or a vegetable like mushrooms, it is simmered in a paprika-rich sauce. Incidentally, Hungarian cooks are very likely to use paprika lavishly. "Use enough to make everything good and red" is apparently their motto.

Most of the paprika used in the United States is of the sweet, milk variety — and quite red. This is the kind we prefer. Some foreign dishes require a nippy paprika. In that case you can "hop-up" paprika with a pinch of cayenne — about one-sixteenth to one-eighth teaspoon cayenne per tablespoon of mild paprika.

Because our paprika does have a mild flavor, don't hesitate to use it with other spices and flavoring ingredients. This familiar "garnish spice" can be used liberally to give an appetizing appearance to a wide variety of dishes, including salads and salad dressings, fish, meat and chicken, soups, eggs and vegetables. Naturally, it is most effective on light-colored foods. Commercially, great quantities of paprika are used in the manufacture of sausages and other meat products, salad dressings, condiments and ready-prepared foods.

Paprika Potatoes

Melt 2 tablespoons butter or margarine in large skillet. Add 18 small new potatoes, 1 tablespoon instant minced onion, 1 cup water, 1 tablespoon paprika, 1 teaspoon salt and 1 bay leaf. Cover and cook over moderate heat until potatoes are tender. Remove bay leaf. Add 1 tablespoon cider vinegar and bring to boiling point. Boil 1 minute. Drain, if necessary. Add $1/2$ cup sour cream. Heat, but do not boil.

Yield 6 portions.

PEACH TART VIENNESE

Poets have written lovingly and dramatically about the beverage called coffee. John Milton: "One sip of this will bathe the drooping spirits in delight beyond the bliss of dreams." Francis Bacon: "This drink comforteth the brain and heart and helpeth digestion." Alexander Pope: "Coffee — which makes the politician wise, And see through all things with his half-shut eyes." An ancient Arab poet: "O Coffee, Thou dost dispel all care, . . . Coffee is our gold . . . Wherever it is served, one enjoys the society of the noblest and most generous men." Both Balzac and Voltaire were great coffee drinkers. The latter remarked that coffee was no doubt a deadly poison, but it acted quite slowly. Since he lived to be eighty-four years old, he suffered little from the "poison" he loved. Our own Robert Frost wrote wittily, "If there is one thing more exasperating than a wife who can make good coffee and won't, then that's a wife who cannot make good coffee and will."

There are a few pleasures in life more satisfying than a good cup of coffee. The great equalizer, coffee brings comfort and warm cheer to peasants and kings, to poets and diplomats, soldiers and housewives.

Did you know that there are 440 million cups of coffee drunk each day in the United States? (I don't know who or when someone sneaked around counting all of these cups, but this is the statistical count for an American coffee day.) However, think not that the U.S. has a corner on the coffee-drinking market. The Arabs have everyone beat with their twenty to thirty cups a day of *gahwa*. However, the Arab coffee cup is never full until the time comes to take leave of coffeehouse or host. A full cup to the Arab means literally, "Finish this cup, then leave."

Of course, every country has a favorite coffee mate. In France it is *cafe* and Crepes Suzettes. In Sweden it is *kaffee* and *lussekake*. In China it is *kia-fey* and *diem sum* (delicacies which touch the heart). But in Vienna the favorite companions for the cups of magic brew are fruit tarts. Peach Tart Viennese is a beautiful dessert to match the aromatic, steaming cup of greatness called coffee.

Peach Tart Viennese

$1/4$	**cup butter or margarine**
$1/4$	**cup confectioners' sugar**
1	**cup sifted flour**
1	**tablespoon cornstarch**
2	**tablespoons sugar**
$1/4$	**teaspoon mace**
$1/2$	**cup orange juice**
$1/2$	**cup currant jelly, melted**
8	**large fresh peaches**
	Whipping cream

Cream butter and confectioners' sugar (adding sugar gradually and creaming constantly); then add flour, mixing to form soft dough. Pat on bottom and sides of a 12-inch pizza pan. Bake in a 350-degree oven for 20 minutes.

Combine cornstarch, sugar, mace and orange juice in a saucepan. Cook over very low heat until thick and clear, stirring constantly. Stir in melted currant jelly. Allow to cool slightly. While glaze is cooling, peel, slice and arrange peaches in a single layer in the baked pie shell. Spoon the glaze evenly over the peaches. Chill in refrigerator. Garnish with whipped cream before serving. Serves 6 to 8 people.

PENNSYLVANIA DUTCH HASH

In the late 1600s a remarkable group of immigrants settled in and around Lancaster County, Pennsylvania. From the Rhineland of Germany, they brought with them a deeply ingrained love for fine food. Although they do not participate in sophisticated, worldly pleasures, they do believe in the fullest enjoyment of the twin necessities of cooking and eating, and with a passion. So great is their cooking of good vittles, they have created gourmet masterpieces which have achieved the heights of epicurean praise. Countless dishes have been created and made famous right where they are, proving the old saying that "if you build a better mousetrap . . ." In this case, if you cook a better casserole, or pudding, or even hash, "the world will beat a path to your door." At the door of the Pennsylvania Dutch every gourmet winds up sooner or later. Let's hope it won't be late for you. What a shame to miss this kind of down-to-earth gourmetmanship when you could be, as the Pennsylvania Dutch say, "eating yourself full."

In spite of the quality, the recipes are economy cooking, as the Dutch are thrifty people. Their recipes consist of no fancy ingredients, only wholesome good food put together with loving care. "Making-do" with what is available and making it into great tasting fare is their specialty. They have a proverb to this effect: "A woman can throw away more with a spoon than her man can bring in with his shovel."

Many Pennsylvania Dutch people speak the language of their homeland, though the dialects vary here and there depending on the county you are in. It makes a delightfully happy and descriptive language as they translate it into a kind of Dutch English. Coming out half and half, the idiom provides such as this: "It makes somesing down like a drizzle," or another favorite expression about the weather, "Look the door out and see if it's puttin' down somesing still." Surely we can all sympathize with the Pennsylvania Dutch woman who told me, "buying so much food reaches me so much in the pocketbook, I bought myself poor." Doesn't it to all the pocketbooks? But on the other hand, they believe that "them that works hard eats hearty," so no problem, because they are very, very industrious people.

On a Pennsylvania Dutch table this recipe would not be the main dish, but only one of the dishes to choose from. Their tables are heavy with every kind of food. A Dutch cook doesn't think she can live up to her true potential as a cook unless she has at least ten to cook for. Meals prepared for any less than that would be considered a mere snack, not a meal. And "to sit down mit yourself alone to eat" is true rejection, an unhappy Pennsylvania Dutchman indeed.

Pennsylvania Dutch Hash

2	tablespoons shortening
1	pound ground beef
2	large onions, sliced
2	green bell peppers
2	cups canned tomatoes
2	cups coarsely crushed pretzel crumbs
1	tablespoon minced parsley
1	teaspoon Worcestershire powder
	Dash of pepper

Melt shortening in a heavy skillet over medium heat. Add ground beef and cook until pink color disappears, stirring with a fork to break up meat into small pieces. Add and sauté the onions and bell peppers for about 10 minutes, stirring occasionally. Stir in tomatoes, pretzel crumbs, parsley, Worcestershire powder, and pepper to taste.

Serve this hash with Dutch Potato Pancakes which are easy to accomplish in the following manner:

DUTCH POTATO PANCAKES

4	tablespoons bacon fat
2	cups grated raw potatoes
1	tablespoon onion, minced
2	eggs
1	teaspoon salt
2	tablespoons flour

Beat eggs until fluffy. Add potatoes, onion and salt. Mix together thoroughly. Stir in flour and drop from a tablespoon into hot bacon fat. Brown, turn, and brown other side. Serve hot.

PENNSYLVANIA DUTCH SHOO-FLY PIE

If you sat down to eat with a Pennsylvania Dutch family, you would soon believe that they invented food, and eating too. So laden is their dining table with great variety, so great a choice do you have, if you are an indecisive person "the food is all, already, so much go et." In Americanese, "all" means gone. You're too late, already.

Nowhere does this variety show up as it does in the desserts. Never are you served one dessert, always two or more. Often your dessert plate comes to the table with two kinds of pie, or two kinds of cake, or cake and pie. Once, after a nine-course meal, I was presented with four kinds of pie, two different cakes, and was told, "Don't eat yourself full, there's pudding back yet."

Pie is, without a doubt, the Pennsylvania Dutch dessert favorite, "to top off on." And of the great number of pie recipes, Shoo-Fly Pie is the most famous to outsiders.

This is their traditional breakfast pie — that's right, breakfast pie! They have complete menus for breakfast: meat, potatoes, eggs, pancakes, or thick bread, relishes, apple butter and preserves, and pie. A teaser of coffee and toast is not for these hard-working, hard-eating people.

I really have never understood why desserts are not more popular breakfast fare. Pie makes a wonderful coffee-mate, to my mind a perfect combination. Reminds me of a time when I had breakfast at a highway diner. In came a tired truck driver who placed an order for chili. The proprietor said, "Chili's not ready so early. How about a hamburger?" To which the truck driver indignantly replied, "Whoever heard of eating a hamburger for breakfast?"

Well, everyone to his own breakfast taste. If you like the pie-for-breakfast idea, you'll like Shoo-Fly pie. It's good anytime, though, and you don't have to be Pennsylvania Dutch to enjoy it.

There are two kinds of Shoo-Fly pie. Both are authentic Dutch recipes and there must be fifty variations of each type pie, with new ones turning up all the time. One type is gooey, a liquid filling, which they refer to as "wet-bottom shoo-fly pie" and the other type is more of a pie-cake construction, crisp and dry for dunking. (Here's where the word "dunking" originated, meaning to dip down with a piece of bread, biscuit, or crust into the "dippy" — liquid, usually meaning gravy.) I wonder if this isn't where our modern word "dip" originated? Probably! Of course, coffee is the "dippy" for which this crusty shoo-fly is intended.

Whether you like gooey or crusty with your breakfast coffee, I think you'll agree with the Pennsylvania Dutch who say "shoo-fly pie sure eats good."

Shoo-Fly Pie
(gooey)

1	9-inch pie shell, unbaked
$^1/_2$	tablespoon soda
$^3/_4$	cup boiling water
$^1/_2$	cup molasses (yellow-label Brer Rabbit)
1	egg yolk, beaten well
$^3/_4$	cup flour
$^1/_2$	teaspoon cinnamon
$^1/_8$	teaspoon nutmeg
$^1/_8$	teaspoon ginger
$^1/_8$	teaspoon cloves
$^1/_3$	cup brown sugar
2	tablespoons shortening
$^1/_2$	teaspoon salt

Dissolve soda into boiling water, add molasses and egg yolk which has been beaten well.

Separately combine the dry ingredients: flour, spices, and brown sugar, then combine dry ingredients with shortening. Work into crumbs using your hands to do so until whole mixture is crumbly.

Line pie plate with pastry. Put liquid filling into pie shell. Top with crumb mixture. Bake in 400-degree oven for about 10 minutes; when crust starts to turn brown, reduce temperature to 325 degrees and bake until the filling is firm.

Shoo-Fly Pie
(crispy)

1	cup molasses (yellow-label Brer Rabbit)
1	cup boiling water
1	teaspoon soda
4	cups flour, unsifted
1	cup brown sugar
$^3/_4$	cup shortening
2	10-inch, or 3 7-inch pie shells, unbaked

Mix the water and molasses. Cool slightly. Add soda. Separately mix the flour, brown sugar, and shortening into crumbs, using your hands to do so until the mixture is crumbly. Fill the pie shells with the molasses mixture. Place crumb mixture on top. Bake for 25 minutes in a 350-degree oven.

PERFECT-RICE GOURMET

The business world tells us that the giving of "that something extra" is the difference between a successful business and a mediocre one. The sciences and the arts prove to us that attention to details is the mark of genius.

The story is told that a friend of Michelangelo once called upon him at his studio. Finding Michelangelo working upon the very same statue the friend had seen him executing months before, he commented, "You have been idle since the last time I saw you, my friend."

"Oh, no," said the great genius, whereupon he pointed out that he had worked over this feature to soften it, brought out vitality in this muscle, polished this part, toned down another part.

"Yes, but are not these only trifles?" asked the visitor. "It may be so," replied Michelangelo, "but remember that trifles make perfection, and perfection is not trifle."

If you aspire to be a perfect cook, or even an improved one, then you must by all means pay attention to the small details — the trifles.

I once was supervising the testing of some recipe when one of the cooks laughed at one of the ingredients. I asked what seemed so funny, and she replied that the recipe called for one tablespoon of water and it just struck her as funny, and what difference could one tablespoon of water make anyway?

I explained: In that particular recipe it was used to crispen the onions, dilute the tomato sauce, and as a liquid base to blend the seasonings together, all of which permeated the meat in proper viscosity, thereby harmonizing the flavors.

As a perfect recipe for rice, I recommend Perfect Rice Gourmet. To showcase this recipe, first petition the following groceries:

Perfect Rice Gourmet

1	tablespoon butter
1	small onion, finely chopped
2	green lettuce leaves, shredded
$^1/_3$	cup sliced mushrooms
1	large tomato — peeled, seeded and chopped
$^3/_4$	cup white rice
1	pimiento, diced
$1^1/_2$	cups hot chicken broth
$^3/_4$	teaspoons salt
	Dash of pepper
2	tablespoons raisins, sautéed in a little butter
2	tablespoons slivered, toasted almonds
	Paprika

Melt the butter in a saucepan and add the onions. Cook until onions are soft, but not yet brown. Add the shredded lettuce, sliced mushrooms, tomato and rice. Mix together well and add the hot chicken broth. Salt and pepper, and bring to a boil. Cover and cook over low heat for 20 minutes. Remove from fire and separate the grains of rice by tossing with a long-tined kitchen fork.

Add the diced pimiento and sautéed raisins. Toss again and serve sprinkled with paprika and slivered, toasted almonds.

Please don't let culinary cowardice take control and eliminate any ingredient from this recipe, even though one or two may seem unusual with rice. But believe me, it is salubrious, just salubrious!

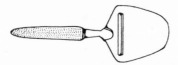

PICCADILLY PIZZA

"Small world, isn't it?" Traveling by jet, we can enjoy a fresh, juicy papaya in Manila for breakfast, jet on to Hong Kong for a lunch of pressed almond duck, while dinner awaits in Tokyo, featuring the popular sukiyaki.

Modern communication makes possible a knowledge of foreign foods and exact formulas for duplicating them which once was only possible for an expert chef. Modern transportation makes possible the actual experiencing of concoctions with a foreign flavor once only heard about or read about in books. All of this has come about since World War II.

The history of foods develops with the history of nations. With conquest, intermarriage, redivided borders, famine, the waxing and waning of empires, and the spirit of adventure, people have naturally migrated to new areas. Newcomers bring new food ideas. Old-timers teach the newcomers their food secrets. Hybrids are thus born.

We have a modern day example of this in the phenomenal growth of the pizza in international popularity. Since World War II, when soldiers returned from Italy, and tourists visited Italy, and Italians migrated to other countries, hardly a nation can be found without a pizza parlor. Hundreds of different "flavors" of pizza are offered to Americans. Pizza invaded England too, but the Englishmen fought back by giving pizza a permutation of their own, using English muffins instead of crust, and putting the British seal of approval on the little pizzas by renaming them Piccadilly Pizza after Piccadilly Circus in London — the swinging city.

Thus, another hybrid was born. Pizza was imported from Italy to England. I have imported the Piccadilly Pizza from London to America. I can definitely recommend that you add these little gems to your repertoire of pizza recipes.

Piccadilly Pizza

6	English muffin halves
1	cup Italian tomato sauce
6	slices mozzarella cheese
6	slices Canadian bacon
1	small can sliced mushrooms
2	tablespoons Parmesan cheese
	Dash of oregano

ITALIAN TOMATO SAUCE:

1	16-ounce can tomatoes
4	tablespoons olive oil
	Salt and pepper
	Dash sweet basil
	Oregano

Place tomatoes in a saucepan, add olive oil, salt and pepper to taste. Add a dash of sweet basil and oregano. Simmer slowly until sauce thickens. Set sauce aside, and toast English muffins on the round side under a hot broiler. Then turn muffins over and on flat side spread some Italian sauce, pieces of mozzarella cheese, pieces of Canadian bacon, and slices of mushrooms. Complete by sprinkling a little Parmesan cheese on top. Place under a hot broiler and heat until the mixture is melted together. A dash of oregano gives the true Italian touch.

These Piccadilly Pizzas are good for outdoor dining, they make excellent cocktail canapes, and in no time they will be a solid family favorite in your home.

POTATO GRUYERE SOUFFLÉ

For all of its modest, dun-colored appearance and expressionless eyes, the potato is the world's largest and most valuable vegetable crop. Potatoes were, in fact, discovered on the slopes of the Andes, in what is now Colombia, in the early fifteenth century. The Spanish conquistadors paid little attention to the brownish tubers grown by the Incas. These soldiers of fortune were looking for gold and silver. Ironically enough, it has been reckoned by a potato historian that today's world potato crop is worth more than all the precious metals taken from the Incan people during the first thirty years of Spanish rule.

Spanish explorers took potatoes to Spain sometime between 1550 and 1570. In Spain, they called them *truffles,* probably because they came from underground. When they reached Italy, the name was changed slightly to *tartufi*. The French called potatoes *cartouffle,* and across the Rhine, they became *kartoffel*.

At first, the potato was regarded with suspicion in many parts of Europe. It grew underground, said one, and that seemed evil somehow. It hadn't been mentioned in the Bible, said others. Adam and Eve were chased from the Garden of Eden for eating potatoes, declared still others. Probably the best reason the potato had a hard time becoming popular is that people didn't know how to cook and eat them. The bland mellow goodness of potato makes it a great go-along with the foods and seasonings of every country. There are quite literally thousands of ways of serving potatoes — soups, appetizers, main dishes and salads.

This recipe is one that I have enjoyed for many years and I believe it will become one of your favorites:

Potato Gruyere Soufflé

3	**cups cooked, diced potatoes**
1/4	**cup soft butter**
3/4	**cup (2 ounces) Gruyere cheeses, grated fine**
3	**teaspoons minced chives**
1	**teaspoon salt**
1/2	**teaspoon ground black pepper**
3	**large eggs, separated**
1	**cup heavy cream, whipped**

Combine potatoes with butter, cheese, chives, salt, and ground black pepper. Fold egg yolks into whipped heavy cream. Fold cream and eggs into potato and cream mixture. Beat egg whites until stiff and fold into potato and cream mixture. Spoon into 6 cups or soufflé dishes. Bake in a preheated moderate oven 350 degrees for 1 hour. Recipe serves 6.

THE POWER OF POSITIVE COOKING

Imitation is the sincerest form of flattery, and I was doubly flattered last month when I opened my television show mail to find two recipes which two different gourmet fans had sent me with the recommendation "you may want to try this on the show sometime." Both recipes were my own and had been given several years ago on "The Gourmet Show." One correspondent said her sister gave her the recipe with high praise, the other related she had the dish at a church dinner and asked for the recipe. Just proves a good recipe gets around, providing pleasurable dining for many along the way. Word of mouth — or word of taste — is the best advertising after all.

Good cooks are always sending me or telling me about recipes. I seem to attract food ideas wherever I go, at home and abroad. Everyone loves good food. It is often impossible, however, to get an exact recipe from a cook. It is true that many good cooks cook from their heads, so they don't write down exact measurements, temperatures, or procedures. Without these specific facts, you get maybe-so-maybe-not results. Mistakes are costly.

You probably have had such an experience as this yourself. You try to get a recipe down in black and white, and you get instructions like "put enough flour in until it is stiff." How stiff? Stiff enough for what? Then they say, "cook until done." How done? When it's brown, thick, bubbling, or alas when it has burned? Or, "add about a handful of sugar." Whose hand? A man's hand, a woman's hand? A giant? A midget? But my favorite is "mix until it looks right!"

Foodstuffs are variable enough without these guessing game measurements. How can these great recipes be preserved for posterity without someone carefully translating them into the language of fine food preparation?

My policy continues to be this, however — if Bonnie and Clyde had a good recipe — you should listen!

So I have often questioned recipe givers at length when I thought I was on the verge of possessing a great recipe. They say, "add a few dashes of cayenne pepper." Well, a little cayenne pepper goes a long, long way. So you ask, "would you say two or three dashes?" Answer: "more than that." "Well, half a teaspoonful?" Answer: "Not that much."

Whereupon the formerly cooperative recipe recommender begins to get nervous — what with all these questions — and tries to sneak away with a "when my mother gave me this recipe, she never really said how much cayenne pepper. Actually, I made it one time and forgot the cayenne and it turned out just fine." Well, you can't win them all.

I'm convinced this is how mixes began. Someone couldn't stand it any longer and vowed he'd give directions in twenty-five words or less of perfectly exact instructions.

But here's one I had the patience to see through until I got the whole, complete, and delicious recipe. This ethereal confection amply illustrates the rewards of patience and dedication, and the power of positive cooking.

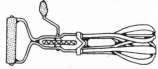

Hunyady Torte

12	egg yolks
1¹/₂	cups sugar
6	squares of bittersweet chocolate, melted
16	ounces chestnut purée (or 24 chestnuts puréed)
12	egg whites
1	pint whipping cream
¹/₄	teaspoon vanilla
3	tablespoons sugar

Beat egg yolks with sugar, add chestnut purée and bittersweet chocolate which has been melted. Beat these ingredients well together. Beat egg whites in a separate bowl. Fold egg whites into the chocolate mixture.

Bake in 3 or 4 layer-cake pans in a preheated 325-degree oven. Beat whipping cream with sugar and vanilla and put between layers, lathering each thoroughly. Save a generous portion of the whipped cream to cover the top of the cake.

DAVID WADE'S PRUNE CAKE

Painting, and composing poems, and sculpting statues, and singing are all art forms which we recognize as art, but they are not the only means of creative expression. I believe cooking is an art and of all the foods which our imaginations can conjure up for taste teasing, cakes rate high in the cooking art world. Cakes are associated with special occasions — birthdays, anniversaries, and seasonal holidays. Almost any reason for celebrating calls for a cake. An abundance of loving, and caring, and giving goes into the making of a cake. Breathes there a man or woman or child with soul so dead who is not pleased and flattered when a cake is baked especially for them?

More's the pity then that creative cake baking is not practiced more today. The recipe I am chronicling for you today is a do-it-yourself from start to finish cake. You'll purchase, measure, and mix all of the items according to the Jet Prune Cake blueprint, and you will reward yourself and your family with a cake that is individual, delicious and, I hope, a new taste which you will want to make a permanent resident of your "best cake recipes" file.

There are only two types of cakes: Butter cakes and sponge cakes. Butter cakes are those made with butter, shortening or oil, and the family of sponge cakes depends upon egg whites for leavening. The Jet Prune Cake is a butter-family cake, although the recipe calls for oil, actually, and not butter.

I have only a few ironclad rules for baking a good cake. 1. Use the very best ingredients. Any cake is only as good as the items you put into it. 2. Measure exactly according to the recipe, and make certain you use the methodology described in the recipe, too. 3. Any cake which will be frosted should be cooled first. Here is where many frostings, which were intended to be the crowning glory of the cake, are ruined. 4. Use the equipment recommended in the recipe.

David Wade's Prune Cake

4	cups sifted cake or all-purpose flour
2	teaspoons baking soda
3	cups sugar
6	whole eggs
2	cups vegetable oil
2	cups buttermilk
2	teaspoons nutmeg
2	teaspoons cinnamon
1	teaspoon salt
2	cups prunes minced, pitted and cooked 10 minutes with water to cover, drain

Sift dry ingredients together. Beat the eggs 1 minute. Add eggs to dry ingredients; mix with remaining ingredients. Beat cake batter for 3 minutes. Pour into 3 greased and floured 9-inch cake pans. Place into preheated 350-degree oven and bake for 35–40 minutes or until toothpick comes out clean.

ICING:

3	**large eggs OR 4 small eggs,** *separated*
2	**cups soft butter (DO NOT SUBSTITUTE)**
	Pinch salt
4	**cups confectioners' sugar**
1	**teaspoon vanilla extract**
1	**teaspoon lemon extract**
¹/₂	**cup chopped nuts (pecans, walnuts, etc.)**

Beat egg whites, adding sugar slowly until they are stiff. Mix in other products except nuts.

Ice cooled cakes. Sprinkle nuts over each layer.

NOTE: By substituting 2 cups applesauce, you will have a delicious applesauce cake. Substituting 2 cups cooked mashed carrots will give you a wonderful carrot cake.

RICE A LA GRECQUE

There is a story about an unemployed schoolteacher who needed a job very much, and right now. He was having an interview with the local schoolboard, and he was fielding each question carefully in order to impress the board members. Finally, he was asked a question which gave him pause. "Sir, will you teach our students that the world is round or flat?" "Well," considered the unemployed teacher deliberately and thoughtfully, "I can teach it either way."

This is about what the world can do with rice — they can cook it — not just either way — but all ways. Teaching rice-lovers only one way to cook rice is an impossibility. It is not even possible to point to one recipe and say, "This, my friends, is the best rice recipe in the world."

Consider for a moment: Rice is the staple diet of more than three-fourths of the world's peoples. For 5,000 years most of the population of earthlings has depended upon rice for life and health. During these centuries nations have invented and created and produced an infinite variety of great rice recipes. Each recipe seems to be almost a self-expression of the people of the nation or region. If one were to gather all the rice concoctions in the world he would truly have a United Nations of Food cookbook.

So, the Spanish have their famous *paella,* the Italians their *rissoto,* the Chinese like it fried, Louisianians like to creole it, the Englishman boils it, the Japanese not only eat it but make a wine — sake — with it. Indians curry it, Mexicans spice it up, too, and call it Spanish Rice, Indonesians stake their claim on the best rice recipe with their *nasi goreng,* and well, you can see what a quandary this puts a gourmet in . . . How could one say that any of these were the only, or the best way, to prepare rice? And the above mentioned are only a world sampling.

What I will say is that Rice a la Grecque is a classic Greek recipe which is fashioned in the Mediterranean style. When you read the recipe you will quickly note that this is more than a "side dish" — it can be a whole meal, but it can also be a sophisticated stuffing for poultry or veal, and complements lamb, veal, or poultry as an entremets.

Epicurus, the Greek philosopher of good living, must have enjoyed this recipe or one much like it, and that is recommendation enough for those of us who enjoy good food, and gets me out of hot water (if you'll pardon a pun) by not having to say Rice a la Grecque is the best rice recipe in the world. Epicurus cannot be reached for comment.

Rice a la Grecque

3	**tablespoons butter or margarine**
1	**onion, chopped**
1	**small clove garlic, crushed**
3	**or 4 leaves green lettuce, shredded**
2	**fresh pork sausages, sliced**
3	**mushrooms, sliced**
3	**tomatoes, peeled, seeded and diced**
1	**cup raw rice**
2	**cups boiling water or chicken broth**
1	**teaspoon salt**
	Dash pepper
¹/₂	**cup cooked peas**
1	**diced pimiento**
2	**tablespoons raisins**
	Butter or margarine

Melt butter or margarine over low heat and add onion. When onion is brown, add garlic, lettuce, sausages, mushrooms, tomatoes, and raw rice. Mix well. Add boiling water or chicken broth, salt, and pepper. Cover tightly and continue cooking for 20 minutes. Mix well with fork. Add peas, pimiento, raisins (which have been sautéed in butter or margarine). Makes approximately 4 cups.

ROAST PHEASANT

Many years ago, I received a letter from a lady in California asking me to settle an argument. "What is the difference," she asked, "between baking and roasting?" My first reaction was one of surprise. Meat is roasted while baking refers to cakes and breads! But then I realized that this was not strictly true. A ham is baked and chestnuts are roasted. A turkey is sometimes baked and at other times roasted, depending on the background of the cook.

But for the present, I think I will just duck the finer points of the argument and consider roasting to be that method of cooking meat by dry heat in an enclosed oven. The old-fashioned covered "roaster" notwithstanding, if meat is covered, it is not roasted, it is braised — even if it is cooked in the oven.

Most of the time I prefer to do my own experimenting and come to my own conclusions about cooking. But when it comes to cooking hundreds of roasts at different temperatures to determine the right one, I am perfectly willing to profit by the experience of the U.S. Department of Agriculture. For that is exactly what they, as well as other experimenters, have done.

Meats have been measured before and after cooking to determine the amount of shrinkage, and the taste preferences of thousands of people have been polled. In experiment after experiment, the results have been in favor of long, slow cooking.

This method produces not only the tenderest, juiciest and most flavorful meat, but also a meat that will shrink only about fifteen percent while the same type meat will shrink as much as fifty percent if cooked at a very high heat. How is that for an economy measure!

High temperature causes protein to become tough. This is the reason that a bloodstain is easily removed in cold water but becomes hopelessly set by hot water. Milk glasses wash more easily if rinsed in cold water and eggs cooked at a high temperature have the delicacy of an old innertube.

Your first step is to make sure you have set your oven thermostat at the right temperature. But a more important step is to make sure the oven temperature is the one you have selected. Few oven thermostats are really accurate (don't blame your oven, it would take a scientific instrument for real accuracy) and the temperature varies in different parts of the oven. It is best to use an oven thermometer, at least occasionally, so you will know where you stand.

If you do not already own a good meat thermometer, I insist that you not let another week go by without one. It is the only way to be sure of properly cooked meats. Time and temperature guides are merely to help plan your time. Size and shape, as well as fat and bone content, affect cooking time.

When you are roasting a pheasant, you don't have to worry a great deal about shape as most pheasants are pretty much the same shape. With lamb, pork and beef, however, you should remember that in terms of minutes

per pound a flat roast will cook faster than a chunky one, and a large roast will require fewer minutes per pound than a small one. Bones conduct heat readily but fat does not. A crown roast may cook in half the time required for a rolled roast of the same weight. A well-marbled roast will take considerably longer to cook than a lean roast. When calculating cooking time, remember to allow for about twenty minutes for the roast to "repose" before carving. Not only will it carve more easily, but the juices will gelatinize and less will be lost.

When choosing a roast, bear in mind that a rolled roast is easier to carve, but the slices are less attractive than those of a bone-in roast. And don't be afraid to choose a large roast. It is more economical for several reasons, one being that a roast under three and one-half pounds or so will shrink excessively. Remember, with a good roast, there are not leftovers, only planned-overs.

Roast Pheasant

1   **2- to 3-pound pheasant**
     Salt and freshly ground black pepper to
        taste
1   **bay leaf**
1   **clove garlic**
     Few celery leaves
1   **slice lemon**
4   **slices bacon**
     Melted butter
     Madeira Sauce

Preheat oven to 350 degrees. Sprinkle the pheasant inside and out with salt and pepper. Place the bay leaf, garlic, celery leaves and lemon in the cavity. Tie the legs together with string and turn the wings under.

Cover the breast with bacon and a piece of cheesecloth soaked in melted butter. Place the pheasant, breast up, on a rack in a baking pan and roast until tender (about 30 minutes per pound), basting frequently with melted butter. Remove the cheesecloth and string.

Serve the pheasant on a bed of rice accompanied by Madeira Sauce.

MADEIRA SAUCE

Remove the pheasant to a warm serving platter and add 1 cup consommé to the pan. Stir over moderate heat, scraping loose the browned particles. Blend 2 tablespoons flour with 2 tablespoons butter and stir into the gravy bit by bit. When the gravy is thickened and smooth, add 2 to 3 tablespoons Madeira wine and the cooked pheasant liver, finely chopped.

ROUNDUP BEANS AND HOMINY CASSEROLE

During roundup time, from early in the autumn to late in the spring, a few big ranches still send out mule-drawn chuck wagons. But gradually the tradition of the chuck wagon is dying out of the Southwestern cowboy culture. Most ranches send a truck now to pick up the riders and bring them into the ranch house for meals.

However, one of the reasons the familiar chuck wagon doesn't go out on the range often is not mechanization, but because ranches can't find experienced cooks to man the range kitchens. The life of a ranch cook is both difficult and rewarding. The number one difficulty is getting up before 5:00 A.M. to begin breakfast and packing up supplies for lunch, moving out to another location, setting up the kitchen again. Sundown finds the camp cooks still serving late riders into camp, and then preparing the night before for a 5:00 A.M. rising the next morning.

On the favorable side, though, he has time for a catnap during the day while the boys are out working. More than anything else, his reward is respect — the better cook he is, the more respect he gets. In the last few years chuck wagon cooks have been highly regarded indeed because they are a vanishing breed. Some cooks of the range have taken lately to store-bought foods — instants, canned and boxed food stuffs. The old veteran cook would wince with shame. Always in the recipe files of the cowboy chef was a version of at least four specialties that the cowboy loves: biscuits (preferably sour dough), chili, son-of-a-gun stew, and beans. Beans cooked that way and this way, and any way, because beans were the easiest to transport and cook of any of the staples available to the ranch cook. Gradually different bean recipes were developed for variety. The following Roundup Bean and Hominy recipe was sent to me by a returned chuck wagon cook. He used to bake it in a Dutch oven set down in a hole pit. Unless you have a hankering to perfect the craft of ranch cook, you may as well take the easy way and bake the recipe in your kitchen oven. On the other hand, someone reading this may yearn for a home on the range and cooking in the wide open spaces. If so, this recipe will get you a job on any ranch you care to cook for. Some ingredients are canned, but with such a recipe no one will ever know, or care!

Roundup Beans and Hominy Casserole

2	tablespoons butter or margarine
1	medium onion
1	clove garlic, minced or mashed
1	can (1 pound) red kidney beans
1	can (1 pound) hominy
1	can (1 pound) tomatoes, broken with a fork
$^1/_2$	cup chopped green bell pepper
3	teaspoons chili powder
$^1/_2$	teaspoon salt
3	slices bacon
4	tortillas, cut in thin strips
$^2/_3$	cup shredded Cheddar cheese

Melt butter in a large skillet over medium heat. Brown onion and garlic in the butter. Add beans, hominy, tomatoes, green bell pepper, chili powder, and salt. Remove from heat after mixed together thoroughly and heated completely, and turn into a 2-quart casserole. Set casserole aside and fry bacon in a skillet and drain. Add to the hot bacon fat, tossing until lightly browned and crisp (about 2 minutes) the tortilla strips. Remove and drain.

Add crumbled bacon to Cheddar cheese. Combine $^1/_2$ of the bacon-cheese mixture with the bean-hominy mixture in the casserole. Sprinkle tortilla strips over the top. Bake in (350-degree) moderate oven for 30 minutes or until thoroughly hot. Do not cover. Makes 6 to 8 servings.

SAUERBRATEN

During midsummer and at evening concerts and music festivals across the country, we may hear Mendelssohn's enchanted *Midsummer Night's Dream*. This was inspired by Shakespeare's play of the same name and the shimmering music of the violin should remind us of the lovely verse which begins:

"I know a bank whereon the Wild Thyme blows,
    Where Oxlips and the woody Violet grows . . ."

In olden times it was thought that "the little people" — the elves and fairies — were particularly fond of thyme. Thyme is a truly venerable herb, known and loved way back in ancient Greece. Among the Greeks thyme was a symbol of elegance. It grew all over Mt. Humettus which is within sight of Athens.

Thyme grows cheerfully in some of the poorest, driest soil that can be found. It is native to the greatest part of the dry land of Europe, not only the mountains of Greece, but in the lower meadows of the Alps, the highest crags of the Pyrenees and, of course, in England.

Thyme was commonly cultivated in parts of England before the sixteenth century. Long before the people of England had access to spices from the Orient, they could grow thyme in their little gardens.

Thyme was not only good, but herbalists of those days said thyme was very good for people. John Parkinson was one of those seventeenth-century herbalists. He wrote, "There is no herb almost of more use in the houses both of high and low, rich and poor, both for inward and outward occasions: outwardly for bathings among other hot herbs and among other sweet herbs for strewings; inwardly in most sorts of broths with Rosemary, as also with other herbs, and to make sauce for diverse sorts of both fish and flesh. It is held by diverse to be a speedy remedy against the sting of a bee, being bruised and laid thereon." Modern medicine has upheld their thinking for the oil from thyme, known as thymol, is an effective ingredient in many brands of modern cough drops.

Getting back home to the range and the spice shelf, thyme has always been one of the favorite herbs in the American cuisine. This love of thyme goes back to the days of the first settlers who brought all kinds of seeds and roots with them for wilderness gardens. Thyme is one of the moderately potent herbs. For a very elusive aroma of thyme, we might use between one-fourth to one-half teaspoon ground whole thyme in a dish to serve six. For a more pronounced taste, use at least a teaspoonful. In the stuffing for a three-pound fish, for instance, we would want about one-half teaspoonful of thyme. In the very delicate oyster stew, a quarter teaspoonful is just about right. It's all a matter of taste: that's what makes seasoning and cooking one of the fine arts. Nothing beats frequent use of the tasting spoon.

Thyme can be had either ground or as whole leaves. This depends on how it is to be used. Ground thyme is a bit more convenient, especially when seasoning heat-to-eat foods. Whole thyme, however, keeps its delectable aroma somewhat longer than the ground product. Whenever possible, delay adding any herbs to a long-cooking mixture until within ten minutes of the end of the cooking period.

Thyme is a famous seasoner of all kinds of seafood, but do use it also with meats, stuffings, croquettes, fricassees and egg and cheese dishes. For inspiration, try this thyme-scented recipe:

Sauerbraten

4   **pounds rump or bottom round of beef**
2   **teaspoons powdered mustard**
2   **tablespoons parsley flakes**
2   **tablespoons grated lemon peel**
1   **teaspoon salt**
$^1/_2$ **teaspoon ground thyme**
$^1/_2$ **teaspoon whole black pepper**
1   **teaspoon Worcestershire powder**
$^1/_4$ **teaspoon ground sage**
6   **whole cloves**
2   **beef bouillon cubes**
$^1/_2$ **cup onion flakes**
$^1/_2$ **cup cider vinegar**
2   **to 3 tablespoons shortening**
    Flour

Place beef in close-fitting pan. Combine mustard and 1 tablespoon water; let stand 10 minutes for flavor to develop. Combine mustard with parsley flakes, lemon peel, salt, thyme, black pepper, Worcestershire powder, sage, cloves, bouillon cubes, 2 cups boiling water, onion flakes, and vinegar; pour over meat. Cool. Place in refrigerator to marinate 24 hours, turning several times. Remove meat from marinade. Brown on all sides in shortening. Add marinade. Cover and simmer until tender, about $2^1/_2$ to 3 hours. Remove meat and make gravy, using $1^1/_2$ tablespoons flour to each cup liquid left in pan.

Yield 8 to 10 servings.

SHRIMP DIABLE

There is an old Creole custom which they call "lagniappe" and it means "to give something extra." Well, there is "lagniappe" in Shrimp Diable. The something extra is "the devil" — diable.

The something extra of Creole cooking was the arrival of the French in what is now Louisiana. Before the coming of Bienville, in 1722, with his small colony of Frenchmen, the cooking of the region was Spanish (Spanish explorers having just recently departed), Negro, and Indian. Frenchmen brought with them over five centuries of skill and appreciation in the culinary arts. From the distillation of hundreds of years of experience in the kitchen arts — a fame which was to go around the whole world — they gave Creole cooking its "lagniappe." The main secret of their talents was the knowledge of the use of spices, and the mastering of the sauce mystique which is still with us today.

Although my Shrimp Diable is not Creole, it is an apt illustration of "lagniappe" in a recipe. Furthermore, much in it can be found in common with Creole cooking. Sauce

Diable will be recognized as one of the famous French sauces, and this sauce more than any other highlights the artful spice blending which has also made Creole cooking famous. The recipe's star is shrimp — so plentiful throughout Louisiana.

Escoffier did not think much of shrimp, apparently, for he says in his writing, "As regards shrimps, their use in Europe is generally limited to garnishes, hors d'oeuvres and the preparation of soups, shrimp butters and creams." I do think much of shrimp, and have found it an absolutely perfect companion for Sauce Diable.

You know, there is another old saying, a cliché, which says there is a little of the devil in all of us. This cliché certainly holds true with food. Often by adding a little of the devil to an otherwise bland creation, the recipe explodes into a taste tempter. My recipe for Shrimp Diable is just such a transformation. This sauce is deviltry itself, but even with the devil added you will find it not too hot, nor too bland, but just right to excite your taste.

Shrimp Diable

1¹/₂	**pounds peeled and deveined shrimp**
4	**tablespoons olive oil**
1	**shallot or green onion, chopped**
1	**clove garlic, chopped**
1	**teaspoon cracked black pepper**
1	**teaspoon of chervil or parsley, chopped**
¹/₃	**cup brandy**
2	**cups rich, brown beef sauce**
1	**tablespoon Worcestershire powder**
	Juice of ¹/₂ lemon
2	**teaspoons dry English mustard**
2	**tablespoons catsup**

Allow peeled and deveined shrimp to thaw completely.

Place the olive oil into a skillet and sauté the shrimp until they are pinkish-red. Next add shallots, garlic, cracked black pepper, and chervil. Briskly sauté this mixture for 3 or 4 minutes. Add brandy, brown sauce, Worcestershire powder, lemon juice, dry mustard, and catsup. Cover the skillet and simmer the shrimp for 15 additional minutes. Serve over a bed of rice. Recipe serves 8.

SCALLOPED SALMON

I always suggest to executives who entertain business associates from time to time that they start with a well-stocked spice shelf and learn how to use it. Expanding your knowledge of spices is fun and essential to become an outstanding host. For example, how many readers are familiar with the herb, marjoram?

Marjoram is a very versatile herb, "the herb of a thousand uses." Use from ¹/₄ to ¹/₂ teaspoon of marjoram in batches of stews to serve four, or in stews, soups, casseroles. Fish and egg dishes are enhanced from the aroma of marjoram, and it gives intrinsic flavor to such vegetables as peas, snap beans, lima beans, spinach, and Swiss chard.

Marjoram comes in whole or ground form. Add the marjoram during the last five minutes when simmering a stew, soup or such slow cooking foods. In a stuffing, naturally, we must add the herb along with other ingredients. When negotiating a roast beef, sprinkle on a flurry of marjoram at the inauguration of the roasting time, then freshen up the intriguing flavor by adding a hint more to the gravy, which is made at the last minute.

People have always loved marjoram as a flavoring for foods, but throughout the ages, it has had many other uses. Marjoram was strewn here and there at public functions and banquets to sweeten the air. Sweet marjoram was also an ingredient in the perfumes the ancients used after the bath. Marjoram attended weddings and funerals. It had countless uses as a medication, especially effective when treating ailments of the head and stomach.

Majoram, like many other herbs, is native to Western Asia and the Mediterranean. The Roman Army, no doubt, hastened marjoram's migration to other parts of Europe. Marjoram came to America with the first settlers. It was a treasured plant in the herb garden.

Marjoram is closely related to oregano, the pizza herb. Both plants are members of the big mint family. Oregano is the Spanish word for marjoram and was once called, "wild marjoram." Marjoram's aroma is sweeter, more delicate than that of oregano, and it is often called, "sweet marjoram," or "garden marjoram."

We import most of our marjoram from France, Portugal, Greece, and Romania. It's fun to become better acquainted with an herb like marjoram. If you are an entertaining executive, it's practically a necessity. I have found that the following recipe demonstrates the unique qualities of marjoram.

Scalloped Salmon

1   can (7³/₄ ounces) red or pink salmon
1   tablespoon lemon juice
1¹/₄   cups cracker crumbs
¹/₃   cup butter, melted
1   teaspoon salt
1   teaspoon powdered mustard
¹/₄   teaspoon ground black pepper
¹/₄   teaspoon instant onion, powdered
¹/₄   teaspoon marjoram leaves, crumbled
1   cup milk, scalded
    Lemon slices for garnish
    Parsley flakes for garnish

Drain the salmon, flake, and mix with lemon juice. Combine cracker crumbs, butter, salt, mustard, black pepper, marjoram and onion powder. Place half of the seasoned crumbs in a 9-inch pie plate over which spread the salmon mixture. Pour milk over all. Top with remaining crumbs. Bake in a preheated hot oven (400 degrees) from 20 to 25 minutes. Garnish with lemon slices and parsley flakes. Recipe serves 4.

SHRIMP NEW ORLEANS

I am often asked by discerning patrons of good food which city in the United States is the food capital. Is it New York, San Francisco, or New Orleans? Each city, of course, stands alone when it comes to its own characteristic skilletry. But there never has been a match for New Orleans when Southern Creole food is demonstrated.

This bewitching city is permeated with the very aroma of food: Bananas unloaded on the docks, strong coffee overtones the air from the roasting ovens, the river giant proffers its pungent smells of crayfish and shrimp, the flower-fragrance of sugar and spice. This crossroads of Old World and New World cultures seemingly bubbles with tantalizing thoughts of food.

Creole cooking was welded together by the French, who brought with them the traditions of centuries of gourmet skill; the Spanish, who brought the exotic trappings which are the hallmark of Creole food; and the Negro, who blended them together in the cooking manner of the Deep Delta.

New Orleans — old enchantress that she is — doesn't leave out atmosphere either: Harbor noises, a tinkling banjo, perfumery from the walled gardens, and a horn wailing out the jazz for which the Queen of the Mississippi is also famous put you into the world of Creole cooking. And the treatment given seafood in New Orleans is enough to forever haunt your hungry moments. See for yourself. Try Shrimp New Orleans.

Shrimp New Orleans

¹/₂   lemon, sliced
4   whole black peppers
3   pounds peeled and deveined shrimp
4   slices bacon
2   tablespoons butter
1   clove garlic, finely chopped
1   cup chopped onions
1¹/₂   cups chopped green bell peppers
¹/₄   cup finely chopped parsley
1¹/₂   cups thinly sliced celery
1   can (1 pound 12 ounces) tomatoes
1   can (6 ounces) tomato paste
1   tablespoon lemon juice
1   tablespoon sugar
1   teaspoon salt
¹/₄   to ¹/₂ teaspoon pepper
¹/₄   to ¹/₂ teaspoon crushed red pepper
1   bay leaf
¹/₂   teaspoon dried thyme leaves
¹/₂   teaspoon file* powder
    Cooked white rice

Bring 1 quart of water to boiling in large saucepan. Add lemon slices, black peppers, and shrimp. Reduce heat; simmer uncovered 3 minutes. Drain the shrimp, reserving 1 cup cooking liquid. In the same saucepan, sauté bacon over low heat, until crisp. Remove bacon; drain on paper towels, and crumble. To bacon fat, add butter, garlic, onion, green bell pepper, parsley, celery; cook, stirring, about 5 minutes, or until vegetables are tender. Add reserved shrimp liquid, bacon, tomatoes, tomato paste, lemon juice, sugar, salt, pepper, red pepper, bay leaf, and thyme. Bring to boiling. Reduce heat; simmer, covered, 30 minutes. Just before serving, stir in file powder and shrimp; bring to boiling. Reduce heat; simmer, covered, 5 minutes. Serve over hot, cooked white rice. Recipe serves 8.

* File (pronounced "fee-lay") is powdered sassafras leaves, and an important accoutrement to Creole cooking. Always add file powder exactly as and when recipe indicates, as it should never be cooked for long periods.

PARSLEY

The
Festive
Cup

Orange Jublius

Equal parts:

Vanilla ice cream
Orange sherbet
Orange juice

Blend in blender.

Balloon Wine

In 1-gallon glass jug (old-fashioned type with small neck) pour one 13-ounce can frozen grape juice. Add 4½ cups sugar (or less if you prefer a drier wine) and sprinkle in 1 package dry yeast. Fill container with water until ½ inch from top. Place child's balloon over neck of jug and secure with rubber band. Store in cool, dark place for 21 days. As wine ferments, it will emit a gas which will cause the balloon to expand. If balloon should burst before 21 days are passed, simply replace the balloon as quickly as possible. Wine will not be harmed. After 21 days, wine is ready to serve. For additional storage time, decant wine into empty, clean liquor bottles with screw on caps.

The Wisconsin

2   **cups milk, cold**
8   **ounces crushed pineapple**
1   **tablespoon pineapple preserves**
1   **scoop vanilla ice cream**
2   **tablespoons shredded coconut**
    Dash nutmeg
    Whipping cream

Combine cold milk, pineapple and pineapple preserves with vanilla ice cream and shredded coconut. Blend in a blender or with a rotary beater until very smooth. Pour into chilled glasses. Top with whipping cream and dash of nutmeg. Serve at once.

Spiced Heaven

1   **pint orange juice**
½   **pound sugar**
4   **eggs, beaten**
1   **tablespoon nutmeg**
1   **pint milk**
1   **teaspoon soda**
½   **tablespoon grated orange rind**
      Dash salt

Mix juice and sugar. Cook over low heat. Add orange rind and salt, soda and nutmeg to milk, then beaten eggs. Combine two mixtures. Serve in chilled glasses with a little ice. Scoop of vanilla ice cream or orange sherbet may be added if desired.

Dairy Treat

2   **eggs**
2   **cups cold milk**
    Dash of salt
4   **teaspoons molasses**
    Nutmeg

Beat egg yolks, add molasses and mix until smooth and thick. Add milk and nutmeg to taste. Beat egg whites stiff; fold in. Sprinkle top with nutmeg for added color. Serve immediately in chilled glasses. Two servings.

New Orleans Evening

2   **cups milk**
8   **ounces pineapple tidbits**
1   **scoop vanilla ice cream**
2   **egg whites, beaten stiff**
¼   **teaspoon vanilla**
2   **teaspoons sugar**

Combine milk, pineapple tidbits and vanilla ice cream in a blender or beat with rotary beater until smooth. Beat egg whites until stiff and combine with vanilla and sugar. Beat to form peaks. Pour pineapple ice cream mix in chilled glass and top with egg whites making large peaks.

Bright Night

1   **ripe banana mashed**
    Juice of one small orange
    Scoop vanilla ice cream
1   **cup cranberry juice (bottled)**
    Dash of nutmeg

Combine orange juice and cranberry juice and beat with mashed banana. Add ice cream and beat until creamy and smooth. Pour into tall, chilled glass and add a dash of nutmeg.

Spicy and Hot

1 quart water
$^1/_2$ cup sugar
8 cloves
1 stick cinnamon
$^1/_2$ cup orange juice
1 cup lemon juice

Mix water and sugar, heat to boiling, stirring until sugar is dissolved. Cover saucepan and boil 2 minutes. Add cinnamon and cloves and continue to cook for about 6 additional minutes. Add juices to this spiced syrup. Let stand few minutes, then remove cloves and cinnamon. Serve warm. This mixture can be reheated, but do not boil again.

The Atlas Drink

1 fully ripe banana
1 cup COLD milk
3 tablespoons vanilla ice cream
$^1/_4$ teaspoon vanilla

Peel banana. Mash in a bowl. Beat with rotary egg beater, electric mixer or blender until smooth and creamy. Add milk, ice cream and vanilla; mix well. Pour into glasses. Sprinkle nutmeg and cinnamon on top and serve immediately. Makes 1 or 2 medium-size drinks.

For a delicious Banana-Nut drink, add 2 tablespoons chopped pecans to above recipe.

Spiced Hot Chocolate

$^3/_4$ cup sugar
$^2/_3$ cup cocoa
1 cup water
$^1/_4$ teaspoon cinnamon
$^1/_4$ teaspoon salt
2 quarts milk, heated
1 quart cream, heated
1 teaspoon vanilla
Marshmallows

Mix first 5 ingredients. Add to heated milk and cream. Stir thoroughly. Place over medium flame and cook until mixture comes to a boil. Remove from flame and add vanilla. With a rotary beater, whip Spiced Hot Chocolate until frothy. Pour immediately into warmed mugs. Top each serving with large marshmallows. Serves 16.

Skier's Warm Up

1 cup brown sugar
$1^1/_4$ cups water
$^1/_4$ teaspoon salt
$^1/_4$ teaspoon nutmeg
$^1/_2$ teaspoon cinnamon
$^1/_4$ teaspoon allspice
$^1/_2$ teaspoon cloves
$^1/_4$ cup raisins
1 quart pineapple juice
2 cups jellied cranberry sauce
3 tablespoons lemon juice
3 cups water
Cinnamon sticks
Pineapple chunks

Mix brown sugar and spices, salt and 1 cup water. Heat to boiling point. With a fork or rotary beater mash cranberry sauce to smooth consistency. Mix pineapple juice, water, lemon juice and add to cranberry sauce. Add raisins and mix with spiced syrup. Heat again and serve very hot in cups garnished with a cinnamon stick stuck through a pineapple chunk.

Cafe au Lait

The French breakfast coffee: scald milk, preferably in a pot that has a pouring spout. Have ready strong, hot coffee. Pour milk and coffee into the cup simultaneously, in a half-and-half mixture.

Turkish Coffee

Into pot put 2 tablespoons pulverized coffee, 4 tablespoons sugar. Stir in 2 cups fresh, cold water. Heat to froth 3 times and allow to settle.

Vienna Coffee

Serve a combination of 2 parts strong coffee to 1 part hot milk, and top each cup with a high mound of whipped cream.

Nocturnal Cup

1   pot hot coffee
1   pot hot chocolate
    Whipping cream
    Shaved French Chocolate

Combine equal portions of hot coffee and hot chocolate in warmed mugs. Top with whipping cream which has been sweetened. Use shaved French chocolate pieces for garnish.

Hot Jungle Punch

2   cups grapefruit juice
1   cup orange juice
1/4 cup lemon juice
1   tablespoon light corn syrup

Combine fruit juices and corn syrup in a saucepan. Heat to just below boiling point. Serve steaming with a cinnamon stick.

Hot Spiced Cider

1   teaspoon cinnamon
12 whole cloves
1   teaspoon allspice
2   quarts cider
2/3 cup brown sugar
    Nutmeg
    Apples quartered
    Swizzle sticks, or toothpicks

Tie spices in cheesecloth to make spice bag. Combine cider and brown sugar in a saucepan and heat. Place spice bag in cider and cook over medium to low flame 10 minutes (longer if a spicier taste is wanted). Remove spice bag and serve very hot in cups or mugs. Dash nutmeg on small pieces of apples on a swizzle stick or toothpick, and float on top of Hot Spiced Cider.

Hot 'N Hearty

1/2 cup grape juice
1/2 cup orange juice
    Cinnamon
    Ginger
1   egg white

Combine juices and heat in saucepan. Add dash of cinnamon and ginger to taste. Beat egg white until stiff and

top heated juice. Serve in mugs or cups, which have been warmed.

1/2 cup pineapple juice
1/2 cup peach juice
1   drop almond flavoring
    Nutmeg
1   egg white

Combine juices and heat in saucepan. Add almond flavoring and nutmeg to taste. Beat egg white until stiff and top heated juice. Serve in cups or mugs which have been warmed.

Good Neighbor Punch

1   quart cider (apple)
1   cup dried apricots
    Juice of one lemon
1/4 teaspoon nutmeg
    Pinch of salt
6   whole cloves for garnish
1   cup prunes
2   tablespoons sugar
1/4 teaspoon cinnamon
    Dash cloves
6   lemon slices

Wash apricots and prunes and dry. Combine fruit with cider in a kettle and heat to boiling. Lower heat and simmer for 30 minutes or until fruit is tender. Add sugar, lemon juice, spices and salt. With lemon slice and a whole clove for garnish, serve hot. If punch is too thick, a little more heated cider may be added.

Good Friend's Cup of Cheer

3   cups cranberry juice
1   cup water
1/2 cup grapefruit juice
1/2 cup sugar
1   stick cinnamon
8   whole cloves
3/4 teaspoon nutmeg
    Orange peel, cut in thin strips and twisted
    Lemon peel, cut in thin strips and twisted

Combine all ingredients in a kettle and simmer about 30 minutes. Strain and pour into mugs or cups. Replace orange and lemon peel for garnish.

When the Crowd Gathers

1 **pound all-purpose coffee grind**
6 **to 8 quarts water (depending on strength desired)**
Cheesecloth bag

Wrap coffee in a cheesecloth bag almost twice the size of coffee grind to allow for expansion. Have a large kettle filled with boiling water. Let coffee bag down into water, moving up and down several times to be sure of full flavor. Leave coffee this way for about 10 to 15 minutes in a warm place. Before serving time, remove coffee bag and cover kettle to keep hot until serving. Serve as soon as possible. Makes about 35 to 45 cups of coffee.

The Wedding Party

1/2 **cup sugar**
1 **cup water**
1 **6-ounce can frozen lemon juice**
1 **6-ounce can frozen orange-pineapple juice**
1 **quart white grape juice**
1 **quart ginger ale**
Small jar maraschino cherries and juice
1 **pint lemon sherbet**
1 **pint pineapple sherbet**
Orange slices
Cherries

Heat sugar and water until dissolved into a syrup. Cool. Add fruit juices, ginger ale, grape juice, and jar of cherries (and juice) to syrup. Mix well and pour into punch bowl. Add ice cubes. Top orange slices with lemon and lime sherbet dips, then top sherbet with a cherry. Add remaining sherbet to punch mixture. Float orange slices with sherbet on surface of punch. Serves about 25.

Thirsty 65

4 **cups water**
8 **cups sugar**
7 **cups lemon juice**
4 **cups crushed pineapple**
1 **cup orange juice**
1 **cup weak tea**
3 **gallons water**
Crushed ice
Orange slices
Lemon slices
Green and red maraschino cherries

Boil 4 cups water and 8 cups sugar for 10 minutes and cool. Add lemon juice, pineapple, orange juice and weak tea. Mix and add remaining water. Pour into punch bowl over crushed ice. Make kabobs of one slice orange, a green cherry, a lemon slice and a red cherry on top threaded on small swizzle sticks or toothpicks. Decorate punch bowl with ivy or garden greens arranged around sides, and daisies or gardenias placed in front and back of serving bowl. Dip lemonade into cups or glasses, topping each one with a kabob from the punch bowl. Have an extra supply to replenish decoration.

(This lemonade is a little strong to allow for melting ice during time of serving. More water may be added in the beginning if necessary.) Serves about 65.

Sunny Day

1 **cup apple cider**
Juice of 1/2 lemon
3 **drops artificial sweetener**
1/4 **teaspoon cinnamon**
3 **tablespoons water**

Mix all ingredients and place in refrigerator tray. Freeze to mushy consistency. Remove, place in bowl and beat until smooth. Serve immediately. Garnish with mint.

Dieter's Delight

2 **cups ice water**
1/3 **cup nonfat dry milk powder**
2 **tablespoons strawberry gelatin powder**
1/2 **cup fresh, washed and hulled strawberries (if you are not using a blender, slice strawberries thinly)**

Combine all ingredients in a blender or bowl. Beat vigorously until smooth. Pour into chilled glass. Garnish with 2 or 3 fresh strawberries.

Fat Man's Favorite

Juice of one lemon
Water, cold
Grape juice, chilled
1 **egg white**
1 **teaspoon sugar**
1/4 **teaspoon vanilla**

Place juice of lemon in glass. Add enough water to fill 2/3 full. Fill with grape juice. Beat egg white, adding sugar and vanilla. Whip into Fat Man's Favorite and serve immediately.

Drink and Smile

1	cup water
1	tablespoon Sucaryl solution
1/4	cup chopped mint leaves
1/2	cup lemon juice
1/2	cup unsweetened pineapple tidbits
1	cup orange juice
1	quart orange beverage (artificially sweetened)
	Crushed ice
	Mint sprigs

Mix water, sweetener and mint leaves in a saucepan. Bring to boil, strain and cool. Add lemon juice, pineapple tidbits, and orange juice. Mix well and add orange beverage. Place crushed ice in tall glasses and pour Drink and Smile over ice. Serve with sprig of mint dusted in powdered sugar. Eight servings.

Why Not?

1/3	cup chilled orange juice
6	ounces cooked, strained prunes
1	cup cold milk
	Dash salt
1	teaspoon fresh lemon juice
1	teaspoon sugar
1	teaspoon brown sugar, light
1	scoop vanilla ice cream

Mix first 3 items, then add salt, lemon juice and sugars. Blend with egg beater and add ice cream. Serve in cool glasses (4 servings) and top with a cherry or a twist of lemon peel.

Taste and See

2	eggs
1/2	cup cold water
6	tablespoons fresh lemon juice
1/2	cup granulated sugar
2	teaspoons grated lemon rind
3	cups cold milk

Beat eggs. Add water, lemon juice, sugar, and lemon rind. Mix well. Add milk, a cup at a time, to lemon mixture. Beat vigorously. Serves 4.

Sis's Toddy

2	heaping teaspoons brown sugar
1/4	cup orange juice, chilled
1	cup buttermilk, cold (no butter flakes)
1	scoop orange sherbet

Mix all ingredients together until smooth. Pour into chilled glasses. Makes 1 large or 2 medium servings.

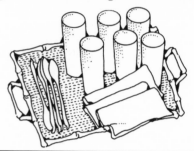

French Coffee

1	rounded teaspoon instant coffee
1	rounded teaspoon sugar
1	cup cold water
	Coffee ice cubes
	Whipping cream
	Cinnamon-Sugar

Combine instant coffee, sugar and cold water. Pour over coffee ice cubes (made by simply freezing coffee in refrigerator tray.) Float whipping cream which has been whipped stiff on top of coffee drink. Sprinkle cinnamon-sugar on top of cream.

Dr Pepper Punch

1	cup sugar
6	lemons
6	limes
1/2	cup grenadine
6	bottles Dr Pepper
2	quarts chilled soda
2	trays Dr Pepper ice cubes
1	cup cherries (with stems)

Boil sugar in 1 cup of water over low flame until sugar is completely dissolved. Cool and add to strained juice of lemons and limes, pouring mixture into chilled punch bowl. Stir in grenadine, Dr Pepper and chilled soda. Add Dr Pepper ice cubes (made by simply pouring Dr Pepper into ice trays, instead of water). Float cherries on the surface or freeze one in each Dr Pepper ice cube.

English Frost

1 cup water (for each glass)
1 teaspoon, heaping, instant tea (for each glass)
Mint, crushed
1 can frozen lemonade concentrate
1 can cold water
1 tablespoon grated lemon rind

Combine frozen lemonade concentrate and cold water. Add lemon rind and put in freezing tray. Freeze to ice crystal point. Mix water, tea and pour mint which has been crushed in glasses. Add 2 large scoops lemon ice crystals and a little extra crushed ice. Stir vigorously and serve at once. Garnish with mint spray which has been dusted in powdered sugar. A little extra powdered sugar may be sprinkled on top for added sweetness and decoration, if desired.

Cranberry Sparkle

2½ cups white corn syrup
3 pints cranberry juice
1½ cups strained lemon juice
3 cups strained orange juice
3 cups carbonated water
Lemon slices

Combine fruit juices and syrup in a bowl. Mix well and chill. When ready to serve add carbonated water and pour into serving bowl over ice. Dip into cups or small glasses and garnish with a lemon slice. Makes about 1 gallon.

Celebration

2 bottles (8 ounces) maraschino cherries and juice
⅔ cup lime juice
1 quart raspberry beverage, chilled
2½ quarts lemon-lime beverage, chilled
1 lime, sliced
Sweetheart roses

Chop cherries finely and combine in a punch bowl with cherry and lime juice. Add raspberry beverage and lemon-lime beverage which have been chilled. Fill glasses and float sweetheart roses on top of lime slice for garnish. Serves about 12 (medium to large servings).

The Floridian

2 cups carbonated cola beverage
4 bottles carbonated cola beverage
2 limes
1½ cups sugar
1 cup water
2 tablespoons white corn syrup
¼ teaspoon mint extract
1 tablespoon lime juice
Sprig of mint

Pour 2 cups of cola beverage into a refrigerator tray. Remove when cola ice crystals are formed.

Mix together in saucepan with lid 1½ cups sugar, 1 cup water and 2 tablespoons white corn syrup. Heat over medium flame for about 4 minutes, covered. Take cover off and boil 4 additional minutes. Set aside to cool; then add ¼ teaspoon mint extract and lime juice. (This mint syrup may be refrigerated for long periods.) To mix The Floridian put ¼ cup of cola ice crystals into four large glasses. Add about 3 tablespoons (more or less according to your own liking) of the mint syrup to each glass. Now fill with bottled cola beverage and juice of ½ lime. Stir thoroughly. Serve at once with large sprig of mint. Glasses may be frosted, or rims frosted by dipping into lime juice (about ¼ inch), then in delicately tinted (green) granulated sugar. Refrigerate glasses to let decoration set. When mixing drinks pour and stir carefully. Serves 4.

The Berry Patch

2 cups boiling water
¼ cup loose tea
1 cup plain corn syrup
3 cups cold water
1½ cups orange juice
¾ cup lemon juice
1½ cups sliced and sweetened strawberries
1 (28-ounce) bottle ginger ale

Pour boiling water over tea leaves, and brew about 5 minutes. Stir, strain, and pour into corn syrup. When cool, add remaining ingredients. Pour into glasses which have been chilled and filled with ice cubes. Strawberry ice cubes enhance this drink, or orange slices may be used for garnish. Makes 3 quarts.

Texas Cooler

1½   cups orange juice
1   cup grapefruit juice
2   tablespoons lemon juice
2   tablespoons light corn syrup
1   pint ginger ale
      Mint and cherries

Blend orange, grapefruit and lemon juice. Add syrup and
mix thoroughly. Make ice cubes with pieces of mint and
cherries. Place ice cubes in glasses. Add ginger ale to
fruit juices and pour mixture over ice. Serve immediately.

Hunter's Punch

1   cup water
1   cup sugar
1   cup strawberries, fresh
1   cup strawberry juice
1   banana, sliced
3   lemons, juiced
2   oranges, juiced
½   can crushed pineapple
1   quart water

Combine sugar and water; boil until syrup is formed.
Cool. Add strawberry, lemon and orange juice, and
crushed pineapple. Chill thoroughly and let stand for 4
hours. Before serving, mix water and fruit mixture. Then
add whole fresh strawberries and banana, sliced, to
punch. Serve with ice.

South Seas

½   cup fresh lemon juice
2½   cups pineapple juice
¾   cup lime juice
½   cup confectioners' sugar
      Ginger ale
      Pineapple rings

Mix lemon, pineapple, and lime juice with sugar. Pour in
even amounts into 6 ice-filled glasses. Fill with ginger ale
and float a pineapple slice on top of each. Insert straws
through pineapple ring and serve.

San Franciscan

1   quart orange sherbet
1   quart vanilla ice cream
2   tablespoons grated orange rind
1   quart orange juice
1   quart ginger ale
      Orange slices

Combine orange juice with orange sherbet and vanilla
ice cream; add orange rind. Mix with rotary beater or
electric mixer. Lastly, add ginger ale. Mix again quickly
and pour this smooth and frosty mixture into chilled
glasses. Top with orange slices and serve immediately.
Or if you choose to serve from a punch bowl, put a little
ice in the bowl and be sure the bowl itself is chilled. Float
orange slices on top.

Roman Coffee

2½   cups strong, cold coffee
5   tablespoons chocolate syrup
1   pint coffee flavored ice cream

Combine all ingredients is a mixing bowl and beat with
rotary beater or blender until smooth. Pour into tall
glasses and serve. Makes 4 servings.

Poor Man's Ale

½   cup sugar
½   cup water
½   cup fresh, frozen or bottled grape juice
¼   cup orange juice
1   tablespoon lime juice
1   pint ginger ale, chilled
      Orange slices
      Cherries

Mix all juices and set aside. Boil sugar and water 5 minutes. Cool, and add to fruit juice. Chill for 2 hours at
least. When ready to serve add ginger ale. Insert cherries
in center of orange slices. Stack orange-cherry slice and
ice cubes, alternating to top of glass. Pour beverage into
glasses and serve.

Ocean Spray

1 cup warm water
1 cup white corn syrup
$^1/_2$ cup fresh lemon juice
$^1/_2$ teaspoon mint extract
Green food color
1 large bottle ginger ale
Minted ice cubes

Mix together water, corn syrup, lemon juice, mint extract and small amount of green food color (for very delicate green tint) and chill. When ready to serve add ginger ale. Into tall glasses put minted ice cubes and pour Ocean Spray punch over cubes. Makes about 6 servings.

Kentucky Julep

6 cups cranberry juice
3 tablespoons lemon juice
Grated rind of $^1/_2$ lemon
$^3/_4$ cup frozen orange juice
Grated rind of $^1/_2$ orange
$1^1/_2$ cups pineapple juice
1 cup weak tea, chilled
2 cups cold water
Orange sherbet

Mix juices and lemon and orange rind. Let stand for $^1/_2$ hour. Strain and pour into glasses or punch bowl over ice. In a punch bowl float dips of orange sherbet on top. If served in glasses top each drink with one generous scoop of orange sherbet. This punch has a tangy, fruit flavor, but if a sweeter punch is desired sugar may be added to taste.

The Trader

2 cups diced ripe cantaloupe
$^1/_4$ cup sugar
2 tablespoons lime juice
1 tablespoon lemon juice
Few grains salt
1 12-ounce can pineapple-grapefruit drink, chilled

Combine cantaloupe, sugar, lime juice, lemon juice and salt in a blender. After blending thoroughly, chill. Then stir in the chilled fruit drink and pour over crushed ice in frosted glasses. Serves 3.

Windsor Punch

1 stick cinnamon
12 whole cloves
3 tablespoons loose tea
2 cups boiling water
$^1/_2$ cup sugar
2 cups grape juice
$^1/_3$ cup lemon juice
1 teaspoon grated lemon rind
1 teaspoon grated orange rind
1 quart ginger ale

Combine spices and tea in large pitcher and add boiling water. Brew uncovered about 10 minutes. Stir, strain and add sugar. Cool at room temperature. Add juices and grated rind. When ready to serve add ginger ale. Pour over block ice into a punch bowl. Serves 8.

Tropic Pleasure

$^1/_2$ cup shredded coconut
$^1/_2$ cup water
$1^3/_4$ cup milk, cold
$^1/_2$ cup cream, cold
1 6-ounce can frozen concentrated orange juice
1 tablespoon shredded coconut
Cherries

Combine orange juice, water and coconut in container (may be blended or whipped with rotary beater). Mix for several minutes until smooth. Add milk and cream. (May be strained if taste of coconut pieces is not desired.) Mix thoroughly and pour into chilled glasses. Top with shredded coconut and 2 or 3 cherries.

The Christmas Cup

Apple cider
Maple syrup
Lemon
Cloves
Cinnamon
Butter

Place apple cider in a kettle or chafing dish and for each cup of cider add 1 teaspoon maple syrup, 3 drops of lemon juice, powdered cloves and cinnamon to taste. Allow mixture to boil and serve hot in mugs. Garnish each cup with thin slice of lemon and a small pat of butter. If stick cloves are used, 2 per cup is desirable.

California Steamer

1	cup water
2	tablespoons sugar
4	whole cloves
1	stick cinnamon
1	tablespoon brown sugar
1½	cups apricot nectar
2	tablespoons lemon juice
2	tablespoons orange juice
2	teaspoons crushed mint

Cook water and sugar over low flame until sugar is dissolved. Add spices and simmer about 10 minutes. Combine apricot nectar, brown sugar, lemon juice and orange juice and add to syrup. Blend thoroughly and heat thoroughly. Pour over mint and let stand about 3 minutes. Strain into cups or mugs and serve hot. Punch may be reheated, but do not boil.

German Mocha

1½ teaspoons instant coffee dissolved in 1
     cup warm water, or extra-strength
     brewed coffee
Rich milk
Whipping cream

Add rich milk to extra-strong coffee. Stir and add whipping cream drifts to float on top. Serve from cups or mugs. Serves 1.

The Southern Colonel

2	cups raspberry jam
1	cup hot water
½	cup lemon juice
1	tablespoon lime juice
4	cups water
	Lemon and lime slices
	Raspberries, fresh or canned

Combine raspberry jam and hot water. Heat and stir for 10 minutes. Add lemon and lime juice, then water. If any lumps remain of unmelted raspberry jam, strain. Chill. Pour over ice into large glasses. Make a kabob of toothpicks with a lemon slice, a raspberry, a lime slice, another raspberry.

The Menehune

½	cup sugar
⅔	cup water
⅔	cup unsweetened pineapple juice
⅔	cup fresh lemon juice
2	tablespoons fresh lime juice
2	unbeaten egg whites
4	cups finely crushed ice

Combine sugar with water and heat for 10 minutes. Remove from heat and chill. Mix pineapple juice, lemon and lime juice together and add to syrup. Pour into shaker or blender. Last, add egg whites and ice. Shake or blend until smooth and creamy. Pour into frosted glasses and serve immediately. Garnish with mint sprigs threaded through pineapple chunks.

Index